THE GOSPELS IN THE NOW

THE FOUR BIOGRAPHIES OF THE GOD-MAN RE-IMAGINED IN MODERN CONTEXT

BISHOP JIM SWILLEY

Scripture quotations marked "NKJV" are taken from the NEW KING JAMES VERSION, © Copyright 1982 by Thomas Nelson, Inc. Used by permission. All rights reserved.

Take note that the name satan and related names are not capitalized, as this author does not recognize him as either supreme nor revered, to the point of violating grammatical rules.

THE GOSPELS IN THE NOW
The Four Biographies of the God-Man Re-Imagined in Modern Context
ISBN 978-0-9787170-3-2
Copyright © 2009 by Jim Swilley

Published by Church In The Now Publishing
1877 Iris Drive, SE
Conyers, GA 30013

Cover artwork, entitled *"The Four Gospels,"* painted by Bishop Jim Swilley
Cover design by A-Grafixx Design Group, www.agrafixx.com

Printed in the United States of America. All rights reserved under International Copyright Law. Contents and/or cover may not be reproduced in whole or in part in any form without the express written consent of the Publisher.

12-09

THE GOSPELS IN THE NOW

THE FOUR BIOGRAPHIES OF THE GOD-MAN RE-IMAGINED IN MODERN CONTEXT

Introduction

Why write a new paraphrase of the Gospels?

1. Because I love Jesus.

I love the real, living Jesus...the outspoken, passionate, confrontational, provocative, liberating, counter-culture, strong and brave and totally secure-within-Himself, fully integrated Jesus...the Word made flesh who became Jesus, the Christ...Jesus in the now...the One who embodies the "I Am," the God who defies definition and description...the manna or the "what is it?" that came down from heaven...the One whose humanity is every bit as beautiful and intriguing and wonderful as is His divinity...the God-man who cannot be bound or limited in any way by religion or philosophy or doctrines or dogma...the firstborn among many siblings in the family of God who live in the 21st century. I love that real Jesus now more than ever and am in no way offended that He says I must eat His flesh and drink His blood to have a revelation of Him!

2. Because I love the Scriptures.

They are a part of me...as absorbed into the fiber of my being as they could possibly be. The words of God vibrate in every cell of my body...they occupy the largest part of my mind...they completely saturate my spirit. The Bible is a miracle—not a book, but a collection of 66 books written by 40 authors over a period of 1,500 years in different languages to different people groups in different generations for different purposes. Therefore, the Scriptures must be *rightly divided* instead of *wrongly connected.* In other words, each book must be judged in its own context and on its own terms, whether it confirms any other book or not. In this way, biblical contradictions are not only acknowledged and accepted...they are expected. I celebrate the tension caused by the conflicting viewpoints of the writers who had different paradigms of God; their contradictions make the Bible literally pulsate with life! And amazingly, in spite of the given contention, the confirmation of Jesus, the Christ, is still the glue that holds the whole collection together!

3. Because I love the Gospels.

> *Also from within it came the likeness of four living creatures.*
> *And this was their appearance: they had the likeness of a man.*
> *Each one had four faces, and each one had four wings....*
> *As for the likeness of their faces, each had the face of a man;*
> *each of the four had the face of a lion on the right side,*
> *each of the four had the face of an ox on the left side,*
> *and each of the four had the face of an eagle.*
>
> Ezekiel 1:5, 6, 10 – NKJV

I love Matthew's Gospel...the Gospel of the Kingdom...the Gospel of the Lion-King...a uniquely important revelation, written for the Jews from a firsthand, up-close-and-personal viewpoint, portraying Jesus as the Messiah so long awaited after Abraham...the King after David. There is a particular and sometimes palpable tension in Matthew, probably because it was written in the name of a Jew whom the Jews hated because he was a collector of taxes for the Romans. But it is written with much love, nonetheless. Matthew was apprehended by Jesus, and was not at all like the other disciples, so the writings that bear his name bring a certain richness to the Jesus narrative that is essential to our understanding of the Son of Man. What the other synoptic Gospel writers call the "Kingdom of God," Matthew calls the "Kingdom of Heaven" (or, better translated: "Kingdom of the Heavens"). "Kingdom of God" says Whose and what it is..."Kingdom of Heaven" says Whose it is and where it's from. Perhaps the most significant contribution of Matthew is the attention to detail in the Sermon on the Mount...the blueprint for the "Kingdom of/from the Heavens." **Matthew...the Gospel that roars!**

I love Mark's Gospel...you can feel the youth and vitality of the man whose name it bears pulsating in every page of it...the Gospel of passion and fire...the most masculine of the Gospels...a Gospel that gets the job done...the "can do!" Gospel. Matthew is symbolized by the Lion, Luke is personified in the Man, John shows us the Eagle...but Mark's is the picture of the Ox...strong...utilitarian...dependable...effective...the Gospel with muscle. No attention is given to Jesus as a baby...those kinds of details are less important here. It's also the shortest of the Gospels...it does more and says less...gets to the point...emphasizes themes like faith and power. Mark's Gospel provides a much-needed paradigm to the big picture...an aspect of the earthiness of Jesus, the Carpenter, who personally builds His Kingdom without fear of getting His hands dirty...a concept that is especially appealing to the Romans, to whom it is written. **Mark...the Gospel that bears!**

I love Luke's Gospel...the Gospel of the fully evolved Man...sophisticated...elegant...educated...intelligent. Luke is a physician with an excellent bedside manner, who writes a thoughtful and lovingly detailed letter to the young Greek, Theophilus, about the amazing God-Man. But in reality, it is written to all the Greeks, who would, in theory, appreciate the culture and refinement of its author and the miracles and philosophy of its Main Character. Luke gives the most attention to the Nativity, because it is the most biographical of the four Gospels...it was also originally combined with the Book of Acts. It brings the synoptic Gospels full circle, showing us the complete spectrum of all that was and is the Son of Man. **Luke...the Gospel that cares!**

I love the Gospel of John...a living, breathing Word, unlike anything else...so different from the three synoptic Gospels. Each of them brings something original to the table, but John's account of the greatest story ever told is in a class all by itself. It is the Gospel written for non-conformists and individualists...for those who can comprehend Jesus outside the box...a flight plan for eagles who exist high above the clouds.

Matthew is written for the Jews, Mark is written for the Romans, Luke is written for the Greeks, but John's writings come from the paradigm of a universalist...he paints his picture in very broad strokes and writes with the global vision of one who sees the whole earth through a bird's eye view. Can you imagine the visionary mind of someone who begins his story with, *"In the beginning was the Word, and the Word was with God, and the Word was God"*? Matthew and Luke open the Jesus-narrative in the little town of Bethlehem...but John begins IN THE BEGINNING...in eternity...in the cosmos...in the now! You could spend a lifetime just discussing that one, wonderful concept and still not be able to fully plumb the depths of its meaning. John's is the Gospel of the Son of God. ***John...the Gospel that soars!***

4. Because I love the diversity among all the translations and paraphrases of the Bible.

Although I wholeheartedly reject the notion of an official "authorized version," I do honor the grandeur and loftiness of the Bible that James, the King of England, authorized for his subjects to read in the 17th century (King James Version). That's why I have memorized vast sections of it. And I love the way James Moffatt could turn a phrase in his translation. I could virtually live in *The Amplified Bible* with all of its shades of meanings and wordy explanations and parentheses and brackets. It's like heaven to someone who loves exploring words and their meanings as I do. When I was young, Kenneth Taylor's beautifully accessible *Living Bible* changed my life and set the course for my whole ministry. Many years later, Eugene Peterson's daring paraphrase called *The Message* affected me nearly as dramatically. In recent years, I have grown to respect the *Today's New International Version* for its modernity and clarity and lack of religious sexism. In my opinion, it is probably the most accurate mainstream translation of them all, even though the small-mindedness of much of the mainstream Church has forced its creators to stop publishing it. I could go on and on about the virtues of the *Concordant Literal New Testament* and the *Khaboris Manuscript*, but I also love the *New English Bible* and *The Jerusalem Bible* for other reasons. I am constantly referring to all of these translations for my teaching and writing, along with some other great ones not mentioned here. You may ask then, "If you love all these translations so much, why write a new one?" My only answer is that this writing is my way to pay homage to those who have already blazed this trail of translation before me. I could not do this if they hadn't done what they did. But this translation is what *I* hear when *I* read and teach these chapters and verses. These are the things *I* have seen...what *I* have read between the lines...for the last thirty-seven years of ministry, and I simply want to submit them to you, the reader, for your consideration.

5. Because I love communication.

Nothing is more important to the life of relationships than communication, and nothing is more gratifying than knowing that you have effectively communicated your message to someone else. I certainly don't claim to know everything about Jesus; in fact, the more that I increase in my knowledge of Him throughout the course of my life, the more mysterious He actually becomes to me. For me, that's not a problem. I'm rather glad that, even though I know Him more intimately than I know anyone else, there is always a part of Him that is past my finding out. I know that I will never reach the limits of the breadth and length and depth and height of Him, ever. But, what I do know about Him is the most wonderful knowledge that I possess, and I have a need to share that knowledge with others.

6. Because I love people.

One of the greatest songs ever written contains the words, "If I can help somebody as I pass along...then my living shall not be in vain." I try to live by the philosophy of that song, so if this book can help someone to rediscover and rethink the Bible—someone who has previously been intimidated or confused or bored by it, regardless of its available translations and paraphrases—then I will have fulfilled at least a part of my destiny. I want to help people know and love Jesus better, but I also want to make them more comfortable with the Bible and with their own interpretations and opinions about it. The Bible is hearty, robust—it is not delicate or fragile—it can withstand a lot of handling by human beings, because it was meant to be people-friendly, and I want to open a door to the house of understanding and let the people in!

7. Because I love living in the now.

More than anything else, I believe that I was specifically put here on this planet to be a good steward of the concept of living in the now. God is in the now because He is always revealed as the I Am. His Word is in the now because people cannot live on bread alone, but on every word that *proceeds* (present tense) out of His mouth. His Kingdom is in the now because it can only be discerned one day at a time by those who take no thought for tomorrow. I will proclaim and defend the doctrine of the "now-ness" of God for as long as I live and will aggressively wage war on every religious idea that tries to relegate God to the past or attempts to project Him into the future. God is always now and my prayer is that, as you read *The Gospels In The Now,* you will walk in a fuller revelation of that. **Now is all that matters!**

Bishop Jim Swilley

Matthew In The Now

Matthew In The Now

Chapter 1

1. This is the genealogy (or natural family tree through His step-father, Joseph) of Jesus, the Christ...the Messiah, Who was revealed and understood in the physical world as both the son of David, and the son of Abraham.
2. To begin with, Abraham was the father of Isaac, Isaac the father of Jacob, and Jacob the father of Judah and his brothers,
3. Judah was the father of Perez and Zerah (whose mother was Tamar); Perez the father of Hezron, Hezron the father of Ram,
4. Ram was the father of Amminadab, Amminadab the father of Nahshon, Nahshon the father of Salmon,
5. Salmon the father of Boaz (whose mother was Rahab), Boaz the father of Obed (whose mother was Ruth), Obed the father of Jesse,
6. and Jesse was the father of King David. David was the father of Solomon (whose mother had been Uriah's wife),
7. Solomon the father of Rehoboam, Rehoboam the father of Abijah, Abijah the father of Asa,
8. Asa the father of Jehoshaphat, Jehoshaphat the father of Jehoram, Jehoram the father of Uzziah,
9. Uzziah the father of Jotham, Jotham the father of Ahaz, Ahaz the father of Hezekiah,
10. Hezekiah the father of Manasseh, Manasseh the father of Amon, Amon the father of Josiah,
11. and Josiah the father of Jeconiah and his brothers at the time of the exile to Babylon.
12. After the exile to Babylon: Jeconiah was the father of Shealtiel, Shealtiel the father of Zerubbabel,
13. Zerubbabel the father of Abiud, Abiud the father of Eliakim, Eliakim the father of Azor,
14. Azor the father of Zadok, Zadok the father of Akim, Akim the father of Eliud,
15. Eliud the father of Eleazar, Eleazar the father of Matthan, Matthan the father of Jacob,
16. and Jacob was the father of Joseph, who became the husband of

Mary, and Mary was the mother of Jesus, Who was and is called, the Messiah.
17. And so it turns out that there were fourteen generations in all from Abraham to David, fourteen generations from David to the exile to Babylon, and fourteen generations from the exile to the Messiah.
18. Now, this is how the physical birth of Jesus took place—how the eternal Word in the now became an actual human being Who lived and moved on the earth. A young woman named Mary was engaged to be married to a man from King David's family whose name was Joseph. But before they were married, and before they ever had sexual relations, she discovered that she was pregnant. But her pregnancy was not a natural occurrence—she had been impregnated by the Holy Spirit.
19. Understandably, Joseph did not believe Mary's story about the supernatural pregnancy, but because he was a good man and did not want to publicly embarrass her, he decided to quietly call off the wedding and move on with his life.
20. But while he was thinking about the best way to break off the engagement, an angel from the Lord came to Joseph in a dream and said, "Joseph, Mary is telling you the truth; as hard as it may be for you to believe, she is still a virgin, even though she is definitely pregnant. She did not ask for this to happen, and she has not been unfaithful to you…she was chosen by God for this miracle. Go ahead and marry her, because the Holy Spirit did, in fact, impregnate her and she is going to need your support through this.
21. "She will give birth to a boy and you, Joseph, are to personally name Him as if He were your own Son; and you are to give Him the derivative of the name Joshua, which is *JESUS*...the name that in Hebrew means "Savior" or, literally, "God saves." This name will be prophetic for Him, for He will save His people (all the people who live on His earth) from their sins."
22. All of this happened to fulfill what the Lord had said through the prophet:
23. *"Look for this to happen: a virgin will get pregnant and still maintain her virginity...and she will give birth to a Son; and they will call His name Immanuel which literally means in the Hebrew language, 'God is with us.'"*
24. When Joseph awoke from this unusual and profound dream he did exactly what the angel of the Lord had commanded him to do and

25. But even after their private wedding ceremony they did not physically consummate the marriage until after she gave birth to the promised Son. And when the Son was finally born, Joseph named Him Jesus.

Chapter 2

1. Now when the man Jesus was born as a baby in Bethlehem of Judea during the reign of Herod the king, astrologers from the East came to Jerusalem to inquire about Him. These astrologers, or "Magi," originated from a religious caste among the Persians who were devoted to divination (or the practice of the magic arts) and to the interpretation of dreams. They came from Southern Arabia where they had long maintained a tradition of Israelite Messianic expectation that had survived in the region since the days of the Queen of Sheba; and this tradition survived alongside their practice of astrology.
2. When they came to Jerusalem, they began to ask around, "Where is He Who has been born King of the Jews? For we have charted His star in the East through our understanding of the zodiac and have come to worship Him."
3. But when the news about these Arabic magicians got to Herod, it worried him greatly and, in fact, troubled all of Jerusalem with him.
4. So he called together all the people who were experts in the Law, and in Messianic prophecy, and asked them where the Messiah was supposed to be born.
5. "In Bethlehem in Judea," the learned men replied, "for this is what the prophet Micah has written:
6. *'But you, Bethlehem, in the land of Judah, are not in any way the least among Judah's rulers, for out of you will come a ruler Who will be the Shepherd of My people Israel.'"*
7. Then Herod called for a secret meeting with the Magi in an attempt to find out if what they knew from their astrological charts lined up with what the Scriptures had predicted.
8. But these magicians had no knowledge of the prophetic Scriptures, so he said to them, "Go to Bethlehem and make a careful search for the Child. As soon as you locate Him, report back to me so that I may go and worship Him."

9. After they conferred with the king, they went on their way and could actually see the star ahead of them. It literally seemed to move, guiding them to Bethlehem until it appeared to stop over the place where the Child was.
10. When they saw the star that they had anticipated for so long, they were absolutely overjoyed. Of all the signs and wonders that they had seen and performed, this was different...this was the most spectacular! And this was proof that the heavens really do declare the glory of God, as David had said, and that even those who were not of the seed of Abraham could see it, even without a knowledge of the Scriptures.
11. On entering the house, they saw the Child with His mother Mary and instinctively bowed down and worshipped Him. While everyone else in Israel was oblivious, these Persian magicians were the very first to recognize and worship the King! Then they opened their treasures and presented Him with gifts of gold, frankincense and myrrh, providing Him and His family with enough wealth to last a lifetime.
12. Then they were warned in a dream not to go back to see Herod and returned to their country by an alternate route.
13. After the wise men had gone, an angel from the Lord appeared to Joseph in a dream and said, "Get up! Hurry and take the Child and His mother to Egypt! Stay there until I tell you to return, because Herod is looking for your Child and wants to kill Him."
14. That very night, Joseph obediently got up and took his wife and baby boy to Egypt,
15. where they stayed until Herod died. So the prophecy came true, just as the Lord had promised and the prophet had said, *"I called My Son out of Egypt."*
16. When Herod became aware that the Magi had more or less tricked him, he was furious. He reacted by giving orders for his men to kill all the boys who lived in or near Bethlehem that were two years old and younger. He based his horrible plan on what he had learned from the Eastern magicians.
17. So another prophecy came true, just as the prophet Jeremiah had said:
18. *"In Ramah a voice was heard crying and weeping loudly. Rachel was mourning for her children, and she was inconsolable because they were dead."*

19. Finally, after King Herod died, an angel from the Lord appeared in a dream to Joseph while he was still in exile in Egypt.
20. The angel said, "Get up now and take the Child and His mother back to Israel. The people who wanted to kill Him are no threat to you now because they are dead."
21. So Joseph obediently got up and left with them for Israel.
22. But when he heard that Herod's son Archelaus was now the ruler of Judea, he was afraid to go there. So the angel spoke to him in another dream and told him to go to Galilee.
23. And, as a result, they went to live there in the town of Nazareth. So yet another prophecy was fulfilled in this action, because the prophet had said, *"He will be called a Nazarene."*

Chapter 3

1. In those days John the Forerunner, who baptized and announced the earthly appearance of the Lamb of God, came preaching in the wilderness of Judea
2. and saying, "It's time for a complete paradigm shift! You must begin to think differently about God and about your relationship to Him, for the Kingdom of/from the heavens—the interior, tangible reign of God through Christ where His will is done on earth (in the physical realm) as it is in heaven (in the spiritual realm)—has now become available and accessible because it has come very near to you!"
3. This is he who was spoken of through the prophet Isaiah: *"A voice of one calling out in the wilderness, 'Prepare the way for the Lord now, and make a straight highway for His entrance!'"*
4. John's clothes were made of camel's hair and he wore a leather belt around his waist. His diet consisted completely of the carob-like pods that came from the locust tree and wild honey.
5. People went out to see and hear him from Jerusalem, all Judea and the whole region of the Jordan.
6. They willingly confessed their sins to him and were baptized by him in the Jordan River.
7. But when he saw many of the religious leaders, both Pharisees and Sadducees, coming to where he was baptizing, he said to them, "You brood of vipers! Who warned you to flee from the coming wrath?
8. "Produce fruit in keeping with the real changing of your minds,

9. and do not think that you have the right to say to yourselves, 'We have Abraham as our father.' I tell you that out of these stones God can raise up children for Abraham.
10. "Even now, the ax is already poised at the root of the trees and every tree that does not produce good fruit will be cut down and thrown into God's purifying fire.
11. "I baptize you in a river of water for transformation through the changing of your minds. But after me comes One Who is much more powerful, Whose sandals I am not worthy to even carry. He will purify you, not in a *physical* river of water, but by baptizing you with the Holy Spirit in a *spiritual* river of consuming fire!
12. "His winnowing fork and fan are in His hand, and He will clear His threshing floor, gathering His wheat into the barn and burning up the chaff in your lives with His unquenchable fire."
13. Then one day Jesus came from Galilee to the Jordan to John to be baptized by him.
14. But John protested passionately, having in mind to prevent Him, saying, "I'm the one who should be baptized by You! What are You thinking by coming to me in this way?"
15. But Jesus replied to him, "John, let's do this; you must allow it to happen now, for this is the appropriate and most meaningful way for both of us to fulfill all righteousness and to perform wholly whatever is holy." His direct words convinced John, and so he permitted Him.
16. And when Jesus was baptized, He came up at once out of the water and immediately the heavens were opened and John saw the Spirit of God descending in the form of a dove and alighting on Him.
17. Just then, a voice from heaven said, "This is My Son, My Beloved, in Whom I take pleasure and with Whom I am completely and absolutely delighted!"

Chapter 4

1. Then Jesus was purposely led by the Holy Spirit out into the solitude of the desert wilderness for an intentionally staged and personal confrontation with the devil (or the adversary) into a place where He could be tempted, tested and tried by him, one-on-one, for Kingdom purposes.
2. And He went completely without food for forty days and forty nights, and at the end of His fast He realized that He was hungry.

3. And at that time the adversary came and said to Him, "If You really are Who You believe and say that You are—the manifestation of God in the physical realm...His own Son—then command these stones to be made into loaves of bread."
4. But He replied, "I will not, because it has been written, *'Man shall not live and be sustained by bread alone, but by every word that comes forth, in the now, from the mouth of God!'*"
5. Then the adversary took Him into the holy city and placed Him on a high gable (or turret) of the Temple sanctuary.
6. And he said to Him, "If You really are the Son of God as You say You are, then throw Yourself down off this tower; for it is written, *'He will give His angels charge over you, and they will bear you up on their hands, lest you strike your foot against a stone.'*"
7. Jesus said to him, "Yes, but it is also written, *'You shall not tempt, test or try the Lord your God!'*"
8. Again, the adversary took Him up on a very high mountain and showed Him in panoramic view all the kingdoms of the world and the splendor and magnificence of them all.
9. And he said to Him, "All of these things I will give You if You will simply prostrate Yourself before me and sincerely worship me."
10. Then Jesus said to him, "All right; that's enough! I have nothing more to say to you. Your purpose here has been accomplished, so you are dismissed—be gone! For it has been written, *'You shall worship the Lord your God and Him alone shall you serve';* so that is that…this episode and this conversation are over!"
11. Then the adversary departed from Him, having been dismissed so matter-of-factly, and ministering angels immediately came to Him and took care of His needs.
12. When Jesus got word that John had been arrested, He left Judea and returned to Galilee.
13. First, He went to Nazareth, then left there and moved to Capernaum, beside the Sea of Galilee, in the region and area of Zebulun and Naphtali.
14. This fulfilled what God said prophetically through the prophet Isaiah:
15. *"In the land of Zebulun and of Naphtali, beside the sea, beyond the Jordan River, in Galilee where there is a great population of Gentiles,*
16. *the people who sat in darkness have now seen a great light. And for*

those who lived in the land where death reigned by constantly casting its shadow, a bright light has shined."

17. From then on, Jesus began to preach, "It's time for a complete paradigm shift! You must begin to think differently about God and about your relationship to Him—you must change your lives by changing your minds—because the Kingdom of/from the heavens has come near enough to you to now manifest in your personal world!"
18. As He was walking by the Sea of Galilee, He noticed a pair of fishermen brothers: Simon, who is also known as Peter, and Andrew his brother, throwing a dragnet into the sea-like lake.
19. And, deliberately interrupting their routine, He said to them, "Come, follow Me…let Me be your life-guide, and as you are disciplined into My world-view, your skills as fishermen will be incorporated into the larger purpose of influencing people, to the point that you will literally 'fish' for human beings and become 'fishermen of humanity!'"
20. His words were so compelling, and the concept of fishing for people was so intriguing to them, that they immediately left their nets right where they were and became His disciples.
21. And going on further from there, He noticed two other brothers: James, the son of Zebedee, and his brother John. They were busy in the boat with their father, mending their nets and preparing them for use, and right then and there He called them, as well.
22. And, finding His concepts and His charisma irresistible, they left the boat and their father at once and also joined Jesus as disciples and followed Him.
23. And He went all throughout Galilee, teaching in their synagogues and preaching nothing but the Good News of the Kingdom and healing every disease and every weakness and infirmity among the people.
24. So His fame as a healer spread quickly throughout all Syria and, as a result, they brought Him all who were sick and those afflicted with various diseases, those who were tormented and seemed to be under the influence of demons, and epileptics and paralyzed people. And regardless of the sickness or disease, or the seriousness of the situation, or the circumstances surrounding the individual, He healed them all, without reservation!
25. So enormous crowds of hurting people began to accompany and

even mob Him, coming from Galilee and Decapolis (the district of the ten cities east of the Sea of Galilee), Jerusalem and Judea, and all the way from the other side of the Jordan.

Chapter 5

1. One day, when Jesus saw how large the crowds were becoming, He climbed up to a high part of a mountainside and just sat down, looking out over them. When the disciples saw Him sitting there, they climbed up to where He was.
2. When they had all come up higher together, He opened His mouth and began to teach them, saying:
3. "Blessed are the poor in spirit—those who have been broken emotionally and whose self-esteem has been severely damaged—for they have the opportunity to rethink their lives and are in a position to receive total restoration by seeking the Kingdom of/from the heavens!
4. "Blessed are those who are in mourning—those whose dreams have been shattered, who have known nothing but heartbreak and disappointment—for they have the promise that they shall be completely comforted!
5. "Blessed are the meek—those who regularly exercise strength under perfect control—for their restraint, humility and self-control will ultimately cause them to literally inherit the earth!
6. "Blessed are those who hunger and thirst for righteousness—the seekers who want more, who refuse to settle for the religious status quo and who earnestly desire to embrace all truth—for they shall be spiritually satisfied!
7. "Blessed are the merciful—the ones who are quick to forgive and move on, who are slow to judge and are unwilling to condemn—for they shall obtain mercy in their own lives!
8. "Blessed are the pure in heart—those who do not live by hidden agendas and ulterior motives…the unpretentious...the real people experiencing the real God in the real world—for they shall be able to see God fully and clearly and without any optical obstruction!
9. "Blessed are the makers and maintainers of peace—the ones who build the bridges, tear down the walls, and are repairers of the breach—for their noble and humanitarian efforts shall cause them to be called the very sons of God!

10. "Blessed are those who are persecuted for righteousness' sake—those who are misunderstood, misquoted and misjudged for their beliefs and are hated for their stand for the truth—for their clear vision will reveal the Kingdom of/from the heavens on the earth!
11. "Blessed are you, even when people revile you and persecute you and say all kinds of evil things against you and make up hurtful and ridiculous rumors about you on My account.
12. "You must see the persecution for what it is and not take it personally. You should actually be glad and even joyful when you experience it, for your reward in heaven is great…strong and intense…and you are in good company, for in this same way people persecuted the prophets who came before you.
13. "You are, in a sense, the salt of the earth; but if the salt has lost the strength of its taste, how can its saltiness be restored? It is then useless…not good for anything any longer but to be thrown out and walked on by oblivious people.
14. "You are also the light of the world…a well-lit metropolis built on a hill that cannot be hidden or ignored in any way.
15. "Think about it: no one lights a lamp and then covers it up and obscures its radiance. On the contrary, a lamp is made to be lit and then fixed somewhere up high on a lamp stand, so that it can burn brightly and illuminate the entire house.
16. "So let your own personal light unashamedly shine before the public that they may see your obvious excellence and the demonstration of your good deeds and acts of kindness, and, as a result, glorify your Father Who is in the heavenly realm.
17. "Look, don't think that I have come to do away with or undo the Law or the prophets; in fact, I have come not to do away with or undo them, but to complete and fulfill them and to make them finally make sense to you.
18. "I tell you in all honesty, until the sky and earth pass away and perish, not one smallest letter or one little punctuation mark will pass from the Law until all the things that it foreshadows are accomplished.
19. "Whoever then does away with or relaxes one of the least important of these commandments and teaches people to do the same shall be called least important in the Kingdom of/from the heavens; his religion will trivialize him. But he who practices them and teaches others to do so shall be called great in the Kingdom of/from the

heavens; he will cause the Law to come alive and accomplish its true purpose in the lives of people.

20. "For I tell you, unless your righteousness is more than that of the superficial scribes and pretentious Pharisees, you will never enter the reign or the Kingdom of/from the heavens.

21. "You have heard that it was said in times past, 'You shall not kill, and whoever kills shall be liable to, and unable to escape the punishment imposed by, the court.'

22. "But I say to you that everyone who continues to be angry with his or her brother or sister, and harbors malice and heart-enmity against another, shall be unable to escape the same punishment imposed by the same court; and whoever speaks contemptuously and insultingly to a brother or sister shall be liable to experience the punishment imposed by the Sanhedrin. And those who are in the habit of randomly saying, 'You stupid idiot!' to others may be inviting unnecessary violence to themselves and could even end up on a heap of garbage and burning rubble in the dump at Gehenna, just outside the city of Jerusalem.

23. "So if and when you are offering your gift at the altar and you remember that your brother has any grievance against you,

24. leave your gift at the altar and go make peace with your brother (you don't need too many enemies), and then come back and present your gift.

25. "Come to terms quickly with your accuser (or with one who is adversarial with you) while you are on the way traveling with him, so that your accuser doesn't decide to hand you over to the judge and the judge to the guard and you be put in prison.

26. "You know how the system works...you will not be released from prison until you have paid the last penny of the fine that you owe.

27. "You have heard that it was said, 'You shall not commit adultery.'

28. "But I say to you that anyone who even looks at someone and fantasizes about committing adultery with them has already done so in his or her heart.

29. "So if looking at someone causes you to lust after them—especially if they are off-limits to you (as in another man's wife or another woman's husband)—then pluck out your right eye and throw it away before your lust gets you into trouble. It is better to lose one of your bodily members than to be stoned for adultery, or killed by a jealous husband or wife, and have your whole body thrown onto the burning

garbage dumb at Gehenna, in the Valley of Hinnom!
30. "And if your right hand serves as a trap to ensnare you, or causes you to steal or to hurt someone, cut it off and cast it from you. Again, it is better that you lose one of your members than that your entire body should be thrown into the garbage-fires of Gehenna and your entire life be thrown away because of some silly foolishness.
31. "It has also been said, 'Whoever divorces his wife must simply give her a certificate of divorce...no questions asked.'
32. "But I tell you, whoever just casually dismisses and divorces his wife for no good or valid reason, such as unfaithfulness or infidelity, will inadvertently cause her to go out and commit adultery herself. And whoever marries a woman who has been divorced in this way will inadvertently commit adultery with her, seeing that she will more than likely still consider herself married to her previous husband.
33. "Again, you have heard that it was said in ancient times, 'You shall not swear falsely, but you shall perform your oaths to the Lord as a religious duty.'
34. "But I tell you, do not foolishly bind yourselves by an oath at all... either by heaven, for it is the throne of God;
35. or by the earth, for it is His footstool; or by Jerusalem, for it is the city of the Great King.
36. "And do not even swear by your head, for it is not absolute; you are not able to make a single hair white or black.
37. "Just let your 'Yes' simply be 'Yes'; likewise, let your 'No' be simply 'No'—no more, no less. Anything more than that implies that you are not honest enough for people to believe that your word alone is your bond. It makes it appear as if you are a liar like the adversary.
38. "You have heard that it was said, 'An eye for an eye and a tooth for a tooth.'
39. "But I want you to see things in a whole new way. I say to you, do not resist the evil man who injures you—choose your battles. If anyone strikes you on the right jaw or cheek, turn to him the other one too, initially. Your moral authority in this case will prove that you are stronger than your opponent and that you don't have to stoop to his level!
40. "And if anyone wants to sue you and take the very shirt off your back, let him have your coat also. It will prove that you see a bigger

picture, one in which your Father in heaven will reward you with new shirts *and* a new coat!

41. "Along the same lines, if anyone forces you to go one mile, go with him two miles. It will prove that God is your strength and that you are nobody's victim!
42. "Give to him who keeps on begging from you and do not turn away from him who would borrow from you. It will prove that you are the prosperous one, the one who knows that God is his source.
43. "You have heard that it was said, 'You shall love your neighbor and hate your enemy.'
44. "But I want you to rethink that. I tell you, love your enemies and pray for those who persecute you,
45. to show that you are the children of your Father Who is in heaven and that love always and ultimately wins. Anyway, the truth, whether you like it or not, is that He makes His sun rise on the wicked and on the good and makes the rain fall upon the upright and the wrongdoers alike.
46. "So if you only love those who love you, where is the reward in that? Don't you know that even the tax collectors do that?
47. "And if you only acknowledge and speak to your own people, what more than others are you doing? Don't you know that even those of the nations do that?
48. "These ideas are new to you and alien to your religious mindset, but you can do all of this because I have declared you to be perfect, even as your heavenly Father is perfect. You therefore must already be perfect, even if you don't realize it yet and even if you don't act like it yet, because I have come to reveal, once and for all, that you are created in the Father's perfect image.

Chapter 6

1. "Be careful not to fall into the trap of doing good deeds publicly, just so you can be seen by the people whose applause and approval you crave. If public opinion is that important to you, you're inevitably going to forfeit the promise of receiving a reward from your Father Who is in the heavenly realm.
2. "So whenever you give to the poor, don't make a lot of noise about it; don't blow a trumpet before you, as the hypocrites in the synagogues and in the streets like to do so that they may be recog-

nized and honored by the public. In all honesty, the accolades and pats on the back that they will receive for their supposed generosity is all the reward that they will get.

3. "But when you give to charity, your motives should be so pure that you will be happy to be absolutely discreet about it. In fact, your low-profile acts of kindness ought to make it seem as though your left hand doesn't even know what your right hand is doing,

4. so that your deeds of charity may be done quietly and your love offerings may be given in secret…even in anonymity. And then your Father Who sees in secret and knows the hidden things of the heart will reward you openly.

5. "Also when you pray, don't be like the hypocrites, for they love to pray standing in the synagogues and on the corners of the streets that they may be seen and heard by the people around them. Again, I tell you in all honesty, they already have their reward in full.

6. "But when you pray—I mean when you really want to talk to God about what's going on in your personal life—do it privately. Find a place where you can be alone…where you can close the door to the world and pray in confidence to your Father, Who dwells in the secret place. And your Father, Who sees into the hidden rooms of the heart, will reward you out in the open light of day. Then, when you emerge strengthened from your private place of individual prayer, you can move into a place of real, effective, public prayer.

7. "And when you pray, do not mindlessly and mechanically mutter maxims and mottos; do not routinely and ritualistically repeat rote religious rhetoric as the Gentile heathen do, for they think they will be heard for their much speaking.

8. "Do not be like them. Really communicate with God, because the thing about prayer is this: your Father already knows what you need even before you ask Him! So prayer is more about building relationship with the One *to* Whom you pray, *for* whom you pray, and *with* whom you pray, than it is about just getting your physical needs met. In other words, it is communication that not only creates a connection in heaven, but also creates a community on the earth.

9. "So pray like this: *Our Father—not My Father…not your Father…but Our Father—Who is in the heavenly realm, may Your name be hallowed by us and always kept holy in our collective consciousness.*

10. *"May Your Kingdom continue to come to us and in us and through*

us. May Your will be done on earth…in the physical realm…as it is in heaven…in the spiritual realm.
11. *Give us—not Me, not you, but us—give us this day our daily bread… just the provision that we need in the now…no more…no less.*
12. *"And forgive us our debts, as we also have forgiven our debtors.*
13. *"And lead us not into temptation, but deliver us from evil—even the evil that we may find within ourselves. For Yours is the Kingdom, the reign, the power and the glory forever. Amen.*
14. "For if you readily forgive the people in your life their thoughtless mistakes and human failures, your heavenly Father will also freely forgive you.
15. "But if you do not forgive others their mistakes and failures, you prevent the Father's forgiveness from flowing into your life, and so you end up going through life having unfinished business with God.
16. "And whenever you are fasting, don't walk around looking sullen, intense and morose like the hypocrites, for they play into religious stereotypes with their dramatics, that their fasting may be apparent to and seen by people. I tell you, honestly, that the attention they get from their audience is their full and complete reward.
17. "But when you fast, see to it that you smell good and look good through the whole process
18. so that your fasting may not be noticed by people, but by your Father (Who sees the secret motives of the heart); and your Father (Who sees what no one else can see) will reward you out in the open where everyone can see.
19. "Do not just accumulate and amass wealth in earthly places where your treasure may be vulnerable to the natural elements. Keep it away from moths and rust—anything that might consume and destroy it—and hold it in a dimension where thieves can never break through and steal it.
20. "But gather up your wealth and deposit it into the heavenly realm where neither moth (anything that might eat it up) nor rust (anything that might cause it to disintegrate) may consume and destroy and where thieves are not able to break through and steal what you have;
21. for where your treasure or wealth is, there will your heart and mind and attention be also.
22. "Your perception ultimately becomes your reality. It's as if the eye is the lamp of the body, because your vision (or the way that you see things) is the light that continually shines on your life-path and

determines its direction. Perception is everything. So if your eye is healthy through singleness of vision—or if your perspective on life is positive and progressive—then your entire body will be full of light…your entire being will be progressively enlightened.

23. "But if your eye is diseased (if your perception is warped), your whole body or self will be full of darkness. And you can't imagine how much darkness you can bring on yourself just by seeing things the wrong way and how dark that darkness can ultimately become if left unchecked!

24. "No one can serve two masters, for either he will hate the one and love the other, or he will stand by and be devoted to the one and despise and be opposed to the other. In a word, you cannot simultaneously serve God and Mammon (the god that people create in their lives through their illusions and delusions about money and possessions).

25. "Therefore, I tell you, stop being perpetually worried and unnecessarily stressed about your quality of life, what you shall eat or what you shall drink. Don't be preoccupied by your body-image and by what you'll have to put on. In the big picture, isn't life greater and more important than food and the body more than clothing?

26. "Just take some time and look at the birds of the air. Haven't you noticed that they aren't preoccupied with the business of sowing and reaping and gathering their harvest into barns? And yet your heavenly Father keeps faithfully feeding them. Don't you think that you are worth much more than they?

27. "And who of you by worrying and being anxious can add any height to his or her frame, or any years, or even minutes for that matter, onto his or her life-span?

28. "And why should you be anxious about clothes? Consider the lilies of the field and learn how they grow; they don't strive with trying to be beautifully adorned, and they don't wear themselves out by staying in a constant spin.

29. "And yet I tell you, even Solomon in all of his magnificent excellence was not arrayed like one of these beauties.

30. "So think about it…if God personally designs the wardrobe and so elegantly clothes the grass of the field (which today is alive and green and tomorrow is tossed into the furnace) will He not much more surely clothe you, O you whose faith needs to be enlarged?

31. "In other words, it's just pointless to worry and be anxious, saying, 'What are we going to have to eat?' or 'What are we going to have to drink?' or 'What are we going to have to wear?'
32. "For the nations are obsessed with these kinds of things, yet the fact remains that your heavenly Father already knows full well that you need them all.
33. "But seek out and search for a revelation of the Kingdom of God in and through every circumstance, and in every situation. And seek it first (or first thing)…before you strive with the circumstance…before you start to worry about the situation…before you fret over it…before you allow yourself to become overwhelmed by it or let it become exaggerated in your mind. And along with your primary search, look diligently for His righteousness (or His *rightness*) to be revealed somewhere in the thing, as well. When you prioritize the Kingdom in this way, then you can be sure that everything in your personal world will come into order and that all you need for your daily provision will just automatically flow into your life and will be added to you as a result of your quest.
34. "So don't worry or be anxious about what may or may not happen tomorrow. Live in the now because the Kingdom is always revealed in the now. Deal with tomorrow and what it may bring when it gets here, knowing that tomorrow will have worries and anxieties of its own. As you live each day as it comes, God will enable you to successfully handle each day's trouble, whatever it may be.

Chapter 7

1. "Don't set yourself up as a judge who takes the liberty of casually condemning others, or even as a critic who thinks that he or she has the right to criticize them, because when you do that, you set a universal law into motion that will inevitably bring negative things back into your own life. In other words, don't judge so that you may not be judged and criticized and condemned yourselves.
2. "For in direct proportion to your judgment, criticism and condemnation of others, you will be personally judged and criticized and condemned. It's just the way the law works. And in accordance with the measure you use to deal out to others…whatever you may deal out…it will be dealt out again to you. You define the terms of your own life in this sense.

3. "And why do you fixate on the very small particle, the tiny speck of sawdust that is in your brother's eye, while you are completely unaware of and oblivious to the huge beam of timber that is in your own eye?
4. "Or how can you obsessively say to your brother, 'Let me try to get that tiny, superficial splinter that I'm preoccupied with out of your eye,' when all the while there is the beam of timber that is obvious to everyone but you lodged in your own eye?
5. "Don't be such a clueless hypocrite! Work on dislodging that beam of timber from your own eye first, because until you can completely remove such glaring, personal obstructions, you're frankly not qualified to take on the responsibility of extracting anything at all from your brother's eye, no matter how big or how small.
6. "Don't treat these holy truths and sacred concepts like scraps that are fit only to be thrown out to the dogs. Rather, value the truths you hold dear and esteem them highly, as if they were exquisite pearls, not as if they are old leftovers to be tossed into a feeding trough for pigs. If you don't discern your audience, or if you are flip with sacred things, you run the risk of presenting priceless pearls to pigs who, when they realize that you have not fed them the slop they desire, will trample the gems and turn and tear you in pieces.
7. "But keep on asking—never stop expressing your desires or challenging the boundaries of your faith—and it will ultimately be given you. Keep on seeking—never abandon your sense of wonder or your inquisitive interest in the mysterious—and you will ultimately find. Keep on knocking—never believe that your possibilities are exhausted or that your opportunities are finite—and the door will ultimately be opened to you.
8. "For everyone in this life who keeps on asking keeps on receiving. And he or she who keeps on seeking keeps on finding. And to him or her who keeps on knocking, doors will continue to be opened.
9. "Or what father is there of you, if his hungry son asks him for a loaf of bread, will ignore the request and instead hand him a stone to eat?
10. "Or if he asks for a fish, will serve him up a snake for dinner?
11. "If you then, with all of your potential for evil, know how to give good and beautiful gifts to your children, how much more will your Father Who is in the heavenly realm lavish the best gifts on those who keep making a demand on Him!
12. "So discipline yourself to live by this simple rule: Whatever you

desire that others would do to and for you, do also to and for them. This not only will set positive things in motion for your life, it will fulfill all the Law and the teaching of the prophets, because this basic principle is the sum of all the writings of the holy books.

13. "Enter into the full blessings of Kingdom-life through the narrow gate of this kind of discipline. For the gate that leads to self-destruction is wide and easily accessible and many are unwittingly entering through it.
14. "But the gate of selfless servitude is narrow and the way is compressed—the way that leads to a fulfilled, Kingdom-life in the now—and few are those who find it.
15. "Beware of false prophets who come to you dressed as sheep but, inside, they are devouring wolves whose only intention is to scatter the sheep and bring division among them.
16. "You will fully recognize them by the fruits of their relationships and their track record with people. Do people pick grapes from thorns or figs from thistles?
17. "Even so, every healthy tree bears good, nutritious fruit, but the diseased and decaying tree bears bad, inedible fruit.
18. "A good or healthy tree can't bear worthless fruit, nor can a diseased tree bear high quality fruit.
19. "So every tree that does not bear good fruit...fruits of love, selflessness, empathy and consideration for others...needs to be cut down and thrown into the fire of purification.
20. "Therefore, you will fully know and discern them by their fruits.
21. "Not everyone who says to Me, 'Lord, Lord' will enter into the blessings of Kingdom-life. Just going through the motions of mechanically calling on My name or religiously praying a prayer does not automatically give one access to the Kingdom of/from the heavens. Only those who do the will of My Father will enjoy the benefits of the Kingdom in the now.
22. "When judgment comes on their lives, many will say to Me, 'Lord, Lord, haven't we prophesied in Your name and driven out demons and done many mighty works in Your name?'
23. "And then I will say to them openly, 'While you've been busily going through the motions of the ministry, you've never developed a real relationship with Me. It's as if I've never known you. You haven't shown Me your love and you haven't loved the people who have partaken of your so-called services. You've done so many

24. *things in My name for the wrong reasons that I want you to keep your distance from Me until you repent and get your priorities in order…until you start really representing Me and living your life the way I want you to live it!'*
24. *"So everyone who hears these words of Mine and acts on them will be like a sensible and wise man who built his house upon bedrock.*
25. *"And all manner of inclement weather bombarded the house…rain fell and floods came and the winds blew and beat against it. But, no matter how bad the weather or how strong the wind, it did not fall, because it had been founded on the stable rock.*
26. *"Likewise, everyone who hears these words of Mine and does not demonstrate them, will be like a stupid man who built his house on the sand.*
27. *"And the rain fell and the floods came and the winds blew and beat against that house, and it fell. And when it fell, the damage was complete and severe."*
28. When Jesus concluded the Sermon on the Mount and finished His teaching, the crowds who had come to hear Him were just astonished and left speechless. They had never heard anything expressed in such a direct manner—so practical and yet so profound—and they were overwhelmed at His teaching,
29. for He was obviously speaking as One Who had authority and was comfortable with it, and not as did the scribes, whose insecurities caused them to hide behind their religion.

Chapter 8

1. When Jesus finished His sermon and came down from the mountain, the mass audience that had become so captivated by His message (and as a result were so enamored with Him) started following along after Him in great throngs as He moved.
2. And as He descended, a leper came up to Him and just fell down before Him, prostrate on the ground, and began to worship Him. And he said, "Lord, if You are willing, I believe that You are able to cleanse me of this horrible disease."
3. And Jesus immediately reached out His hand and fearlessly touched the untouchable, saying, *"I am able and I am willing…and I call you clean!"* And instantly, as Jesus said these words, the man's leprosy disappeared and his body became completely whole.

4. And Jesus said to him, "Look, don't go around telling everyone you see about this, because it will bring you more unwanted attention and publicity than you can imagine. Just go and show yourself to the priest and present the offering that Moses commanded, for a testimony and as validating evidence to the people who will inevitably find out about it on their own."
5. As Jesus went into Capernaum, a high-ranking Roman officer who was a centurion (one who was responsible for a century of men in the Roman army) came right up to Him and very politely but directly asked for His help,
6. saying, "Master, I have a servant who is lying at my house paralyzed and in intense, physical pain."
7. And Jesus said to him, "No problem. I'd be more than happy to come with you right now and restore him to health."
8. But the centurion replied to Him, "Sir, I really don't feel right about asking You to come under my roof, because I don't worship Your God—I worship the many gods of Rome—and it would be unseemly of me to invite You into a home that You might consider pagan or unworthy. I don't want to dishonor You like that. But I believe that if You will just speak the word, my servant will be cured."
9. "See, I, like You, am a man who *has* authority because I am *submitted* to authority. I have men who are over me and I also have approximately one hundred soldiers who are completely under my command. I know that I explicitly follow the orders of my superiors and if I just say to any one of those hundred men under me, 'Go!' he goes...no questions asked...no hesitation...no modification of the order whatsoever. I never have to second guess the command or do any follow up on him, because I am confident that my directives will be carried out precisely as I gave them. To another of my men I may say, 'Come!' and when I speak, he drops what he is doing and comes immediately. And when I say, 'Do this' to one of my servants, You can be sure that he follows my orders and does it. The continuity of this command system is the strength of our military power and, in the same way, I see that You have authority over the words of life. Words are Your servants because You are submitted to the creative word of a Higher Authority. If You tell one of Your words to do something, that word will absolutely do it because of Your obedience to the commands given You by the One You call 'Father.' The point is, I believe that if You command one of Your servant-

words to take Your healing power to my manservant, it will follow Your orders and do exactly what You tell it to do!"

10. When Jesus heard this, He said, "Well, that's just marvelous! Seriously, I am literally marveling at what you just said! I mean, since I have been in this dimension, I haven't heard anyone in all of Israel say anything that even comes close to your expressed insight and understanding!" Then He turned to those who were following Him and said, "I want you all to know that I haven't found faith like the faith of this polytheistic idol-worshipper anywhere in this whole nation!

11. "And I tell you that in the very near future, many more like him will come from eastern lands, as well as from the west...literally from everywhere in the world...and will sit down at the table of covenant with Abraham, Isaac and Jacob in the Kingdom that comes from heaven.

12. "Meanwhile, the original heirs to the Kingdom will be driven deeper into the dark blindness of their elitist, nationalistic religion where they will weep and grind their teeth in anger at the obvious fact that My covenant is not exclusive or limited to the people of this belief-system or of this geographical region."

13. Then to the centurion Jesus said, "Go...there's nothing more to say. You have exactly that for which you have believed." And, sure enough, the servant was fully restored to health at the very instant the healing-word was dispatched.

14. Later, when Jesus went into Peter's house, He saw his mother-in-law lying ill with a fever.

15. So He touched her hand and instantly the fever left her. She immediately got up and began waiting on Him as her guest.

16. When evening came, they brought to Him many who seemed to be under the power or influence of demons, and He expelled any and all such rebel spirits with a simple, authoritative word and restored to health all who were sick.

17. And by doing this He fulfilled what was spoken by the prophet Isaiah who said, "He Himself personally took our weaknesses and infirmities and bore away all our diseases."

18. Now Jesus, when He saw that the great throngs around Him were growing unwieldy, gave orders to cross to the other side of the lake.

19. And as He was about to get into the boat, a religious scholar rushed up to Him and said, "Master, I want to follow You wherever You

go."
20. And Jesus replied to him, "Are you sure about that? You see, foxes have holes in which to live and the birds of the air have their nests, but the Son of Man has no permanent place to lay His head. The urgency of My message keeps Me constantly on the move and rarely allows Me to rest. And it forces those who want to keep up with Me to have to rough it most of the time because of our vagabond lifestyle."
21. Another of the disciples standing nearby said to Him, "Lord, my father is old and sick and probably very near death. I need to stay with him until he goes, and once I have buried him and have gotten everything in my house back in order, I'll catch up with You."
22. But Jesus said to him, "If you really are a disciple of Mine, you'll just follow Me in the now and deal with whatever you need to deal with when the time comes; your schedule and plans will be built around life and not around death."
23. Then He got into the boat and His disciples accompanied Him.
24. And He immediately fell into a deep sleep once the vessel was launched and, almost as immediately, there arose a violent storm on the sea-like lake. The boat was nearly being submerged by the huge waves, but Jesus was completely undisturbed by what was happening around Him.
25. So they frantically woke Him up and said, "Lord, You've got to get up and do something about this storm or we're all going to die in it!"
26. And, rubbing the sleep from His eyes, He said to them, "Why are you men of the sea so hysterical because of a typical, natural storm? And, more importantly, why is your faith so small?" Then He got up and matter-of-factly told the winds and the waves to settle down, and suddenly the atmosphere became silently still and the surface of the water became perfectly placid. Then He lay back down and went to sleep.
27. And the men just stood there looking at each other, stunned and bewildered and said "What kind of man is this? What kind of authority does He have? Not only do demons and diseases obey Him, even the winds follow His orders and the sea does what He tells her to do!"
28. And when He arrived at the other side in the country of the Gadarenes, two insane men under the control of rebel spirits came out of the tombs to meet Him. They were so fierce and savage that

they terrorized anyone who tried to pass that way.

29. And they screamed at Him, "What have You to do with us, Jesus, Son of God? Have You come to torment us before the appointed time when every knee will bow and every tongue will confess Your Lordship?"
30. Now at some distance from where they were, a herd of pigs was grazing.
31. And the demonic rebels begged Him, saying, "If You tell us to leave the bodies of these men, we'll have to do what You say, but will You at least not make us leave this local area? Command us to take up residence in the bodies of those pigs over there and we'll go where You tell us to go."
32. And He said to them, "Get out of these men right now!" So they came out and went into the pigs and, when they did, the whole herd rushed down the steep bank into the sea and died in the water.
33. The shocked herdsmen immediately fled, went into the town and reported everything they had seen, including what had happened to the men under the power of the demons.
34. Then the whole town got together and sent a representative group out to meet Jesus and, as soon as they saw Him, they begged Him to depart from their locality.

Chapter 9

1. So Jesus stepped back into the boat with His disciples and crossed over to return to His hometown.
2. And as they were stepping out of the boat, some men brought a paraplegic lying on a stretcher right up to them and set him down directly in front of Jesus. When He saw how their faith in Him was manifested by this bold action, He said to the man, "Not to worry My son...be happy today...I forgive all of your sins!"
3. Upon hearing this, some of the teachers of the Law who stood nearby said to themselves, "Who does this arrogant blasphemer think He is?!"
4. Perceiving their innermost thoughts, Jesus said them, "Why do you embrace such an evilly negative and limited paradigm?
5. "Let Me ask you experts something: which do you think is easier...to say, 'Your sins are forgiven' or to say, 'Get up off that stretcher and walk?'

6. "But just so you will know that the Son of Man, indeed, has authority on earth to forgive sins, listen to this." Then He turned to the paralyzed man and said, "Get up now, pick up your own stretcher and go home."
7. Then the man just got up and went home, exactly as Jesus had commanded.
8. When the crowd saw this miracle, they were collectively filled with awe and spontaneously and instinctively began to praise God Who had given this kind of authority to human beings.
9. As Jesus went on from there, He saw a man named Matthew sitting at his work in the tax collector's booth. He moved to the front of the tax line and said to him, directly, "Follow Me." And, without any question, Matthew got up and followed Him, leaving his business behind him.
10. Some time later, while Jesus was having dinner at Matthew's house, many other tax collectors and disreputable people who were known as sinners came and ate with Him and His disciples.
11. When the Pharisees saw this, they asked His disciples, "Why does your Teacher fraternize and even sit down and eat with people like this...tax collectors...sinners...the scum of the earth?"
12. Jesus, overhearing this, indignantly retorted, "Who do you think needs a doctor...the healthy or the sick?
13. "If you really want to understand My connection with these people, then go figure out what this Scripture means: 'I'm all about mercy, not religious pretense.' Don't you see? I'm here to minister to the sick ones...not reinforce the delusions of the self-righteous!"
14. Then the disciples of John came and said to Him, "The Pharisees subject themselves to fasting often and we certainly do, as well, but, as far as we can tell, Your disciples do not. Tell us...why is that?"
15. "Well, it's like this," Jesus answered, "the guests of the bridegroom cannot mourn while he is with them. But the time will come when the bridegroom will be taken from them, and then they will fast.
16. "No one sews a patch of cloth that has not been shrunk on an old garment, because the patch will pull away from the garment, making the original tear even worse.
17. "Neither do people pour new wine into old wineskins, because, if they do, the skins will burst and the wine will run out. As a result, the wineskins will be ruined. That's why they pour new wine into new wineskins...that way, both are preserved."

18. While He was saying this, a prominent synagogue leader came and knelt before Him and said, "My daughter has just died, but I believe that if You will come and put Your hand on her, she will live again."
19. Without any hesitation, Jesus just got up and went with him, as did His disciples.
20. Almost immediately, a woman who had been hemorrhaging for twelve full years came up behind Him and grabbed the border of His coat.
21. She had the courage to do this because she had been continually saying to herself and within herself, "I believe that if I can just make physical contact with Him…even if I'm only able to touch the edge of His clothes…I will be healed!"
22. Jesus turned and saw into her, and said, "Celebrate what has just happened within you, daughter; it's your own, daring faith that has healed you." And the woman was healed from that very moment.
23. When Jesus entered the synagogue leader's house and saw the noisy crowd and the professional mourners playing pipes,
24. He said, "Every one of you needs to leave this room right now. The girl is not dead as you perceive death…but in another reality she is simply asleep." But they mocked this concept and laughed at Him.
25. But they were expelled from the room anyway and, after the entire crowd had vacated the premises, He went in and took the girl by the hand. When He touched her, life came into her body and she got up.
26. Understandably, news of this event spread quickly throughout the whole region.
27. As Jesus went on from there, two blind men followed Him, calling out, "Son of David, have mercy; have mercy on us!"
28. When He had gone indoors, the blind men came to Him and He asked them both, "Do you believe that I am able to do this?" "Absolutely, Lord," they replied.
29. Then He touched their eyes and said, "According to your own, persistent faith, let it be done to you now,"
30. and their sight was restored. But Jesus warned them quite sternly, "I don't want you to tell anyone about what has happened here."
31. But they couldn't keep quiet about it and went right out and spread the news about Him and His healing power all over the surrounding area.
32. Not long after that, a man who had been struck speechless by a controlling, evil spirit was brought to Jesus for help.

33. And when the spirit was driven out, the man who had been mute clearly spoke. When the crowd heard him, they were amazed and said, "We've never seen things like this happen in all of Israel!"
34. But the Pharisees were unimpressed, as usual, and said, "If this so-called miracle is even real at all, it is because He has made a pact with the prince of evil spirits."
35. But Jesus kept performing miracles, anyway. He went through all the nearby towns and villages, teaching in their synagogues, proclaiming the Good News of the Kingdom and confirming its reality by healing every disease and sickness.
36. When He saw how the crowds kept coming and how broken they were, collectively as well as individually, He had compassion on them. Not only were they sick and unhealthy, but they were scattered and without an identity as a people. They lacked effective, spiritual leadership, so were like sheep without a shepherd.
37. Then He said to His disciples, *"The harvest is abundant and has so much potential, but the workers are few.*
38. *"Ask the Lord of the harvest, therefore, to send out workers into His harvest field (which is the whole world) who can discern the fullness of it."*

Chapter 10

1. And in direct answer to the prayer for harvest hands, Jesus summoned to Himself His twelve disciples and gave them power and authority over rebel spirits, to evict and expel them and to cure all manner of disease, weakness and infirmity.
2. Now these are the names of the original twelve apostles: first, Simon (who is called Peter or "Rock") and Andrew his brother; James the son of Zebedee, and John his brother;
3. Philip and Bartholomew (a.k.a. Nathaniel); Thomas and Matthew (known as "The Tax Man"), James son of Alphaeus, and Thaddaeus (a.k.a. Judas...not Judas Iscariot);
4. Simon the Canaanite (who was a Zealot and perhaps Jesus' most controversial pick because of his radical political connections and agenda), and Judas (Iscariot), who eventually betrayed Him even though he had been given the same anointing and authority that the other eleven had received.
5. Jesus sent out this very diverse and eclectic group, charging them

with these words: "This Gospel is ultimately for the entire world—that's the big picture—but it has to begin somewhere. So, for the time being, go nowhere among the Gentiles and do not go into any town of the Samaritans;

6. go, instead, to the lost, confused people right here in the house of Israel...the people who speak your language and have your world-view.
7. "And tell them, plainly, that the Kingdom of/from the heavens is here! Say to them, 'the Kingdom is "at hand," or as close to you as is the hand at the end of your arm!'
8. "And to drive home your point, bring health to them when they are sick. Raise the dead. Touch the untouchables. Take the dominion away from their demons and set them free. You have been treated generously, so live generously; freely you have received the Kingdom, so freely you should give it away!
9. "And don't worry about how you're going to finance your travel and expenses. In fact, don't even take any money with you.
10. "You don't need a lot of paraphernalia...just travel light...walk by faith...stay in the now. Everything you need is already inside you, so just do your work and remember that a good worker is worthy of his food. In other words, don't worry about going hungry...you'll have everything you need in the external world because of the abundant overflow from your internal world.
11. "And into whatever town or village you go, ask around until you find someone who is open to your message and in the flow with you, and wait for a door to open for you to stay with that person. And then stay there until you leave that vicinity.
12. "And as you go into their house—or into any house, for that matter—speak a Kingdom blessing over that house.
13. "Then, if the people in that house are open to your words, let peace and prosperity come to the entire household. But if they are religiously close-minded, and reject you and your message, then your words will not produce fruit for them and your very own blessing will return to you and will bless you!
14. "In fact, if you are so rejected, don't just leave the house...leave the entire town and shake the dust from its streets off of your shoes.
15. "I tell you, honestly, that when judgment comes on this nation, it will be more tolerable for the land of Sodom and Gomorrah than for that town.

16. "I say all of this to you because you need to know that I'm really sending you out like sheep in the midst of wolves. And to be able to survive this hazardous work, you're going to have to develop the flexibility to be wary and wise as serpents when necessary, and still be innocent and guileless as doves. I realize that no two animals are less similar in temperament than a snake and a dove, so I'm really asking you to do the impossible.

17. "So you can't afford to be naïve. You must be on guard against men whose way or nature is to rebel against God and the inevitable changes that His Kingdom brings; for they will deliver you up to councils and actually flog you in their synagogues,

18. and you will be brought before governors and kings for My sake, as a witness to bear testimony before them and, ultimately, to the nations.

19. "But when they deliver you up in this way, do not worry, or even be anxious about how or what you are to speak. You'll know exactly what to say when the time comes, because it will be given to you as revelation in the eternal now.

20. "And, aside from what will be happening at that moment in the natural realm, in the larger context, it will cause you to realize that it really is not even you doing the speaking; you will have the awareness that it's the Spirit of your Father speaking through you!

21. "But when you begin to colonize the earth with this message of the Kingdom (the Nation of Heaven), a clash of cultures will occur here and chaos will ensue. Brother will deliver up brother to death and the father his child; and children will take a stand against their parents and will have them put to death.

22. "Initially, it will seem as though you will be hated by all for My name's sake, but he or she who, in spite of this resistance, perseveres and endures to the end—who stays strong until they see the full manifestation of the Omega of God—will be saved from destruction.

23. "But, at the same time, use wisdom. If you need to flee to another geographical location to avoid the persecution, then do what you have to do to survive. But I promise that you will not have resorted to going through all the places of refuge in Israel before the revelation of the Son of Man comes.

24. "The bottom line is this: A disciple is not above his teacher nor is a servant above his master. In other words, this inevitable persecution only reveals how very connected you are to Me.

25. "So, if you look at the whole thing correctly, you should be content—even pleased and satisfied—that you, My students, get the very same treatment that I get! Don't you see the implication here? Obviously, it means that when the public sees you, they see Me... just as when they see Me, they see the Father! And if they have been brutish enough to call Me, the Master of the House, 'Beelzebub, the Lord of the Flies from the Outhouse,' what can you expect them to call you?

26. "But, at the end of the day, none of that stuff even matters. So have no fear of them; take your cues from Me and refuse to be intimidated by any of it. Eventually, everything that needs to be revealed will be revealed, and truth will triumph!

27. "And what I now say to you in the dark, I want you to begin to tell in the light...and what you hear whispered in the ear, I want you to fearlessly shout from the housetops.

28. "And do not be afraid of those who can only kill the temporal, physical body, because they can't touch the part of you that is both internal and eternal. If you were going to fear anyone, you would have legitimate reason to be afraid of Him Who has the power to destroy that part of you which is internal and to then throw the external part onto the garbage dump at Gehenna!

29. "So you can be fearless in spite of persecution, because the only One Who actually has the power to destroy you is your loving, caring Father! Are not two little sparrows sold for a mere penny? And yet not one of them will fall to the ground without your Father's consent and notice.

30. "And you are each so uniquely special and important that even the individual hairs growing out of your head are actually all numbered.

31. "So don't fear anyone or anything; the Father Who keeps inventory of your hairs obviously considers you to be much more valuable than many sparrows.

32. "But even though you are so loved, your actions will define your terms with Me because of the universal laws of sowing and reaping. So everyone who acknowledges Me before men and confesses Me regardless of the repercussions, I will also acknowledge him before My Father Who is in heaven.

33. "But whoever denies Me before men in their hour of persecution, I also will deny before My Father in their hour of need.

34. "This relationship is a two-way street, so don't think that I have

come to just bring unconditional peace upon the earth. Let Me be clear: I am demanding your total allegiance. So, in a sense, I have not come to bring peace, but a sword,

35. because My standard of discipleship, especially during this time of national transition, could potentially part asunder a man from his father, and a daughter from her mother, and a newly married wife from her mother-in-law.

36. "The demand that I am making on you could create a scenario in which a man's foes will be the very members of his own household.

37. "See, I want you to love me with the same abandon with which I love you. So he who loves and is loyal to father or mother more than Me is not worthy of Me; and he who loves and takes more pleasure in son or daughter more than Me is not worthy of Me.

38. "The thought of you possibly having to choose between your family or Me may be as painful for you as a death on a cross. But he who does not take up his cross and follow Me is simply not worthy of Me.

39. "Why does it seem that I am making it so difficult for you with such high expectations of commitment? It's because I want you to walk in a higher, more exalted kind of life. Whoever compromises to find his lower life will lose the higher life, but whoever loses his lower life on My account will ultimately find the higher life.

40. "But here's the payoff for walking in such loyalty to Me: It will give you a place of honor in the Kingdom that will create a new reality...a reality in which he who receives and welcomes and accepts you receives and welcomes and accepts Me. And it follows that he who receives and welcomes and accepts Me, receives and welcomes and accepts Him Who sent Me.

41. "In this new Kingdom reality, he who receives and welcomes and accepts a prophet simply because he is a prophet, will actually receive a prophet's reward. And he who receives and welcomes and accepts a righteous man simply because he is a righteous man, shall receive a righteous man's reward.

42. "The coming of this Kingdom (for which you may indeed be persecuted) is going to change everything...so much so, in fact, that whoever gives to one of these 'little ones'—one of those who has seemed insignificant and unimportant in the natural world—even a cup of cold water just because he is My disciple, will be openly and permanently rewarded. When you think of it in this way, you will

realize that anything you may go through for the advancement of the Kingdom will be worth it!"

Chapter 11

1. After Jesus had finished charging His twelve disciples and preparing them for what they were possibly facing, He went on from there to teach and preach in the towns of Galilee.
2. John, meanwhile, had been locked up in prison on orders of Herod Antipas (in reaction to his condemnation of Herod's marriage to Herodias, the wife of his brother), and the effects of his incarceration had put John through some changes, both mentally and emotionally. So when he heard in prison what the Messiah was doing, he sent his disciples
3. to ask Him personally, "Are you really the One Who was to come, the One the prophets talked about, the One we've been expecting…the Christ? Or should we part with our illusions concerning You and start to look for someone else to fit that description?"
4. Jesus, without being defensive, non-emotionally replied to them, "Just go back and simply tell John what you hear and see;
5. all he needs to know is that the blind are receiving their sight, the lame are walking, those who have leprosy are being cleansed, the deaf are hearing, even the dead are being raised, and the Good News is being proclaimed to the disenfranchised and the destitute.
6. "And blessed is anyone who accepts this as My validation, without offense because of their perception of Me, and does not even think of asking such a question."
7. But as these disciples were leaving to take Jesus' pointed reply back to John, He began to speak to the crowd about him…before anyone could form a negative opinion because of this exchange of words...before anyone could bring an accusation against John due to his obvious doubt and insolence. He said to them, "Just what did you think you were going to see out there in the wilderness? A little weakling who doesn't speak his mind...a reed swayed by the wind?
8. "If not, then what did you go out to see? A man dressed in fine clothes...a sell-out for the religious establishment? No, those who wear fine clothes are in kings' palaces, and a shaky reed would never have the nerve to challenge Me in this way.

9. "Then what did you go out to see? A prophet? No doubt...that's what you wanted to see and that's what you did see. But I tell you, this man—regardless of the mental battle he may be having right now in that lonely prison cell—is still a prophet...more than a prophet...in fact, a prophet and then some.
10. "This is the one about whom Malachi wrote: *'I will send my messenger ahead of You, who will prepare Your way before You.'*
11. "This is the absolute truth, among those born of women there has not risen anyone greater in history than John the Forerunner. Yet, ironically, in this Kingdom which he introduced to you—in this new paradigm where the first shall be last, and the last shall be first—the order of things will be so radically changed that whoever is perceived to be the least important—the least significant…the least worthy in the Kingdom of/from the heavens—is actually greater than he!
12. "You see, for a long time now—even from the days when John the Forerunner was at the height of his influence…right up until this very moment—the Kingdom of/from the heavens has been subjected to a kind of violence, as it were. People have tried, in one way or another, to literally force themselves into God's Kingdom through their own efforts. Men of passion, like John, have demonstrated this 'violence' and, frankly, it has been allowed because there was basically no alternative.
13. "For all the prophets and the Law prophesied the coming of this Kingdom, up until John appeared on the scene and manifested their prophecies into this reality. They spoke it into spiritual existence, but he literally opened it up for you in the material world.
14. "And if you are able and willing to grasp this concept, he is actually the Elijah who was to come.
15. "Whoever has discernment, let him perceive what I mean by that.
16. "Speaking of discernment and perception, to what can I compare this generation? They are like spoiled, unhappy children...clueless about how blessed they are...sitting in the marketplaces and whining to others:
17. 'We played dance music for you and you did not dance like we wanted you to; we sang sad songs for you and you did not cry hard enough.' In other words, they are never satisfied with the message, regardless of how the messenger brings it.
18. "For when John appeared on the scene, he became well-known in the

community, not just for his message, but for his very disciplined, ascetic lifestyle. He had no social life…in fact, he lived as a hermit out in the wilderness, fasting and being a teetotaler. But instead of being impressed by his commitment to such an exemplary moral code, the religious community misinterpreted his model behavior and dismissed him as being a social misfit and even a demoniac. And, in so doing, they completely missed the point he was trying to make.

19. "The Son of Man, on the other hand, came with a completely different modus operandi and packaged the message quite differently. I willingly accepted the invitations for every party to which I was invited…openly eating with anyone who welcomed Me, even drinking with them…no matter who they were or what they were doing. And still, the religious were unimpressed and incoherent. The same ones who said that John had a demon because he didn't eat a lot, said that I was an out-of-control glutton because I did! They said, 'He has a drinking problem and has no standards, because He hangs out with tax collectors, lowlifes and the worst of the worst!' But those who possess wisdom know that she is a lady who doesn't have to convince anyone of who and what she is…and, most importantly, her children know the truth about her."

20. Then Jesus began to denounce the towns in which most of His miracles had been performed, because the places where He had done the most work had changed the least. The miracles hadn't even altered their perception of Him.

21. "Destruction is coming to you as a city, Chorazin! It's coming to you, too, Bethsaida! If half the miracles that were performed in you had been performed even in Tyre and Sidon, they would have had a complete paradigm shift and would have fallen on their knees!

22. "But I tell you, it will be more bearable for Tyre and Sidon than for your communities on the day that judgment comes to this nation.

23. "And you, Capernaum…will you be exalted up to the skies? No, you will go down to the depths. If the miracles that were performed in you had been performed in Sodom, it would still be a thriving city to this day.

24. "But I tell you that what happened to Sodom will pale in comparison to the judgment that is coming to you as a city."

25. Then suddenly Jesus shifted into prayer mode, and said, "I praise You, Father, Lord of heaven and earth, or of the invisible and visible

realm, because You have hidden these things from those who have preconceived ideas about You and are smug enough to think that they have all of Your ways figured out. You have revealed them, instead, to the open and unpretentious...to those who, unlike the spoiled children that I mentioned earlier, are like beautiful children who don't have to fully understand something to accept it.
26. "Yes, Father, this is the way of revelation which pleases You."
27. After the prayer, Jesus resumed speaking to the people, but with a change in tone, He said, "Try to understand that all things have been committed to Me by My Father. Whether you think I am the One that you have been expecting or not, the fact is that no one knows the Son except the Father, and no one knows the Father except the Son and those to whom the Son chooses to reveal Him...and I choose to reveal Him to anyone who will listen.
28. "So just come directly to Me, all you who are weary of labor...who are tired of trying to take the Kingdom by force and are burned out from the violence which that effort requires. Come to Me, all you who are burdened heavily with these same questions and frustrations expressed by John, and I will refresh your spirit and will give your mind the rest that it needs.
29. "Take upon yourself the yoke that is on Me...be yoked to Me as I am yoked to the Father and learn from Me. You will find—in spite of things such as John's probing questions or these ominous, prophetic warnings to the unrepentant cities—that I am personally serene and peaceful of mind because I know Who I am. This is why My internal world is unaffected by the external and, so, in learning from My example, you will find for yourselves serenity and quality rest for your souls.
30. "For the yoke that is upon Me is pleasant—it allows Me to live stress-free…free and easy—so if you connect yourself to it, you will live the same way. And even though the responsibility of bringing the Kingdom is very great, the burden that is on Me is actually quite light."

Chapter 12

1. One particular Sabbath around this time, Jesus was strolling with His disciples through a field of ripe grain. While they were talking with one another, the disciples, who were hungry, just pulled off some

heads of grain and snacked on them.
2. Somehow the ever-critical and perennially vigilant Pharisees saw this and, when they did, they said to Him, "Just look at Your disciples! They are breaking the Law right here on the Sabbath!"
3. He calmly answered, "Relax. Haven't you read in your own Law what David did when he and his companions were hungry?
4. "He entered the house of God and he and his company ate the holy, consecrated bread, which, as I'm sure you know, was not lawful for them to do, because only the priests were allowed to partake of it.
5. "Or haven't you read in the Law that the priests on Sabbath duty in the Temple break rules like this all the time and it doesn't even matter? In fact, it's not even held against them!
6. "But the main point—the point that your legalism is causing you to miss—is that One greater than the Temple is right here in front of you!
7. "If you had comprehended what these words mean: 'I desire mercy, not sacrifice,' you would not have condemned the innocent.
8. "For the bottom line is that the Son of Man is Lord of the Sabbath."
9. Going on from that place, He went into their synagogue,
10. and a man with a shriveled hand was there. As always, the religious leaders were looking for a reason to accuse Jesus of something, so they asked Him, "Is it lawful to heal on the Sabbath?"
11. Instead of directly answering their question of entrapment, He said to them, "Let Me ask you this: If any of you has a sheep and it falls into a pit on the Sabbath, will you not take hold of it and lift it out?
12. "Well, how much more valuable is a person—a human being—than a sheep? Therefore, we can say that it is lawful to do good on the Sabbath."
13. Then, to validate His point and to take the conversation out of the limited realm of natural, religious law, He said to the man, "Stretch out your hand, friend." So the man stretched it out and immediately it was completely restored to the same soundness of the other hand.
14. But, as usual, the Pharisees were unfazed by the miraculous. So they went out and plotted how they might kill Jesus because, once again, He had embarrassed them and had made their rules and regulations seem silly and irrelevant.
15. Aware of this, Jesus withdrew from that place to keep a lower profile, but a large crowd followed Him anyway. And when the sick ones among them approached Him for help, He didn't turn any of

them away. In fact, He healed every last one of them.
16. But He warned them not to tell others about Him or of the miracles that He performed for them.
17. And this scenario fulfilled what was spoken through the prophet Isaiah:
18. "Here is My Servant Whom I have personally chosen...the One that I love so very much and in Whom I absolutely delight; I will put My empowering Spirit on Him, and He will proclaim justice to all the people of all the nations.
19. "He will not have to yell louder than anyone else to be heard, and no one will need to hear His voice crying out in the streets, because His message will resonate with the heart.
20. "A bruised reed—that one who is fragile and weak, broken or about to be broken—He will not break. And a smoldering wick—that one who has no strength left to bear up with what life has been throwing against him or her and has been left battered to the point that he or she has lost the sense of self-worth—He will not snuff out. He will minister in compassion, sympathy and empathy, till He brings justice to all...till He leads that justice to victory.
21. "In His name all the people of all the nations will ultimately put their hope."
22. Then they brought Him a man who was under the control of a spirit of blindness and was also mute, and Jesus healed him so that he could both talk and see.
23. All the people were impressed to the point of astonishment and said, "Could this be the Son of David?"
24. But when the typically cynical Pharisees heard this, they dismissed it and said, "It is only by Beelzebub, the Lord of the Flies, that this charlatan exorcises spirits."
25. Jesus saw right through them, knowing what they were thinking, and said to them, "Every kingdom divided against itself will be ruined, and every city or household divided against itself will not stand.
26. "If Beelzebub drives out Beelzebub, he is divided against himself. How then can he maintain his domain over the flies of the dunghill?
27. "And if I expel darkness by his authority, then how do your exorcists drive it out? So then, they will be your judges.
28. "But if it is by the Spirit of God that I drive out darkness, then the now-ness of the Kingdom of God has been revealed to you.
29. "How can anyone enter a strong man's house and carry off his

possessions without first tying up the strong man? Then his house can be plundered.

30. "Whoever is not in the flow with Me rejects the authority of My Kingdom...and My authority over darkness sets the captive free. So if you're not helping to bring about Kingdom purposes, you're making things worse for everybody.

31. "Speaking of Kingdom authority, let Me tell you about the power of words...specifically, the power of your words to create by the ability and influence of the Holy Spirit. You see, every sin and blasphemy can be automatically forgiven people because of the mercy extended to the limited flesh, but when you are filled with the Holy Spirit, your words become so effective that they literally create your reality. So when you speak things out of your mouth which are contrary to the purpose and nature of the Holy Spirit, you actually speak blasphemy against Him; and He can't forgive you in order to prevent those words from coming to pass because He has empowered you to have what you say. You'll just have to deal with the consequences of whatever you've said, whether for good or for evil.

32. "You can speak against Me as the Son of Man and I'll automatically forgive you of your wrong words; but when you are empowered by the Holy Spirit, the words that you speak against His nature will have to stand just as you said them. They will not be erased through forgiveness in this dimension or in the one to come.

33. "If a tree is good and full of life, its fruit will be good and life-giving...if the tree is bad and full of death, its fruit will be bad and deadly, for a tree is recognized by its fruit.

34. "You brood of vipers, how can you who are motivated by the evil side of religion say anything good? For out of the abundant overflow of the heart, the mouth speaks.

35. "People of good intention bring good things out of the treasure stored up in them, and people of evil intention bring negative things out of the dark thoughts stored up in them.

36. "And on the day that you give an account for the quality of your life, you will realize its outcome was determined by your every word, and you will have to explain why you didn't create a higher standard by speaking higher ones.

37. "In that respect, your words will either make or break you."

38. Then some of the Pharisees and teachers of the Law said to Him, "Teacher, we want to see a sign from You."

39. He answered, "An immature and manipulative generation asks for a sign! But none will be given it except the sign of the prophet Jonah.
40. "For as Jonah was three days and three nights in the belly of a huge fish, so the Son of Man will be three days and three nights in the earth's heart.
41. "The people of Nineveh will stand up when this generation is judged and accuse it; for they repented at the preaching of Jonah, and now One greater than Jonah is here.
42. "The Queen of the South rises in judgment with this generation and sentences it; for she came from a faraway land to listen to Solomon's wisdom, and now one greater than Solomon is here.
43. "When an evil spirit comes out of a person, it goes through arid places—places that have not been watered by the water of the Word—seeking rest, and does not find it.
44. "Then it says, 'I think I will return to the house I left.' And when it arrives, it finds the house vacant and unoccupied, swept clean and put in order.
45. "Then it goes and takes with it seven other spirits even more wicked than itself, and they go in and live there. And so the final condition of that person is worse than the first. That is how it will be with this wicked, unaware generation."
46. While Jesus was still addressing the crowd, His mother and brothers came and stood outside, wanting to speak privately with Him.
47. So someone interrupted Him and said, "Your mother and brothers are standing outside, wanting to speak to You right this minute!"
48. But He calmly and rather matter-of-factly replied to him, "Who, exactly, is My mother, and who really are My brothers?"
49. Then, pointing to His disciples, He said, "Right here are My mother and My brothers.
50. "For true family is not defined by name or blood or genetics. As far as I am concerned, whoever does the will of My Father in heaven is My brother and sister and mother."

Chapter 13

1. On the same day, Jesus went down to the beach and simply sat by the water to meditate in solitude.
2. But when the people saw that it was Him, they began to gather around Him in such great numbers that He got into a boat and

remained sitting there, while the huge crowd stood on the shore and stared at Him in silent expectation.

3. So He began to teach by telling them many things in didactic allegories or parables, saying, "A sower went out to sow.

4. "And as he sowed, some of his seed fell by the side of the road and the birds came and ate them up.

5. "Still other seeds fell on rocky ground where the soil was so shallow that it was virtually nonexistent, and immediately they sprang up because they had no depth of soil.

6. "But when the sun rose, they were scorched, and because they had no root system to nourish and anchor them, they just dried up and withered away.

7. "And other seeds fell among thorns and the thorns grew up and suffocated them.

8. "But other seeds fell on good soil and yielded healthy grain. Some produced a hundred times as much as was sown, some sixty times as much and some thirty.

9. "He who has spiritual ears, let him listen and let him perceive, discern and comprehend by spiritual hearing."

10. After the conclusion of this teaching, His disciples came to Him and asked, "Why do You speak to them by telling these stories?"

11. And He replied, "I have unveiled the secrets of the Kingdom of/from the heavens to you first, but not yet to others.

12. "You see, this is the way it (the Kingdom) works: Everyone who uses what he/she already has within himself/herself (because the Kingdom is within you) will attract even more to himself/herself. But people who don't utilize what they already have within, will lose even what little they have already manifested without.

13. "When I teach, I use allegories, or 'stories' as you call them, because they force My listeners to activate their inner vision and to hear My words in their spirit. When they look only with the natural eye, they cannot see, and when they listen only with the external ear, they cannot hear or understand.

14. "In this sense is the process of fulfillment of Isaiah's prophecy, which says, *'You shall indeed hear and hear but never grasp and understand; and you shall indeed look and look but never see and perceive;*

15. *for this is about what is happening right now in this nation…and this nation's heart has grown grossly fat, their collective mind has*

become dull, their ears are heavy with prejudice so that they have difficulty in hearing, and their eyes they have intentionally and tightly closed. If this were not the case, they could see and perceive, they could hear and comprehend, and, most importantly, they could grasp and understand with the heart what can never be seen or heard with eyes and ears. If they allowed for this kind of insight and perception, I could turn and easily heal every one of them of the disease resulting from their self-inflicted blindness and deafness.'

16. "But you are blessed in spite of all that because your eyes have chosen to see, and your ears are purposefully open so that you can actually hear what I am saying now.

17. "You don't even realize the full impact of this, but it's true anyway. Many prophets and seers—righteous men and women of old who longed to see into the future—actually yearned to see what you are seeing right now. They believed for it but did not see it. They wanted to hear what you are hearing, but they were not able to connect with it.

18. "So listen with your heart, then, to the meaning of The Tale of the Sower:

19. "You see, while anyone is hearing the Word of the Kingdom with nothing but the external ear, they fail to grasp and deeply comprehend it. So when something or someone, who is adversarial to the Word that they have heard, challenges their revelation of it, that adversary is like an evil one who comes and snatches away the seed that should have been sown in the heart. Regardless of how much life-potential the planter scatters, when the seed remains un-sown—when it just sits lightly on the surface—it is vulnerable to enemies. This is symbolic of what was sown along the roadside.

20. "As for what was sown on the thin and rocky soil…this is a similar issue. This represents the one who hears the Word (even beneath the surface), because he/she actually has the ability to comprehend the Kingdom on a deep level. So immediately this one welcomes and accepts the Word with joy and embraces the revelation of it.

21. "But even though he/she can recognize and receive Kingdom revelation, this person has no real internal root system because he/she has formed no genuine relationships in the Kingdom. As I have already told you, the Kingdom comes in corporate revelation, so the 'roots' here are the relationships that nourish and anchor an individual. So, because this one is isolated (and therefore rootless),

he/she is inconstant and only lasts a little while. When affliction or trouble or persecution come to challenge the Word, at once he/she is caused to stumble and just falls away because of his/her own disconnection.

22. "As for what was sown among thorns, this is he or she who truly 'hears' the Word...this one has both the required roots of relationship and the desired depth of discernment. But even though this one has everything that is needed, he/she fails to consistently get rid of what isn't needed. And, so, the cares of the world (the wrong perception of the daily duties of life) and the deceitfulness of riches (the wrong idea that riches are something external) simply choke out and suffocate the God-breathed Word. In this case, someone who obviously should be fruitful and flourishing becomes bleak and barren just by ignoring regular, basic garden maintenance.

23. "As for what was sown on good soil, this is he/she who hears the Word with the heart (or with spiritual ears) and grasps and comprehends it! This is the one who holds onto their roots and gets rid of their weeds (they keep the relationships and let go of the cares), instead of the other way around. This one indeed bears fruit and yields in one case a hundred times as much as was sown, in another sixty times as much, and in another thirty. In other words, a person's harvest is ultimately determined by the quality of their soil, not by the amount of seed that is sown into them."

24. Another similar allegory that He shared with them (as a visible symbol representing an abstract idea) went like this: "The Kingdom of/from the heavens is like a man who sowed good seed in his field.

25. "But while he was sleeping, an enemy of his came and sowed darnel (weeds that closely resemble wheat) among the real wheat that the man had planted. Then the enemy went on his way.

26. "The man, of course, had no idea that his field had been sabotaged, but, when the plants sprouted and formed grain, the darnel appeared right along with the wheat—the false growing in tandem with the real.

27. "So the man's servants came to him and said, 'Sir, didn't you sow good quality seed in your field? How, then, is it possible that it has darnel shoots in it?'

28. "He replied to them, 'Obviously, an enemy has done this in an attempt to compromise the harvest.' So the servants said to him, 'Well, then, do you want us to go and weed them out so that the field

29. "He said to them, 'No, don't do that, because if you go in there focused only on removing the weeds (or what is false in the field) you'll inadvertently root up the true wheat (or what is real) along with it.
30. 'Just let them grow together until that field's harvest-time, because then I'll tell the reapers to gather the darnel first and bind it in bundles to be purged in the fire, but gather the wheat that remains after the purging into my granary.'"
31. He created for them yet another visual image by way of story-telling, again using the symbolism of a seed, saying, "The Kingdom of/from the heavens is like a grain of mustard seed, which a man took and sowed in his field.
32. "Of all the seeds, it is actually the smallest, but when it has grown, it becomes the largest of the garden herbs…literally becomes a tree big enough for the birds of the air to come and find shelter in its branches." In this way He revealed that the Kingdom begins in the small things, but, because it is a living, growing thing, it increases day by day.
33. He also described the all-pervasive and powerful influence of the Kingdom to them using this simile: "The Kingdom of/from the heavens is like leaven (or sour dough yeast), which a woman took and covered over in three measures of meal or flour till all of it was leavened, or until all of the yeast had risen." In this way He described the Kingdom as something that has authority in three dimensions.
34. All of these ideas were presented to the crowds as Jesus spoke to them in allegorical stories, using these kinds of similes. In fact, He basically said nothing to them without employing this style of story-telling and teaching technique.
35. Again, this was in fulfillment of what was spoken by the prophet: "I will open My mouth and tell My stories, and hidden within the simple plotlines of each one will be the revelation of mysteries which have been hidden since the foundation of the world."
36. Then He left the throngs and went into the house. And His disciples came to Him saying, "Please, explain to us the story of the darnel in the field."
37. He answered them, "All right...the one who sows the good seed is the Son of Man.

38. "The field is the whole world as you know it, and the good seed are the children of the Kingdom. The darnel represents what was planted in the children by the enemy.
39. "And the enemy who sowed it is that one who is an adversary to the authority of the Kingdom. The harvest is the close and consummation of this present age or eon, and the reapers are angels.
40. "Just as the darnel is gathered and burned with fire, so it will be at the close of this age when judgment comes on this nation.
41. "But in the larger context (the field is the world), this is about more than just the judgment coming on this nation and the end of this present era. Ultimately, the Son of Man will send forth His angels and they will cull out of His Kingdom all that which causes the practice of lawlessness in the children*
42. and will cast it into the consuming fire of God, where the pain of the purification process will cause them to weep and grind their teeth until its ends are accomplished.
43. "Then the righteous—those who are righteous by faith, along with those who have been purified by fire—will shine forth like the sun in the Kingdom of their Father. Let him who has ears to hear be listening, and let him consider and perceive and understand by hearing.
44. "The Kingdom of/from the heavens is like something precious buried in a field which a man found and hid again; then, in his joy, he goes and sells all he has and buys that field.
45. "Again, the Kingdom of/from the heavens is like a man who is a dealer in search of fine and precious pearls,
46. who, on finding one single pearl of great price, went and sold all he had and bought it.
47. "And again, the Kingdom of/from the heavens is like a dragnet that was cast into the sea and gathered in a diverse array of fish…fish of every sort...in fact,
48. when it was full, men dragged it up on the beach, and sat down and sorted out what was good from the catch into baskets, but that which was worthless they threw away.

*see Jeremiah 31:33, 34 and Hebrews 8:8-12

49. "So it will be at the close and consummation of this age when judgment comes on this nation. But, again, as was the concept in the story of the wheat and darnel, the angels will go forth and ultimately separate all that which is wicked and unnecessary from all that which is righteous and eternal,
50. and cast the refuse into the furnace of fire, where, again, the purging process will cause weeping and wailing and grinding of teeth in those who are being purged.
51. "Now, as I have created a panorama of truth through the telling of these stories, I ask you: have you comprehended these conceptual tales taken together?" They said to Him, "Yes, Lord."
52. He said to them, "All right then...every teacher and interpreter of the sacred truths who has been instructed about and trained for Kingdom-life and has become a disciple, is like a householder who brings forth out of his storehouse treasure that is new and old…that which seems fresh and newly born as well as that which seems ancient and familiar."
53. When Jesus had finished this series of comparisons in story form, He left there.
54. And coming to His own country of Nazareth, He taught in their synagogue with such unprecedented understanding and conspicuous confidence that they were amazed with bewildered wonder. Upon hearing Him, the people said, "Where in the world did this man get this kind of wisdom...and from where does He derive these miraculous powers?
55. "Isn't this just the local carpenter's son? Isn't His mother called Mary? Aren't His brothers James and Joseph and Simon and Judas?
56. "Don't all of His sisters live right here in this very town? We know His family...all of them...and we know how ordinary they all are...so what has made this man so special? He obviously didn't get all this from His family...so where is all this coming from?"
57. And, instead of being intrigued by this and interested in finding out more about Him, they took offense at Him. They fought in their minds what seemed to them unfamiliar and unexplainable, and so were repelled by what those from the other towns and villages were drawn to. Their natural knowledge of Him hindered them from acknowledging His authority and caused them, instead, to stumble at His ministry. But Jesus said to them, "Once again this truth is confirmed: a prophet is not without honor except in his own country

and in his own house."
58. And He did virtually none of the amazing works of power that He had become known for there in His hometown because of their limited perception of Him. Their own lack of vision, and inability to see beyond the physical realm, kept them from receiving what He had to offer them.

Chapter 14

1. About this time, King Herod was hearing reports about Jesus and about the remarkable things that were occurring around Him and because of Him.
2. So he told his officials, "I think this man must be the re-incarnation of John the Baptist! The man that we executed has come back from the dead in the form of this Jesus and that's apparently why He has the power to work these miracles!"
3. Herod was very aware of John, the Forerunner, because earlier he had arrested John and had him chained and put in prison.
4. He did this because John (outspoken as he was) had told him, "It isn't right or appropriate for you to take Herodias, the wife of your brother Philip."
5. Herod wanted to kill John for daring to confront him in this way, but the people thought that John was a prophet and Herod was afraid of what they might do if he touched him.
6. But when Herod's birthday came, the teenage daughter of Herodias danced for the guests at his celebration, particularly directing her movements toward her uncle/stepfather. And Herod was seduced by the dance and was greatly pleased by it...
7. so much, in fact, that (in an outburst of passionate reaction to her) he publicly swore to give her anything she wanted.
8. But the girl's mother (who had been incensed at the words of John) told her to say to him, "Right here on this platter, I want the head of that John the Baptist!"
9. And immediately the king regretted what he had said in the heat of the moment, but he didn't want to break the promise that he had made in front of his guests. So he ordered a guard,
10. "All right, then...do it...go to the prison right now and cut off John's head."
11. And sure enough, John was then decapitated, and his severed head

was taken on a platter to the girl and she presented the gruesome trophy to her mother.

12. Shortly thereafter, John's followers took his headless body and buried it. Then they went and told Jesus about the horrible thing that had happened.
13. After Jesus heard the shattering news about John, He crossed Lake Galilee to go to some place where He could be alone to grieve silently and try to process what had happened, in His own way. But, as usual, the crowds found out that He was moving and followed Him on foot from the surrounding towns.
14. When Jesus got out of the boat, He saw the large, needy throng and, instead of resenting their lack of sensitivity to His suffering or focusing on His own feelings, He immediately was moved with compassion for them. So He translated His heartbreak into healing by curing everyone there who was sick. He sacrificed His own need for solitude for the sake of service, and in this way He soothed His own sorrow.
15. And this impromptu healing service went on for so long that it turned into an all-day meeting. So as evening set in, the disciples came to Jesus and said, "This place is desolate and it is already late. We really need to end this unplanned assembly and let the crowds leave so they can go to the villages and buy some food."
16. But Jesus replied, "No, don't make them leave. Why don't you give them all something to eat?"
17. But they said to Him, "Look, the only food we have here is five small loaves of bread and two fish!"
18. Jesus calmly asked His disciples to bring the little bit of food to Him,
19. and then He told the crowd to just sit down on the green grass (Psalm 23:2). Once they were all seated, Jesus took the five loaves and the two fish, looked up toward heaven, and simply blessed what He had to work with. Then He broke the bread and handed it to His disciples and, somehow, within the transition of the bread going from His hands to theirs, there was enough for them to give to all the people!
20. Not only did everyone eat, but they ate all that they wanted...the food wasn't rationed and no one was told to eat sparingly. So, after everyone had eaten until they were full, Jesus' disciples moved through the enormous crowd and picked up twelve large baskets of leftover food that hadn't even been touched.

21. So, at the end of the day, all had been healed and all had been fed. But when the disciples tried to estimate the number of people involved in this miracle, there were so many that they just counted the men, which were about five thousand strong, and didn't even attempt to count the women and children.
22. As soon as the disciples had finished collecting the baskets, Jesus made them get into a boat and start back across the lake. But He stayed there to personally send the people away and remained until the crowd had completely dissipated.
23. Then, according to His original intention, He went up on a mountain where He could be alone and pray, which He did into the wee hours of the morning.
24. By this time, of course, the boat was a long way from the shore, and it was going against the wind and was being tossed around by turbulent waves.
25. And just a little while before the break of dawn, Jesus came walking towards His disciples along the surface of the water, strolling across the waves as if they were little hills of terra firma.
26. When they saw Him, they thought that He was a ghost and literally went into hysterics, screaming like terrified little children.
27. Immediately, Jesus called out to them, "Settle down, boys! I AM Jesus! There's no reason for you to be afraid!"
28. And, Peter, being the most spontaneous and the first one of them to come out of panic mode, shouted out, "Lord, if it is really You, tell me to come out there to You on the water!"
29. "Come on...you can do it!" Jesus said. And at this responsive and very direct word, and before he had a chance to really think about it, Peter jumped out of the boat and started walking on the water toward Him.
30. But once he got out there and saw how strong the wind was, he shifted his focus from Jesus to the impossibility of the situation. And when he did that, fear instantly set in, his mind resorted to logic, and his understanding of natural law (which dictates that men can't walk on water) superseded his ability to embrace the supernatural. In that instant he started sinking and, re-entering panic mode, he screamed out "Save me, Lord!"
31. Right away, Jesus reached out His hand, pulled him up and said to him, "Peter, what happened? You were walking on the water! Where did your faith go?"

32. But Jesus and Peter arrived back at the boat, anyway, and when they got in, the wind died down.
33. Then the men in the boat worshiped Jesus and said, "You really are the Son of God!"
34. Jesus and His disciples crossed to the other side of the lake and came to shore near the town of Gennesaret.
35. And, once again, the people found out that He was there and they sent word to everyone who lived in that part of the country to bring their sick to Him, which they did.
36. And the people who came begged Him to let them just touch His clothes—the fringe around the bottom of His garment—and everyone who did was healed.

Chapter 15

1. After that, some Pharisees and religious scholars made the trip all the way from Jerusalem for the sole purpose of critically confronting Jesus about something that they considered vital. When they found Him, they said to Him,
2. "We want to know why You allow Your disciples to transgress and violate the important rules handed down by the elders of the past! They don't practice ceremonially washing their hands before they eat as they're supposed to!"
3. He replied to them, "Look, if you really want to start examining the keeping of rules and regulations—especially if you actually care about their purpose—I could just as easily ask you why you transgress and violate the commandment of God for the sake of the rules handed down to you by the same elders!
4. "For God gave this commandment: 'Honor your father and your mother,' and also, 'He who curses, reviles, speaks evil of, or abuses his father or mother, let him be put to death.'
5. "But you have found a legal loophole to honoring them by saying, 'If anyone tells his father or mother that he can't take care of them in their old age because his money is already dedicated as a gift to God, then he is exempt and no longer under obligation to honor and help his father or his mother.'
6. "So, for the sake of this tradition of yours, you have ignored the Word of God, depriving it of force and authority and making it of no effect…you have missed the point of the commandment by

7. "You obnoxious bunch of phonies! Isaiah hit the nail on the head about you when he prophesied:
8. *'These people draw near to Me with their mouths and honor Me with their lips, but their hearts are total strangers to Me.*
9. *'Their worship of Me is useless, for they invent self-serving commands that are obviously manmade, and then obsess over them, elevating them to the status of God-inspired doctrines.'"*
10. Then Jesus called the crowd together and said to them, "Listen, I'm going to say something to you that you really need to grasp...I want you to take this to heart, and get it into your thinking.
11. "Very simply put, it is not what goes into the mouth of a person that pollutes him or her...it is only what comes out of the mouth of that person that has the potential to pollute him or her."
12. Later the disciples came to Him and said, "Hey, did You know that the Pharisees were very offended by what You said and are really upset about it?"
13. Unfazed, He answered, "Look, everything which has not been planted by My heavenly Father will ultimately be torn up by the roots.
14. "So stop paying so much attention to them or worrying about their constant offenses and irrelevant ideas. They are just blind guides and teachers...blind men leading other blind men right into a ditch."
15. But Peter said to Him, "Okay...whatever about them...but can You at least make it plain for us and interpret this saying of Yours?"
16. And He said, "Seriously, Peter...is this really so difficult for you to understand? It just isn't that complicated...the truth never is.
17. "Don't you understand that whatever goes into the mouth passes into the digestive system and is eventually eliminated?
18. "But whatever comes out of the mouth originates in the heart…and when the thoughts and ideas of the heart are put into words, they are given physical reality...and this is what has the potential to pollute a person.
19. "For out of the heart can come destructive thoughts, divisive arguments which can even lead to murder, infidelity, uncontrolled sexual appetites and dysfunction, theft, lies, slander and all sorts of hate-speech.
20. "These are the things that can pollute a person and cause him or her to be unclean. Eating with unwashed hands is just a basic hygiene

issue and has no real bearing on what can actually defile someone or make any difference in the grand scheme of things."
21. And from there, Jesus withdrew to the district of Tyre and Sidon.
22. He had hardly arrived in the area when a woman, who was a Canaanite from that district, came down from the hills and made her way directly to Him. "Have mercy on me, O Lord, Son of David!" she urgently cried out in a loud voice. "My daughter is miserably tormented and afflicted by an evil spirit!"
23. But Jesus didn't answer her, and so she kept crying out to Him. In fact, the longer He ignored her, the louder she got until, finally, His disciples asked Him, personally, to deal with her. They said, "Look, if You're not going to do anything for this Canaanite, then please send her away, because she won't shut up and now she's begging us to help her...and she's really overbearing, obnoxious and out of line!"
24. But He answered them, "She's ahead of schedule; it's not time yet for Me to be revealed to the rest of the world and to be accessible to people like her. Right now I am solely focused on My call to minister to the lost sheep of the house of Israel."
25. But, undaunted by this, she came and knelt before Him and worshipped Him. And she said to Him, "Lord, I don't know anything about that...about Israel, or lost sheep, or the world, or even some 'schedule'...I just know that You can help me now, and I need Your help now! Please help me!"
26. And, finally acknowledging her, He said, "Lady, you know that the Israelites consider your people to be dogs...so because I have My hands full in dealing with them as a nation at the moment, to help you would be like taking the children's bread and throwing it to the dogs...at least that's true as far as they're concerned. Now, do you think that 'dogs' should take away bread from the children?"
27. But she said, "Look, right now I don't care about what the Israelites think. I just want my daughter well. So to answer Your question... I would say, yes, Lord, even the 'dogs' eat the crumbs that fall from their master's table."
28. Then Jesus, impressed with her fierce persistence and dogged determination, and moved by her ability to rise above offense at an insult in order to focus on getting results, answered her. He said, "Oh woman, your faith is great and powerful! By faith you have reached into the future to when My Spirit will be poured out on all

flesh, including the Canaanites, and you have pulled your miracle into the now...regardless of procedure...regardless of propriety...regardless of prejudice. Be it done for you just as you have declared it." And her daughter was completely cured in that instant.

29. Jesus went on from there and passed along the shore of Lake Galilee. Then He went up into the hills and sat down in a particular place, quieted Himself, and just remained there in a meditative state.
30. And in practically no time the local people started to sense His presence there and began to be attracted to the spot where He sat. They gathered until, eventually, a massive throng completely surrounded Him. And they brought with them paraplegics, the blind, the maimed, the mute—people with all kinds of health issues—and they pushed the very sick ones up to the front of the huge crowd to see what He would do with them. And the flow of healing power became so strong there on that spot that they were all made well.
31. And the whole crowd was amazed when they saw the mutes speaking, the maimed made healthy, the paraplegics walking and the blind seeing. It should be noted that on this particular day there were no people there from His hometown to doubt or defy Him...no angry Pharisees to confront or challenge Him...just happy, healed people who were grateful to be there, who were too blessed and too thankful for what they had received to waste the experience in any unnecessary analysis of it. On that day, on that hillside, people just praised and thanked and glorified the God of Israel for His goodness.
32. In fact, the gathering was so glorious that the multitudes refused to leave the locale. They stayed there for three whole days until Jesus finally called His disciples to Him and said, "I'm really touched by this crowd; I hurt for them and am deeply moved by their devotion, because they have been with Me now three days without anything to eat. I don't want to send them away empty; I don't want them to be weak, hungry or faint on their journey home."
33. But the disciples said to Him, "Where are we going to get enough food to feed all these people in this isolated place?"
34. Jesus then asked them, "How many loaves of bread do you have?" They replied, "Seven...and we have a few small fish."
35. At that, Jesus ordered the entire crowd to sit down on the ground, wherever they were, right where they were,
36. and He took the seven loaves and the fish and gave thanks for what He had in His hand. Then He began to break up the food and started

doling it out to the disciples, who, in turn, started passing it to the people.

37. And, as had happened in the previous, similar miracle, every person there ate heartily, until they were completely full. And, just like before, the disciples began to move around the crowd, picking up all the leftovers, this time gathering up seven large baskets full.
38. And, again, there were so many people fed there that day that they only counted the men—this time about 4,000 of them. So, including all the women and children, several thousand people were miraculously fed from a few loaves of bread and some little fish.
39. Then He dismissed the full and contented crowds—these people with whom He had so connected—and got into a boat headed for the district of Magadan.

Chapter 16

1. Now the relentless Pharisees and Sadducees came up to Jesus, yet again, this time asking Him to show them a sign, or a spectacular miracle from heaven, that would validate His divine authority.
2. He replied to them, "Look...when it's evening, you have a tradition of saying, 'We'll have fair weather, because the sky is red,'
3. and in the morning you say, 'It will be stormy today, because the sky is red and looks threateningly gloomy.' You obviously know how to interpret the meaning of the sky's appearance, but you can't interpret the signs of the times!
4. "Only a shallow and clueless generation is wicked enough to constantly crave a sign, but no sign shall be given to it except the sign of the prophet Jonah!" And without any commentary or further explanation, He left them and went away.
5. When the disciples reached the other side of the lake, they realized that they had forgotten to bring along any bread.
6. During the boat ride, Jesus had said to them, "Be careful and on your guard against the Pharisee/Sadducee yeast or leaven,"
7. so they reasoned among themselves about it in hushed tones, wrongly assuming that Jesus was annoyed with them for traveling without food supplies.
8. But He, aware of this, asked, "Why are you worriedly whispering among yourselves the fact that you have no bread and trying to hide it from Me? Honestly, sometimes I'm just amazed at how little faith

you men have!

9. "How is it possible that you have already forgotten that we literally fed thousands, just the other day, with only five loaves of bread? Don't you remember gathering up the twelve whole baskets of leftovers after everyone was full?

10. "And surely you recall that a little later we also fed another several thousand people with only seven loaves. Can it really be that you don't remember also gathering baskets of leftovers that day, as well?

11. "But even that's not the issue...My real question is this: How can you, at this point, be so out of touch with what I'm talking about, in general? Why would you even think that I was talking about bread in the first place? How many feeding miracles is it going to take for you to realize that food-supply isn't the problem? The problem is what's inside the out-of-touch religious community, which is why I said (and say) to beware of the Pharisee/Sadducee yeast!"

12. Then, at last, they got it. They understood that He was warning them to not be void of discernment as the Pharisees and Sadducees were. They finally made the connection that He did not tell them to beware of the leaven of bread but of the empty teaching of those two misguided religious groups.

13. Now when Jesus went into the region of Caesarea Philippi, He called His disciples together and pointedly asked them, "Who do people say that the Son of Man is?"

14. And they answered, "Well, some say that You are the reincarnation of John the Baptist or even that of Elijah; and others believe that You are Jeremiah of old, miraculously appearing in this present time, or that You are a modern manifestation of one of the other prophets."

15. With no surprise at their answers or response to their observations, He pressed them further, asking, "But who do you, yourselves, say that I am?"

16. Simon Peter, almost always the first one of them to speak up, replied, "I say that You are the Christ, the Son of the living God!"

17. Then Jesus answered him, "You are truly blessed, Simon, Son of Jonah, because flesh and blood—or natural, human reasoning—has not revealed this to you. You have gained this insight through tapping into the perspective and paradigm of My Father Who is in the heavenly dimension.

18. "And since My Father has revealed to you Who I really am, I'm going to reveal to you who you really are. So I tell you, your name

is now *Peter/Rock,* or as the Greeks say, 'Petros' (the masculine form of the word 'Petra'). In other words, others may see you merely as a rolling stone, but you are cut from The Rock, or the 'PETRA,' nonetheless; and it's on this Rock—this massive formation like the Rock of Gibraltar—that I will build My Church! Yes, My Church will be built on a mammoth, unshakable and unmovable revelation of the I AM, from which you have spoken...and the gates of death and of everything else from the dark side of the unseen realm (or 'Hades,' as the Greeks call it in their mythology) shall not be able to overpower it or be strong enough to hold out against the magnitude of it!

19. "And through this revelation, I will give people like you the very Keys of the Kingdom of/from the heavens. So with this power to unlock or lock up heaven on earth, as it were, whatever you declare to be improper and unlawful in this dimension must be what is already declared improper and unlawful in the heavenly realm. In the same way, whatever you declare to be lawful on earth must be the standard norm in the heavenly realm. You can actually bind or loose...forbid or permit...lock or unlock with the authority that comes from these revelation-keys!"

20. Then He strictly charged the disciples to tell no one that He was Jesus, the Christ, so that each individual would have to know Him by their own revelation, as well, and not by means of hearing it from "flesh and blood."

21. At that time Jesus began to unveil the big picture to His disciples of what was coming. He made it clear to them that He was going to Jerusalem to submit Himself to an ordeal of suffering at the hands of the very religious leaders with whom He had so often contended, even going so far as to disclose that He was going to be killed and would be raised from death on the third day.

22. But Peter, stunned by this revelation, took Him aside to rebuke Him, privately, saying, "Don't ever say such a thing again, Lord! There is absolutely no way that we would ever allow or tolerate something like that to happen to You!"

23. But Jesus, in an effort to resist being swayed by the natural affection of a friend, turned away from Peter (both physically and emotionally) and, over His shoulder, said to him, "Get behind Me, Satan! You are a hindrance in your attempt to prevent Me from walking in My higher purpose! You have no idea what's really

happening here; your human perception can't protect Me from the will of God!"

24. Then Jesus said to His disciples, "Look, if anyone really desires to be My disciple, he or she is going to have to resist and deny any attempts at self-preservation, which are at odds with his/her divine destiny...or, I could put it this way...he or she is going to have to take up his or her personal 'cross'...whatever that represents to that person...and, choosing to do the right thing above doing the easy thing, follow Me.

25. "For whoever is bent on saving the temporal life...temporal comfort...temporal security, at any cost, is potentially going to sacrifice what is eternal...or lose the better blessings of the eternal life. Likewise, whoever releases their grip on the lower luxuries of the temporal life for My sake shall find the excellence of the eternal life.

26. "The bottom line is this: It is ultimately unprofitable for an individual to compromise himself/herself in order to get everything he/she wants and then lose himself/herself in the process. What's the point of gaining the whole world if you have to lose your very essence—your sense of self...your purpose...your soul—to do so?

27. "So see beyond the scenario of My (your/our) short-lived suffering and realize that the Son of Man is going to come in the glory and majesty and splendor of His Father with His angels—nothing and no one can prevent it—and when that happens you'll get everything you have coming to you as a personal gift.

28. "And I'm not just placating you with platitudinous promises; the benefits of the eternal life are not held for you in the sweet by and by...I'm talking about Kingdom blessings in the now. In fact, some of you standing here are going to see it take place...your eyes will see the Son of Man revealed in Kingdom glory!"

Chapter 17

1. And, as it turned out, just six days later the first three of them actually did, indeed, see that glory, just as Jesus had prophesied. The way that it happened was this: With no warning to them of what was about to occur, or any explanation at all for that matter, Jesus took with Him Peter and James and John, his brother, and led them up on a high mountain by themselves.

2. Once they reached the top, almost immediately His appearance began to undergo a complete metamorphosis right before their very eyes! His visage seemed to literally change from the inside out, causing His face to shine with the intense, blinding light of the sun! Even His clothing began to morph into a surrounding aura that was as white as light!

3. And as this supernatural light continued to emanate and radiate from every part of Him, it seemed to burn off some kind of layer or membrane, which then allowed the disciples to suddenly and literally see into another dimension...and what they saw was two men standing right there with Jesus, holding a conversation with Him. And somehow, inexplicably, they just knew that the two men were Moses and Elijah! They had obviously never seen them before (since both men had lived on the earth centuries before this) and yet, as these two prophets continued to commune with Jesus, the disciples not only recognized them, they were totally comfortable in their presence...not at all alarmed or surprised that they were seeing living people from another time and era right there on the mountain...in the now!

4. Then Peter, always the first to speak up regardless of whether or not it was appropriate, said to Jesus, "Lord, this is an amazing and unforgettable moment in time! If You approve, I'd like to put up three booths right here...to build three memorials...one for You and one for Moses and one for Elijah!"

5. But while he babbled on about this notion of memorializing the moment with mere mementos, a shining cloud, completely composed of transcendent light, emerged and overshadowed all of them. And a deep, thunderous voice from within the cloud began to speak, saying, "This is My Son...My Beloved, with Whom I am and have always been delighted! Listen to Him!"

6. And even though the disciples hadn't been startled by Jesus' transfiguration or the appearance of two people from the distant past whom they had considered long dead, for some reason, when they heard this voice, they fell flat on their faces in fear.

7. But Jesus, now back in His normal, physical form, came and touched them and said, "All right, get up. Stop being so afraid of these things."

8. And when they opened their eyes and looked around, they not only saw that Jesus was no longer in an altered state, but they realized that

He was no longer accompanied by the other two men.

9. So they got up and descended the mountain in somewhat of an awkward silence, which was finally broken when Jesus spoke up and said, "Look, I don't want you to say anything at all about what just happened here on this mountain to anyone…at least not until the Son of Man has been raised from the dead."

10. The disciples then asked Him, "Why do the religious scholars say that Elijah must come first?"

11. He replied, "Well, they're right about that; Elijah is, in fact, the one who is supposed to come first and get everything restored and ready.

12. "But what they don't grasp is that Elijah actually has come already…they just didn't know or recognize him when he came. So, seeing him only with natural eyes, they did to him in the flesh what flesh-minded and flesh-limited people would naturally do. And what I've been trying to get you to understand is that they are going to treat the Son of Man exactly the same way."

13. Then, in a rare and short-lived moment of insight, the disciples understood that He was really speaking to them about John, the Forerunner.

14. As was typical for Jesus and His disciples by this point, a crowd of needy people was waiting for them at the foot of the mountain. As they approached the throng, a man came up to Him, fell on his knees before Him and began to beg, saying,

15. "Lord, please have mercy on my son! He has a terrible condition that causes severe, epileptic-type seizures which manifest frequently and, when they do, he becomes suicidal and tries to find relief by ending his life. He has burns all over his body because he has run into an open fire on several occasions, and many other times he has attempted to drown himself!

16. "Previously, I brought him to Your disciples to see if they could help him, but they weren't able to do a thing for him."

17. In extreme frustration, Jesus answered, "Oh, you unbelieving, clueless and backward generation! How long am I supposed to demonstrate dominion before you? How many miracles is it going to take before you realize the power that you already have?! Bring him here to Me."

18. Then He addressed the boy's condition as a rebel or demonic spirit and evicted it from his ravaged body. As soon as it was expelled, the young man who had been so tormented was made instantly well,

both mentally and physically.
19. Later, when the disciples had Jesus off to themselves, they asked Him, "So why couldn't any of us, no matter how hard we tried, do for him what You so easily did?"
20. He said to them, "Because of the littleness of your faith...because you force your faith to remain in tiny seed-form. The truth is, if you have faith that is like a seed...say, like a grain of mustard...all the faith that you'll ever need is already resident within that small, insignificant thing. If you just allow the seed to grow and mature, and stop striving with it—stop trying to make things happen in the flesh—that seed will naturally and organically produce after its kind. Just trust the nature of the seed! As the grain of mustard doesn't try to grow into a tree, but rather lets the growth process take its course in its time, you have the seed-potential to say to this mountain from which we have just descended, 'Move!' and that mountain would move! It's already all inside you. Seriously, if you can embrace this concept, nothing at all will be impossible to you!"
21. [Verse 21 does not exist in any original manuscripts.]
22. As they were regrouping in Galilee, Jesus said to them, "Listen, you don't seem to be comprehending this yet, but I'm telling you again that the Son of Man is about to be betrayed and turned over into the hands of carnal men.
23. "You need to prepare yourself for this and accept the fact that they will murder Him...but you also need to prepare yourself for the other part of this scenario...as I've told you, three days later He will be raised alive!" This time it began to sink in with the disciples a little more, and, even though they couldn't fully accept it, they believed it enough to feel horrible about it.
24. When they arrived in Capernaum, the tax men came to Peter and asked, "Does your Teacher pay taxes?"
25. Peter replied, "Yes, I'm sure that He does." But as soon as they were in the house together, Jesus confronted him, saying, "Simon, what do you think? When a king levies taxes, who pays...his children or his subjects?"
26. He answered, "His subjects, of course." Jesus said, "Then the children are tax-exempt, right?
27. "But so that we don't upset them needlessly, go down to the lake, cast in a hook, and pull in the first fish that bites. Open its mouth and in it you'll find the required tax money. Take it then and give it

to the collectors to pay what is owed, according to their system, by both you and Me."

Chapter 18

1. Then the disciples came up and asked Jesus, "Who, in Your estimation, is really the greatest in the Kingdom of/from the heavens?"
2. But instead of directly answering their question, He first called a little child over to Himself and placed him in the center of the room,
3. and, once they had focused on the child, He said to them, "Boys, I really and truly want you to get this: Unless you change the way you think about things—until your mind is cleansed from your cynicism and competitiveness with one another...until you have a paradigm shift that moves you from the silliness of being 'childish' so that you can enter the freedom of becoming 'child-like'...and until you grasp the difference between these two concepts—you're never going to be subjects in My Kingdom at all!
4. "Whoever will remove the mental clutter of adulthood so that he or she can re-connect with what is the best part of childhood—the simple, basic ideas of trust, humility, love, forgiveness, imagination—that person will rank very high in the Kingdom of/from the heavens.
5. "Furthermore, you should know that I am so identified with these little ones, I can tell you that whoever receives and loves and welcomes and celebrates one little child like this for My sake, and in My name, receives and loves and welcomes and celebrates Me.
6. "On the other hand, whoever hurts one of these precious ones—or abuses them in any way...or takes advantage of their simple trust...or causes them to grow up and be less than what they should have been—it would actually be better for that individual to have one of those huge grinding-stones that they use in the mills fastened around his neck and to be sunk in the depth of the sea.
7. "The world suffers terribly because of those who bring this kind of sin into it. Children are going to have a difficult enough time learning to make right choices for themselves, without selfish adults making it even harder for them to do so. The on-going struggle to choose the right path is a fact of life and a rite of passage, but those strong ones who cause the weak ones to go astray bring a certain

kind of curse on themselves!

8. "So, let Me put it this way: Your desire to be a good example should be such that if, say, your hand or your foot causes you to stumble and sin, you would be willing to just cut it off and throw it away. It would, in fact, be better for you to go through life maimed or lame than to have two hands or two feet and your very existence become so worthless that you end up being thrown into the fires at the garbage dump outside Jerusalem, which never go out.

9. "By the same token, if your eye causes you to stumble and sin, you should be willing to pluck it out and throw it away from you. Again, it would be better for you to go through life with only one eye than to have two eyes and live in such a way that would cause you to end up being thrown into the fires of Gehenna.

10. "This may sound extreme to you, but you need to comprehend the importance of this point. It is simply unacceptable to damage one of these little ones...or even to resent or despise them in any way. Remember this: Their personal angels are constantly in touch with My Father in the heavenly realm.

11. [Verse 11 does not exist in any original manuscripts.]

12. "Now think about this: If a man has a hundred sheep and one of them has gone astray and gets lost, won't that man (if he's a true shepherd) leave the ninety-nine on the mountain and go in search of the one that is lost?

13. "And then, if he finds it, doesn't he make far more over it than over the ninety-nine who haven't wandered off?

14. "Well, your Father in the heavenly realm feels exactly the same way about people, especially these little ones. He doesn't intend to ever stop searching for those who are lost, until every single one is found!

15. "So, since your Father is so relentless in His love for you, you should be relentless in your love for one another. For example, if your brother or sister wrongs you in any way, you should have the integrity to go and tell him or her about it directly, and keep the conversation and the whole matter between the two of you. And if he/she 'hears' you...I mean listens to and receives what you have to say...you have won back your brother or your sister.

16. "But if the offender refuses to listen to you, don't give up your pursuit of reconciliation, yet. Take along with you one or two others so that every word may be confirmed and upheld by the testimony of two or three witnesses...and try again.

17. "If that doesn't work and he or she still won't listen or receive you, then, and only then, go public with it. Get up and tell the whole church what's going on between the two of you. And if that still doesn't work, and you still can't work out a way to re-connect with that person in relationship, then you may have no choice but to stop your physical efforts and just pray for him or her. In that case, you will have to love the one who hurt you from afar, as you would a pagan or a tax collector.

18. "Let Me tell you why this is so essential. First, as I have already told you, whatever you forbid and declare to be improper and unlawful on earth must be what is already forbidden and declared unlawful in the heavenly realm. In the same way, whatever you permit and declare proper and lawful on earth must be what is already permitted in the heavenly realm.

19. "This is why relationships are so important. See, if two of you on earth come into the kind of agreement that exists between those in the heavenly realm, you create a supernatural harmony together that makes a symphony...and that kind of harmony is the music of God, the ONE song or the 'Uni-Verse,' no discord, no dissonance, no instrument out of tune with the others. And when that symphony is played, the agreement causes whatever (anything and everything) they may ask to come to pass and be done for them by My Father in heaven.

20. "Because wherever at least two or three are gathered or drawn together in and into My name—when that kind of harmony takes place—there is a revelation of the Christ, and there the I AM is in the midst of them."

21. Then Peter, intrigued by all this talk of reconciliation and harmony, came up to Him and said, "Lord, how many times may my brother sin against me and I forgive him and just let it go? I mean, You're talking about a relentless pursuit of reconciliation so that people can be in harmony with one another...so...should I go so far as to forgive him seven whole times?"

22. Jesus answered him, "Oh, Peter, you're way off; I say that you shouldn't stop at seven times, but that you should forgive seventy times seven…and by that I mean into infinity! You never, ever stop forgiving.

23. "Let Me explain it this way: The Kingdom of/from the heavens is like a human king who wanted to settle accounts with his attendants.

24. "When he began the accounting, it became apparent that someone owed him a huge amount of money. So the man who owed so much was found and brought to him, and when all of his debts were added up it was discovered that he owed the king several million dollars.
25. "Well, the man didn't have anywhere near that kind of money, so the king ordered him to be sold into slavery, along with his wife and his children and everything that he possessed, so that at least some of the debt could be repaid.
26. "So the man, overwhelmed with the enormity of the debt and the severity of the situation, fell on his knees and just begged the king, pitifully. He said, 'Please, sir, don't destroy my family by selling us into slavery. I beg you to have mercy and patience with me, and I promise that somehow I will pay you everything.'
27. "And the man seemed so sincere that the king's heart was moved with compassion for him. So, as a gesture of good will he released him and forgave him of the entire debt!
28. "And would you believe, the very same attendant got up and went to find one of his fellow attendants who owed him about twenty dollars. And when he found him, he grabbed him by the throat, started wringing his neck, and demanded, 'Pay me right now what you owe me!'
29. "So his fellow attendant, startled by this attack, fell down and begged him earnestly, saying, 'Please, just give me time and I promise to pay you back!'
30. "But he wouldn't hear of it, and he went out and had the man put in prison till he could pay the debt.
31. "As you can imagine, when his fellow attendants saw what had happened, they were indignant, and so they went and told everything that had taken place to the king.
32. "So the king called the man back in and said to him, 'I've never in my life seen anything like this display of ingratitude and wickedness on your part! Out of the goodness of my heart I forgave and cancelled all that huge debt of yours because you begged me to, and I felt sorry for you.
33. "How is it possible that you could leave here and go straight to this man and treat him the way that you did? You received so much mercy from me...where was the mercy you should have given him?'
34. "And the king was understandably incensed and irate with this insensitive ingrate and turned him over to the torturers in the jail

until he should pay all that he owed.
35. "The point of the story is this: My heavenly Father expects every one of you to be as forgiving as you have been forgiven; don't force Him to treat you the way the king treated the man because of his unwillingness to show the same mercy that was shown him!"

Chapter 19

1. When Jesus had finished saying these things, He left Galilee and went into the part of Judea that is on the other side of the Jordan.
2. And great throngs followed Him there, and so He healed them there.
3. And while He was in the area, the Pharisees came to Him again and put Him to the test by asking, "Is it legal and right for a man to dismiss his wife...to divorce her for any reason that he may have?"
4. He replied to them, "Have you never read in your Scriptures that He Who made them from the beginning made them male and female?
5. "This is why a man has to leave his father and mother at some point and be united and bonded to his wife…and when that happens, the two of them become, in a sense, one single entity,
6. so that they are no longer two separate physical bodies, but actually become one new one. And if a particular union between a man and a woman is, indeed, God-ordained, then no human being should do anything to create a disconnect between what God has put together."
7. They shot back at Him, "Well if marriage is so special…if, indeed, it is a God-created thing, then why did Moses make it so practical and easy to get a divorce? According to his law, all a man has to do to get out of a marriage is to send his wife a written notice and then just simply dismiss her from his life and be done with her altogether."
8. He said to them, "Moses set up this system basically because of the hardness of your hearts…specifically, your insensitivity to women. He permitted you to simply dismiss your wives with no regard for required responsibility to them because you have had no concept of covenant. But in this Moses did not have the heart and mind of God, considering that this self-serving male convenience was not in God's original plan.
9. "But I say to you that whoever just casually dismisses his wife for no legitimate reason, and marries the next available woman who comes along, really is only committing adultery with her. His shallow flippancy in such a case shows that he has no understanding of the

seriousness of covenant. The situation is somewhat different if the wife has been unfaithful to her husband, but the real issue is still about the apparent disregard of covenant. So, if a man marries a woman just because she was dismissed for her unfaithfulness to her husband, he is still just committing adultery with her if there is no genuine commitment to the covenant of marriage."

10. The disciples, listening in on this conversation, said to Him, "If that's really what marriage is about...if covenant is really that important...if God takes it that seriously...then no man in his right mind would ever want to get married! What would be the point of limiting your options by binding yourself to that kind of commitment?"

11. But He said to them, "Marriage is for men...not for boys. That's why not all men can accept this concept. It's for those who are mature enough to understand and appreciate the value of human, adult relationships.

12. "But it also requires a certain kind of maturity to understand that this kind of relationship isn't for everyone. There are some asexual men who, from birth, never seem to give women or marriage a thought. Other men may have been intentionally emasculated for cultural purposes or for other reasons. And still others are single and celibate for spiritual pursuits...as if they were married only to the Kingdom of/from the heavens. Whatever the case, it requires insightful maturity to comprehend that not everyone takes the same path or has the same needs in these matters. If you can receive this, you will be able to live and let live."

13. When this unusual exchange ended, people started bringing their little children to Jesus, requesting that He put His hands on them and pray for them. But the disciples, thinking that this was unimportant, or beneath Jesus or was a waste of His time, openly rebuked those who brought them.

14. But He stopped them immediately and said, "You leave these children alone! Allow every single one of these little ones to come to Me, and don't you ever forbid or restrain them again. Not only are they important…they are what the Kingdom of/from the heavens is all about!"

15. And He laid His hands on them, and after He had prayed for all of them, He went on His way.

16. Another day a man came up to Jesus and asked, "Teacher, You're

good, so I ask You: what good thing must I do to be in full possession of eternal life?"
17. Jesus said, "Why do you question Me about what's good; in fact, why do you even call Me good? God is the only One Who is good. If you want to enter the life of God, just practice His precepts...keep His commandments...and you will manifest His goodness in your life."
18. This statement was too general for the man, so he probed a little further, saying, "Okay, then...which commandments, in particular, should I keep?"
19. Jesus said, "All of them are important—don't murder, don't commit adultery, don't steal, don't lie about people, honor your father and mother—basically all the different ways of simply saying 'love your neighbor as you love yourself.'"
20. The young man said, "That's it? That's all there is? I've kept all these commandments practically my whole life and I'm still not good. What am I missing?"
21. Jesus said to him, "Look, if you're really that serious about manifesting the character of God in your life, then go sell everything that you have, give everything that you make from the sale to the poor, and then you'll be free to become one of My disciples. The entirety of your possessions will then be in the Kingdom and all that you own will be deposited into the heavenly realm."
22. But Jesus went too far for the young man on this point. The idea of selling everything—this suggestion of total abandon—just seemed too extreme for him, especially because he was wealthy and had a lot of possessions. Jesus' words not only caught him off guard, they also overwhelmed and depressed him...and so, not knowing what to say, he turned around and walked away in convicted silence.
23. As Jesus watched him go, He said to the disciples who were standing there with Him, "I tell you, truthfully, it is really quite difficult...extremely hard...for a rich man to become a subject in the Kingdom of/from the heavens.
24. "In fact, it's easier for a camel to go through that little gate that they leave open at night in the walls of Jerusalem called 'the Needle's Eye'...the gate that is so low and narrow that a large animal can only pass through it on its knees and unencumbered with baggage. It's symbolic of the way a rich man has to enter the Kingdom."
25. For some reason, the disciples were staggered by these words. They

said to Him, "Well, then, if that's the case, who has any chance at all of being fit for the Kingdom?"
26. Jesus looked straight at them, and into them, and said, "Things like this are virtually impossible when only using human strength...but with God's help, anything and everything is really possible!"
27. Then Peter spoke up and said, "Well, now that You mention it, we may not have had the kind of wealth that young man has, but we've left everything that we did have to follow You. What are we going to get for our sacrifice?"
28. Jesus said to them, "Yes, you have, in fact, followed Me fully, and so I say to you that in the new age...when the earth is reborn into the revelation of the Christ...when the Son of Man is enthroned in glory...you will be enthroned, as well! In fact, all who have followed Me will rule and have dominion, starting with the twelve tribes of Israel.
29. "And this is the part the wealthy young man didn't stick around long enough to find out: Anyone who sacrifices home, family, property, whatever—because of their desire to follow Me—will get every bit of it back a hundred times over! And this is in addition to the promise of the full blessings of eternal or 'now-life!'
30. "And in this there is a great reversal coming; many of the so-called 'first' ones will actually end up being the last to walk in this. And, by the same token, many who are considered to be the 'last' to come in will, in reality, be the first to obtain it.

Chapter 20

1. "For the Kingdom of/from the heavens operates like this: Imagine that the owner of an estate with a winery went out very early in the morning to hire workers for his vineyard.
2. "And the workers that he found agreed to accept the modest, daily wage that he offered them and then went right to the task at hand.
3. "A little later that morning (around nine o'clock) he went to town and noticed that there were some able men who were standing around, doing nothing.
4. "So he said to them, 'Hey, if you're looking for work, I have some; go over to my vineyard and get started, and I will pay you whatever is appropriate.' And they went.
5. "He went out again around noon and did the same.

6. "And again, at about five o'clock (or what is referred to in the workplace as 'the eleventh hour'), he went out and found still others standing around, and he asked them, 'Why do all of you just hang out like this all day long, doing nothing?'
7. "And they answered him, 'Because no one is hiring right now; there's no work for us to do.' So he told them, 'All of you go over to my vineyard and start working, and I'll pay each of you a fair wage.'"
8. "At sundown, when the workday was over, the owner of the vineyard said to his manager, 'Call every one of the workmen and pay them their wages, beginning with the last ones who have come in and ending with the first.'
9. "So, those who had been hired at five o'clock (the eleventh hour) came and received their day's wages.
10. "Now when the first ones came to be paid, they understandably supposed that they would get more than the 'last' people, but each of them received the very same amount that the other group received.
11. "And when they looked at their pay, they angrily protested to the owner of the estate,
12. saying, 'this isn't fair! These men who came in at five worked no more than an easy hour, and yet you've compensated them exactly the same as you have those of us who worked so hard...all day long...out in the scorching heat!'
13. "But he calmly answered the irate group's spokesman, saying, 'Buddy, I'm not being unfair with any of you. We agreed on a wage and that's exactly what you were paid. Right?
14. 'So take your pay and just be happy with what you've got. If I choose to give to this man hired last the same as I give you, what difference does it make? No one is taking anything away from what is rightly yours.
15. "'Am I not allowed to do what I choose with what is mine? It's my vineyard and my money...and, furthermore, I never told you that I wasn't going to hire other people. As long as it doesn't affect you negatively, why do you resent my generosity to others or my philosophy of equal-opportunity employment?'
16. "Once again, I'm showing you this concept of a great reversal, as it were...My Kingdom operates on these principles. Many who you would consider to be the first in line will actually end up being the last, and (as I've told you already) many whom you would consider

to be the last will, in the big picture, actually be the first."
17. And as Jesus was going up to Jerusalem, He took the Twelve disciples off to the side of the road and said to them,
18. "All right, I need you to listen to Me carefully. We're not just on our way to Jerusalem...we're heading toward the consummation of everything that's been happening for the last three years...the grand finale to My time and purpose in this dimension. So I want to re-iterate: When we get to the city, the Son of Man will be betrayed to the religious leaders and scholars, and they're going to sentence Him to death.
19. "Then they will hand Him over to the Romans to be mocked, tortured and crucified. But, as I've been telling you, on the third day He will be raised up alive. I keep telling you this so that it will sink in...so that you won't be taken by surprise when it all begins to happen."
20. Around this time the mother of the Zebedee brothers came with her two sons and knelt before Jesus, telling Him that she wanted to make a certain request.
21. He looked down at her and asked, "What do you want?" She answered Him, "I want You to give me Your word that these two sons of mine will be awarded the highest places of honor in Your Kingdom. I want You to put one of them in a position at Your right hand and one in a place of recognition at Your left hand."
22. Jesus responded to her, "Lady, you have no idea what you're asking." Then He looked over to James and John and said, "Do you boys think that you're even capable of drinking the cup that I'm about to drink?" They said to Him, "Of course we are!"
23. Then Jesus said, "Yes, in reality you are going to drink My cup, even though you still don't fully comprehend what's about to happen. But as to awarding places of honor, I've put Myself into such a place of submission to the Divine will that that's not even My business now. My Father is taking care of that."
24. When the other ten disciples got wind of this conversation, they were thoroughly disgusted with the two brothers and their opportunistic mother.
25. So Jesus got them all together to settle things down a bit. He said to them, "Look, you've all seen how insecure, ungodly, power-drunk rulers throw their weight around, tyrannizing those who are 'under' them...

26. well, it just can't be that way with you. My Kingdom is bringing about a new order in the earth...a new reality in which whoever wishes to be great among you must be your servant,
27. and whoever desires to be in charge of everyone else must be willing to serve as everyone else's slave!
28. "Don't you see, this is precisely what the Son of Man has done; He came to serve, not to be served...He came to give away His life in exchange for all those who are held hostage by death."
29. And as they were going out of Jericho, a huge crowd followed along after Him.
30. And suddenly they came upon two blind men sitting beside the road. When they heard that it was Jesus passing by, they yelled out, "Lord, please have mercy on us! Have mercy, Son of David!"
31. For some reason the crowd tried to shut them up, but their attempts to stifle the men only caused them to get louder. They lifted up their voices, again crying, "Lord, have mercy on us! Mercy, Son of David!"
32. Jesus, ignoring the crowd's vain efforts to quiet them, stopped and called out to the two men, asking, "What do you want Me to do for you?"
33. They answered Him, "Lord, we just want our eyes to be opened!"
34. And Jesus, deeply moved by their persistence, as well as their simplicity, walked over to them and touched their eyes. And when He did, they instantly received their sight and jumped up and joined the procession.

Chapter 21

1. When they came near to Jerusalem and had reached Bethphage at the Mount of Olives, Jesus sent two of His disciples on ahead,
2. saying to them, "Go into the village that is across from you, and there you'll find a donkey tied and a colt with her. When you locate them, untie them and bring them to Me.
3. "If anyone should object to you taking them, you just need to say, 'The Lord needs them!' You will have no resistance from anyone to whom you say these words."
4. This happened to fulfill what was spoken by the prophet,
5. "Say to Zion's Daughter (the inhabitants of Jerusalem), 'Look at this! Your King is coming to you, riding on a donkey and on a colt,

the foal of a donkey.'"
6. Then the disciples went and did exactly as Jesus had directed.
7. They brought the donkey and the colt to Jesus and laid their coats across them, and He seated Himself on the donkey.
8. And the majority of the crowd took a cue from the disciples and began to spread their garments on the road, laying down a sort of community-created red carpet for Him. Others kept cutting branches from the trees and scattering them on the road to make a widespread welcome mat.
9. And the crowds that went ahead of Him, and those that followed along behind Him, kept shouting, "Hosanna! Save, Lord! Hosanna to the Son of David! Blessed is He Who comes in the name of the Lord! Hosanna in the highest heights of the heavenly realm!"
10. By the time He entered the gates of Jerusalem, the excitement created by this whole scenario had escalated to fever-pitch...the entire city seemed to be electrified and buzzing with one, universal question: "Who in the world is this?"
11. And the people who were part of the parade called out to those who asked, "This is the prophet, Jesus, from Nazareth of Galilee!"
12. Once inside the city, Jesus went straight into the Temple and began throwing out anyone and everyone who had set up shop there to buy and/or sell. Without any warning, He started kicking over the tables of the loan sharks, as well as the stalls of dove merchants who profited from the sales of sacrificial animals.
13. He quoted this text to them: *"My house was designated to be a house of prayer; but you have degraded it down to nothing more than a hangout for thieves!"*
14. And once this area was cleared out, the blind and the lame came to Him in the porches and courts of the Temple, and at once He seamlessly transitioned from prophetic-warrior mode into that of compassionate healer. As He had driven out every last one of the shady business people with His own hands, so He restored every last one of those who were in need of His healing touch.
15. But when the religious leaders saw the wonderful things that He was doing, and witnessed how the young people, including little boys and girls, were excitedly running through every part of the Temple crying out "Hosanna to the Son of David!" they were furious.
16. And so they said to Him, "Do You hear what these out-of-control children are saying?" And Jesus replied, *"Of course, I hear them...*

17. have you not read in your own Scriptures, 'Out of the mouths of the children and even the babies You have provided perfect praise?'"
17. And, having had enough of their predictable protests for the day, He left the city for Bethany, where He spent the night.
18. Early the following morning, as Jesus was returning to the city, He realized that He was hungry.
19. And as He saw a single, leafy fig tree beside the road, He went over to it to find a breakfast of figs, but found nothing on it but leaves. So He said directly to the deceptive-looking tree, "Never again shall fruit grow on you!" And at these words, the fig tree withered right there on the spot, becoming nothing but a dry stick protruding from the ground.
20. The disciples who were walking with Him saw this and rubbed their eyes in disbelief, saying, "Did we really see what we just saw?! One minute there's a perfectly healthy tree standing right in front of us and the next just a dry stick is there!"
21. But Jesus, as usual, was matter-of-fact about the miraculous. He said to them "Look, if you simply embrace this Kingdom life and don't doubt God, you'll not only be able to perform minor feats like this (I do these kinds of things all the time), but you'll also easily triumph over huge obstacles, as well. This mountain, for example... you'll tell it what to do or where to go, just as I told the fig tree what to do, and it will do exactly as you say.
22. "In fact, this kind of dominion can become second-nature to you to the point that the power of your intention—or whatever you ask for in prayer, having faith—will enable you to receive that for which you believe."
23. And when He entered the Temple, the ever-vigilant religious leaders came up to Him as He was teaching and asked, "By what power of authority are You doing these things, and who gave You this power of authority?"
24. Jesus answered them, "This time I will answer your question with another question, and if you give Me the answer, then I also will tell you by what power of authority I do these things...
25. the baptism of John...from where did it originate? Did it come from heaven or did it come from men?" This immediately set a private meeting into motion among them, in which they said to one another, "Watch out...this is a trick question; if we say that the baptism originated in heaven, He will no doubt ask us, 'Why then did you not

believe him?'
26. "But if we say, 'It is of mere human origin,' we're going to receive so much flak from the people, for they all regard John as a prophet."
27. So they had no choice but to answer Jesus, "We don't know." And He said to them, "Fair enough; so neither will I tell you by what power of authority I do these things."
28. Then He said, "All right, tell Me what you think of this story: A man had two sons, and one day He went up to one of them and said, 'Son, go out for the day and work in the vineyard.'
29. "But the son answered, 'I just don't want to,' but later on he changed his mind and went.
30. "Then the father gave the same command to the second son and he answered, 'Sure, Dad, I'd be glad to go'...but, in fact, he never went.
31. "I ask you: which of the two sons did what the father asked?" They said, "Well, obviously, the first son." Jesus said, "You are correct... and that's why I tell you that the crooks and the whores are going to precede you into God's Kingdom!
32. "See, John came to you showing you the right road to take, but you turned up your pious, religious noses at him. And yet, at the same time, the crooked law-breakers and the women who sell themselves into prostitution somehow believed him. But even though you witnessed this phenomenon—you saw their receptivity as well as their changed lives—you still didn't care enough to allow for a paradigm shift and believe him for yourselves.
33. "And here's another story to consider: There was a prominent landowner who planted a vineyard and put a hedge around it, dug a wine vat in it and built a watchtower there. Then he rented out the vineyard to some tenants and moved somewhere else.
34. "When it was time to harvest the grapes, he sent his servants back to collect his profits.
35. "But the tenants took his servants and beat up one of them, killed another, and stoned yet another.
36. "So again he sent some of his other servants to the vineyard, more even than the first time, and they treated them the very same way.
37. "Finally he sent his own son to them, saying, 'surely, they will respect my own son and not treat him the way that they have treated my servants.'
38. "But, as it turned out, when the tenants saw the son, they said to themselves, This is the heir to the fortune...let's kill him so that we

39. "And, sure enough, they took him and threw him out of the vineyard and killed him right then and there.
40. "Now when the owner of the vineyard comes back, what do you think he'll do to those horrible, murderous tenants?"
41. They said to Him, "Of course he should immediately put them all to a miserable death and then rent the vineyard to some tenants who will hand over the profits to him when it's time."
42. Jesus said, "Indeed." Then He asked them, "Have you never read in your Scriptures: 'the very Stone which the builders rejected and threw away has become the Cornerstone; this is the Lord's doing, and it is marvelous in our eyes?'
43. "That's why I tell you that, for this reason, the Kingdom will be taken away from you and given to people who will produce the fruits of it by living a Kingdom-life.
44. "And whoever stumbles on this Stone will be shattered to pieces, but he on whom it falls will be crushed to powder, scattering him like dust."
45. And when the religious leaders heard His dark, illustrative stories that day, they perceived that He was talking about them.
46. This particularly intense exchange was somewhat of a defining moment for them. At once they were now angrier and more determined than ever to arrest Him...but, at the same time, they were absolutely intimidated by public opinion. So, for the time being they held back, because most of the people perceived Him to be a prophet of God.

Chapter 22

1. Jesus responded by telling even more of His special kind of stories, saying,
2. "The Kingdom of/from the heavens is like a king who threw a wedding banquet for his son.
3. "He sent out his servants to call in all the invited guests, but they just wouldn't come!
4. "Then he sent out another round of servants, instructing them to tell the guests, 'Look, everything is on the table right now...the beef has been butchered and all the side dishes that go with it have been prepared to perfection. You are invited to come as you are to this

amazing feast and celebrate with us!'

5. "But these rude and clueless invitees basically shrugged their shoulders, ignoring the opportunity before them, and went off...one to weed his garden and another to work in his shop.

6. "The rest weren't just indifferent...they were openly hostile and aggressive. For no apparent reason, they beat up on the messengers and then killed them.

7. "When the king heard about this, he was understandably infuriated and sent his soldiers to put those ungrateful murderers to death and to burn down their whole city.

8. "Then he said to his servants, 'Here we've prepared this gorgeous wedding banquet, sparing no expense, but the ones who were initially invited didn't want our company, insulted our hospitality, and refused to join in our celebration. But we planned a wedding with a party and so we will have the wedding...and we will have our party!

9. "'I want you to go out into the busiest intersections in town where all kinds of people interact with one another, and invite anyone and everyone you find to our beautiful banquet!'

10. "So the servants took to the streets, searching every highway and back alley, rounding up anyone and everyone they laid eyes on, regardless of who they were, where they were, or what they were doing at the time. And so the banquet was on and every seat at the table was filled, as was every available spot on the dance floor and every corner of the reception hall.

11. "But when the king entered the banquet and looked over the whole scene, he saw a man who wasn't dressed in the appropriate, traditional attire that a gentleman would normally wear to a wedding feast at that time, in that culture.

12. "So he went to him and said, 'My friend, what makes you think that just because you were invited to my banquet, you can come in here ignoring protocol and insulting our customs?' The man was completely speechless and just looked at him, offering no excuse or explanation for this breach of etiquette, as if he had been muzzled or gagged.

13. "Then the king said to his servants, 'I want him out of here this instant! In fact, just so he won't try to come back in and disrupt my celebration, tie him up and make him sit outside in the dark; keep him away from the rest of my guests so they will be spared having to

see him snarl at them and grind his teeth in anger simply because they are having a good time and he was put out of the party.'

14. "For many in this nation are called; you, as a people, have all been invited, in fact, but out of that great number, relatively few of you are eligible for Kingdom-life."

15. After this, the Pharisees went and plotted together how they might entangle Jesus in His talk, causing Him to slip up and say something that they could use against Him.

16. So they sent some of their own disciples to Him, along with a few of Herod's followers mixed in to ask, "Teacher, we know that You have integrity, that You teach the way of God truthfully, regardless of possible consequences, that You are uncompromising in Your ethics, and that You don't pander to Your audience.

17. "That being said, tell us what You think about paying taxes…is it lawful to pay the tribute levied on individuals to Caesar or not?"

18. But Jesus replied, "Do you big phonies honestly think that I don't see through these kinds of bogus questions? Surely you can't be simple enough to assume that I would be rendered gullible by your empty compliments. That kind of flattery may work on you, but it doesn't on Me…why do you keep trying to trap Me with these tired old tricks?

19. "All right…I'll play along with your silly game. Do you have a coin? Let Me see it." They handed Him a silver piece.

20. "Okay…this engraving…whose likeness and image is it? And whose name is on it?"

21. They said, "Caesar's." Then He said to them, "Well, then, it should be obvious, shouldn't it? Pay to Caesar the things that are due to Caesar and pay to God the things that are due to God. It's that simple."

22. The Pharisees didn't have a comeback. Once again the profound simplicity of His words had left them speechless, so they went away shaking their heads.

23. The same day some Sadducees, who say that there is no resurrection of the dead, came to Him with a question of their own.

24. "Teacher," they began, "Moses said that if a man dies, leaving no children, his brother should marry his widowed sister-in-law and raise a family for his brother with her.

25. "So, let's say there were seven brothers and the first married and died and, having no children, left his wife to his brother.

26. "Then, the second brother also died childless, and the third, down to the seventh.
27. "Now...stay with us on this...let's say that, last of all, the woman died also.
28. "This is our question: in this scenario, in the resurrection, to which one of the seven brothers will she be wife, since she was married to all of them?"
29. But Jesus replied to them, "Not only is your premise implausible—quite a stretch to say the least—but your entire question is wrong-headed. It exposes a basic flaw in you: that you are ignorant... ignorant of the Scriptures...ignorant of God's power.
30. "For in the resurrection, neither men nor women get married, nor are they considered married when they enter the resurrected state...in that sense they are like the angels who live in the heavenly realm.
31. "But as to the larger question...the very reality of the resurrection of the dead...have you never read what was declared to you by God, Himself?
32. "He clearly said, 'I AM (not, "I was...") the God of Abraham and the God of Isaac and the God of Jacob!' Don't you get it? By Him saying I AM their God, He is revealing that He is the living God...not of dead people, but people who are alive!"
33. And when the crowd that had gathered around Him heard these words, His message of life bore witness with them and they were filled with amazement at His teaching.
34. Now when the Pharisees discovered that He had gotten the best of the Sadducees, as well, they gathered together with them, joining forces for an all-out assault.
35. So they chose one of their religion scholars who was a lawyer to speak for them, posing a question to Him that they hoped would finally show Him up.
36. He approached Jesus and said "Teacher, about the commandments... as You well-know, some are light and some are heavy...which command in God's Law is the most important one?"
37. Without missing a beat, Jesus answered, "'Love the Lord your God with all of your heartfelt passion, your willed intention, and your complete intellect or intelligence.'
38. "This is the most important...the one at the top of the list.
39. "But there is actually a second one which ranks so high that it is virtually part of the same commandment: 'Love others as

unconditionally as you love yourself.'
40. "These two commandments (which are three, really, because in the second one is the implied commandment to love yourself...so think of them, in a sense, as 'three in one') are like nails (or a nail) in a wall; and everything...and I mean everything...in God's Law and the prophets hangs from them."
41. Now while the Pharisees were still standing there, pondering this and regrouping, Jesus came back at them with a question of His own.
42. He pointedly asked them, "What do you think about the Christ? Whose Son is He?" They said, "He is David's son."
43. Jesus replied, "Well, if the Christ is indeed David's Son, how do you explain that David (under the influence of the Holy Spirit) calls Christ his 'Lord?'
44. "Because he (David) said, 'God said to my Master' (or, literally, 'the Lord said to my Lord'), "Sit here at My right hand until I make Your enemies Your footstool.'"
45. "Now if David calls Him 'Master' or 'Lord,' how can He at the same time be his son?"
46. Once again they were stumped, legalistic literalists that they were. But, on this occasion, they finally realized that there was just no way to win one of these Scriptural sparring matches with Jesus. So, reluctantly accepting the fact that all of their trick questions had backfired on them, and unwilling to continue to risk losing face again in one of these public exchanges, they quit asking questions for good from that day on.

Chapter 23

1. After that, Jesus turned to address His disciples, along with the great crowd that had gathered there with them.
2. He said to them all, "Look, when it comes to teaching the Law of God strictly from a legal standpoint, the religion scholars, particularly the scribes and Pharisees, are completely competent. In that sense, they sit on Moses' seat of authority.
3. "So, if you're just interested in being informed about the letter of the Law, they're the ones to see. In fact, you won't go wrong in following their teachings on Moses, but following them is a different story. The bottom line is, they don't practice what they preach because they don't have a relationship with God...and without

relationship, keeping 'the rules' just becomes a pointless exercise in absurdity.

4. "That's why they continually bundle up heavy loads, which are hard to bear, and place them on your shoulders, loading you down like pack animals. Then they seem to take pleasure in watching you stagger under these burdens of endless rules and regulations... commandments that they themselves can't and don't even keep...and never think of lifting a finger to help you try to figure out how to live up to this impossible lifestyle-standard which they have created.

5. "And the laws that they do in fact keep, they only do so to be seen of people. That's why they make their phylacteries (which are typically just small cases enclosing certain Scripture passages and worn during prayer on the left arm and forehead) so big and obvious! And even though all male Israelites, according to the command, wear fringes on their prayer garments, they make theirs extra long! It's as if they've totally missed the point of these external things and have turned something that should actually be meaningful into an empty fashion show.

6. "And then there's the whole other aspect of it which has to do with their love for public places of honor and having the best seats in the synagogues, which really speaks to their insatiable need for validation;

7. and they bask in the sunlight of public recognition and flattery, going beyond the normal use and appropriateness of titles. Their love for being called 'Rabbi' is an entirely different thing; it's as if their whole identity is wrapped up in the power that comes from that title.

8. "But the title of 'Rabbi' is irrelevant for you; you don't need to be put up on a religious pedestal, nor is the approval of men necessary or essential for you. Simply put, you have one Teacher and you are all brothers.

9. "Furthermore, don't even call anyone on earth 'father.' You obviously have earthly fathers to honor and mentors who are father figures in your life, but concerning the things of God, you have one Father—one Parent Who watches over your life and has rightful authority over you—Who is manifested in the heavenly realm.

10. "I'm helping you change your perspective on who and what is important in the Kingdom; that's why I even say that you must not be called 'Masters' or 'Leaders' or even 'Teachers;' if you have Kingdom authority, it will be recognized without the trappings of

human notoriety; your gift will make room for you, you won't have to convince anyone of your importance by demanding that they recognize you by a title. But the real issue at hand is that you have one Master/Leader/Teacher...the Christ!

11. "In the Kingdom there is a new order; in a word, whoever is greatest among you shall be your servant. The way to stand out is to step down.
12. "In the Kingdom, whoever exalts himself/herself—the person who puffs up himself/herself publicly with pride—will be publicly humbled and brought low. But whoever humbles himself/herself and is content to just be real and authentic and keep his or her importance in perspective, will be raised to a place of real honor.
13. "What sorrow you bring upon yourselves, you scribes and Pharisees, you frauds and pretenders; your obsession with control prevents your followers from entering the Kingdom of/from the heavens. It's not enough that you yourselves refuse to enter in...you don't want anyone else to enter in, either.
14. [Verse 14 does not exist in any original manuscripts.]
15. "What sorrow you bring upon yourselves, you scribes and Pharisees, you frauds and pretenders; you travel halfway around the world to make one convert and, when you find one and turn him or her to your way of thinking, you make that victim twice as fit for ending up in Gehenna, the garbage dump, as you are!
16. "What sorrow you bring upon yourselves, you blind guides who say that if anyone swears by the sanctuary of the Temple, it's no big deal...the oath isn't binding; but, at the same time, you say that if anyone swears by the gold of the sanctuary, that person is totally bound by his oath!
17. "Do you honestly not see how ridiculous your religious rules have become? Your preoccupation with the precision of these points of order has turned you into fools and has blinded you from seeing what really matters to God. Anyone with any sense would know that there is no logical way to decide which is greater...the gold, or the sanctuary of the Temple that has made the gold sacred.
18. "Then you say that whoever swears by the altar is not bound to keep his or her promise, but whoever swears by the offering on the altar is absolutely bound by their oath.
19. "How could men like you, who are supposedly intelligent, allow yourself to become so dumbed down by details like this? It's a silly

question, but which is greater...the gift, or the altar which makes the gift sacred?

20. "I mean, if you're going to split hairs over this issue, a simple observation would cause you to conclude that whoever swears by the altar swears by it and by everything on it.

21. "Furthermore, whoever swears by the sanctuary of the Temple swears by it and by Him Who dwells in it.

22. "And whoever swears by heaven swears by the throne of God and by Him Who sits upon it.

23. "Again, what sorrow you bring upon yourselves, you scribes and Pharisees, you frauds and pretenders. You're faithful to pay your tithes—meticulous about it, even—but you have neglected and omitted the weightier and more important matters of the Law, which are righteousness and justice and mercy. Look, I'm not saying that you shouldn't tithe...in fact you should...but not at the expense of missing the big picture. Everything that you care about, including tithing, should be about your relationship with God...without that, none of the religious mechanics matter.

24. "Your misguided myopia has degenerated into total blindness. Your thoughtless theology has caused you to become so trivial that you're like someone who constantly filters his drinking water to avoid swallowing a gnat, but has become so insanely compulsive about the filtering process that he doesn't even notice when he swallows a whole camel!

25. "What sorrow you bring upon yourselves, you scribes and Pharisees—you frauds and pretenders—you worry yourselves silly over how things look on the outside...things like the appearance of cups and plates...but you completely ignore all of the gross filthiness that is inside those spotless-looking containers.

26. "How could you have descended into such blind insanity? First, scrub the insides, and then the clean appearance on the surface will actually matter!

27. "What sorrow you bring upon yourselves, you scribes and Pharisees, you frauds and pretenders; you are like tombs that have been externally whitewashed...you look impressive on the outside and appear as beautiful memorials to the lives of the men and women buried within, but, in fact, on the inside there is only the harsh reality of death...only dead men's bones and inevitable decomposition.

28. "The people look at you and think that you are authentic, but beneath

the surface there is nothing about you that is real.

29. "What sorrow you bring upon yourselves, you scribes and Pharisees...you frauds and pretenders...you build these great granite tombs for your prophets and these magnificent marble monuments for your saints.

30. "And all the while you say that had you lived in the days of your forefathers, you would not have aided them in shedding the blood of those prophets and saints.

31. "Truth be told, you shouldn't even mention your forefathers in this context, because everyone knows that you're just like them, and when you protest too much and try to make yourselves look good in everyone's sight, it makes it obvious to all that you are their descendants.

32. "In fact, you are even now doing the very same things your ancestors did...you add to the death-count of the prophets daily.

33. "Let Me put it this way: you're just a bunch of snakes...vipers, full of the dangerous poison of dead religion! How do you not see that this whole, obsolete system of yours just needs to be dismantled and thrown into the garbage dump at Gehenna?

34. "It's because of people like you that I keep sending prophets and seers and scholars who actually understand the Law, and what it is and isn't; I send them generation after generation, but you never discern them, and when you hear them speak new truth and greater ideas to you, you automatically go into attack mode. You only know how to kill what threatens you and to destroy what you don't understand.

35. "Look, all of this treatment of the prophets is going to come back on your own heads...the blood of the righteous shed on the earth, from the blood of Abel to the blood of Zechariah, son of Barachiah, whom you murdered while he was praying between the sanctuary and the altar of burnt offering.

36. "I'm telling you, the harvest from all this is about to come down hard on this nation, and on this generation.

37. "Jerusalem! Jerusalem! Murderer of prophets...killer of the ones who brought you God's gospel throughout the ages! Do you have any idea how often I've literally ached to embrace your children the way a mother hen gathers her little chicks under her wings? Yes, I admit it...I wanted to love you like that, but you just wouldn't let Me.

38. "And now look at you...your own stubbornness has left you forsaken and desolate and abandoned.
39. "So, what is left to say? I only have a few more hours in this dimension, walking in the incarnation in which you now see Me. On one level, I weep for you—you have no idea of the destruction that's about to come on you as a nation—and yet you will see Me again in the revelation of the Spirit...I mean, really 'see' Me...and when you do, you'll say, 'Blessed, adored, exalted is He Who comes in the name of the Lord! Let us worship the One Who has brought God's rule to the earth!'"

Chapter 24

1. Jesus then left the Temple area and was going on His way when His disciples came up to Him and began to discuss the buildings of the Temple and how imposing and impressive they thought the architecture to be.
2. But He said to them, "You may be rightfully impressed with what you see before you...the Temple is, indeed, something to behold. But the truth is, there is not one stone in that magnificent building that is not going to end up in a pile of rubble."
3. Later, as He was sitting alone on the Mount of Olives overlooking Jerusalem, His disciples came to Him and said, "Tell us more about the destruction of the Temple that You mentioned before. When are these things going to happen? Will that be the sign of Your fully coming into power and of the completion and consummation of this age and era?"
4. Jesus said to them, "Be careful that no one deceives or misleads you on these points...understand these beginning events marking the period between My resurrection and the Temple's destruction,
5. for during this time, many will come in falsehood claiming, 'I, alone, am the Christ,' and they will lead many away from the truth of Who and what the Christ is, in reality.
6. "Also, during this time you will hear of wars and rumors of wars; see that you are not frightened or troubled, for this must take place; wars will come and go as they always have, but the end of the age is not yet.
7. "And nation will fight nation, ruler will fight ruler, famines and earthquakes will occur in various places, as they always have.

8. "These events are a part of the natural order of things...but, in another sense, they are also the birth pangs of the destruction that is coming on this nation.
9. "And they will hand you over to suffer affliction and tribulation and even put you to death. You should know this now: a period of time is coming when you will seemingly be hated by all nations because you carry My name.
10. "In fact, the conflict will become so intense that many will be offended and repelled and will stumble and fall away from My truth, even betraying one another and pursuing one another with hatred because of My testimony.
11. "And in all the confusion, false prophets will rise up in opportunism and deceive a lot of gullible people.
12. "And, worse yet, the love of the majority of people will grow cold because of the multiplied chaos and iniquity.
13. "But whoever endures until the end of this period of time will find that their salvation is real, durable and fully intact.
14. "And this Good News of the Kingdom will be preached throughout the entire, known world as a testimony to all the nations (Colossians 1:5, 6, 23; Romans 1:8, 10:18) and then will come the end of the age...the end of the Temple and its sacrificial system...the consummation of the Law...the end of the covenant nation of Israel...in a word, the end of the world as you now know it.
15. "So when you see the sacrilege and the appalling abomination spoken of by the prophet Daniel—the desecration set up in the Temple sanctuary when armies come to destroy both Jerusalem and the Temple—let the one who has read the prophecy take notice and realize that this is its fulfillment.
16. "And if you're living in Judea at the time, you'll need to run for the hills.
17. "If, at that time, you're up on the roof of your house, or working in your yard, don't even go into the house to get anything.
18. "If you're out in the field, don't go back to get your coat.
19. "Unfortunately, pregnant and nursing mothers will have it especially hard during this time of persecution.
20. "Even though this is inevitable, you should pray that it won't happen during the winter or on a Sabbath.
21. "Seriously, what's about to happen to this Temple...this city...this nation will be on a scale beyond what the known world has ever seen

or will see again.

22. "In fact, if this Great Tribulation—these dark days of destruction—were left to run their course, nobody would survive. But on account of the ones that God has chosen, the trouble will actually be cut short.

23. "But, if during this period anyone says to you, 'Look, this person right here is the Christ!' or 'That man over there is the Christ!'...do not believe it for a second.

24. "For after My resurrection and ascension, the Christ will no longer be manifested and revealed as an individual person; so when these singular false Christs and false prophets arise, be aware of what's really happening. And don't be deceived by their tricks, for some of them will show great signs and wonders so as to lead many astray and to cause many to view them as an individual Christ. In fact, if it were possible, they would attempt to deceive even the ones that God has chosen as the first-fruits of salvation.

25. "Now, see and remember...I have warned you of all of this beforehand.

26. "So, if they say to you, 'Look, He's out there in the wilderness,' don't even bother to go out there and look. And if they tell you, 'He's in some secret place,' do not believe it.

27. "This revelation—the true appearing of the Son of Man—isn't something you can go somewhere to see. On the contrary, it comes to you as fast as lightning!

28. "But, in the same way that a gathering of vultures indicates that there is a carcass nearby, so these signs will reveal that the end of an era is near."

29. Then, speaking to them in poetic, prophetic vocabulary, or in a symbolic language of prophecy that His audience understood from their familiarity with the Law and the prophets (Genesis 1:14-16; Isaiah 13:9, 10; 34:4; Amos 8:9; Ezekiel 32:7, 8), He said, "Immediately after this Great Tribulation, the sun will be darkened, and the moon will not shed its light, and the stars will fall from the sky, and the powers of the heavens will be shaken." (In this way He used the same imagery that the prophets of old had employed to speak of the downfall of earthly authorities and governors).

30. And He went on to say, "Then the sign of the Son of Man will appear in heaven, or in the heavenly realm...the sign indicating that this destruction of Jerusalem and the Temple means He is now

enthroned in heaven, ruling over the whole earth...this cataclysmic series of events will show that the Kingdom has been taken away from a visible nation and given to an invisible one...that the destruction of the natural Temple has made way for a Temple of the Spirit to be built in the heavenlies." And, once again using the imagery of the prophets of old (Psalm 104:3; Isaiah 19:1; Nahum 1:3), He said, "And all the tribes of the earth will repent with great emotion when they see the Son of Man coming on the clouds of heaven (an almost commonplace Scriptural symbol for His presence, judgment and salvation) with power and great glory!

31. "And He will send out His messengers—ministers of the gospel who will sound out His Good News like a loud trumpet call—and they will gather His chosen ones—the ones He has chosen in Him from the foundation of the world—they will call them in from the four winds, from every part of the earth...into His New Temple in His New Nation, His New Synagogue of the Spirit...from one end of the universe to the other.

32. "From the fig tree, learn this lesson: as soon as its young shoots become soft and tender and it starts to put out leaves, you know for a fact that summer is near.

33. "And so it is with you...when you see all these things coming to pass, you'll know the full revelation of Him is at the door.

34. "I'm telling you the truth, so do not take this lightly or assume that this is some far-off, futuristic prophecy that has no relevance to you. I'm not saying all this for some generation that will live hundreds of years from today. This is for all of you who are alive right now! And this era continues until all these things take place.

35. "Count on the validity of these words...the sky and the earth will fade away before any of My words do, because My words are eternally and absolutely true.

36. "I've told you these things to prepare you for the imminent judgment coming on this nation, but concerning the full revelation of the Son of Man and when, exactly, it will occur, no one knows, not even the angels of heaven, nor the Son, but only the Father.

37. "But I can tell you what I do know about it: this great, global revelation of the Son will take place in times like Noah's.

38. "It will be just as it was in those days before the flood...there were no signs...nothing out of the ordinary happening...everyone was carrying on as usual, eating and drinking, marrying and being given

in marriage, until the day when Noah went into the ark.

39. "The population, at large, knew nothing of God's intention until the flood hit and swept everything that was unrighteous away; only the righteous were left behind. The revelation of the Son of Man will be like that, only this time it will be a flood of grace.

40. "As the darnel will be separated from the wheat in you...as the catch in the dragnet will be divided in you, so 'two men,' as it were, will be working in the field...one will be taken, one left behind. The full revelation of the Son of Man will take away from you the man that needs to be purged and will leave behind the real you, the righteous you, the man that He has chosen.

41. "In the same way, 'two women' will be grinding at the mill...one will be taken in the Son of Man's flood—the part of that woman that is subject to His judgment—but one, the real one, will be mercifully left behind, safe in the ark of His redemption.

42. "Even so, regardless of the promise that the real you will ultimately be left behind, you should stay awake and alert. You have no idea when this revelation will come, so, until it does, you should make every effort to live righteously.

43. "In fact, you should be as vigilant as a homeowner looking out at all times for a burglar.

44. "You have no idea when the Son of Man is going to be revealed, so you should live in a prepared state of expectation at all times, simply because you want to please Him.

45. "Who is a faithful, thoughtful and wise servant whom his master has put in charge of his household to give to the others the food and supplies at the proper time?

46. "Blessed, indeed, is that servant whom, when his master comes, he will find so doing.

47. "Without a doubt, he will set him over all his possessions.

48. "But if that servant acts wickedly and says to himself, 'My master is delayed and is going to be gone a long time...and besides, he's always going to take care of me, regardless of what I do,'

49. and begins to beat his fellow servants and to eat up all the food that should be going to the hungry, and stays drunk all the time,

50. the master of that servant will come on a day when he does not expect him and at an hour in which he has let down his guard and is clueless,

51. and will judge him harshly, cutting him off from what he should

have been paid as a steward, and will put him out of the house, along with the other pretenders...outside in the cold, where his teeth will chatter as he weeps over what he has lost.

Chapter 25

1. "Now, back to the subject of the Kingdom of/from the heavens...it's comparable to ten young bridesmaids who took oil lamps and went out to greet the bridegroom.
2. "Five of them were silly and undiscerning, and five were smart and perceptive.
3. "The five who didn't have a clue took lamps, but no extra oil.
4. "The intelligent bridesmaids took flasks of oil to keep their lamps burning for an extended period of time.
5. "Well, the bridegroom didn't show up when expected, so as they sat around waiting for him, the bridesmaids all fell asleep.
6. "But sometime in the middle of the night someone yelled out, 'He's here! The bridegroom's here! Go out and greet him, as is customary for dignitaries, and accompany him into the city, and to the wedding feast!'
7. "Then all ten of the bridesmaids got up and readied their lamps for use.
8. "But the five who were irresponsibly unprepared said to the other ones, 'Our lamps are going out; lend us some of your oil.'
9. "They answered them, 'There might not be enough to go around; you need to go buy your own.'
10. "And they did go to buy their own, but while they were out making the purchase, the bridegroom arrived. When everyone who was there to greet him had gone into the wedding feast, the door was locked.
11. "Sometime later, the other bridesmaids, the silly ones, showed up and knocked on the door, saying, 'Sir, we're here. Let us in.'
12. "But he answered, 'Do I know you? I don't think I know you.' And he treated them as strangers.
13. "Now, obviously the Son of Man knows the people who are His own creation (the foolish ones as well as the wise ones), but I use this illustration to remind you to stay alert at all times. The operation of the Kingdom is very much about personal responsibility, and you have no idea when a visitation, an answer, a missing piece, a

'bridegroom' for a wedding, if you will, might arrive. So keep your eyes open and stay ready for Kingdom manifestations!

14. "And, speaking of personal responsibility, I could also say that the Kingdom operates like a man who was about to take a long journey and called his servants together and entrusted them with his property and investments in his absence.

15. "To one he gave about $5,000, to another he gave about $2,000, and to another he gave $1,000...to each in proportion to his own personal ability. Then he departed and left the country, leaving the whole operation of the business with them.

16. "The one who had received $5,000 got busy immediately and, in a smart investment deal, quickly made another $5,000.

17. "Likewise, the one who had received $2,000 used his skills to double his money, as well.

18. "But the one who had received $1,000 just decided to maintain (rather than to multiply), so he went and dug a hole in the ground and hid his master's money in it.

19. "Now after a while, the master of those servants returned and settled accounts with them.

20. "And the servant who had received $5,000 came and brought him $5,000 more, saying, 'Master, you entrusted to me $5,000, and here I have made another $5,000!'

21. "His master said to him, 'Nicely done, you good and faithful servant! You have been faithful and trustworthy over a little bit of finance and, now that I see what you're capable of, I will put you in charge of a lot more. Consider yourself promoted to live the lifestyle that your master enjoys...consider yourself a master, as well!'

22. "And then the one who was given $2,000 came forward, saying, 'Master, you entrusted $2,000 to me, and here I have gained $2,000 more!'

23. "His master said to him, 'Nicely done, you good and faithful servant! You have been faithful and trustworthy over a little bit of finance and, now that I see what you are capable of, I will also put you in charge of a lot more. Consider yourself also promoted to live the lifestyle that your master enjoys...and consider yourself a master, as well!'

24. "Then the one who had received $1,000 also came forward, saying, 'Master, I knew you to be a harsh and hard man, reaping where you did not sow and gathering where you had not winnowed the grain.

I knew that you were just lucky in life, and that's why you have what you have.

25. 'so I was afraid, and I went and hid your money in the ground. But you'll be happy to know that every penny of it is here!'

26. "To his surprise and dismay the master answered him, 'You lazy, good-for-nothing loser! Do you indeed know that I "reap where I have not sown and gather grain where I have not winnowed?"

27. 'You don't know the first thing about how I acquired my wealth, but you at least should have invested my money with the bankers so that at my coming I would have received what was my own, with interest! Did you honestly think that I would be impressed with the hole in the ground idea?

28. 'All right, here's what's going to happen. The two of you who doubled your money can keep what I gave you, along with your profits. But take the $1,000 away from this guy and give it to the one who has the $10,000!'

29. "And the master spoke something that is indicative of how the Kingdom works, for he said, 'To everyone who has will more be given, and he will be furnished richly so that he will always have an abundance. But from the one who does not have, even what he does have will be taken away from him.

30. 'And throw the good-for-nothing servant outside in the cold where he will weep over his missed opportunities and grind his chattering teeth in regret!'

31. "One more thing...when the Son of Man is fully revealed in all His glory, and all His messengers with Him, then He will sit on the throne of Kingdom authority.

32. "And the people of this nation will be gathered before Him, along with those from every other nation, and He will cause a separation in them as a shepherd separates his sheep from the goats.

33. "And He will have that which is compassionately righteous and sheep-like in them to be at His right hand, but that which is wickedly indifferent and goat-like to be at His left.

34. "Then the King will say to those who appear to be at His right hand, 'Come, you blessed of My Father, inherit as your very own the Kingdom prepared for you from the foundation of the world.

35. 'For I was hungry and you fed Me, I was thirsty and you gave Me something to drink, I was a stranger and you welcomed, entertained and took Me into your home,

36. I was naked and you clothed Me, I was sick and you visited Me and ministered to Me, I was in prison and you didn't forget to come to see Me.'
37. "Then the just and upright people will answer Him, 'Lord, when did we ever see You hungry and gave You food, or thirsty and gave You something to drink?
38. 'And when did we see You as a stranger and welcomed and entertained You? When did we see You naked and clothed You?
39. 'And when did we see You sick or in prison and came to visit You?'
40. "And the King will reply to them, 'this is the absolute truth: in so far as you did any of these things for one of My brethren, especially for one of the least in the estimation of men—one of the disenfranchised, one of the unfortunate ones, one who is overlooked and ignored—you did it for Me. My Kingdom is built on these principles.'
41. "Then He will say to those who appear to be at His left hand, 'It's a different story with you...this part of you that is cold and uncaring needs to be gone and cursed, purged in the fires of judgment!
42. 'For I was hungry and you gave Me no food, I was thirsty and you gave Me nothing to drink,
43. 'I was a stranger and you did not welcome Me or entertain Me, I was naked and you did not clothe Me, I was sick and in prison and you did not remember to visit Me, nor did you care at all about ministering to Me.'
44. "Then they also will answer, 'Lord, when did we ever see You hungry or thirsty or a stranger or naked or sick or in prison, and did not minister to Your needs?'
45. "And He will reply to them, 'This is the absolute truth: in so far as you failed to do it for the least of these in the estimation of men—as you failed to care, as you didn't even notice the suffering going on all around you—you failed to do it for Me. In your callousness you have violated the most basic principles of My Kingdom in which the first will be last and the last will be first!
46. 'Then those who are uncaring, indifferent, unfeeling, will go into the fire for a period of time—into a fiery trial that will ultimately burn out everything in them that is beastly and goat-like—until, at last, they are empathetic and compassionate to "the least of these," until they are like righteous sheep, humble and fit for the Kingdom—and then all those who are just and upright and in right

standing with God will enjoy the fullness of the eternal life.'"

Chapter 26

1. When Jesus had finished this discourse, He turned to His disciples and said,
2. "Now listen...you know that the Passover is in just two days, so I want you to be braced for what I've been telling you is going to happen...you know what I mean...in the next few hours the Son of Man will be betrayed, and handed over for crucifixion."
3. Even while He was trying to prep the disciples with these solemn words, the high priests and other religious leaders were already meeting in the chambers of the chief priest named Caiaphas,
4. working on a strategy to arrest Him so that they could secretly put Him to death.
5. But after much discussion, they agreed that the plot should not be carried out during Passover Week, for fear that, if the news of it was leaked, there could potentially be a riot among the people.
6. So Jesus went back to Bethany, as an invited guest in the house of Simon the Leper.
7. And while He was there having dinner, a woman came up to Him with an alabaster flask of some of the rarest and most expensive perfume that money could buy at that time...and, without warning or asking His permission, she opened it up and poured the entire contents of it all over His head as He reclined at the table.
8. When the disciples saw this very bold and extravagant display, and that Jesus didn't seem to be put off by her dramatic gesture or the obvious wastefulness demonstrated by it, they were absolutely indignant: "This is ridiculous! What purpose could it possibly serve to squander such valuable perfume like this?
9. "If this woman wanted to really do something worthwhile, she should have donated this valuable substance to the ministry, and we could have sold it and given the proceeds to the poor!"
10. But Jesus, fully aware of everything that was happening in this scenario—and of every one's perspective and motivation—said to them, "Why are you giving this fine lady such a hard time? She should be praised, not reprimanded, because she has done a beautiful thing to Me.
11. "Look, no matter how much you give away to the poor, and

11. (cont.) regardless of how much you minister to them, you are always going to have the poor here with you—needing you, expecting you to help them—but you're not always going to have Me in this incarnation, in this dimension, as I am now.
12. "In pouring this perfume out on Me, regardless of the expense of it, she has actually done something to prepare Me for My burial, whether she realized what she was doing or not.
13. "In fact, this gesture of hers was so prophetic and timely, that anywhere the Good News of the Gospel is preached in the entire world, her lovely act of worship will be told as a part of the story...she will be memorialized forever because of this one simple act of obedience."
14. But this event served as a kind of defining moment for Judas Iscariot, and he left immediately and went to the chief priests
15. and said to them, "What are you willing to pay me if I hand over Jesus to you?" And, without hesitation, they weighed out and gave him thirty pieces of silver to carry out the act of betrayal.
16. So, since there was no turning back for him at this point, from that moment on he began to devise a plan and look for an opportunity to do the deed.
17. Now on the first day of Unleavened Bread, or of Passover week, the disciples came to Jesus and asked, "Where do You want us to prepare for You to eat the Passover supper?"
18. And He said to them, "I want you to go into the city, to a certain man, and simply say to him, 'The Master says that His time is near and He will keep the Passover at your house with His disciples.'"
19. And, without question, the disciples did as Jesus had directed them and quietly prepared the Passover supper.
20. So Jesus came and celebrated with them at the appointed time, but at a certain point in the evening as He was reclining at the table with all twelve of them,
21. He said, "I have something very serious to share with all of you: one of you sitting here at this very table is going to betray Me!"
22. Well, these words hit them hard; they were already extremely stressed because of what Jesus had been saying to them about His impending death, but this revelation took the tension in the room to another level. After a few moments of stunned silence, they began to say to Him, one after another, "You can't be talking about me, can You?...Please tell me that You don't mean me!"

23. But He soberly replied, "The one who has just dipped his hand in the same dish with Me is going to betray Me!
24. "Everything is happening to the Son of Man just as it is written of Him...but what great sorrow is coming to that man by whom the Son of Man is betrayed! And even though everything that is happening right now is necessary and is unfolding according to the plan, considering what the betrayer is going to experience emotionally in the next few hours, in a sense it would have been better for him if he had never been born!"
25. At this, Judas sprang up from the table and said to Him, "Surely You can't be referring to me...can You, Master?" But He said to him, "Your words have already located you."
26. Now as they went on with the meal, Jesus took bread and gave thanks and blessed it, and when He had broken it, He gave it to the disciples, saying something to them that He had never said at any other meal that they had previously shared. Looking straight into each of their eyes, He said, "Take, eat; this is My body" (a statement that had meaning on many levels: "this bread is My body"..."this assembly of friends around this table is My body"..."this" gathering..."this" event..."this" moment is My body!)...
27. and then He took a cup and, when He had given thanks for it, He also gave it to them, saying, "Drink all of it...all of you" (again, making a meaningful statement, using the word "all"—all of the cup...all of the covenant...all of the disciples, including Judas).
28. "For this is My blood of the new covenant, which ratifies the agreement that forgiveness is being poured out for all in the Atonement.
29. "And I say to you, I will not drink wine again like this until the day I drink it with you as the New Wine of the Spirit, manifested in the Kingdom promised by My Father."
30. And when they had sung a well-loved and familiar song of praise together, they went out to the Mount of Olives.
31. Then Jesus said to them, "I might as well tell you that you will all be shaken in your loyalty tonight; you are going to fall into a state of mind where you will distrust Me, and even desert Me, because it's written, *'I will strike the Shepherd, and the sheep of the flock will be scattered.'*
32. "But after I am raised to life again, I will go ahead of you to Galilee and meet you there."

33. Then Peter stepped forward and said to Him, "Listen, they may all fall apart and turn on You, but You can count on me; I'm not like any of the rest of them...I will never leave You for a minute!"

34. But Jesus said to him, "Oh, buddy, I know that you think you mean what you say and that you can make good on your promise of faithfulness...but I have to tell you that this very night—before a single rooster crows—you're going to deny and disown Me three times."

35. Refusing to accept this, Peter said to Him, "There's no way that could happen; look, even if I have to die with You, I'm just not capable of denying or disowning You!" And then all the disciples started declaring the same thing.

36. But Jesus had nothing more to say...nothing else to set in order...nothing more for which to prepare them...so, with no further discussion, He led them all to a place called Gethsemane and there He told them to just sit down and wait while He went to a separate part of the garden to pray.

37. But He did take with Him Peter and the two sons of Zebedee and, once He chose a spot to pray, He immediately began to go into a state of intense grief and distress, with waves of despair and depression washing over Him.

38. But He managed to say to them, "Oh, you have no idea how much pain and darkness I have in My soul at this moment; the sorrow is so heavy that I feel like I'm already dying. Please, I need your support; I need you to be here and stay awake and keep watch with Me."

39. And going on a little farther, He threw Himself down on the ground, falling face-first, and began to pray, saying, "My Father, My Father, if it is possible...if there is any other way...please let this cup pass away from Me. But if not—if there really is no alternative—then let Your will, alone, be done...not what I will...not what I desire...but only as You will and desire."

40. Then He got up and came back to the disciples, finding them sound asleep in the spot where He had left them, and He shook Peter and said, "I don't believe this! Are you so full from the food and wine that you can't stay awake and keep watch with Me for just one hour?

41. "Seriously...all of you have got to stay awake and watch and pray, so that you are able to face what's about to happen. The spirit indeed is willing, but the flesh is weak."

42. Then He went away a second time and prayed, "My Father, if this

ordeal is indeed inevitable, if this cup can't pass by unless I drink it, then Your will be done!"

43. And again He got up and came and found them sleeping, this time realizing and accepting they simply could not stay awake that night.
44. So, leaving them yet again, He went back to the spot and prayed for the third time, using basically the same words.
45. Then He got up and returned to the disciples and said to them, "Boys, are you still sleeping? Open your eyes; the time has arrived...the Son of Man is betrayed into the hands of sinners."
46. "Come on...get up...let's go! My betrayer is here!"
47. As He was still speaking, Judas came right up to Him, along with a huge crowd carrying swords and clubs...a throng that had been commissioned by the chief priests and elders of the people.
48. Judas had already told them, "The One that I greet with a kiss is the Man...as soon as I kiss Him, seize Him."
49. And, sure enough, he came up to Jesus and said, "Greetings and good health to You, Master...I'm so glad to see You!" Then he embraced Him and kissed Him with feigned warmth.
50. Jesus just looked at Him and said, "Friend, what have you come for?" Then they rushed Jesus and grabbed Him and arrested Him.
51. And immediately violence broke out between the disciples and the crowd, and one of them with Jesus drew his sword, striking the servant of the high priest on the side of the head, and cut off his ear.
52. But Jesus said to him, "No, put away your sword; this isn't a physical battle to be fought with physical weapons and, anyway, those who draw the sword just end up dying by the sword.
53. "Besides...don't you know that if I wanted to, I could cry out to My Father this minute and He would dispatch thousands and thousands of ministering spirits to come to My aid?
54. "But if I did that...if I took the easy way out...then how would the Scriptures be fulfilled which say that it must happen this way?"
55. Then Jesus turned to the crowds and said, "Have you really come out here with swords and clubs as you would against a dangerous criminal to capture Me? I mean, day after day I was out in broad daylight teaching in the porches and courts of the Temple, and you did not arrest Me then. What is all this sudden show of force about?
56. "Ah, well...I know what it's about...all this has to take place so that the Scriptures of the prophets might be fulfilled." Then, exactly as He had predicted, all the disciples panicked and deserted Him,

fleeing on foot as fast as they could.

57. But those who had seized Jesus took Him straight to Caiaphas, the high priest, where the scribes and other religious leaders had assembled.
58. But Peter followed along after Him from a distance, at least as far as the courtyard of the high priest's home. He even went inside and sat with the guards to see how everything was going to play out.
59. Now the chief priests and the entire Sanhedrin conspired to obtain false witnesses to testify against Jesus, so that they would have some legal reason to put Him to death.
60. But, as it turned out, they found none, though many witnesses came forward and tried to come up with some damaging evidence against Him. Finally, two men came forward with something that the council thought they could use to build a case for His execution.
61. They said, "We heard this Man say that He was able to tear down the sanctuary of the Temple of God and build it up again in three days!"
62. And the high priest jumped up, pointed to Him, and said, "Do You have anything to say in answer to these charges of blasphemy?"
63. But Jesus just stood there and said nothing. So the high priest, waxing even more dramatic, said to Him, "I call upon You to swear by the living God and tell us whether or not You are the Christ, the Son of God!"
64. Jesus calmly said to him, *"You have already stated the fact."* Then, once again using the prophetic imagery that He had previously employed, He said, *"Furthermore, I tell you that in the future you will see the Son of Man seated at the right hand of the Almighty, riding on the clouds of judgment, revealed in the heavenlies."*
65. Well, that did it! Jesus said this to force a reaction, and He definitely got one. The high priest tore his clothes and exclaimed, "Sacrilege! Profanity! Blasphemy! What further evidence do we need? You have all heard His damnable words!"
66. Then he asked the council, "What is your ruling on the matter?" They answered him, "Undoubtedly, He deserves to be put to death!"
67. Then they all suddenly went into a kind of frenzy...spitting in His face...pummeling Him in the face with their fists...slapping Him over and over again,
68. saying, "Prophesy to us, You Christ!" And they kept slapping Him, each time demanding that He prophesy who it was that struck Him.
69. Meanwhile, Peter was sitting outside in the courtyard, and a young

girl came up to him and said, "You were also with Jesus, the Galilean!"
70. But he openly denied it, saying, "I don't even know what you're talking about."
71. Then he stood up and walked out to the porch, and when he did another girl spotted him and she said to the bystanders, "Hey, this guy was with Jesus, the Nazarene!"
72. And, overhearing her, he denied it again, saying, "Damn it, woman...I don't even know the Man!"
73. A little later the same bystanders came up and said to him, "Look, we know for a fact that it's you...it's pointless to try to cover it up...even your accent betrays you."
74. Then Peter lost it and began to let out a string of obscenities, while even more vehemently denying that he had ever met Jesus...and at that very moment a rooster crowed.
75. And immediately he remembered Jesus' words when He had said, "Before a single rooster crows, you will deny and disown Me three times." And he went outside and wept bitterly from the deepest place in his soul.

Chapter 27

1. A few hours later, at the break of dawn, the priests and religious leaders met to work out the final details of Jesus' execution.
2. And they tied Him up and led Him away to be handed over to Pilate, the Governor.
3. When Judas saw the evidence on Jesus' body of the physical abuse that He had suffered throughout the night, the realization that Jesus was actually condemned crashed in on him, and he immediately fell into a state of overwhelming remorse, almost going mad with guilt. At once he went back to the priests, carrying the silver coins with him,
4. saying, "Dear God, I've sinned; I've done a terrible thing by betraying innocent blood! Please, take your money back...call it off...I made a mistake...Jesus is innocent...I should have never come to you...I don't want to be a part of this...I can't bear the guilt of what I've done!" But they replied, "We don't care a bit about your stupid guilt; you did what you did...there's no turning this thing around...it's even out of our hands now...deal with it!"

5. So, as the stranglehold of utter regret devolved into a suffocating sense of total hopelessness, Judas threw all of the silver pieces right back at the smirking religious leaders and went off to commit suicide by hanging.
6. But the chief priests, picking up the pieces of silver, said, "It's not legal to put this money back in the treasury, because it was the payment for betrayal and murder."
7. So, after some consultation, they bought with the pieces of silver the Potter's Field...a place where nameless, unidentified strangers are buried.
8. And that's why that piece of ground has been called the "Field of Blood" to the present day.
9. Then Jeremiah's prophetic words were fulfilled and became history: *"They took the thirty silver pieces, the price of the One priced by some sons of Israel,*
10. *and purchased the Potter's Field. And so, without realizing it, they confirmed the word of the Lord."*
11. Now Jesus found Himself standing before Pilate, the Roman Governor, who asked Him, "Yes or no...are You the king of the Jews?" Jesus simply replied, "It is as you have said."
12. But when the priests and other leaders started hurling their accusations at Him, Jesus remained silent.
13. Pilate demanded, "Surely You hear all of these serious charges that they are bringing against You; don't You have anything to say in Your defense?"
14. But Jesus remained calm and quiet and centered. His transcendence and focus at this point made all of the charges and accusations a non-issue, and Pilate marveled at how serene He remained in such an intense situation.
15. Now it was the Governor's custom each year during the Passover celebration to release one prisoner to the crowd—anyone they wanted, regardless of the crimes they had committed.
16. And this particular year there was a well-known and notorious prisoner, a man named Barabbas, who was up for consideration for release.
17. So as the crowds gathered in front of Pilate's official residence that morning, he came out and asked them, "Which of these men do you want me to release to you...Barabbas, or Jesus Who is called Christ?"
18. The bottom line was, he knew very well that the religious leaders

had arrested Jesus out of envy and because He had embarrassed them (it wasn't about blasphemy or protecting The Law—it was personal).

19. Then, while Pilate was sitting there on the judgment seat, his wife sent him this message: "Leave that innocent Man alone. I had a terrible nightmare about Him last night."
20. Meanwhile, the priests and religious leaders were working hard to influence the crowd to ask for Barabbas to be released and for Jesus to be put to death.
21. So Pilate asked once again, "Which of these two do you want me to release to you?" And the crowd shouted back to him, "Barabbas!"
22. Surprised, Pilate responded, "Then what should I do with Jesus Who is called Christ?" And they shouted back to him, "Crucify Him!"
23. "But why?" Pilate demanded. "I don't understand; what crime has He committed?" But by that time the crowd's mentality had taken on a life of its own and the mob roared even louder, "Crucify Him!"
24. Pilate could see that he wasn't getting anywhere and that a riot was developing, so he sent for a bowl of water. When it was brought to him, he washed his hands before the crowd, declaring, "I am officially innocent of this Man's blood; the responsibility of this is all yours!"
25. Unmoved, the people responded with something that had more than one meaning, they yelled, "Good! We take full responsibility for His death; let His blood be on us and on our children!"
26. So Pilate reluctantly released Barabbas to them and ordered that Jesus be flogged with a lead-tipped whip. Then he turned Him over to the Roman soldiers to be crucified.
27. Then the soldiers took Jesus into the palace and gathered the entire battalion about Him.
28. They stripped off His clothes and put a scarlet robe on Him (the kind that Roman officers of rank wore as a garment of dignity),
29. and weaving a crown of long, spiky thorns, they forced it down on His head and scalp and put a reed in His right hand to symbolize a staff. And kneeling before Him, they mocked Him, saying, "All hail, all hail, great King of the Jews!"
30. Then they started spitting on Him and took the stick-like reed and began to strike Him on the head with it.
31. When they grew tired of this exercise in mockery and degradation, they stripped Him of the robe and put His own clothes back on Him and led Him away to be crucified.

32. As they were proceeding in the death-march, they came upon a man of Cyrene named Simon, and they forced him to carry the cross of Jesus for awhile.
33. When they came to a place called *Golgotha*, which means "the Place of a Skull" (called that because the rock formation on the side of the hill actually resembles a human skull),
34. they offered Him a mild painkiller to drink (a concoction of wine mixed with gall or myrrh), but when He tasted it, He refused to drink it.
35. Then they nailed Him to a cross and started the long, gruesome process of watching Him die a slow and horrible death. To amuse themselves and pass the time, they divided and distributed His clothes among themselves and threw dice for them, again fulfilling the words of a prophet: "They parted My garments among them and over My apparel they cast lots."
36. And once this was done, they sat down to keep watch over Him.
37. Eventually one of them climbed up to the top of the cross and, over His head, put up a sign. This was in keeping with the tradition of displaying something over the accused that publicly identified the reason for execution. But in Jesus' case, the sign just read "This is Jesus, the King of the Jews."
38. At the same time, there was a line of crosses along the road in front of Golgotha, each holding a condemned and dying man. On this particular day there was a thief being crucified on His right hand and one on His left.
39. And those who passed by on the road didn't miss the opportunity to jeer at the dying men and to verbally abuse them—Him especially—making faces and vulgar gestures,
40. saying, "So, You were going to tear down the sanctuary of the Temple and rebuild it in three days, were You? Hey, "King of the Jews," if You're so mighty and powerful, why not rescue Yourself from death? If You really are the Son of God as You claim, then hop down from that cross and convince us all!"
41. And the priests, scribes, and virtually all of the religious leaders who were there or came by, wasted no time in joining in with the general public in making sport of Him, saying,
42. "He rescued others from death, why can't He rescue Himself? This pitiful, impotent and dying Man is the King of Israel? If He really is, let Him come down from the cross now and then we'll abandon our

religion and believe in Him!

43. "Supposedly He trusted in God, so let His God deliver Him now if He cares for Him! Then we'll have Him for King. Remember, He's the One Who said, 'I am the Son of God!'"
44. And the thieves who flanked Him on either side also joined in the abuse and in reproaching Him. They made sport of Him in the same way, so that He was completely surrounded by hatred and accusation and condemnation and shame.
45. Then, at around noon, everything went dark and the darkness remained all over the area until about three o'clock in the afternoon.
46. About that time, Jesus, Who had been suffering silently, suddenly began to cry out with a loud voice, saying, *"Eli, Eli, lama sabachthani?"* which, in His native tongue meant *"My God, My God, why have You abandoned and forsaken Me in My time of need?"*
47. And some of the bystanders, misunderstanding and misinterpreting His words right up to the very end, said, "This Man is calling for Elijah!"
48. And, for some reason, one of them immediately ran and took a sponge, soaked it with sour wine vinegar, put it on a reed, and was about to give it to Him to drink.
49. But some of the others said, "Wait a minute! We heard Him call for Elijah; let's see if Elijah will come and save Him from death!"
50. And that was it. After this last display of insolent ignorance on the part of the public, Jesus cried again with a loud voice and gave up His spirit.
51. And at the split second that He did that, the curtain of the sanctuary of the Temple was ripped in two from top to bottom, opening up the Holy of Holies once and for all, removing all barriers—all division...all exclusiveness of religion—and releasing the presence of God...the glory of God to fill all the earth and to be universally accessible. In fact, what happened in the Temple was so powerful that it had seismic consequences in the surrounding area; the earth literally shook and huge rocks close by were broken into pieces.
52. And nearby tombs were opened by the shaking, and life came into many of the recently buried corpses of saints in the area.
53. And they left the cemeteries and went into the holy city and appeared to many people there.
54. Once the earthquake had stopped and things began to settle down a

little, the centurion and those who were with him keeping watch over Jesus became terrified and filled with awe, and said, "This absolutely was God's Son!"

55. And quite a few women were there, looking on from a distance, many of whom had accompanied Jesus from Galilee to minister to Him.
56. Among them were Mary Magdalene, Mary the mother of James and Joseph, and the mother of Zebedee's sons.
57. And when evening came, a rich man from Arimathea named Joseph (who also was a disciple of Jesus) arrived on the scene to assess the situation.
58. Then he went to Pilate and asked for the body of Jesus, and Pilate ordered that it be given to him.
59. And Joseph took the body and carefully rolled it up in a clean linen cloth, the kind used for swathing dead bodies.
60. And he laid it in his own freshly made and unused tomb, which he had just had carved out of the rock, and he had a big boulder rolled in front of the door of the tomb. Then he went away.
61. But Mary Magdalene and the other Mary just sat where they could watch the tomb for an indefinite period of time.
62. Early the next day (the day after the day of Preparation for the Sabbath), the chief priests and the Pharisees assembled before Pilate
63. and said, "Your honor, we remember how that lying imposter said while He was still alive, 'After three days I will rise again.'
64. "And because some of these imbalanced followers of His still believe His ridiculous words, we'd like for you to give an order to have the tomb made secure and safeguarded until the third day. The reason we want you to do that is we're afraid that His zealous disciples will come and steal Him away and tell the people that He has risen from the dead. If that were to happen, the effects of His fraud and deception would be worse than ever...and He could become even more of a local hero than He already is!"
65. Pilate, resigned to their ceaseless hatred and fear of Jesus, said to them, "All right, gentlemen, whatever...you have your guard and your soldiers...take them and go make it as secure as you can."
66. So they hurried off to the gravesite, happy that Pilate had once again taken their demands seriously. And they made the tomb secure by sealing the boulder and by posting a guard of soldiers to remain and keep watch.

Chapter 28

1. Now after the Sabbath, as the first light of the dawn of a new week began to break, Mary Magdalene and the other Mary went to visit the tomb to see how everything there looked.
2. But just as they were entering the garden that surrounded it, the earth beneath their feet began to shake violently, and an angel of the Lord simultaneously emerged from the heavenly realm and began to roll back the massive boulder. Once the angel had completely opened up the tomb's entrance, he sat on top of the stone.
3. His appearance was like lightning, with blazing shafts of light radiating from him. His garments glistened and shimmered like freshly-fallen snow in the sunlight.
4. When the guards at the tomb saw this incredible sight, they were so overtaken with fear that they went limp and fell on the ground like dead men.
5. Ignoring them, the angel said to the amazed women, "There is absolutely no reason to fear! I know that you have come looking for Jesus, Who was crucified,
6. but He is not here! He has risen, exactly as He said He would do! Please...come and see the place where His body was!
7. "And now that you have seen what has happened here, go quickly and tell His disciples, 'He is risen from the dead and He is going on ahead of you to Galilee as He said He would do! You will see Him there...alive!' Remember this message and deliver it just as I have said."
8. So the women, still in a state of shock, yet completely overjoyed, quickly left the tomb to tell the disciples the news, just as the angel had commanded.
9. And while they were en route, to their utter amazement, the newly resurrected and glorified Jesus met them and said, "Good morning, ladies!" And this unexpected encounter finally just overwhelmed them; they fell to their knees, grabbed Him tightly around His feet and ankles, and began to worship Him with all their might.
10. After a few moments of allowing this intense, emotional reaction to Him, Jesus said to them, "All right, all right, calm down... everything's fine; I'm here and there's no reason to be afraid. Now get up and go and tell My brothers to go into Galilee and they will

see Me there."
11. So they did as they were told, but at the same time that they were on their way, some of the guards who had collected themselves were going into the city to tell the chief priests everything that had occurred at the tomb.
12. And when the priests had gathered with the elders and had consulted together, they actually paid off the soldiers with a substantial amount of money,
13. and said to them, "If anyone asks, just tell them that His disciples came at night and stole His body away while you were sleeping.
14. "And don't worry about Governor Pilate hearing of it; if he does, we'll take care of everything and make sure that you're not held accountable."
15. So the soldiers took the money and did as they were instructed, and this story is still circulated among the Jews to the present day.
16. Meanwhile, the remaining eleven disciples went to Galilee, to the mountain to which Jesus had directed them and had made an appointment with them.
17. And when they at last saw Him, they immediately fell down before Him and worshiped Him with abandon. But, believe it or not, some of the people there on that mountain—people who had seen Jesus die a bloody and horrible death...people who knew that He had been in the grave for three whole days...people who saw Him standing right there before them in a resurrected incarnation—actually doubted!
18. But, regardless of this fact, Jesus freely approached them all and openly declared, even to the doubters, "All authority, all power, all rule, all dominion in heaven and on earth has been given to Me! Not some of it...ALL of it! ALL of it is mine!
19. "So, *because* all the power is mine, you are authorized and qualified to go and make disciples of all the nations, baptizing them into the Name of the God Who has been revealed throughout history as The Father (Who has been revealed to this nation as the Son and Who will now be revealed to the whole earth as the Holy Spirit),
20. teaching them to observe everything about life in the Kingdom that I have commanded you, teaching them as I have personally taught you...and always be aware of this: I am with you all the days of your life...every minute of every day and on every occasion...to the very close and consummation of the age...but this is not the ending, this is only the beginning! Amen...so let it be."

Mark In The Now

Mark In The Now

Chapter 1

1. The beginning of the earth-revelation of the Good News...the manifestation of the Gospel in the now...seen in this dimension in the person of Jesus Christ, the Son of God.
2. Living out His earth-life exactly as it was written by the prophet Isaiah: *"Watch this! I send My messenger before Your face, who will make Your path ready for You,*
3. *a voice of one crying in the wilderness, shouting out the message in the desert, which is: 'Prepare the way of the Lord! Make His entryway smooth and straight and level!'"*
4. And, as Isaiah had prophesied, John, the Forerunner, did appear in the wilderness-like desert, preaching the need for a paradigm shift, which he symbolized by publicly performing the rite of water baptism.
5. And his unusual ministry so caught the attention and imagination of a spiritually-starved people that the masses thronged to him from Judea and Jerusalem and, as they voluntarily confessed their sins, were baptized by him in the Jordan River into a new reality.
6. Everything about John, including his appearance and diet, was unusual. He wore clothing woven entirely of camel's hair and had a large, leather belt strapped around his waist. He was vegetarian and basically only ate the carob-like pods that came from the tops of the locust tree, and wild honey.
7. As he preached, he said, "I am delivering an important message to you, but there is One about to come on the scene Who is stronger and more powerful and has more authority than I; in fact, I am not even worthy or fit to stoop down and unloose the straps of His sandals.
8. "I can and have baptized you with water for the changing of your life by the changing of your mind—altering your perception is what you can do...the part that you can play to enter the Kingdom—but He will baptize you with the Holy Spirit...a work that He will do for and in you that you cannot do for yourselves! The baptism in water is a great start—it is the genesis of the Kingdom—but the baptism of the

Spirit is about a finished work...it brings the ultimate revelation of the Kingdom!"

9. During the time that John was saying these things, Jesus came from Nazareth in Galilee and was baptized by John in the Jordan.
10. And at the moment He came up out of the water, He perceived that the sky was split open and God's Spirit—the Holy Spirit, in a visible incarnation of that of a dove—came down on Him and remained there until it (He) was absorbed into Him.
11. And when that happened, an other-worldly voice began to speak loudly, saying, "You are My Son...My Beloved...chosen and marked by My love...in Whom I take pleasure and with Whom I am completely and absolutely delighted!"
12. And immediately the pulsating force of this same Holy Spirit from within virtually forced Him out into the wild...driving Him to go to a desert place, both physically and spiritually, where He could experience complete and total solitude.
13. And for forty days and nights He was out there alone, being tested in His thoughts by the Adversary...exposed to the elements and the wild beasts. But, during the entire trial period, angels took care of Him.
14. Now after John was arrested and put in prison for confronting Herod about his adulterous relationship, Jesus came into Galilee preaching the Good News of the Gospel of the Kingdom of God,
15. saying, "The time is fulfilled and the Kingdom of God is here now... as accessible and close to you as your own hand! Change your mind—rethink everything—and believe completely in a message of good news...the Good News of the Gospel!"
16. One day, as He was walking along the beach of Lake Galilee, He saw Simon and his brother Andrew skillfully fishing with nets. Their expertise made it obvious that they were professional fishermen.
17. And Jesus, taken by their command of the art of fishing, said to them, "Hey, let Me cast this vision to you: come with Me and be My disciples, and I will make a new kind of fisherman out of you! I'll show you how to catch people for the Kingdom of God, using the same methods and ability that you currently have at your hand."
18. And the persuasiveness of His words, the presentation of this concept and the perfection of the timing of it all, caused them to drop what they were doing right then and there and start following Him, no questions asked.

19. He then went on just a little farther down the beach and saw James, the son of Zebedee, and John his brother, who were in their boat putting their nets in order and mending them.
20. And being equally impressed by how diligent and detailed these young men were in their work, He called out to them, making the same offer. And, as the other men had done, they abandoned what they were doing, leaving their father Zebedee, the boat, and the hired hands and followed Him.
21. Their first destination together was Capernaum, and the Sabbath came while they were there so Jesus went into the synagogue and began to teach.
22. The people who came that day were amazed at His manner and delivery because He taught them as One Who had authority...as One Who made a real connection with the Scriptures and Who understood the purpose and intent of the Law within the context of the big picture. This was remarkable to those who regularly attended, because the men who typically spoke there sounded nothing like this.
23. As Jesus was delivering His message, a man in the synagogue who was under the control of a rebel spirit began to cry out,
24. "What do You want from us, Jesus of Nazareth? Have You come to terminate our tenure and to put an end to our rule so that You can set up Your Kingdom? I know Who You are...You are the Holy One of God!"
25. "That's enough! Stop being so loud and obnoxious...and stop interrupting My teaching session!" said Jesus sternly. "In fact, I want you to come out of him right now!"
26. And the spirit was reluctantly obedient to Jesus' authority, shaking the man violently and coming out of him with a shriek.
27. Well, this encounter just amazed the people that much more and they asked each other, "What is this all about? Not only does He teach with fresh revelation, He does so with complete confidence! And He openly converses with those from the spirit world, even giving them orders...and they recognize and confess His lordship over them and bow their knees to Him!"
28. And it goes without saying that the news about Him spread quickly over the whole region of Galilee.
29. As soon as they left the synagogue that day, they went with James and John to the home of Simon and Andrew.

30. Simon's mother-in-law was sick in bed with a fever and they immediately told Jesus about her.
31. So He very matter-of-factly went to her, took her by the hand and just helped her up. And with this simple gesture, the fever left her and she immediately felt so much better that she insisted on making dinner for all of them and serving it herself.
32. That evening after dinner, many local people who had received word that He was in the neighborhood brought to Jesus those who were sick and/or were under the influence of a rebel spirit.
33. Eventually it seemed as though the whole town had gathered at the door of His hostess' home,
34. and Jesus went right into healing mode, curing many who had various diseases. He also expelled many rebel spirits, but He wouldn't permit them to say anything, because they knew too much. They immediately recognized Who He was, so He wouldn't allow them to publicly say things about Him that He, Himself, wasn't ready to say.
35. And even though this went on for several hours (very late into the night), He was up before the first light of dawn. He left the house and went off to a solitary place where He could pray.
36. Simon and his companions got up a little while later and went out to look for Him.
37. When they finally found Him, they exclaimed: "Everyone is already looking for You this morning!"
38. Jesus replied, "Then let's go somewhere else...to all the nearby villages; I need to preach in each of them also because that's why I have come into this physical dimension."
39. So they began to travel throughout Galilee, and He preached in their synagogues and dismissed any rebel spirits that He encountered from their respective assignments.
40. In one of the villages a man with leprosy came to Him and begged Him on his knees, "If You are willing, You can make me clean."
41. Jesus was indignant. "What do you mean 'If I am willing'? I am always willing!" But to show that He was also able, He reached out His hand to the man and simply said, "Be clean!"
42. And immediately the leprosy left him and his diseased skin was completely cleansed.
43. But Jesus sent him away with a strong warning.
44. He said, "Look...I really don't want you to tell anyone about this.

Just go and discreetly show yourself to the priest and offer the sacrifices that Moses commanded for your cleansing, as a testimony to them."

45. But the man did just the opposite; the rebel spirits in the area did exactly as they were told, but the local people usually did not. The man went out and began to talk freely to everyone he met about his miracle, spreading the news everywhere. And, as a result, Jesus could no longer enter a town openly because the crowds were becoming uncontrollable. From that time on He had to stay outside in lonely places and, even then, the people still found Him and came to Him from everywhere.

Chapter 2

1. A few days later Jesus returned to Capernaum and, as was typical, the word got out that He was staying at someone's house.
2. So when it became publicly known whose house it was, people started gathering there...so many, in fact, that there wasn't room for all of them, not even around the doors. So everyone just stood wherever they could (practically piling in on top of one another) while He was inside discussing the Word.
3. Then four men came to the location, carrying a paraplegic on a stretcher. They had picked the man up and brought him there with the intention of getting him to Jesus.
4. But the crowd around the house was so thick and impenetrable that there was no way for even one of them to get through. So they climbed up on the roof and dug through it directly above Him. And when they had made a large enough opening, they let down the man's stretcher through it.
5. And when Jesus saw the boldness of their faith, the compassion that they had for their paralyzed friend along with their undaunted determination and spontaneous ingenuity, He stopped what He was doing and immediately acknowledged them. But He said something quite unusual and unexpected to the paralyzed man; instead of speaking to his obvious physical condition, He said to him, "My son, all of your sins are completely forgiven and removed from you!"
6. Well, some of the local religious scholars happened to be there in the crowd and, when they heard these words, they started whispering among themselves, saying,

7. "Wait a minute...He can't talk that way! That's total blasphemy! God and only God has the power and authority to forgive sins!"
8. Jesus, of course, knew what they were thinking and saying—He had made this statement to evoke such a reaction from them—so He said, "Why do you have such a problem with this?
9. "I mean, which is simpler...to say to the paraplegic, 'I forgive your sins,' or to say to him, 'Get up, take your stretcher and start walking'?
10. "I'll answer the question for you and at the same time make it clear to you that the Son of Man is authorized, beyond the shadow of doubt, to do either or both...and to reveal that the word of forgiveness and the word of healing are basically the same thing!" Then He focused on the paralyzed man, and said to him,
11. "Get up! Pick up your stretcher, carry it out of this house, and walk home!"
12. And instantly the man got up, grabbed his stretcher and walked out as Jesus had commanded, with God and everyone there watching him. The religious scholars were speechless, but everybody else there was absolutely amazed. They started praising God, saying, "We have never in our lives seen anything like this!"
13. After this, Jesus went out beside the lake again and a large crowd came to Him there and He began to teach them.
14. When He finished, He took a walk, and as He strolled along He saw Levi, the son of Alphaeus, sitting at the tax collector's booth. People typically avoided the tax collector if at all possible, going out of their way to walk as far as they could from his booth, but Jesus went right up to him with no hesitation and said to him, "Follow me!" This bold action on Jesus' part was so unprecedented and surprising, that Levi just got up and followed Him.
15. That night Jesus was having dinner at Levi's house and many other tax collectors (who usually were never invited to dinner parties) were there, along with many other people who had the reputation of being sinners (and were seemingly always at a party), all eating with Him and His disciples, enjoying lively conversation and having a good time. At this point in Jesus' ministry there was quite a large, eclectic group that followed Him.
16. When the religious leaders (namely the Pharisees) saw Him openly socializing with and befriending this strange mix of characters—all disreputable for different reasons—they asked His disciples: "Why

does He unashamedly eat with tax collectors and sinners? Doesn't He know that He is being seen with all the wrong people?"

17. On hearing this, Jesus quickly shot back, "It's not the healthy ones who need a doctor, but those who need healing. You might as well know that I have not come to call the ones you call righteous, but rather the ones that you call sinners."

18. Now John's disciples—in contrast to those who were following Jesus—were intense and very serious, and they and the Pharisees were fasting. Some people who noticed the difference came and asked Jesus, "Why is it that John's disciples and the disciples of the Pharisees are fasting, but Yours are not?"

19. Jesus calmly answered, "How can the guests of the bridegroom fast while he is celebrating with them? They can't do it as long as he, the guest of honor, is still at the party.

20. "But the time will come when the bridegroom will be taken away from them and then, and only then, will they fast.

21. "Look, I'm giving you a whole new way to think about these things. No one sews a patch of unshrunk cloth on an old garment, do they? No, because if they do, the new piece will pull away from the old, making the tear even worse.

22. "And to further illustrate My point...you know that people do not pour new wine into old wineskins. That's because, if they do, the wine will burst the skins and both the wine and the wineskins will be ruined and unusable. No, they pour new wine into new wineskins—new garments...new wineskins...new thoughts...new perspectives—that's what I'm talking about!

23. "But old wineskins (old ways of thinking) aren't so easily done away with." Case in point: one particular Sabbath Jesus was going through the grain fields and His disciples were walking along with Him. At a certain point they became hungry and, without giving it a thought, began to pick some heads of grain there in the field and started eating them.

24. The ubiquitous and ever-vigilant Pharisees were scandalized by this and said to Him, "Look...look...Your men are doing what is unlawful on the Sabbath! Why would they do such a thing?"

25. Jesus just looked at them for a minute and then said, "Gentlemen, have you never read what David did when he and his men were hungry and in need?

26. "Go look it up...in the days of Abiathar the high priest, he entered the

house of God and ate the consecrated bread, which is lawful only for priests to eat. Not only that, but he also gave some to his companions to eat."
27. Then He said, "Don't you get it? The Sabbath was made for people...people weren't made for the Sabbath! You need to align your priorities with what is actually important to God!"
28. And if that bit of new wine was difficult for them to swallow, He made it even more challenging for their old wineskin-mindset by saying, "I can say this with all confidence because the Son of Man is Lord, even of the Sabbath!"

Chapter 3

1. Once again, Jesus went into the synagogue and a man was there who had a disabled hand.
2. And the Pharisees (who at this point were closely watching His every move) were just waiting to see whether or not He would heal the man on the Sabbath. The possibility of this happening was of great interest to them, particularly because of Jesus' claim that He was the Lord of the Sabbath. Their plan was to catch Him in an infraction of the Law concerning the Sabbath so they might discredit Him and have a charge to bring against Him, formally.
3. And, sure enough, Jesus didn't waste any time walking right into a confrontational situation. He boldly said to the man with the deformed hand, "Stand up and walk out here where everyone can clearly and plainly see you."
4. Then, with the same air of confidence, He said to the Pharisees, "Let Me ask you: Is it lawful and right on the Sabbath to do good or to do evil...to save life or to take it?" But they were deathly silent.
5. And He stared for a few moments at each of them, waiting for at least one of the religious leaders to make some kind of intelligent or insightful statement. And when they didn't, He began to experience an intense emotional mix of anger and sorrow...anger at their lack of openness to the truth and sorrow at how insensitive religion had made them to the suffering of humanity. Then, getting past His feelings, He said to the man, "All right, hold out your hand!" And he held it out and, when he did, the use and appearance of his hand was completely restored.
6. Then the Pharisees rushed out and went immediately to hold a

consultation with the Herodians (those who supported Herod, the King) discussing how they might come up with a legal means to exterminate Him.

7. After this occurrence, Jesus took His disciples to the lake to just get away with them and relax, but a great throng of people from Galilee who were constantly aware of His whereabouts followed Him there. But there were also people following Him from Judea...

8. and from Jerusalem and Idumea, and from beyond the Jordan River, and from the area around Tyre and Sidon. In a word, His fame had now taken on a life of its own and vast numbers—hordes of people who were hearing all the time about all that He was doing—came to Him, wanting to see for themselves if what they had heard was true.

9. So He told His disciples to have a little boat ready for Him so He could escape in the event that mass hysteria set in and the crowd literally crush Him.

10. The throngs now were regularly so massive that they were basically becoming unmanageable; the people were being more and more physically aggressive with Him, especially those who were very sick and in need and, on occasion, some were so intent on personally touching Him that they were out of control.

11. And more and more rebel spirits were recognizing and acknowledging Him and, when they did, they fell down before Him and kept screaming out, "You are the Son of God!"

12. But Jesus was persistent in His refusal to allow these spirits to fully reveal Him, so again and again He made them shut up in public.

13. When things calmed down a bit, He climbed a mountain and invited those He wanted to officially work with Him, and they accepted the invitation and climbed up, too.

14. Out of all those who were following Him, He settled on twelve and, designating them Apostles (or special messengers), He sent them out to preach the Good News of the Gospel,

15. and to have authority and power to heal the sick and to expel rebel spirits.

16. And these are the Twelve: Simon, whom He later called Peter;

17. James, the son of Zebedee, and John, the brother of James. He gave these two a very special name: Boanerges, which literally means "Sons of Thunder";

18. Andrew, Philip, and Bartholomew (also known as Nathaniel), Matthew, Thomas, and James (the son of Alphaeus), Thaddaeus,

Judas (not Iscariot), and Simon the Canaanaean (also called *Zelotes* or "The Zealot" because of his radical political persuasions and underground connections),

19. and Judas Iscariot, who later betrayed Him. These men—including Simon, who came from a group of anarchists and assassins, and the infamous Judas Iscariot—were all called and authorized to be apostles, preachers, healers, deliverers...by Jesus, Himself.
20. After this He went to someone's house for dinner, but a throng heard about His visit and converged on the house, literally shutting down any possibility of a social occasion. The people were so demanding that night that Jesus and His disciples couldn't even eat.
21. And when His family (who was already concerned about how His popularity was getting out of hand and was becoming completely uncontrollable) heard about this, they felt they were forced into taking some kind of action. So they got together and planned an emergency intervention, with the expressed intention of having Him committed. They rationalized that He was their responsibility, saying, "He's clearly lost His mind by buying into and encouraging this mania, and it's up to us to do something about it; we have to put Him away!"
22. And to make things worse, the scribes who came down from Jerusalem said, "He is possessed by Beelzebub ('the Lord of the Flies') and with the help of demons He is casting out demons and practicing black magic!"
23. But Jesus this time called a meeting with them to do a little damage control and to confront their superstitious slander with an illustration, saying, "Tell Me...how can demons drive out other demons?
24. "Furthermore, if a kingdom rebels against itself, that kingdom cannot stand.
25. "In the same way, if a house is divided, or split into factions, that house will not be able to last.
26. "And if the Adversary is adversarial to the Adversary, he will ultimately self-destruct!
27. "Look, no one can go into a strong man's house, if he's home, and walk off with his possessions, unless he first ties up that strong man; but if he does tie the man up, then indeed he may thoroughly plunder his house.
28. "These are all authority issues and, speaking of authority, here's

another thing you should know. Every sin and blasphemy can be automatically forgiven people because of the mercy extended to the limited flesh;

29. but when you are filled with the Holy Spirit, your words become so authoritative and effective that they literally create your reality. So when you speak things out of your mouth which are contrary to the purpose and nature of the Holy Spirit, you actually speak blasphemy against Him, and He can't forgive you in order to prevent those words from coming to pass, because He has empowered you to have what you say. You'll just have to deal with the consequences of whatever you've said, whether for good or for evil. The words that you speak against His nature in you will have to stand just as you said them. They will not be erased through forgiveness in this dimension or in the one to come and, in that sense, they bear eternal consequences."
30. Jesus went out of His way to explain all of these things because they persisted in saying, "He has an evil spirit."
31. Then, while He was still talking about this, His mother and His brothers came for the intervention that they had discussed. They stood outside and sent word to Him, calling for Him.
32. And some of the people who were there heard them and said to Him, "Your mother and Your brothers and Your sisters are outside asking for You."
33. And, intuitively sensing the alienation from His natural family—even without actually hearing them say that they thought He had lost His mind—He replied, "Who, really, are My mother and My brothers?"
34. And looking around at those who were there in support of Him, He said, "See! Right here are My mother and My brothers and My sisters!"
35. And, completely ignoring His family's demand for a meeting with Him, He went on to say, "For whoever does the things that God wills is My real brother and real sister and real mother!"

Chapter 4

1. Again Jesus went back to teaching by the lake, and a huge crowd gathered around Him. So once again He got into an offshore boat in order to sit in it on the water, and everyone either stood or sat along

the lakeside on the shore.
2. And He taught them many things that day in His signature story-telling style, using illustrations and comparisons, and in His teaching He said,
3. "Listen to this! One day a sower went out to plant seeds in his fields.
4. "And as he scattered the seed, some of it fell on the road and the birds came and ate it right up.
5. "Some of the same kind of seed fell in the gravel where there wasn't much soil and it just sprang right up but didn't put down roots because it had no depth capability;
6. so in the heat of the sun it was scorched and, because it had not taken root, it withered away just as quickly as it had come up.
7. "Other of the same kind of seed fell among the weeds, and the thistles grew and pressed together and suffocated the life right out of it and it became utterly useless.
8. "And still other seed of the same kind fell into good, healthy soil and produced grain, growing up and increasing, yielding up to thirty times as much in some spots...and sixty times as much in other areas...and even a hundred times as much as had been sown in some places."
9. And He said to them, "If you have an ear to hear what I'm saying, then hear it...consider it...comprehend it!"
10. As soon as He was alone with the Twelve after the session had ended, they began to ask Him about the illustration.
11. And He said to them "You've been given insight into the mysteries of God's Kingdom...a revelation of its inner workings...an understanding of its day-to-day operation. But those who can't see it yet are intrigued by My stories, but that's all they are to them at this point...stories...illustrations without introspection, metaphors without meaning.
12. "These are the ones spoken of in the Scriptures: they indeed look and look, but they do not see and perceive; they hear the words over and over again, but do not grasp and comprehend them. But as soon as they open their hearts to the Light, they will turn to Me and be forgiven of their willful rejection of the truth."
13. Then He said to them, "Surely you understand this story; I mean, if you don't get this one, how are you going to understand any of them? The whole truth is incrementally revealed in prophetic

14. pictures...sort of like a puzzle put together piece by piece. Do I really need to spell it out for you?
14. "All right, then...the sower sows the Word.
15. "The ones along the roadside are those who have the Word sown in their hearts, but when they hear it only with their intellect, the Adversary comes immediately and steals the message that was sown in them.
16. "And in the same way, the ones sown on the gravelly ground are those who, when they hear the Word, are at once sort of infatuated with it and have an emotional response to it;
17. but they have no real root in themselves—no sense of covenant relationship to the Word—and so they endure for a little while, but when trouble or persecution arises on account of the Word, they immediately become resentful and basically fall apart.
18. "And the ones sown among the thorny weeds are others who hear the Word with some real comprehension;
19. but the daily cares and anxieties of the world just sort of wear them out, and so they get distracted by the illusions of the age, looking for pleasure and false glamour elsewhere, being deceived by the empty promises of riches, and so, without even noticing it, the craving and passionate desire for other things creep in and strangle the Word and it becomes fruitless in their lives.
20. "And, finally, those sown on the good, well-prepared soil are the ones who hear the Word and openly receive it, accepting the personal responsibility for their own soil-maintenance. They welcome it and have a mature relationship to it, and so they bear fruit; for some it's thirty times as much as was sown...for others it's sixty times as much...and for still others who fully embrace these concepts, it's even a hundred times as much!"
21. Then He went on to say, "Look, does anyone bring a lamp home and then put it under a basket or hide it under the bed? Of course not! The lamp's purpose is to be put up high somewhere...like on a lamp stand where everyone can benefit from its light.
22. "The mysteries of the Kingdom are hidden temporarily; they must be sought first as a revelation or a new birth. But the bottom line is this: there is no hidden spiritual truth that won't eventually be revealed...every part of the truth is meant to be known, either now or later.
23. "So again I say...if you have a spiritual ear to hear, then listen deeply

and perceive and comprehend these things."

24. Then He added, "You really need to pay attention to everything you are hearing. Guard the gate, because the ear is a major gate to the understanding; the measure of thought and study you give to the truth you hear will be the measure of Kingdom-life you manifest. That's why I say, 'if you have an ear' (singular)...not 'if you have ears' (plural). It's not just what you hear, but how you hear it that determines the reality that is ultimately created in your life.

25. "Let Me put it this way: to him who has will more be given...and from him who has nothing, even what he has will be taken away. Hear this only with your spiritual ear and you will understand it."

26. Then He said, "Here's something else you should know about how the Kingdom of God works: think of it as being like a man who scatters seed upon the ground,

27. and then he releases it—he doesn't sit there in the field, looking at the spot where he planted the seed, waiting and worrying about how and when it's going to produce something. In fact, in a way, he forgets about it...continuing to sleep and rise night and day, while the seed just naturally does what it was destined to do...it grows! And the man doesn't try to over-think the laws of nature...he just embraces the mysterious wonder of it.

28. "Meanwhile, the earth produces by itself...living and thriving alone on the original word that created it in the first place. And the miracle of the seed is then manifested through a process...first a simple, inedible blade of grass appears...then a bud with only the promise of grain comes...then the full, mature grain eventually ripens and is then ready to be harvested.

29. "Then and only then the man returns...still not fully understanding how it all worked, but recognizing a potential harvest when he sees it. And then he eagerly puts in the sickle and reaps what he sowed.

30. "Now, let's see...what other picture of the Kingdom can I paint for you? What other story can I tell you that will make you see it from another perspective?

31. "How about this? It's like a grain of mustard seed which, when sown in the ground, is the smallest of all the seeds on the earth;

32. yet after it is sown, defying all natural logic, it grows up and becomes the greatest of all garden herbs and puts out huge branches...so big that even eagles come and nest in it!"

33. And with many other such stories or word-pictures, Jesus spoke the

Word to them, as they were able to really "hear" it...or as was fitting to their experience or maturity level.

34. In fact, He basically explained everything like this to them in story form...but privately to His disciples He interpreted the meaning of each story or illustration, making sure that they didn't overlook the deep profundity housed in the elemental simplicity of each of them.
35. On that same day when evening had come, He said to them, *"All right...that's enough story-telling for one day. Let's go over to the other side of the lake now."*
36. And leaving the throng, the disciples piled into the boat in which He was sitting and, along with some other boats, they all launched out into the deep.
37. But when they got out into the middle of the sea-like lake, a furious storm of hurricane proportions unexpectedly arose and the waves started beating into the boat so violently that it filled up with water in just a few minutes.
38. Meanwhile, Jesus had disappeared from their company into the stern of the boat and had fallen into a deep sleep there on a leather cot. The frantic men found Him and woke Him up, saying, "Master! Does it even matter to You in the least that we're all about to die?!"
39. Giving no response to their indicting question, He calmly stood up and ordered the wind to settle down and said to the sea, *"All right... hush now! Be still!"* And immediately the wind ceased its raging and there was a great calm...an entirely different scene, with clear, peaceful skies and a lake that looked as if it was made of glass.
40. Then He turned around and looked at His astonished staff and said to them, *"Why are you so fragile and fearful? You're not strangers to the sea or to storms...how is it possible that you sometimes seem to have no faith at all?"*
41. And this just took their awe of Him to a whole other level. Stunned, they stood there in the quiet peacefulness and could think of nothing to say to Him in their defense. But as He went back to finish His nap, they looked at one another and said, "Who is this? What kind of Man gives orders to the wind and the water...the storm and the sea...and gets them to obey Him?"

Chapter 5

1. They arrived some time later on the other side of the lake, in the country of the Gerasenes.
2. And as soon as He stepped out of the boat, a madman under the influence of a rebel spirit came right up to Him from out of the cemetery.
3. This man actually lived outside among the tombs, and no authority could subdue him anymore, even with chains.
4. In an effort to control his violent and antisocial behavior, he had been bound on many occasions with handcuffs and shackles on his feet, but every time he wrenched the cuffs apart and broke the shackles in pieces. No one seemed to have the strength to restrain or tame him, so they just left him alone to live in the graveyard.
5. Night and day he was out there among the tombs on the mountainside, shrieking and screaming and mutilating his naked body with stones.
6. But when he saw Jesus from a distance, he ran and fell on his knees before Him in reverent submission; the spirit controlling him recognized Jesus, as the spirits always did, and true to form, its first instinct was to bow before Jesus in worship.
7. And, crying out with a loud voice, the spirit spoke through the man, saying, "What business do You have here with me, Jesus, Son of the Most High? Why has the Son of God come here? I beg You not to torment me!"
8. Jesus immediately recognized that the worship and honor was coming from the disembodied spirit and not from the man, so He said, "Come out of this man, you controlling spirit!"
9. And He asked him, "What is your name?" And the spirit responded simultaneously in the singular and in the plural, because in the spirit realm they are most always the same. And, mixing his pronouns he said, "'My' name is Legion, for 'we' are many!"
10. Being typically resistant to change or movement as rebel spirits usually are, he kept begging Him urgently not to send him/them away out of that region.
11. Now an enormous herd of hogs was grazing there on the hillside while this exchange was happening.
12. So "Legion" begged Him, saying, "Please, Sir, grant us permission to go to the hogs, that we may go into them!"

13. So He did give them the permission, being fully aware that they could do nothing without it. And the spirits came out of the man and entered into the hogs. And the entire herd (numbering about 2,000) immediately rushed headlong down the steep slope into the lake and were drowned in the water.
14. Terrified, the hog feeders ran away and told everyone they met in the town and in the country about the bizarre incident. And practically everyone they told came to see what had taken place.
15. And they came to Jesus and looked with amazement at the man who had been previously controlled by the spirits, just sitting there, clothed, calm, and completely lucid—the very same man who had been controlled by the Legion of spirits called demons—and they were seized with alarm and struck with fear.
16. And those who had seen it related in full what had happened to the man who had lived in the cemetery and to the hogs.
17. And they began to beg Jesus to leave their neighborhood.
18. So He did, and when He had stepped into the boat, the man who had been liberated kept begging Him that he might go with Him and be with Him...now worshipping Him on his own accord and not under the influence of any other entity.
19. But Jesus said to him, "No, friend...you'll be more effective if you go home to your own family and friends and tell them all that the Lord has done for you and how He has had mercy on you. They need to see for themselves what has happened to you!"
20. And the man departed and immediately began to publicly proclaim in Decapolis (or the region of the Ten Cities) how much Jesus had done for him, and his testimony was indeed very effective, for all the people were astonished and marveled when they heard him!
21. When Jesus had crossed in the boat back to the other side, a large crowd met Him at the lakeside.
22. And there on the shore, something unprecedented happened: from out of the crowd, one of the rulers of the synagogue came up to Him (Jairus by name), but this religious leader wasn't there to discuss the Law or to confront Him about some perceived infraction of it. On the contrary, when this man saw Him, he prostrated himself at His feet.
23. And he begged Him earnestly, saying, "Sir, my little daughter is at death's door; please come and lay Your hands on her so that she may be healed and live."

24. And, without question, Jesus went with him, the whole crowd tagging along, pushing and pressing in, almost suffocating Him in their excitement and desire to see, up close, what was going to happen.
25. And while they were en route, there appeared a woman who had suffered from a debilitating condition of hemorrhaging for twelve years.
26. A long succession of physicians, including some quack doctors, had treated her to no avail. Not only were they all incompetent (powerless to help her), but they also had taken advantage of her desperate vulnerability...taking all her money, bleeding her dry financially, and leaving her worse off than before she had the condition.
27. But when she started hearing the reports about Jesus, she was energized with hope...and when she realized that He was actually in close proximity to her, a sense of faith motivated her to come up behind Him in the throng and touch His garment.
28. So she started thinking and saying out loud to herself, "I believe that if I can just put my finger on His robe, I will get well!" And the more she said it, the more she believed it...and the more she believed it, the more she said it.
29. The words she kept speaking built her confidence and increased her physical strength, enabling her to push through the mob of people and finally make a connection with Him, both physically and spiritually. And, on contact, her constant flow of blood was immediately dried up at the source. It was undeniable...she could feel the change and knew, instantly, that her long nightmare was over and done with.
30. Interestingly, at the very same moment, Jesus felt healing power discharging from Him...He sensed when His flow of energy stopped her flow of blood. So He turned around to the crowd and asked, *"Who just touched My robe?"*
31. His disciples said, "Are You kidding? How can You possibly ask *'Who touched Me?'* when hundreds of hands are all over You in this mass of people?!"
32. But He wouldn't let it go. He kept on asking about it, knowing that something very unusual had just happened. He stopped in His tracks and just stood there, looking intently through the crowd until He finally zeroed in on the woman.

33. But she, finally feeling the full impact of it all, just fell down before Him and emotionally gave Him the whole story.
34. When she finished giving her testimony, Jesus compassionately continued the miracle by calling her "Daughter" in front of the whole crowd...and, in that one word, He reversed the stigma spelled out in Levitical Law, that was attached to the kind of female reproductive problem that she had dealt with for over a decade. Reconnecting her to a world that would have normally ostracized her, He said, "Daughter, you took a risk of faith, and it has paid off for you! You're healed, and more than that...you're whole! Live well, be blessed and be continually healed of your plague."
35. But while He was virtually in mid-sentence, some people came from the house of Jairus and said to him, "We have bad news: your daughter is dead. Come with us...why bother the Teacher any more?"
36. But Jesus, overhearing what they said, looked straight at Jairus and, before he could react to the news...before he could say a word...before he responded with any emotion, whatsoever...said to him, "Jairus...look at Me...don't say anything...don't feel anything... don't grieve...don't cry...don't be seized with alarm or struck with fear. Do one thing and one thing, only...only believe!"
37. And from that point, He permitted no one to accompany Him except Peter and James and John, the brother of James.
38. And when they arrived at the house of the ruler of the synagogue, He looked around at the large number of people who had already gathered there—family, friends, and even the professional mourners—all weeping and wailing loudly together.
39. And He was very direct with them, even abrupt, saying, "What's all this drama about? Everyone needs to settle down right now; this child isn't dead...she's just sleeping!"
40. And the people in the room switched, almost automatically, from crying to laughing...laughing at Him, that is...jeering at Him and sarcastically telling Him that He was out of touch with reality. But He was unfazed by their negative reaction to His creative words and He ran them all out of the house. Then, taking the child's father and mother, and those who were with Him, He went into the room where the little girl was lying.
41. And, gripping her firmly by the hand, He said to her in His native tongue, *"Talitha cumi,"* which translated is, "Sweetheart (or Little

girl), I say to you, arise!"

42. And at these simple words, this girl of twelve was up and walking around! Her family, understandably, were all amazed and beside themselves with joy.
43. But as they were rejoicing and embracing their living daughter, He gave them strict orders that no one was to know what had taken place in that room. Then He said, "All right now, go find this precious one something to eat."

Chapter 6

1. Then Jesus left there and went to His hometown of Nazareth, accompanied by His disciples.
2. And when the Sabbath came, He began to teach in the synagogue and many who heard Him were utterly amazed and astonished, saying, "Where did this Man get all this? What is the source of the intelligence, insight and wisdom which He has obviously acquired? And how has this wisdom given Him the ability to work these mighty miracles?
3. "Isn't He just a local carpenter? Isn't this Mary's son...the brother of James, Joseph, Judas and Simon? Don't His sisters live right here in the neighborhood with us? Who in the world does He think He is?" And they were offended that He attempted to be something that, in their opinion, He was not—the natural knowledge of Him was an unavoidable roadblock to their being able to acknowledge His authority—and so they just shut down on Him, mentally and emotionally.
4. But Jesus said to them, "You know, only in his hometown, among his own relatives, friends and acquaintances, is a prophet without honor."
5. And because of their limited collective perception of Him, He could not do any miracles there...at least none of His more impressive manifestations of power. He was only able to lay His hands on a few sick people in order to help them feel a little better.
6. And He was astounded at their unbelief...really surprised by their lack of faith in Him. But He let it go and went around the surrounding villages and continued teaching.
7. And He called to Him the Twelve and began to send them out on their own, in pairs, as His personal ambassadors. He also gave them

8. And He instructed them to basically take nothing with them on their journey—no external equipment—so that they would have to rely, solely, on the internal gifts which He had imparted to them.
9. He allowed them to wear their sandals, but told them not to even take a change of clothes with them, wanting them to keep it simple and to learn to use their own faith for their self-preservation.
10. And He encouraged them to make real connections with the people to whom they would minister, telling them, "Wherever you go into a house, just stay there until you leave that area.
11. "But if any community will not receive, embrace and welcome you…if they refuse to listen to you…then get out of there. And when you depart, make a grand gesture of shaking off the dust from their streets that is on your feet, for a visible testimony against them."
12. And when this unlikely and somewhat limited group of men hit the road under His authoritative command, they preached a powerful and urgent message, joyfully proclaiming the possibility of a radical life-change.
13. And their message was effective: rebel spirits were expelled everywhere they went, and they brought wellness and wholeness to the sick, anointing them and healing them, spirit, soul and body.
14. King Herod heard of what was happening, for Jesus' name and reputation by this time had become very well known. In fact, he was so taken by the reports he was hearing of Jesus' ministry, that he and the members of his court said, "John the Baptizer has apparently been raised from the dead! That can be the only explanation of why these mighty powers and abilities of His to perform miracles are at work!"
15. But others were saying, "No…it's not John…it is Elijah!" And still others said, "He is obviously a prophet, like one of the prophets of old."
16. But Herod was convinced. He insisted, "Seriously…I'm telling you, this is the very same John whom I beheaded…he has been raised from the dead!"
17. Herod was the one who had sent for and seized John and bound him in prison for the sake of Herodias, his brother Philip's wife, after he had married her.
18. The reason for this was that John had publicly told Herod, "It's not right or lawful for you to have your brother's wife like this!"

(Note: item 8 continues from previous page beginning with "authority and power over rebel spirits and any other evil opposition.")

19. And, as a result, Herodias was incensed with him and held a grudge that eventually turned into a desire to kill him; but she couldn't make that happen,
20. for Herod had a reverential fear and awe of John, believing that he was truly a holy man. Because of that, he continually kept him safely guarded. When he heard John speak, he actually became miserable with guilt...and yet he was strangely attracted to, and respectful of, John's fearless message...as if he had sort of a love/hate relationship with the prophet.
21. But one eventful evening, an opportunity came for Herodias when Herod, on his birthday, threw a party for his nobles and the high military commanders and chief men of Galilee.
22. That night, when the daughter of Herodias came in and seductively danced for him, she ignited a kind of palpable passion in Herod and his guests...and the king, in a moment of desire, said to the girl, "Honey, you can ask me for whatever you desire...anything at all...and I'll give it to you!"
23. He even went so far as to put himself under oath to her, reiterating in front of everyone, "I mean it...whatever you ask for, I will give it to you...even to the half of my kingdom!"
24. So she left the room and excitedly said to her mother, "What should I ask for?" And Herodias bitterly replied, "Ask for the head of John the Baptizer!"
25. And without missing a beat, she rushed back in to the king and made her dark request, saying, "I want you to give me the head of John the Baptizer on a platter right now!"
26. And the king immediately sobered up, instantly experiencing profound regret and remorse over his thoughtless oath. But even though he was deeply pained and grieved by this, because of his oath and his guests, he did not want to be seen as someone who was too weak to keep such a promise.
27. So he sadly and reluctantly sent off one of the soldiers of his bodyguard and gave him orders to decapitate John at once and to bring his head. And the guard followed orders and left immediately to behead him in the prison,
28. and, according to the horrible request, brought his head on a platter and handed it to the girl. And the girl then gave it to her heartless mother.
29. When John's disciples heard the tragic news, they came and took his

body and laid it in a tomb.
30. After this, the apostles came back and rendezvoused with Jesus, reporting on all that they had done and taught since He had commissioned them to go out on their own.
31. When they were through comparing notes, Jesus said to them, "Well done, gentlemen...now you need to get some well-deserved rest; come away by yourselves to a secluded place and take it easy for a little while." He wanted them to start taking better care of themselves, for they were continually coming and going, being so involved in the work of the ministry that they regularly didn't even take time to eat.
32. So, according to instructions, they got in a boat and went off to a remote place by themselves.
33. But it had become virtually impossible by this point for them to have any real privacy; they were now as famous and as recognizable as Jesus. As a result, many people spotted them and saw where they were going, and they ran there on foot from all the surrounding towns, getting there ahead of those in the boat.
34. And Jesus went with them, too, but as His boat landed, He saw the great crowd waiting there. And instead of being resentful of this intrusion on what was supposed to have been a time of relaxation with His disciples, He was actually moved with compassion for them. He saw them as being like sheep without a shepherd, so He got out of the boat and just began to teach them many things right then and there.
35. And this spontaneous teaching evolved into an all-day seminar, lasting until very late in the afternoon. So as dusk began to set in, His disciples came to Him and said, "This place is desolate and isolated, and the day is almost over.
36. "We need to send the crowds away so that they can go into the nearby country and villages to buy themselves something to eat."
37. But He replied to them, "No, let's not do that; why don't you just give them all something to eat right here?" And they said to Him, "Are You suggesting that we take money and go ourselves to buy them enough bread to eat and then get back here before dark to serve it to them?"
38. But He said to them, "No...how many loaves do you have here right now? Go and see." And when they looked around at what was on hand and available, they came back to Him and said, "It looks like

we have five loaves of bread and two fish."
39. When He heard this, He instructed the people to sit down on the green grass, organizing them by companies.
40. So they cooperatively separated themselves into ranks of hundreds and fifties, spreading out all over the hillside.
41. Then, taking the five loaves and two fish, He looked skyward, gave thanks, blessed the bread, and started breaking it. And He kept on breaking loaves and breaking them again and again, handing them to the disciples to give to the people. He also miraculously divided the two fish among them all.
42. And everyone ate, and everyone was completely satisfied.
43. After they all were full, reclining on the ground, the disciples filled up twelve whole baskets of broken pieces from the loaves and of the fish.
44. And when they counted the people by companies, they discovered that those who ate the loaves were 5,000 men, accompanied by women and children.
45. Immediately following this, He insisted that the disciples get into the boat and go on ahead of Him to the other side to Bethsaida, while He personally finished dismissing the crowds.
46. After the last of them had moved on, He went off by Himself into the hills to pray.
47. By late evening, the boat was out in the middle of the lake and Jesus was alone on the hillside.
48. From where He was standing, He could see that His men were experiencing great difficulty with the rowing because the wind was strong and against them. So, sometime after midnight, in the very early hours of the morning, He came out to them, walking directly on the surface of the water. Initially, He just casually walked by them, as though taking a leisurely stroll on the lake in the middle of the night; in fact, He would have just passed by them and walked on if they hadn't noticed Him.
49. But they did, in fact, notice Him walking by, only they thought He was a ghost and began to scream and cry like scared little children.
50. But He said to them, *"All right, boys, calm down…it's Me! There's no reason for you to be afraid!"*
51. And He climbed into the boat with them and the wind settled right down. And, even though they had just seen the miracle of the loaves and fish—and even though they had been performing miracles

themselves—they were still apparently astonished beyond measure by the miraculous.
52. It was as if the feeding miracle that had occurred only a few hours earlier had never even happened. Observing supernatural manifestations had not enlarged their capacity for understanding spiritual things, nor had it increased their tolerance level for the suspension of natural law. They were still glaringly underdeveloped in these areas and so they were still quick to panic and become overwhelmed by fear when faced by natural challenges.
53. But there was no more discussion about it this time and, when they had crossed over, they reached the land of Gennesaret and came to anchor at the shore.
54. And it didn't take long for the action to begin again. In fact, as soon as they got out of the boat, the people recognized Jesus,
55. and started running from everywhere, carrying around sick people on their sleeping pads to any place where they heard or thought that He might be.
56. And, for that window of time, wherever and whenever He came into villages or cities, they would lay the sick in the marketplaces and beg Him to walk by so that the people could touch the fringe of His outer garment. And, sure enough, as many as touched Him were completely restored to health.

Chapter 7

1. Now the Pharisees, along with some other religious leaders and scholars who had come from Jerusalem, gathered around Him.
2. And, seeing everything in their world from a legalistic perspective, they were keenly aware that some of His disciples seemed to have no apparent regard for the observance of ceremony, specifically that of ritual washings before meals.
3. The Pharisees, in keeping with strict, Jewish legal tradition, do not eat unless they first wash their hands diligently...up to the elbow...with clenched fist. This practice is observed merely for ceremonial reasons, but to them, the careful and faithful adherence to doing it just right is of the utmost importance and is to be taken very seriously.
4. Furthermore, when they come from the marketplace, they will not eat until they completely purify themselves according to the Law.

And there are also many other traditions having to do with washing and eating...manmade rules handed down to them over the centuries...which they honor faithfully and without question, such as the scouring of every cup and wooden pitcher and wide-mouthed jug, along with every utensil of copper.

5. So the Pharisees and scribes, unable to imagine a world without all these rules to keep, kept asking Jesus, "Why do Your disciples flout the rules...the hallowed traditions handed down to us by the forefathers? How can they eat their food with hands unwashed and ceremonially not purified?"

6. But He said to them, "The prophet Isaiah hit the nail on the head about frauds like you...pretenders and hypocrites...and so it is written: *'These people make such a big deal out of doing and saying the right thing, supposedly to honor Me with their lips...but, in reality, nothing they do is motivated from the heart, and so their hearts are actually very far away and distant from Me.*

7. *'Their so-called worship of Me is pointless and fruitless, because their top priority is teaching the commandments and precepts of men, demanding that they be obeyed as if they were the doctrines of God.'*

8. "In fact, you disregard and dispense with the actual commandments of God—the things that really matter to Him—and hold on for dear life to the empty traditions of men, keeping them carefully and faithfully as if they really make any difference in the big picture."

9. And He went on to say to them, "You've really developed a sophisticated system of manipulation: you keep the people under your authority constantly uneasy about their approval rating with God and, in so doing, have guaranteed that you'll always have a place of importance in this society. Your desire for significance, or just simple job security, has caused you to reject, thwart and nullify the commandment of God...so you place inappropriate importance on keeping your tradition and your own human regulations!

10. "For example, Moses said, *'Honor your father and your mother,'* and, *'He who curses, reviles or mistreats his father or mother is worthy of death!'*

11. "But you have devised a legal loophole, saying, 'A man is exempt from having to provide for his parents in their old age if he tells his father or his mother that the money he would have used for their care and upkeep is "Corban," meaning that it is a gift already designated

for and given as an offering to God.' And then this money that is freed up is, in essence, coming to you.

12. "In doing this, you no longer are permitting a man to do anything for his father or mother, but are letting him off the hook from his rightful responsibilities.

13. "This little trick nullifies and makes void the purpose of the commandment, and the enforcing of it enables the traditions of men to make the very Word of God completely impotent and ineffective. And this is just one of many things like this that you are doing all the time."

14. Then He called the people who were in close proximity to Himself again and said to them, "I want you to listen to Me...every one of you...and I want you to understand what I say.

15. "All this ceremonial cleansing that the religious leaders think is so vital is harmless in and of itself...but you should all know that there is not one thing from the outside world, which by going into a man or a woman, can pollute and defile him or her. It's the things which come out of a person—the fruit of the internal world—which have the potential to defile him/her and make him/her unhallowed and unclean!

16. "If any of you can hear Me, then listen to what I'm saying...really listen with perception and comprehension!"

17. After this He left the crowd and went into the house where He was staying and, once inside, His disciples began asking Him about the illustration He had used.

18. And He said to them, "Please tell Me that you're not so unintelligent and dull of hearing that you don't understand this simple premise! Just think about it...whatever goes into a person from the outside cannot possibly make him or her filthy or unclean,

19. since it doesn't go to his heart. It's the heart that determines the real standard of cleanliness in a person, so the heart is all that ultimately matters. Don't you realize that whatever is physically ingested automatically goes toward a person's digestive tract and then is inevitably eliminated, passing into the place designed to receive waste?" And with this straightforward reference to human biology, He made and declared all foods to be ceremonially clean; in judging everything edible as being kosher, He abolished the ceremonial distinctions of the limited Levitical Law.

20. And He reiterated His point, saying, "It's what comes out of a person

that determines what makes him or her unclean or renders him/her unhallowed.
21. "Instead of worrying about filtering or washing what comes in from the outside, you should be concerned with sanitizing what comes out of your internal world. For from within that place...that is, out of the heart...can come base and destructive thoughts, sexual dysfunction, stealing, murder, adultery,
22. jealousy, endangerment to others, deceit, indecent conduct, obsession with what others have, slander, malicious misrepresentation, abusiveness, pride, recklessness, thoughtlessness, and so on.
23. "All these evil purposes and desires can originate from deep within an individual, and these are the things that can make a person truly unclean."
24. And, having finished this exchange, Jesus left this place and went to the region of Tyre and Sidon. And there He entered into a certain house and didn't want anyone to know He was there. But, of course, it wasn't possible for Him to keep any sort of low profile by this time...He simply could not be hidden from public notice.
25. So, practically as soon as He arrived and the local buzz started about Him being in town, a woman whose little daughter was under the control of a rebel spirit got word about Him and came and literally flung herself down at His feet.
26. What was particularly interesting about this woman coming to Him in this way is that she was a Greek...a Gentile...a Syro-phoenician by nationality. But their ethnic differences seemed to be a non-issue with her. With absolute absence of pride or awkwardness, she begged Him in a very demonstrative way to expel the spirit and to end its authority over her daughter's life.
27. But, seemingly unfazed by her demeanor, He said to her, "You're ahead of schedule…it's not time yet for Me to be revealed to the rest of the world and to be accessible to people like you. Right now I am solely focused on My call to minister to the lost sheep of the house of Israel. You know that the Israelites consider your people to be dogs…so, because I have My hands full in dealing with them as a nation at the moment, to help you would be like taking the children's bread and throwing it to the dogs…at least that's true as far as they're concerned. It's not right that the 'dogs' should take bread away from the children."
28. But she answered Him, "I don't care about what the Israelites think.

I just want my daughter well. So I would humbly disagree with You…I would say, 'but Lord, even the "dogs" eat the crumbs that fall from their master's table!'"

29. And He said to her, "You know what? Because of what you just said and how you said it, you can go in peace; the spirit has released control of your daughter and has left her, permanently!"
30. So she went home and, sure enough, she found her daughter resting peacefully on the couch and the rebel spirit was nowhere to be found.
31. Right after this, Jesus, coming back from the region of Tyre, passed through Sidon on to Lake Galilee through the region of Decapolis, or "The Ten Cities."
32. And there they brought to Him a man who was deaf and had great difficulty in speaking, and the people who were with him begged Jesus to just place His hand upon him.
33. But Jesus took the man aside from the crowd to minister to him privately and in a very unconventional manner, even for Him. He authoritatively thrust His fingers into the man's ears and then He spat into His hand, dipped His finger into His own saliva, and touched the man's tongue with it.
34. Then, looking up to the sky, He groaned from somewhere deep within Himself as He said in His native tongue, *"Ephphatha!"* which means, "Be opened!"
35. And immediately the startled man's ears were opened and he began to speak perfectly…with no impediment at all.
36. Then Jesus brought him back to the crowd and sternly ordered the people who had brought him to tell no one about what had just happened. But, as it turned out, the more He commanded the people to be quiet about the miracles, the more zealously they seemed to proclaim it.
37. They were too overwhelmed and amazed by it all to remain silent. "He has done everything with excellence!" they said. "He even causes the deaf to hear and the mute to speak!"

Chapter 8

1. Not long after this, another immense crowd gathered to hear Him and again the meeting went long…so long, in fact, that it turned into a three-day event. And, as was the case before, they had nothing to

eat because they had not been prepared for the length of the meeting. And once again Jesus called His disciples to Himself and told them,

2. "I really feel for these people; My heart goes out to them for they have been with Me now three whole days and have nothing left to eat;
3. "I can't send them away hungry, trying to get back to their homes on empty stomachs. I don't want them and their children to faint on the road. For some of them it's quite a journey; many of them have come a very long way."
4. And, even though they had fairly recently seen Him multiply a little bit of food and feed thousands with it, His disciples replied to Him, "How can anyone adequately feed these people with a few loaves of bread out here in the middle of nowhere?"
5. And, again ignoring their finite concept of abundance and supply, He asked them, "How many loaves do you have here?" And they very matter-of-factly replied, "Seven."
6. And, as before, He commanded the multitude to spread out on the ground and then took the seven loaves of bread, gave thanks for what He had to work with, and started breaking them apart. And, also as before, He kept on breaking them and giving them to His disciples to serve to the hungry people. And as the bread multiplied, they placed it before the crowd.
7. And they also discovered that they had a few small fish there, so He took them, as well. And when He had praised God, given thanks, and blessed them, He ordered that they should also be served to the people, along with the bread.
8. And the crowd ate and all the people were satisfied. Afterward, the disciples took up seven large provision baskets full of the broken pieces left over.
9. This time there were about 4,000 people there. And after He had finished feeding them, He dismissed them,
10. and immediately got into a boat with His disciples and went to the district of Dalmanutha, also known as Magdala.
11. And when He arrived at His destination, the Pharisees found Him and went right into questioning and cross-examining Him, trying to start an argument, badgering Him, and demanding a sign—the performance of a miracle that would validate Him in their estimation and judgment.
12. But instead of going into debate mode, or making any pointless

attempt at self-defense, He just groaned and sighed deeply in His spirit and said, "What is it with this generation...and why do you need to see yet another sign? There's nothing I could say to you...no sign I could show you...that would cause you to see Me in a different light. So, suffice it to say, no sign will be given this generation."

13. And He just ended it there and left them. And, getting into the boat again, He departed to the other side.
14. And the disciples boarded the boat with Him, but they had completely forgotten to bring any bread and had only one loaf with them.
15. But Jesus, still thinking about what had just occurred, looked at them and said, "Listen, you all really need to look out and keep on your guard against the contaminated yeast of the Pharisees—and beware of the yeast of Herod and his followers, as well."
16. After He had said this, they began to discuss His use of words and came to the conclusion that He was chastising them in a roundabout way for not bringing any bread with them.
17. And being aware of how utterly they had missed His point, He said to them, "How could you possibly assume that I said what I said because you have no bread? I mean, really...do you not yet discern or understand? The Pharisees demanded a sign for proof...you've actually seen plenty of signs and yet you still don't seem to get it! Are your hearts really that petrified?
18. "You obviously have eyes, but you don't really see with them; and you clearly have ears, yet you don't hear or perceive or understand the sense of what I say. But I ask you: don't you at least have the capacity to simply remember?
19. "When I broke the five loaves for the 5,000, how many baskets full of broken pieces did you take up?" And they said to Him, "Twelve."
20. "And when I broke up the seven loaves for the 4,000, how many baskets full of broken pieces did you collect afterward?" And they said to Him, "Seven."
21. Then He asked, "How many miracles is it going to take before you begin to walk in some kind of understanding of all this?"
22. Then they came to Bethsaida and, when they got there, some people brought to Jesus a blind man and begged Him to just touch him.
23. And He took the blind man by the hand and led him away from the people, as He had done previously with the deaf man. In fact, He led him out of the village and, when they were completely alone, He spit

on the man's eyes and put His hands on him. Then He asked him, "Do you see anything at all?"

24. And the man looked up and said, "I think I see people, but they look more like trees than people...yes, I see people who look like walking trees!"

25. Then Jesus put His hands on the man's partially-healed eyes again and the man opened them and started looking around with the ability to focus—he could fix his eyes on definite objects—and he realized that he had been completely restored. He could see everything distinctly and perfectly.

26. And Jesus sent him home, telling him directly, "Don't enter the village at all, and don't tell anyone there what just happened here."

27. Then Jesus went on with His disciples to the villages of Caesarea Philippi, and on the way He said to them, "I want to ask you something: who do people say that I am?"

28. And without even having to think about how to answer Him they said, "Well, generally, people say that You're the reincarnation of John, the Baptizer...but others think and say that You're Elijah appearing in the now...and still others just believe and declare that You're 'one of the seers.'"

29. Then He responded to them, "All right, so who do you yourselves say that I am?" And, without missing a beat, Peter spontaneously replied to Him, "You are the Christ...the Anointed One!"

30. But He warned them to keep this revelation quiet...not to even breathe a word of it.

31. Then He went right into teaching and explaining to them that it was necessary for the Son of Man to experience an ordeal of suffering, to be tested and rejected by the elders, priests and other religious leaders...and to be ultimately put to death. He also revealed that after three days He would rise again.

32. And He took His time in spelling all this out for them, speaking very plainly and explicitly, making sure that they fully grasped what He was actually saying. But Peter, in spontaneous protest, grabbed Him by the hand, took Him aside and began to openly rebuke Him for saying these things.

33. But turning His back to Peter, and seeing how His disciples were responding to all this, He returned the rebuke, saying, "Peter, you're completely out of line; get behind Me, you adversary! You are seeing and hearing only with your physical, natural senses; you are

oblivious to what is happening, and what needs to happen, in the spirit realm, which is why you are responding like this. The will of God is bigger than your perception or opinion of what I have said is going to happen to Me!"

34. Then Jesus called the throng with His disciples to Himself and said to them, "Look, if any of you intend to follow after Me, you're going to have to deny the lower life with its selfish agendas and instinct for self-preservation...and you're going to have to take up your own 'cross'...your own gateway to the larger life...the life motivated by a love unafraid to make hard choices...the life of personal sacrifice...a resurrected life, born out of a death of selfishness.

35. "For whoever wants to save his higher, spiritual, enlightened life will lose the lower, natural, limited life which is lived out only in the physical realm. By the same token, whoever gives up the life lived only in the physical realm for My sake and the Gospel's, will save his/her higher, spiritual life in the eternal Kingdom of God.

36. "For what does it profit an individual to gain everything the physical world has to offer and forfeit his spiritual, visionary life in the eternal Kingdom of God?

37. "For what could a person ever give as an exchange or compensation for his/her blessed, enlightened life in the Kingdom?

38. "And this is a great concept...nothing to be ashamed or afraid of! In fact, whoever is embarrassed in this dimension of Me and My words, of him or her will the Son of Man also be embarrassed when He is revealed in the glory and majesty of His Kingdom...and before His Father and the holy angels."

Chapter 9

1. Then He took this concept of the revelation of the Kingdom to another level by saying, "This is the absolute truth: Some of you who are standing right here are going to see it happen; you're going to see the Kingdom of God arrive in full force and power."

2. And, sure enough, six days after this, His prophecy came to pass for three of them. He took with Him Peter, James and John, and led them up to the top of a high mountain, apart by themselves, and was transfigured right in front of their eyes—His appearance morphed and changed from the inside out, becoming luminous with near-blinding brightness.

3. His clothes began to glisten with a white intensity...whiter than any launderer on earth could bleach them in a thousand washes.
4. As this was happening, the Prophet Elijah suddenly stepped out of linear time—out of the perceived past...out of their history and into their now—and appeared alive to them. Amazingly, he was accompanied by Moses, and both of them entered talking; they broke through to where the disciples physically existed, already in mid-conversation with Jesus!
5. And somehow Peter instinctively and instantly connected with transcendence and joined right in this cross-dimensional conference, saying, "Master, it is a beautiful thing for us to be here to witness this! Let us make three memorials: one for You, one for Moses, one for Elijah!"
6. He spoke before thinking, but when he said these words, it dawned on his mind what he was seeing and saying, and "reality" set in. And this perception took him immediately to a place of violent fright and dread, connecting him with the fear that the rest of the disciples were already experiencing.
7. But before any of them could begin to process any of this, a cloud threw a shadow upon them, and a voice came out of the cloud, saying, "This is My Son, the blessed and beloved One! Listen to Him always...listen and obey!"
8. And in an instant the disciples were looking around, rubbing their eyes, trying to mentally accept this seemingly surreal experience and seeing nothing but Jesus—no Moses, no Elijah, no blinding light, no cloud—only Jesus.
9. Then, as they were coming back down the mountain, He swore them to secrecy, saying, "Listen, right now I really don't want you to tell anyone about what you just saw here. But after the Son of Man rises from the dead, you're free to talk about it."
10. So they faithfully kept the matter to themselves, as He had instructed. In fact, keeping quiet about the strange experience was easy for them because there really was no way to adequately explain it, anyway. The part of what He said, however, that they did have a problem with was the thing about "rising from the dead." They really had no idea what on earth He meant by it.
11. Meanwhile, they were asking Him, "Why do the religious leaders and scholars insist that Elijah has to come first?"
12. And He said to them, "Well, they're right about that; Elijah does

have to come first to restore all things and set them right...to get everything ready for the revealing of the Son of Man, Who will suffer many things and will be despised and rejected by the people.
13. "But in reality I tell you that Elijah has already come and the people abused him in much the same way, just as the Scriptures predicted."
14. And when they came back down the mountain to re-join the other nine disciples, they saw a huge crowd around them and the religion scholars obviously arguing with them about something.
15. But as soon as the crowd saw Jesus, His face still slightly glowing with the residue of the glory from the transfiguration, they were amazed and instantly drawn to Him, and they all flocked to Him and greeted Him with great excitement.
16. And He warmly received them, asking, "What's going on down here? What's all the commotion about?"
17. From out of the crowd a man spoke up and said, "I'll tell You what's going on: I brought my son to You because he is under the influence of a spirit that has struck him dumb.
18. "And not only has it silenced him, verbally, it also frequently sends him into violent convulsions, causing him to foam at the mouth and grind his teeth, after which he falls into a motionless stupor. This thing is literally making him waste away, so I asked Your disciples to end its authority over his life, but they weren't able to do it."
19. To which Jesus responded, "Oh, what a faithless and unaware generation! How many times do I have to go over these things with you? At what point are you going to start walking in your own authority? Bring your boy to Me, sir."
20. So the boy was brought to Him, and when the controlling spirit saw Jesus and recognized Who He was (as the spirits always did), it started showing off, attempting to rebel and resist Jesus' authority. It threw the boy into a seizure, causing him to writhe on the ground and foam at the mouth, just as the father had described.
21. Ignoring the spirit's dramatic display, Jesus asked the boy's father, "How long has this been going on?"
22. "Ever since he was a little boy," the man said. "And I didn't tell you this part, but sometimes it even causes him to attempt suicide; it tells him to jump into an open fire or to drown himself in the river, and he tries to do what it tells him to do! We're really in trouble here, so if you can do anything to help us with this thing, please have a heart and do it!"

23. Jesus answered him, "You say 'if' to Me—'if' you can help us—and and I say 'if' right back to you—'if' you can believe—'if' you can believe, anything is possible!"
24. And before Jesus could completely finish the sentence, the man cried out, "YES! YES! I do believe! I mean, I have some doubts I have to deal with—I'm tired, physically and emotionally, frustrated with this thing that's been plaguing my son for so long—but deep in my heart, I really do believe! That's why I came to You in the first place!"
25. Jesus noticed that an even larger crowd was forming to see what was going on and He refused to let the spirit gain any more attention. So He said, "All right, that's enough, you controlling spirit! Leave the boy's life, and never bother him again!"
26. And the spirit screamed and convulsed him...then it obeyed Jesus and departed. But it left the boy spent and seemingly lifeless, lying still on the ground, so the people started saying, "He's dead."
27. But Jesus gripped his hand and, in one swift motion, pulled him up off the ground and he stood on his own.
28. After arriving back home, His disciples cornered Jesus and asked, "Okay, why couldn't we drive out the spirit?"
29. And He answered them, "Look, I've authorized you all to do everything that I do, but you can't let rebel spirits intimidate you and make you think that you're weak...or that they're strong. You have to maintain your confidence in who you are in God to have dominion in the spirit realm...and you can do that by staying in constant communication with Him. In that sense, you could say that these kinds of spirits can only be expelled through the self-awareness resulting from the strength of your own prayer life."
30. So they went on from there and passed along through Galilee, but He didn't want anyone to know where they were or where they were going.
31. His reason for wanting to keep such a low profile was that He was particularly focused on teaching His disciples at this time. As they traveled, He said to them, "I want to prepare you all for something: You need to know that the Son of Man is about to be betrayed and delivered into the hands of enemies and they will put Him to death; but after He has been killed...in fact, three days after He has been killed...He will rise from death."
32. But even though He spelled it out for them like this, they had

absolutely no comprehension of what He was saying, and for some reason were afraid to ask Him to explain it further.

33. Eventually, they arrived at Capernaum, and when they were all together in the house, He confronted them about something, asking them, "What were you boys discussing and arguing about on the road?"

34. But they all froze and didn't say a word, because on the road they had argued and debated with one another as to who among them was the greatest.

35. So He sat down and called all twelve of His disciples together and said to them, "Look, I want you to understand this Kingdom principle: the bottom line is this...if anyone desires to be first, he must be last of all, and servant of all."

36. And to drive home His point, He took a little child who was there in the house with them, put him in the center of the group and, taking him in His arms, He said to them,

37. "Remember this: whoever in My name and for My sake accepts, receives and embraces a child like this, also accepts and receives and embraces Me. And, it follows, that whoever receives Me receives not only Me, but Him Who sent Me."

38. Then John said to Him, "By the way, Teacher, the other day we saw a man who does not follow along with us—You didn't appoint him or sanction him or approve him...You don't even know him—but he was driving out rebel spirits in Your name, and we told him that he was completely out of line to do that and commanded him to stop it immediately because He is not one of us...and not one of Yours!"

39. But, to their surprise, Jesus said, "Oh, you really shouldn't have done that. Don't ever restrain or forbid someone like him from doing something like that; for no one who does a mighty work in My name will soon afterward be able to speak evil of Me.

40. "But that's not even the point...what you must realize is that he who is not against us is for us. It's just that simple!

41. "And, furthermore, the truth is that whoever gives you a cup of water to drink just because you bear the name of Christ—just because you are making a difference in the world through His power and authority—will be guaranteed a sure reward. A basic act of kindness like this is, in the big picture, an important contribution to the Kingdom...driving out spirits...giving a cup of water...it's all the same and it's all valid.

42. "Whoever hurts one of these little ones—or abuses them in any way, or takes advantage of their simple trust, or causes them to grow up to be less than what they should have been—it would actually be better for that person to have one of those huge grinding-stones that they use in the mills fastened around his or her neck and to be sunk in the depth of the sea.
43. "Let Me clarify this: your desire to be a good example before the young should be such that if, say, your hand causes you to stumble and sin, you would be willing to just cut it off and throw it away. It would, in fact, be better for you to go through life maimed than to have two hands and your very existence become so worthless that you end up being thrown into the fires at the Gehenna garbage dump outside Jerusalem, which never go out."
44. [Verse 44 does not exist in any original manuscripts.]
45. "By the same token, if somehow your foot is a cause of stumbling and sin to you, you should also be willing to cut it off, as well! Again, it would, in fact, be better for you to go through life lame, than to have two feet and your very existence become so worthless that you end up being thrown into the fires at the Gehenna garbage dump outside Jerusalem."
46. [Verse 46 does not exist in any original manuscripts.]
47. "In the same way, if your eye causes you to compromise your good example before one of these little ones, be willing to pluck it out! It is more advantageous for you to enter the Kingdom of God with one eye than to go through life with two eyes and end up being thrown onto the garbage dump,
48. that horrible, maggot-infested place where dismembered limbs and cadavers are discarded and burned constantly.
49. "The reason I'm making this point using such extreme, conceptual language is that I want you to realize that everyone must take responsibility for their own lives and for the example they set...but, one way or another, everyone is going to go through a refining fire...sooner or later every person will be tried by the flames...if not in Gehenna, then by the trials of life...but when you pass through the fire, you ultimately will be preserved.
50. "Salt is a good preservative, but if the salt has lost its saltiness, it is worthless...how can it be restored? So have salt within yourselves; by that I mean, what you need to preserve you in the fire is already within you...you just have to locate it. And those who have passed

through the fire will ultimately be at peace and live in harmony with one another...their inner preservative will enable them to preserve the peace."

Chapter 10

1. Then Jesus left that place and went into the region of Judea and across the Jordan. And again crowds of people came to Him and, as was His custom, He went right into teaching mode.
2. And some Pharisees who were in the crowd came to Him again and put Him to the test by asking, "Is it legal and right for a man to dismiss his wife…to divorce her for any reason that he may have?"
3. He answered their question with another question, asking, "What did Moses command you?"
4. They replied, "Moses permitted a man to simply write a certificate of divorce and just send her away, no strings attached."
5. "Moses set up this system basically because of the hardness of your hearts…specifically, your insensitivity to women. He permitted you to easily dismiss your wives with no regard for required responsibility to them, because you have had no concept of covenant," He said to them.
6. "But, in this, Moses did not have the heart and mind of God, considering that this self-serving male convenience was not in God's original plan; at the beginning of creation, God 'made them male and female.'
7. "This is why a man has to leave his father and mother at some point, and be united and bonded to his wife.
8. "And when that happens, the two of them become, in a sense, one single entity, so that they are no longer two separate physical bodies, but actually become one new one.
9. "And if a particular union between a man and a woman is, indeed, God-ordained, then no human being should do anything to create a disconnect between what God has intentionally put together."
10. When they were in the house again, the disciples asked Jesus to explain this further.
11. He answered them, "Whoever just casually dismisses his wife for no legitimate reason, and marries the next available woman who comes along, really is only committing adultery with her. His shallow flippancy in such a case shows that he has no understanding of the

seriousness of covenant.

12. "The situation is somewhat different if the wife has been unfaithful to her husband, but the real issue is still about the apparent disregard of covenant. So if she divorces her husband and marries another man for no good reason, she commits adultery, as well, because there is no genuine commitment to the covenant of marriage."

13. Around this time people were beginning to bring their little children to Jesus for Him to place His hands on them and bless them when He was ministering; but when they did, the disciples would insult them by preventing them to do this.

14. One day it happened and when Jesus saw what the disciples were doing, He was furious with them. He said, "You let these little children come right to Me, and don't you dare tell them that they aren't allowed or welcome! Childlikeness is the standard for the Kingdom of God, so, in essence, the Kingdom belongs to such as these.

15. "The truth is that anyone who will not perceive and receive the Kingdom of God like a little child will never enter it in the first place."

16. Then He stopped what He was doing and saying and started taking the children who were there in His arms, placing His hands on them affectionately, and taking the time to bless each one of them.

17. As Jesus went out into the street, a young man came running up to Him, greeted Him reverently, and asked, "Good Teacher, what must I do to experience the fullness of eternal life?"

18. Jesus answered him, "First of all...why do you call Me good? No one is good except God alone.

19. "And secondly, you already know the commandments...'Do not murder, do not commit adultery, do not steal, do not give false testimony, do not defraud, honor your father and mother, etc.'"

20. "Yes, Teacher," he responded, "I do know the commandments and I have devoutly kept all of them to the letter since I was a boy."

21. Jesus looked at him—looked beyond his religious pretentiousness and misguided concepts of discipleship—and just very simply loved him. "All right, if you're really that serious about inheriting the Kingdom—about walking in the fullness of eternal life—then do this one thing: go, sell everything you have and give all the profits and proceeds to the poor, and you will have treasure in the heavenly realm. Then come, and follow Me!"

22. At this specific word the young man's face fell. Unable to recognize the possibility that Jesus was uniquely offering him, he went away very sad because he had great wealth and his great wealth had him.
23. Then Jesus looked around and said to His disciples, "You know, for some reason it is really difficult for the very rich to enter into the Kingdom-life."
24. The disciples were amazed at His words because of the illusions that they themselves held concerning the supposed invincibility of the rich. But Jesus said again, "Children, what great discipline is required to enter the lifestyle of the Kingdom of God!
25. "It is easier for a camel to go through the gate in Jerusalem called the eye of the needle, through which it cannot pass unless it first stoops and has all its baggage removed. After dark, when the main gates are shut, travelers or merchants have to use this smaller gate, through which the camel can only enter, unencumbered and crawling on its knees."
26. The disciples were even more amazed at these words. This scenario had unearthed some very wrong ideas that they obviously had held; it revealed that they considered the very rich to be in another class, altogether, and not necessarily in need of the same saving grace as the poor to whom they regularly ministered. They said to each other, "Well, if the rich have this much trouble connecting with the Kingdom, who then can be saved?"
27. Jesus looked at them and said, "With man—or rather from a merely human perspective—this is indeed impossible...but not with God; when the rich bow their knees to Kingdom authority, they are equally blessed with the poor...and the bottom line is that, regardless of how much wealth someone has or doesn't have, when it comes to entering the Kingdom, all things are possible with God!"
28. Peter said to Him, "Well, none of this really even applies to us, anyway, because we have left everything to follow You!"
29. "Look, here's the truth about that," Jesus replied, "no one who has left home or brothers or sisters or mother or father or children or fields for Me and the Gospel
30. will fail to receive a hundred times as much in this present age... homes...brothers...sisters...mothers...children...fields...and, yes, with them, persecutions. The Kingdom-life requires that you rethink your current definitions of wealth and poverty...all these things you will abundantly receive now (as the young man who left would have

received, had he received the word I gave him) and, in the age to come...in the era of manifestation...a full revelation of all that the realization of eternal life has to offer!
31. "But many who in this culture and world-system seem to be first, will be last, and many who now appear to be last, will be first."
32. After this they were on the way going up to Jerusalem, and Jesus was walking ahead of them with a distinct sense of purpose and direction in His stride. At this point they were all beginning to second-guess their commitment to follow Him at any cost. Some of the things He had been saying had left them bewildered and perplexed, and those who were still following were becoming more and more unsettled and afraid over what was potentially on the horizon for them all. So He took the Twelve aside again and began to tell them exactly what was about to happen to Him.
33. He said, "Look...I don't want anything that is about to happen to take you by surprise, so here is the full plan: We are going up to Jerusalem, and there the Son of Man will be turned over to the religious leaders and the scribes...and they will condemn and sentence Him to death and turn Him over to the Roman government.
34. "And they will mock Him, spit on Him, whip Him and put Him to death. But after three days, He will rise again from the grave."
35. The disciples had no response to these startling and very specific words, but James and John (the sons of Zebedee) later approached Him and said to Him, "Teacher, we desire You to do for us whatever we ask of You."
36. And He replied to them, "Well...what is it that you desire Me to do for you?"
37. And they said to Him, "We want You to promise us that we may sit, one at Your right hand and one at Your left hand, in Your glory...when Your majesty and splendor are finally revealed."
38. But Jesus said to them, "You boys don't even know what you are asking. Do you honestly think that you are able to drink the cup that I drink, or be baptized with the baptism of affliction with which I am about to be baptized?"
39. And they immediately replied to Him, "Without a doubt we are able!" And Jesus told them, "All right, the cup that I drink you will drink and you will be baptized with the baptism with which I am baptized...
40. but to sit at My right hand or at My left hand is not Mine to decide;

41. as the Son of Man, I am completely submitted to a Higher authority, but that honor will be given to those for whom it is divinely ordained and prepared."
41. When the other ten disciples got wind of this exchange, they began to be resentful and even furious with James and John.
42. But Jesus called them all together to Himself to settle things down, saying to them, "You've all seen how ego-centric rulers throw their weight around...you experienced, firsthand, how when people get a little authority they easily become power-drunk.
43. "Well, it can't be that way with any of you...not if you're going to live the Kingdom-life; in this new world order, whoever desires to be great among you must become your servant,
44. and whoever desires to be most important—whoever wants to be first in rank among you—must be willing to act like the slave of all when it comes to fulfilling the law of love.
45. "For even the Son of Man did not come to have service rendered to Him; on the contrary, He came for no other purpose than to serve...to ultimately give His life as a ransom for, or rather instead of, many."
46. Then they came to Jericho and spent some time there. But as Jesus and His disciples were leaving the city, they passed a blind man by the name of Bartimaeus, which means "son of Timaeus," sitting by the roadside, begging.
47. When Bartimaeus heard that it was Jesus of Nazareth, he began to shout out as loud as he could, "Jesus, Son of David, have mercy on me!"
48. And many who were in the crowd following Jesus immediately rebuked him and told him to shut up. But he ignored them and shouted even more loudly, "Son of David, have mercy on me!"
49. Jesus stopped and said, "Don't shut him up...call him over here!" So they called to the blind man, "Hey, beggar man, things are looking up for you! Get up on your feet...Jesus is calling for you!"
50. Instantly, the man tore off his coat, jumped to his feet and found his way over to Jesus.
51. "Okay...what do you want Me to do for you, friend?" Jesus asked him. The blind man said, "Teacher, I want to see!"
52. "All right, then...go!" said Jesus, "Your own faith has healed you!" And immediately Bartimaeus received his sight and began following Jesus along the road with everyone else.

Chapter 11

1. As they neared Jerusalem and came to Bethphage and Bethany on the Mount of Olives, He sent two of His disciples ahead.
2. And He gave them very specific instructions, saying, "I want you to go into the village ahead of you, and as soon as you enter it you will find a young colt tied which has never been ridden by anyone. When you find it, I want you to unfasten it and bring it here to Me.
3. "If anyone should ask you, 'Why are you taking this animal which doesn't belong to you?' just say to them, 'The Lord needs it, but He will send it right back here when He's through with it.'"
4. So they went on their way, and, sure enough, they found a colt tied at the door of a house as soon as they entered the village and they went right up to it and loosed it.
5. And some who were standing there said to them, "What do you think you're doing? Why are you untying this man's colt?"
6. And they said to the people exactly what Jesus had told them to say...and it worked! The people allowed them to go without saying another word.
7. And they brought the colt to Jesus and started throwing their outer garments on it, creating a sort of festive, makeshift saddle...and He sat on it.
8. And many of the people who were around took their cues from the disciples and began to spontaneously spread their garments on the road. Still others joined in with the impromptu decorating and scattered a layer of leafy branches which they had cut from the fields along the route on which He would be traveling.
9. And still others formed a parade of praise, preceding Him on the road and crying out joyfully and triumphantly, "Hosanna! Save, Lord! Praised and infinitely blessed is He Who comes in the name of the Lord!
10. "Praised and blessed in the name of the Lord is the coming Kingdom of our father David! Hosanna! Save, Lord! Hosanna in the highest!"
11. And this is the way Jesus entered into Jerusalem. Once He was inside the city, He went into the Temple enclosure. Walking in, He looked around, surveying everything...taking it all in...and He made some serious observations about what He saw there. But it was getting late in the day, so He went out to Bethany together with the

Twelve.

12. On the following day, when they had come away from Bethany, He realized that He was hungry.
13. And, seeing in the distance a fig tree covered with leaves, He went to see if He could find any edible fruit on it (in fig trees, fruit appears at the same time as the leaves). But when He came right up to it, He found nothing but leaves, because the natural fig season had not yet arrived.
14. And, immediately reacting to this natural limitation, He calmly said to it, "Fig tree, no one will ever eat fruit from you again." And His disciples overheard what He said.
15. So they kept on walking and, as they came to Jerusalem, He went again into the Temple area. And as He entered the porches and courts, acting on instinct, He began to personally and violently drive out those who sold and bought in the Temple area, overturning the four-footed tables of the money changers and the seats of those who dealt in doves for sacrifice.
16. He wouldn't even permit anyone to carry any household equipment through the Temple enclosure, because it turned the Temple area into a short-cut traffic lane and contributed to the general disrespect that the public had for such a sacred place.
17. And He began to declare to them, "Is it not written, *'My house shall be called a house of prayer for all nations'*? But you have denigrated this hallowed place—a place set aside for such universal worship—into nothing more than a den of petty robbers!"
18. And the religious leaders and the scribes got wind of this occurrence and, as a result, became more aggressive in seeking some way to destroy Him. They feared Him, intensely, because the entire population was awe-struck at His revolutionary and revelatory teaching.
19. And when evening came, He and His disciples, as was their custom, went out of the city.
20. In the morning, when they were passing along, they noticed that the fig tree He had so casually spoken to was completely withered away, dead down to its roots.
21. And Peter remembered it right away and said to Him, "Master, look! The fig tree which You sentenced to barrenness has withered away!"
22. And Jesus, replying, said to them all, "Realize that you have the very faith of God resident within you...don't just try to 'have faith in

God'...embrace, instead, the inherent God-faith that you already have.

23. "Let Me reveal this truth to you: You're impressed with what happened to the fig tree, but the fact is that you have the power and ability to say to this entire mountain, 'Be lifted up and be thrown into the sea!' and see it obey you! You've seen Me actually speak to a storm...or command the dead to live again...well, in the same way, if you can connect the God-kind of faith that is in your own heart with the creative ability that is in your own mouth...if you say what you believe and believe what you say...you can produce these kinds of results!

24. "This is why I am telling you, whatever you ask for in prayer...whatever you decree...BELIEVE...accept the reality that it exists in another, unseen dimension, simply because you say it. Don't suspend or delay belief until you see it manifested in the physical realm, because what is unseen is more real than what is seen. Be confident that your request is granted to you, and you will get it...your own irresistible faith will attract it to you.

25. "But when you enter into a season of prayer, remember that it's meant to be much more than simply making a list of declarations and petitions. Your prayer-life is more about changing *you* than it is about getting God to change things *for* you. It's about creating personal transformation so that you can change what needs to be changed in the world around you. So, for that reason, prayer should affect your horizontal relationships as much as it does your vertical relationship; that's why I tell you that whenever you stand praying, if you have anything against anyone at all, you need to forgive him or her and just let it drop...leave the past in the past...let it go so that you can pray in the now, without having all the emotional baggage from yesterday drag you backwards. When you set these things in order, it's as if your Father Who is in heaven is forgiving you your own failings and shortcomings and letting them drop, leaving you mentally and emotionally cleansed from distractions.

26. "But if you do not forgive, you set negative, universal laws into motion that prevent you from receiving the blessing of forgiveness from your Father in the heavenly realm."

27. And they came once again to Jerusalem, but this time the religious leaders, scribes and elders were there in the Temple. So when Jesus was walking around in the courts and porches of the Temple area,

they came to Him;
28. and they said to Him, "We want to know by what authority are You doing these things...who gave You the right to do them?"
29. Jesus said to them, "I will answer your question with another question. If you can give Me a legitimate answer, I will tell you by what authority I do these things.
30. "Was the baptism of John a supernatural product of the heavenly realm, or was it simply a manmade ritual? Tell Me what you think."
31. And they stepped aside and conferred and argued with one another, saying, "If we admit that we think it was heavenly, no doubt He will say, 'Why then didn't you believe him?'
32. "On the other hand, how can we say that we think it was merely an idea that originated from the mind of a man?" They knew they couldn't say that because they were afraid of the people, and practically everyone considered and held John to be a prophet.
33. So they came back to Jesus and said, "We don't know what to tell You." And Jesus said to them, "Fair enough...so neither am I going to tell you by what sort of authority I have done and do these things."

Chapter 12

1. Then Jesus began to speak to His audience in allegories, saying, "There was a man who planted a vineyard. He built a wall around it, dug a pit for the winepress, and then built a watchtower. Then he rented out the vineyard to some farmers and moved away to another place.
2. "At harvest time he sent one of his servants to these tenants to collect from them some of the harvested fruit of the vineyard.
3. "But, to his surprise, they wouldn't hear of it. They seized him, beat him up, and sent him back to where he came from with nothing but a black eye and a bloody nose.
4. "Then the man sent another one of his servants to them, but they took the violence up a notch with this man. They struck him hard on the head, and just generally brutalized him for a while.
5. "So, finally, he sent yet another servant, but this one they murdered in cold blood. In fact, over a period of time he sent many others, and some of them they beat up and still others they killed.
6. "As a last resort he sent a son, whom he loved, saying to himself 'Surely, they will respect my son.'

7. *"But, on the contrary, the tenants said to one another, 'This is the man's heir...come on, let's kill him, too, and the entire inheritance will be ours.'*
8. *"So, indeed, they took the son and killed him and threw his dead body out of the vineyard.*
9. *"What, then, will the owner of the vineyard do in such a case? Certainly he has the right to come and kill those bloodthirsty tenants and give the vineyard to others.*
10. *"Haven't you read the passage of Scripture that says, 'The stone that the builders rejected has become the cornerstone;*
11. *'the Lord has done this, and it is marvelous in our perception'?"*
12. Then the religious leaders, teachers of the Law and the elders looked for a way to arrest Him because they were at least intelligent enough to realize that He had spoken the extended metaphor against them. But they were cowards, afraid of the crowd, so they just left Him and went away.
13. But they sent some Pharisees and followers of Herod to bait Him, in an effort to catch Him saying something incriminating.
14. They came up to Him and said, "Teacher, we know that You have integrity, that You are impartial...enlightened...indifferent to public opinion. So, because You don't pander to Your followers but teach the way of God accurately, please tell us...in Your estimable opinion...is it lawful to pay taxes to Caesar or not?"
15. Of course He saw right through this trick question and the pretentious motivation behind it. So He said to them, *"Why do you keep trying to engage Me in your nonsense, playing these mind games with Me? Okay, I'll bite...bring Me a coin and let Me look at it."*
16. They quickly handed Him one and He said, *"The engraving on this coin...who does it look like? And, more importantly...whose name is on it?"* "Caesar," they replied.
17. Jesus said to them, *"Then the answer is simple and obvious: give Caesar what is his, and give God what is His."* And, once again, they were left utterly speechless by the clarity and candor with which He conveyed complex concepts.
18. Then, after this episode with the Pharisees, next came the Sadducees (who say there is no resurrection) with another provocative question for Him.
19. "Teacher," they said, "Surely You're aware that Moses wrote that if

a man's brother dies and leaves a wife but no children, the man must marry his widowed sister-in-law and raise up offspring for his brother.

20. "Now, let's say, hypothetically, that there were seven brothers and the first one married and died without leaving any children.
21. "Then let's say that the second one married the widow, but he also died, leaving no children. And the same scenario occurred with the third.
22. "And so it went, but none of the seven brothers left any children. Then, finally, the woman died, too.
23. "Now, at the resurrection, whose wife will this woman be, seeing that she was married to all seven men?"
24. Jesus replied, "Your implausible premise is way off base because clearly, in asking this question, you reveal that you are ignorant of both the Scriptures and of the power of God.
25. "The fact is that in the next life when the dead are raised up, they will have a completely different paradigm of human relationships... the concepts of sexuality, gender and procreation will be rendered altogether obsolete, so, in that dimension, they will neither marry nor be given in marriage...in that sense they will be in an exalted state like the angels in the heavenly realm.
26. "But as to the main point of your question about the dead rising...have you not read in the Book of Moses, in the story of the burning bush, how God said to him, *'I AM* (not "I Was" or "I Will be") *the God of Abraham, the God of Isaac, and the God of Jacob?'*
27. "In so revealing Himself, He has declared that He is not the God of the dead, but of the living; your ideas about the finality of death have caused you to completely miss the point!"
28. While this exchange with the Sadducees was still in progress, along came a religion scholar who heard the tail end of it and was impressed with Jesus' knowledge and the good answer that He had given them. So he asked Him, "Of all the commandments, can You tell me which one is the most important?"
29. "The most important one is about the one true God," Jesus answered, "It's this: 'Hear, O Israel: The Lord our God, the Lord is one.
30. 'Love the Lord your God with all your passion, and with all your emotion, and with all your intelligence, and with all your energy.'
31. "But there is a second one which is technically the same commandment: 'Love your neighbor as much as you love yourself.'

There is no commandment greater than this one revealed in these two integrated dimensions."

32. "Beautifully stated, Teacher," the man replied. "And You are absolutely right in saying that God is one and there is no other but Him...

33. and that to have the full revelation of that, you must love Him with all your passion, with all your intellect, and with all your ability, and love your neighbor with the same love you have for yourself. Embracing this is more important than all burnt offerings and sacrifices."

34. When Jesus observed that the man had answered with such insight, He said to him, "You, sir, are on the very cutting edge of the Kingdom of God!" And from that point on no one had the nerve to ask Him any more questions.

35. And as Jesus taught in one of the porches of the Temple, He said to His audience, "Think about this...how can the scribes say that the Christ is David's Son?

36. "David himself, in a Holy Spirit-inspired declaration, said, 'The Lord said to My Lord, "Sit at My right hand until I make Your enemies a footstool under Your feet."'

37. "The point is that David himself calls Him 'Lord'...so how can it be that He is his Son?" The huge crowd that was there that day was completely delighted with the way He challenged the pretentious scribes and their conventional wisdom.

38. And in the course of His teaching, He went on to say, "Beware of the scribes who like to go around preening in long robes, basking in public flattery and generally acting piously superior;

39. sitting at the head table in every public forum...expecting a place of honor at every feast.

40. "That in itself can be dismissed simply as a basic human weakness in them that manifests itself in a dysfunctional need for attention...it is what it is. What makes it so reprehensible with this group, however, is that all the while they are playing to the crowd publicly, they are secretly exploiting widows...preying on them...going into their houses and devouring what little they have. And yet to distract the public from discerning their dark deeds, they make long prayers and elaborate speeches which make them sound intimidatingly holy. Be assured they will receive the heavier sentence of condemnation."

41. Later, He sat down opposite the treasury and witnessed firsthand

how the crowd was casting money into it. That day many rich people were obviously throwing in large sums.
42. And somewhere within the stream of people who were giving, a poverty-stricken widow came and unassumingly put in two copper mites, the smallest of coins, which added together are the equivalent of half of a cent.
43. And He called His disciples over and said to them, "Here's the truth about this little woman: she has demonstrated the relativity of giving because, even though she is poor, she has put in more than all those contributing to the treasury.
44. "The others all casually threw their money in from out of their vast wealth and apparent abundance...they won't even miss the money. But she, out of her deep poverty, has put in everything that she had...in fact, she has sacrificed all that she had on which to live, which is why she has given the most."

Chapter 13

1. As Jesus was leaving the Temple area that day, one of His disciples said to Him, "Teacher, just look at these magnificent buildings with their imposing and impressive architecture!"
2. Jesus replied, "You may be rightfully impressed with what you see before you...the Temple is, indeed, something to behold. But the truth is, there is not one stone in that building that is not going to end up in a pile of rubble when this city is destroyed."
3. Later, Jesus sat alone on The Mount of Olives across the valley from the Temple. And Peter, James, John and Andrew came to Him and said,
4. "Tell us more about the destruction of the Temple that You mentioned before. When are these things going to happen? Will that be the sign of the completion and consummation of this age and era?"
5. Jesus said to them, "Take care that no one deceives or misleads you on these points...understand these beginning events which mark the period between My resurrection and the Temple's destruction...
6. for during this time many will come in falsehood, claiming, 'I, alone, am the Christ,' and these deceivers will lead many away from the truth of Who and what the Christ is, in reality.
7. "And during this time you will hear of wars and threats of wars...see

8. "Nation will fight against nation…ruler will fight against ruler…earthquakes will occur in various places, as well as famines, as they always have. But this is only the first of the birth pangs…the beginning of a new order.

9. "These events are a part of the natural flow of things, but when they begin to happen, pay attention to their significance! It means that some of you will be handed over to suffer affliction and tribulation and will literally be beaten in the synagogues. You will stand trial before governors and kings because you are My followers, but this can be your opportunity to demonstrate the power of the Gospel.

10. "For this Gospel…this Good News of the Kingdom…will be preached throughout the entire, known world as a testimony to all the nations.

11. "But when you are arrested and stand trial, don't worry in advance about what you're going to say. Just say what God tells you at that time…speak in the now…for it will not be just you speaking, but the Holy Spirit with, in, and through you.

12. "During this upheaval, brother will betray his brother to death, and a father will even betray his own child…children will rebel against their parents and cause them to be killed.

13. "For a time, it will seem as though everyone hates you because you are My followers. But whoever endures until the end of this period of testing will find that their salvation is real, durable and fully intact.

14. "The day is coming when you will see the sacrilege and the appalling abomination spoken of by the prophet Daniel…the desecration set up in the Temple sanctuary, where he should not be; watch for this, because when this city and Temple are destroyed, those in Judea must flee to the hills.

15. "A person out on the deck of his or her roof must not go down into the house to pack or to even collect any belongings.

16. "A person working out in the field must not return even to grab a coat.

17. "And worse, yet, is how terrible it will be for pregnant women and for nursing mothers during that period.

18. "Even though this is inevitable, you should pray that it won't happen during the winter.

19. "What's about to happen to this Temple…this city…this nation…will be on a scale beyond what the known world has ever seen since the beginning of creation, or will see again.
20. "In fact, unless the Lord intervenes and shortens that time of calamity, not a single person in this nation will survive…but for the sake of those who have responded positively to His choosing, He will mercifully limit the number of those days.
21. "And then if anyone should say to you, 'See…here is the Christ…this person is the Messiah!' or 'Look…there He is…that one individual is Christ!' do not believe it for a minute.
22. "False 'Christs' and false prophets will always come and go...but, especially during this time, many of them will arise and even show signs and seem to work miracles to validate their claims. They will do this in an effort to deceive people into thinking that one person alone can be the Christ. They will even attempt to lead astray those of you who have already responded to God's call.
23. "So don't fall for this just because I won't be here in the bodily form that you recognize. Be on your guard…you may be vulnerable in My physical absence. Just remember that I have told you all about this beforehand."
24. Then, speaking to them in poetic, prophetic vocabulary—or in a symbolic language of prophecy that His audience understood from their familiarity with the Law and the prophets [Genesis 1:14-16; Isaiah 13:9, 10; 34:4; Amos 8:9; Ezekiel 32:7, 8]—He said, "Immediately after this Great Tribulation, the sun will be darkened and the moon will not shed its light...
25. and the stars will fall from the sky, and the powers of the heavens will be shaken." (In this way, He used the same imagery that the prophets of old had employed to speak of the downfall of earthly authorities and governors).
26. "Then they will see the Son of Man appearing in heaven (or in the heavenly realm), the sign of clouds indicating that this destruction of Jerusalem and the Temple means He is now enthroned in heaven, ruling in kingly power and glory; this cataclysmic series of events will show that the Kingdom has been taken away from a visible nation and given to an invisible one.
27. "And then He will send out messengers who will gather together His elect (those who have willingly responded to His gracious call) from the four winds, as it were, or from the farthest bounds of the known

world to the farthest bounds of the heavenly realm.

28. "Now learn a lesson from the fig tree: as soon as its branches become tender and put forth leaves, you recognize and know that summer is near.

29. "In the same way...when you see these things happening, you may recognize and know that He is near...the manifestation of His Kingdom is at the door.

30. "And this is why you need to hear this now; I'm not talking about some far-off, futuristic event that you would deem to be irrelevant to your life. On the contrary, this generation—the whole multitude of people living at this time—will not pass away before all these things take place.

31. "The earth and sky may pass away, but these words of Mine will not perish or pass away until they are fulfilled.

32. "But no one knows the day or the hour that all of these calamities will begin to come on this nation—not the angels in the heavenly realm nor the Son of Man in His present physical manifestation—but only the Father.

33. "So remain vigilant and pray with vision, for you don't know when the time will come for the beginning of this nation's destruction.

34. "It is like a man going on a journey...when he leaves home, he puts his servants in charge of things, each with his or her own particular task. And he gives orders to the doorkeeper to be constantly on the look-out.

35. "So pay attention and keep your eyes open, for you don't know when the 'Master of the house' is coming to shift the power that rules this nation...in the evening...at midnight...in the morning.

36. "So, again I say, maintain the practice of visionary prayer; or, to put it another way, watch and pray! Otherwise, He may come suddenly, even in another manifestation, and find you asleep.

37. "And what I say to you about the destruction of the Temple and of this nation I say to everybody about their own experiences: this event, as I said, will happen in your lifetime, but the admonition to be watchful and visionary is universally relevant and eternally important!"

Chapter 14

1. By this time the Passover and the Festival of Unleavened Bread were only two days away, and the religious leaders and teachers of the Law were actively looking for some way to easily and justifiably arrest Jesus and kill Him.
2. "It has to be done," they said, "but not during the Festival. If we make our move during an especially holy time like this, the people may riot."
3. Meanwhile, in Bethany, Jesus was having dinner in the home of Simon the Leper. After the meal, while He was reclining at the table, a woman came in with an alabaster jar of very expensive perfume made of pure and rare spikenard. Without asking permission or explaining her actions, she walked up to Him, broke the jar, and poured the perfume on His head.
4. Some of the guests who witnessed this were indignant and said to one another, "Why this extravagant display and waste of such expensive perfume?
5. "This rare and costly substance could have been sold for as much as (or more) than a whole year's wages and the money be given to the poor!" And they railed on the woman without restraint.
6. Jesus lashed out at them immediately, saying sharply, "All of you...leave her alone! Why are you bothering her...rebuking her for doing such a beautiful thing to Me?
7. "The bottom line is this...if you're really that concerned with helping the poor, you can relax; this isolated event isn't going to keep you from trying to wipe out poverty altogether! But the truth is, no matter how much you help the poor, you will always have the poor with you...and you can help them any time you want. But you will not always have Me, at least not in this physical incarnation.
8. "She did what she could...acting out of what she knew to do. You can't even grasp the symbolism of this, but she poured perfume on My body beforehand to prepare Me for My burial.
9. "I don't want to overstate the importance of this gesture, but, truth be told, wherever the Gospel is preached throughout the world in the future, what she has done will also be told in memory of her."
10. But that event was a turning point, especially for Judas Iscariot. As soon as this happened, he went to the religious leaders to betray Jesus to them.

11. And this was the opportunity for which they had waited, so they were delighted to receive him. They also promised to give him a significant amount of money, so he began to watch for an opportunity to hand Jesus over to them from that moment on.
12. When the first day of the Festival of Unleavened Bread arrived—the day when it was customary to sacrifice the traditional Passover lamb—Jesus' disciples asked Him, "Where do You want us to prepare for You to eat the Passover meal?"
13. In answer to their question He sent two of His disciples, saying to them, "I want you to go into the city and, when you get there, a man carrying a jar of water will meet you. Just follow him wherever he goes.
14. "Whatever house he enters, enter as well and say to the owner of it, 'The Teacher asks, "Where is My guest room? Where may I eat the Passover with My friends and followers?"'
15. "When you say those words, he will show you a large room upstairs, furnished and already ready. Make the preparations for the meal there."
16. So the disciples did as they were told, went into the city and walked right into the scenario exactly as Jesus had described it. And there they prepared the Passover supper.
17. At evening time, Jesus arrived with the rest of the Twelve.
18. And they partook of the supper, but while they were reclining at the table eating, as was their custom, He said to them, "I need to tell you the truth about a situation which is about to unfold in the next few hours: simply put, one of you is going to betray Me...one of you sitting right here, eating with Me."
19. They were taken aback by these startling words and then immediately were depressed by them, knowing that He always spoke the truth. So, bypassing denial altogether and going right into acceptance of His prediction, one by one they said to Him, "Please, Lord, tell me that it's not me!"
20. "All I can tell you is that it is one of the twelve of you," He replied, "And I will tell you that it is the one who dips bread into the bowl with Me.
21. "Everything that I've said would happen to the Son of Man will happen to Him...it is inevitable at this point...it's already written down. But the one who betrays the Son of Man will be irreparably damaged by his actions...at least in this dimension. In fact, this

22. Having no further response to these troubling words, the disciples just sat and ate in awkward silence. Then, while they were eating, Jesus took bread and, when He had given thanks for it, He broke it and gave it to His disciples, saying, "Go ahead...take it...and as you eat it I want you to have a paradigm shift...I want you to see beyond the appearance of the bread...visualize a new reality...I want you to know that 'this'—this group...this fellowship...this occasion...and even this bread—is My body."

23. Then He took the cup of wine and, when He had given thanks for it as He did for the bread, He also served it to them...and they all drank from that one, common cup, Judas included.

24. As they were passing the cup around the table, He said "This is not just a common cup of wine...this is My blood of the covenant...the blood that creates a common bloodline...the covenant which provides atonement for the common man.

25. "And the truth of it is, I will not drink again of the vineyard's harvest until I experience it through your new revelation of the Kingdom of God."

26. And when they had sung a familiar worship song, they all went out to the Mount of Olives.

27. "Initially, you're all going to respond very badly to what's about to happen to Me; in fact, each one of you is going to fall apart because of it," Jesus told them, bluntly. "I say this because there's a Scripture that states, *'I will strike the Shepherd and the sheep will be scattered.'*

28. "But after I have risen from the dead, I will go ahead of you into Galilee and there we will open a new chapter in the story."

29. Peter blurted out, "I don't know about the rest of these guys, but I can assure You that if every one of them panics and deserts You, You can still count on me. I'm not like the rest of them...I'll never leave You...not even for a minute!"

30. "Oh, buddy...I know that you think you mean that," Jesus answered, "but the truth is that today...actually tonight...before the first rooster crows twice, you're going to completely disown Me three times."

31. But Peter emphatically insisted, "I don't think You understand how committed I am to You...even if I have to die with You, I will never

disown You...it's just not possible." And at these words, all the others joined in and said the same.

32. Then there was no more discussion about it...they didn't know what else to say. In silence they followed Jesus to a place called Gethsemane, and there He said to them, "Just sit here and meditate while I pray."

33. Then He took Peter, James and John along with Him and, as they walked deeper into the garden, a sense of overwhelming and unspeakable dread began to settle in on Him.

34. "My soul is entering into a stark realization of death," He said to them. "I'm connecting with the death of all who are condemned, and there's no way to describe to you the pain and darkness of it all...please, stay here and keep watch...I need your support through this."

35. Then, going on a little farther, He fell like a dead man to the ground...and, as the conflicting voices of both the Son of God and the Son of Man began to contend for His destiny, He prayed that He might just circumvent the hour altogether.

36. "Abba...Father," He cried out, "everything is possible for You. Just take this cup away from Me! I can't...I won't drink it!" Then, in virtually the same breath, the visionary love of the Son of God overrode the natural survival instincts of the Son of Man, and Jesus said, "Never mind...I won't submit to the limitations of the human will...I accept the infinite possibilities of the divine will...of Your will...and of all that goes with it."

37. Then as the conflict between the human and the divine began to gradually taper off, He returned to His disciples and found them sleeping. "Simon," He said to Peter, "are you really asleep? Now, of all times? Couldn't you just keep watch and support Me for one hour?

38. "You should be praying with vision and insight so that you do not succumb to the limitations of your humanity. The spirit is willing, but the flesh is weak."

39. Again, He went away and prayed the same thing, as the tension created by the opposition of two potential realities temporarily resurfaced.

40. And again when He came back, He found them sleeping because they were exhausted. They woke up again, but didn't know what to say to Him.

41. Returning the third time, He said to them, "Still?! You're still sleeping? Oh well...that's enough...it doesn't matter now, anyway. The hour has come. Take a good look...the Son of Man is delivered into the hands of rebels.
42. "Come on! Let's go! Here comes My betrayer...it all starts now!"
43. Even as He was saying these words, Judas appeared, accompanied by a huge crowd armed with swords and clubs. It was an unnecessarily large crowd, considering that they had come to arrest just one man. They were commissioned by the religious leaders, chief priests, teachers of the Law, and the elders.
44. Now the betrayer had arranged a signal with the crowd. He had said to them "The one that I kiss is the Man you want...arrest Him and lead Him away under guard."
45. So, walking right up to Jesus, Judas said, "Rabbi!"...and with these words he kissed Him.
46. Immediately the plan went into action. The men seized Jesus and arrested Him right on the spot.
47. As some of them grabbed Him and began to shove Him around, roughing Him up a bit, one of those standing near drew his sword and struck the servant of the high priest, cutting off his ear.
48. "Seriously? This is the way it's going to be?" asked Jesus. "Am I leading a rebellion so dangerous that you think you have to come out with swords and clubs to capture Me?
49. "I was with and among you every day...completely accessible... teaching in the Temple courts. Why didn't you arrest Me then? I'll tell you why...it's because none of this even makes sense unless you define it by what is written in the Scriptures, and the Scriptures must be fulfilled."
50. At these words everyone who was with Jesus, namely His disciples, deserted Him and fled.
51. A young man, wearing nothing but a sheet-like linen garment, was following Jesus and, somehow in all the chaos, they seized him, as well.
52. But they inadvertently pulled the garment off of him, and he ran away, naked, leaving them holding the sheet.
53. Then they took Jesus straight to the high priest, and all the chief priests, elders and religious leaders came together for an impromptu trial.
54. Peter followed along after Him at a distance, right into the courtyard

of the high priest, where he sat with the guards and warmed himself by the fire.
55. The chief priests and the whole Sanhedrin were scrambling to find some credible evidence against Jesus so that they could put Him to death, but there was none to be found.
56. Many people stepped up to testify falsely against Him, but their statements could not be corroborated.
57. Others, trying to get in on the action, stood up and gave this false testimony against Him:
58. "We heard Him say, 'I will personally destroy this Temple made with human hands, but in three days I will build another one that is not made with hands.'"
59. But even their stories did not match up.
60. Seeing that entertaining these bogus testimonies was getting them nowhere, the high priest stood up before them and asked Jesus, directly, "Aren't You going to answer? What do You have to say to the accusations that these people are bringing up against You?"
61. But Jesus remained silent...detached...giving no answer and appearing as though He was only there physically. Again the high priest addressed Him, asking, "Are You the Messiah, the Son of the Blessed One?"
62. At this Jesus seemed to come back from wherever He had been, mentally, and said, "I am...and you will see the Son of Man sitting in the place of authority...the seat of the Mighty One...coming on the clouds of the heavenly realm."
63. And at this statement, the high priest tore his clothes in reaction and protest to what he perceived to be blasphemy. "I think it's obvious that we don't need to hear any more witnesses," he declared.
64. "You have heard the obscenity for yourself; what do you think should be done?" They unanimously decided that He was worthy of death.
65. And then a kind of frenzy set in among them. Some began to spit on Him, and they blindfolded Him and began to violently pummel Him with their fists, all the while they were saying "Prophesy!" Then the guards took Him away and started another round of beatings.
66. Meanwhile, while Peter was down below in the courtyard, one of the high priest's serving maids walked outside to where he was sitting.
67. And when she saw him warming himself, she just stopped in her tracks and stared at him. Unable to take her eyes off him, she said,

"Hey, you were with Jesus of Nazareth, too."

68. But he completely denied it, saying, "Lady, I don't even know what you're talking about." And getting up from there, he went outside the courtyard and walked into the vestibule. Just as he entered, he heard a rooster crow.
69. The girl spotted him again and began to say to the bystanders, "This man is one of them...one of Jesus' close followers!"
70. But again he denied it, insisting that he didn't know Him and had never even met Him. After a short while, the bystanders began to say to Peter, "Come on, man...admit it...you really are one of them...you are a Galilean...your dialect shows it!"
71. Then he sharply retorted, "May I be damned if I'm not telling the truth! And you're all a bunch of damn liars! I'm telling you I don't know the son of a...I mean the man...I swear I don't know the man you're talking about!"
72. And as these harsh words were still lingering in the air, a rooster crowed for a second time. When he heard it, Peter instantly remembered how Jesus said to him, "Before the rooster crows twice, you will utterly deny Me...you will deny any connection to Me three times." And when the realization of what he had just said came crashing in on him, Peter broke down and cried loud and hard.

Chapter 15

1. Very early in the morning, after having deliberated through the night, the chief priests, elders and religious leaders, along with the entire Sanhedrin, reached a decision. So they bound Jesus and led Him away to be handed over to Pilate.
2. When He finally stood before the governor, Pilate asked Him, "Are You the King of the Jews?" Jesus calmly replied, "I am to each man whoever he says that I am...if you say that I am the King, then to you I am the King."
3. At these words the chief priests started in with another litany of charges and accusations against Him.
4. When Pilate had heard enough, he stopped them and turned his attention back to Jesus, asking Him, "Aren't You going to answer Your accusers and defend Yourself? Don't You see how many indictments they are bringing against You?"
5. But Jesus by this point had said all He wanted or needed to say about

what was unfolding; He was still...He was silent...He was serene. Pilate was amazed at how someone Who appeared to be so resigned to His fate could at the same time seem to be in charge of everything that was happening around Him.

6. Now it was the custom at the Festival to release one prisoner... anyone that the people requested, regardless of his crime.
7. And a man named Barabbas was in prison with the insurrectionists who had committed murder in an uprising against Rome.
8. So the crowd assembled before Pilate and asked him to do for them what he usually did during the Festival.
9. "What is your pleasure?" asked Pilate. "Do you want me to release to you the King of the Jews?"
10. He made the suggestion, knowing that it was out of envy that the chief priests had handed Jesus over to him.
11. But the chief priests were already moving through the crowd... stirring them up...influencing them to have Pilate release Barabbas instead.
12. "Well, what do you suggest I do, then, with the One you call the King of the Jews?" Pilate asked them.
13. "Crucify Him!" they shouted in unison.
14. "Crucify Him? Why? What crime has He committed?" asked Pilate. But by now a mob mentality had set in and the people assembled were just mindlessly chanting louder and louder, "Crucify Him!"
15. And, wanting to satisfy the crowd, Pilate released Barabbas to them. Then he had Jesus brutally flogged and handed Him over to be crucified.
16. Then the soldiers led Him away to the courtyard inside the palace known as the Praetorium, and they called together the entire battalion of soldiers.
17. And they dressed Him in a purple robe that someone found and wove together a crown of long, spiky thorns and forced it down over His scalp and forehead.
18. Then, in an attempt to completely humiliate Him, they began to mock-worship Him, saying, sardonically, "Hail, King of the Jews!"
19. As they said this, they smacked Him repeatedly all over His head with a staff made of a bamboo-like reed and continually spat in His face until it was drenched and dripping with their hot saliva. All the while they kept blasphemously bowing their knees in homage to

Him.
20. And when they finally grew tired of abusing Him and making sport of Him…when they had run out of profanities and had no more obscene gestures to make towards Him…they yanked the purple robe off of Him and covered His bloody nakedness up with His own clothes. Then they drug Him out of the city to crucify Him.
21. At one point, when His strength failed and He collapsed under the weight of the heavy cross-beam He was carrying, they forced a passerby, Simon of Cyrene (the father of Alexander and Rufus), who was coming in from the country, to carry it for Him.
22. And they led Him to Golgotha (which in Latin is called *Calvary*), meaning "the Place of a Skull," because of the strange rock formation on the side of the hill there that eerily resembled the face of a human skeleton.
23. In a brief and rare moment of compassion, they attempted to give Him a painkiller consisting of wine mingled with myrrh, but He refused it.
24. So then they just did it…as if being prompted and animated by a force greater than any of them, collectively or individually, they crucified Him. And as hunters seeking a trophy from the kill, they divided His garments and distributed them among themselves, throwing lots for them to decide who should take what.
25. It was about nine o'clock in the morning when they finally did the deed.
26. Now it was customary to place an inscription of accusation over the head of each crucified prisoner…but since Jesus was personally innocent of any crime, individually…and yet guilty by association of every crime, universally…the one they hung above His head simply and poignantly read, "The King of the Jews."
27. And with Him they crucified two convicted thieves, one on His right side and one on His left.
28. With this, the Scripture was fulfilled which says, *"He was just a number among the transgressors."*
29. Since the crosses were lined up along the street there in front of Golgotha, He was very accessible to the moving traffic, and the people who walked by kept cursing Him and swearing at Him, using the worst and vilest kind of language imaginable. They shook their heads and made faces at Him, saying, "Just look at You! You Who bragged that You would destroy the Temple and build it back in

three days…

30. if You're such a powerful big shot, why don't You show us what You've got? Rescue Yourself and jump down from that cross!"
31. Even the chief priests, with the scribes, joined in the mass mockery, saying, "What do we have here? Someone Who rescued others from death, but can't even lift a finger to rescue Himself!
32. "Let's all watch to see if the Christ…the Messiah…the King of Israel…can come down now from His pitiful cross. If He can do that, we'll all fall down and worship Him and believe that He is Who He says He is!" Even those who were crucified on either side of Him swore at Him and railed on Him with hurtful insults and all manner of verbal abuse, until it seemed as if the entire creation was cursing Him in unison.
33. When it was about midday, a mysterious and ominous darkness began to settle in over the entire surrounding area and remained there until about three o'clock in the afternoon.
34. At about this time, Jesus cried with a loud voice in His native Aramaic, *"Eloi, Eloi, lama sabachthani?"* which means, *"My God, My God, why have You forsaken Me?"*
35. And some of those standing by heard it and completely misunderstood, saying, "Listen to that! He is calling for the prophet Elijah to come and help Him!"
36. Then one man ran, and, filling a sponge with a mixture of sour wine vinegar and water, put it on a staff made of another bamboo-like reed and gave it to Him to drink, saying, "Wait…wait! This is gonna be good! Let's see whether or not His friend Elijah does come to take Him down!"
37. And with that Jesus uttered a loud cry from the depths of His being and exhaled His earth-life.
38. And at this exact instant, the curtain of the Holy of Holies in the Temple—the veil which symbolically divided all things holy from all things ordinary—was somehow torn in two from top to bottom, creating a new reality concerning where the presence of God could officially abide.
39. When the centurion who stood facing Jesus saw, up-close and personal, how elegantly He breathed out His own physical life in the midst of His own unbearable torture, he said, "Now I see it…really, this Man was God's Son!"
40. Now some women were also nearby, looking on from a distance,

among whom were Mary Magdalene, Mary the mother of James the younger and of Joses, and Salome.

41. These women were a part of Jesus' large female following and were in the habit of accompanying and ministering to Him when He was in Galilee. Aside from them, there were also many other women who had come up with Him to Jerusalem.
42. As evening had already come, and since it was the day of Preparation or the day before the Sabbath,
43. Joseph of Arimathea, a nobleman of honorable rank and a respected member of the Sanhedrin—a man who had revelation of the Kingdom of God—dared the consequences, worked up his courage, and went to Pilate to ask for custody of Jesus' corpse.
44. But Pilate found it hard to believe that He was dead so soon, so he called the centurion and asked him to verify the actuality of Jesus' death.
45. And when he was assured by the centurion that He was indeed dead, he gave the body to Joseph.
46. And Joseph bought a fine linen cloth—the kind that was used at that time for swathing dead bodies—and carefully and gently took the lifeless body down from the cross. Then he rolled it up in the linen cloth and placed Him in a tomb which had been recently chiseled out of a rock. Then he rolled the very large stone, which had been fashioned to serve as a protective door, against the entrance.
47. And Mary Magdalene and Mary, the mother of Joses, were both attentively observing where the body was laid to rest.

Chapter 16

1. And when the Sabbath was over (which, technically, was just after sunset), Mary Magdalene, Mary, the mother of James, and Salome went to purchase sweet-smelling spices that they could use to anoint the body of Jesus.
2. And very early, before the dawn of the first day of the week, they got up and went to the tomb. By the time they arrived, the sun had risen.
3. As they were entering the garden area, they said to one another, "One thing we haven't thought of...how are we going to roll back the stone that fits into the groove at the floor of the entrance to the tomb? Do you think we can find someone to help us move it?"
4. But even as they said these words while approaching the tomb, they

looked up and saw clearly that the stone was already rolled back completely (which was remarkable because it was very large).

5. Amazed, they just walked right into the tomb without any hesitation. Once inside, they saw a young man calmly sitting there on the right side of where the body had been, clothed in a long, flowing robe of white. When they got a good look at him, they were stunned into a terrified silence.

6. The young man turned to them and said, "Ladies, there's absolutely nothing here to fear. You've come looking for Jesus of Nazareth Who was crucified, haven't you? Well...He's not here, at least not in the form to which you are accustomed. But He's very much alive! See...here's the place where they laid Him...

7. "You should go now...there's nothing else here to see. Go...tell the disciples, including Peter, that He is going before you all into Galilee. You will be able to see Him there, just as He told you."

8. They didn't waste any time. They went out of the tomb in a frenzy... running as fast as they could...fluctuating between being in a state of shock and being in a state of hysterics. And they said nothing about it to anyone, because they were too excited...too panic-stricken...to even say a word!

♦ This is where Chapter 16 and the entire Gospel of Mark ends in all original manuscripts. Typically, *The Gospels In The Now* do not include non-original text, but, to give the story proper closure, the author has made an exception...

9. Now Jesus, having freshly risen from death early on the first day of the week, appeared initially to Mary Magdalene, from whom He had expelled seven rebel spirits which had controlled her.

10. She went immediately and reported it to His followers...those who had been with Him in His earth-walk...as they were in complete grief mode, weeping and mourning.

11. And when they heard her news that He was alive and that she had actually seen Him, they didn't even consider the possibility of it... even though she was verifying exactly what He had told them would happen, they didn't believe it for a second.

12. Later, He appeared in a different form to two of them as they were walking along the road into the country.

13. And after these two were finally somewhat convinced, they returned

14. to Jerusalem and told the others, but they didn't believe them either.
14. So then He appeared to the remaining eleven apostles as they reclined at the table and, as soon as He manifested, He began to severely reprimand them for their unbelievable lack of faith and the impenetrable hardness of their hearts. He rebuked them for refusing to believe those who had seen Him up close after He had risen from death.
15. But He said to them, "Here's My last word on this...one of you betrayed Me...one of you denied Me...all of you abandoned Me...none of you believed I was alive...but not one of you is disqualified because of what he did or didn't do. Now go into all the world and preach the Good News of the Gospel to every creature of the entire human race!
16. "Whoever believes the Gospel that you proclaim, and is baptized to demonstrate and act on their revelation of it, will be delivered...but whoever misses the opportunity of faith—whoever doesn't believe the Gospel—will invite unnecessary destruction into their lives.
17. "And these signs of confirmation will accompany those who believe: in My name they will have authority to drive out rebel spirits, they will speak in new languages and communicate My message in new and innovative Spirit-ways;
18. "If a snake bites them while they're in this flow, they won't be harmed by it at all, and if they accidentally drink anything poison, it won't hurt them. They will also lay their hands on the sick, and they will get well."
19. So then Jesus, after He had said all these things to them about their future, was translated into the heavenly realm...and He sat down in the place of God's authority.
20. And they were all energized and inspired to go out and preach everywhere, while the Master kept working with them and through them, continuously confirming the message by the attesting signs...the irrefutable evidence...brought about through the world of the miraculous which they created together. Amen – so be it!

Luke In The Now

LUKE IN THE NOW

Chapter 1

1. It's a known fact that so many have tried their hand at telling this amazing story from their own perspective. Because those who have been transformed by the potency of it wanted to be a part of the propagation of it, they have undertaken to draw up an official account…a story of record…of the things which have been fulfilled among us.
2. And these who have added their own voices to the narrative have honored the oral tradition of the eyewitnesses of Jesus' earth ministry—of those who were actually there and who ministered alongside Him—embracing what those followers remember about it from its inception. And they have told their version of the story as a confirmation to the truth of it.
3. But it seemed desirable to me, also, to write an account of it through my own paradigm, while being careful to maintain the integrity of what has already been said concerning what happened from the beginning…and my motivation was to write it for you, most excellent Theophilus, friend of God.
4. I personally took on this responsibility, doing the research and investigation myself, because it was important to me that you know the full truth, beyond any shadow of doubt, of the things you have been taught. In other words, I wanted to be sure that you knew these things really happened.
5. And this is where I'll begin the story: In the time of King Herod's reign in Judea, there was a priest named Zechariah who belonged to the priestly division of Abijah. He was married to a woman named Elizabeth, who was also a descendant of Aaron.
6. By all accounts, both of them lived very honorable and fulfilling lives that were pleasing in the sight of God. They observed the commandments and basically had reputations which were above reproach.
7. It seemed that the only thing they lacked in their lives was a child of their own. For some reason, Elizabeth had never been able to conceive and, at the time in which the curtain rises on this drama,

they were both well advanced in years.
8. Anyway, one day when Zechariah's particular division was on duty and he was serving as priest before God,
9. he was chosen by lot (a custom of the priesthood) to go into the Temple of the Lord and burn the incense.
10. So when the time for the burning of the incense came, all those who had assembled to worship that day were just quietly praying outside.
11. All of a sudden, an angel of the Lord appeared to Zechariah, standing at the right side of the altar of incense!
12. Well, when Zechariah got a good look at this imposing, celestial creature, he nearly collapsed from fear.
13. But the angel very calmly and directly said to him: "Do not be afraid, Zechariah…your prayer has been heard…the secret desire of your heart has been granted. Your wife Elizabeth is going to bear a son and you are to call him John.
14. "And this boy of yours is going to bring you so much joy…you can't even imagine! In fact, his birth will bring a dimension of sheer delight to many, many people.
15. "And he will achieve unprecedented greatness in the sight of the Lord and will never desire to drink his fill of wine or any other alcoholic beverage, because he will be born fully filled with the Holy Spirit!
16. "He will effectively bring back the relevance of the real God to many of the people of Israel.
17. "And in the sight of the Lord, he will be Elijah—or the Elijah of his day—because he will reunite the hearts of the generations…his message will resonate with both the parents and the children and, so, it will re-connect them and make them as one. Even the skeptics and the doubters, the cynics and the indifferent, will be changed and motivated by the sense of expectancy created by his preaching. He will literally make people ready for a revelation of the real God."
18. Ironically, as the angel was speaking of doubters and skeptics, Zechariah's own sense of reason caused him to suddenly flee in his mind to the seat of his natural logic, despite the fact that an angel was standing in the Temple prophesying to him! So he asked the supernatural messenger, "How can I be sure that what you're telling me is the truth? I mean, I'm an old man (if you know what I mean); I lost my virility long ago, and I'm married to an old woman well past the change of life."

19. The angel said to him, "Don't insult me, Zechariah...I am Gabriel! I live in the very presence of God and have been sent here to speak to you and to tell you this good news. If there were any possibility that this thing wasn't going to happen, in spite of the biological facts of your life, I wouldn't be standing here!
20. "How can you second-guess the very thing for which you have prayed? God has decreed this reality in the heavenly realm, but you must permit it to manifest on the earth by your agreement with Him. So this is what I will do—so that you won't inadvertently abort your own baby by your doubt-filled speech—I will protect the seed from the destructive potential of your own words. I will cause you to be totally mute until the day of your son's birth!"
21. Meanwhile, the people were still waiting outside for Zechariah, wondering why it was taking him so long to come out.
22. When eventually he did emerge, he couldn't even make a sound. But somehow, through his own, makeshift kind of sign language, he was able to convey to them that he had seen a vision in the Temple, and somehow they comprehended.
23. When his time of service was completed, he silently returned home.
24. And, sure enough, after some time his wife Elizabeth actually became pregnant, as if she were a young woman married to a young man, just as the angel had said. The whole thing, particularly the pregnancy, was such an adjustment...such a shock to her, really... that for five months she remained in complete seclusion.
25. But during that whole time she never wavered in faith; "The Lord has done this for me," she said. "In these strange days He has shown His favor and has created this whole new reality for us!"
26. Then, in the sixth month of Elizabeth's pregnancy, God sent Gabriel to a town in Galilee called Nazareth,
27. to a little teen-age girl who was engaged to be married to a man named Joseph, who was a descendant of King David. The young girl was a virgin, and her name was Mary.
28. The angel just went right into her house and said to her, "Greetings, you who are highly favored! The Lord is with you."
29. Mary was not only startled by his appearance, she was also troubled by his declarative words and wondered what he meant by his greeting.
30. But Gabriel said to her, "Do not be afraid, Mary, I am here because you have found favor with God.

31. "You are going to conceive today and in a few months will give birth to a Son, and you are to name and call Him 'Jesus.'
32. "And your baby boy will become great and will be called the Son of the Most High. The Lord God will give Him the throne of His father David,
33. and He will reign over the house of Jacob forever; His Kingdom will never end…it will exist in the eternal now."
34. After collecting herself and gaining her composure, Mary asked the angel, "How can I conceive a child today? I am engaged to a man, but I am a virgin; I have not slept with my fiancée, or any other man for that matter, and have no plans to do so today!"
35. But the angel answered, "You are about to have an unprecedented encounter with the Holy Spirit that is going to affect your natural body and, when that happens, the power of the Most High will literally overshadow you and permeate your entire being. This encounter will cause you to conceive, so that the Holy One to be born will be called the Son of God!
36. "And your cousin Elizabeth is also going to have a child, even in her old age. She has never been able to conceive throughout her whole life, but she is already six months pregnant!
37. "I know this seems impossible to you…and, in fact, it is biologically and naturally impossible. But, with God, nothing in any realm is or ever will be impossible!"
38. Then Mary said, "You must understand that I can't even begin to comprehend or process all this with my mind, but in my spirit I say 'Here I am, may it be to me, not according to logic or reason, but according to your word! I submit myself to the eternal, now Word of God that makes all things possible!'" And when Mary said that, the angel left her.
39. So Mary, realizing that the big picture of this miracle involved much more than just what was happening in her, wasted no time in making her way into the hill country to a town of Judah.
40. And when she got there, she went immediately to the house of Zachariah and, entering it, called out with great excitement for her cousin, Elizabeth.
41. Now she was in another part of the house, but at the instant in which she heard the sound of Mary's voice, the baby in her womb very forcefully jolted and, when this occurred, Elizabeth was filled, energized and thoroughly permeated with the power of the Holy

Spirit.
42. And this simultaneously spiritual and physical action and reaction somehow released a prophetic cry out of Elizabeth, as she approached Mary and exclaimed to her, "Blessed! Favored of God above all other women are you! And blessed and favored of God is the supernatural Fruit of your womb!
43. "And how is it that I have been so honored as to have the very mother of my Lord come and visit me?
44. "My dear, the very instant the sound of your sweet voice reached my ears, the baby in my womb literally leaped for joy!"
45. Then she went on to say, "Blessed is she who believed, without reservation, the creative word of the Lord—impossible as it may seem in the natural realm...unexpected as it most certainly was—you are forever blessed simply for believing!"
46. At these words, the music of Mary's internal praise and thanksgiving was released into an audible anthem of adoration, and for the first time she fully acknowledged the enormity of what was happening. She sang out, exuberantly, "My soul...my internal self...magnifies and worships the Lord,
47. and my spirit...the very essence of my eternal self...rejoices in God my Savior,
48. for He has looked upon the very simple and seemingly unimportant little life of His handmaiden and has created an entirely different existence for her. From now on, all generations...all ages...will call me blessed and will recognize the very special and unique place that I will hold throughout all of human history!
49. "For He Who is absolutely almighty has done great things for me... and holy is His name...excellent is His reputation!
50. "And His mercy, His compassion, His kindness toward the disenfranchised and the forgotten—the ones who think and feel that they are completely invisible—is on those who worship Him with a sense of awe, from generation to generation and age to age.
51. "He has flexed the mighty muscle of His arm; He has scattered the abusers of the defenseless through sheer intimidation, exposing and thwarting the imaginations of their hearts.
52. "He has put out of position the seemingly invincible ones and has promoted those whose value has been hidden to the public eye.
53. "He has filled and satisfied the hungry with delicious things, and the rich who have built their fortunes on the backs of the oppressed He

has sent away empty-handed.
54. "He has embraced and supported His servant Israel to help him, to remind him of His mercy,
55. just as He promised our forefathers...to Abraham and to his descendants forever."
56. When Mary finished the song, she decided to stay with Elizabeth for awhile, and so she did for about three months and then returned to her own home.
57. So when it was time for Elizabeth to have her baby, she gave birth to a son, just as the angel had said.
58. As you can imagine, it was quite an event in the neighborhood. Friends and relatives from all around heard of how God had lavished this miracle of mercy upon her, and they shared her joy and celebrated with the family.
59. On the eighth day, as was customary, they came to the Temple to circumcise the baby...and everyone just assumed that they were going to name him after his father Zechariah.
60. But Elizabeth spoke up and said, "No! He is going to be called John!"
61. And those that she told said to her, "John? What kind of name is that? It's certainly not a family name...what's the meaning of this?"
62. Then they gestured to Zechariah (who was still completely mute, by the way), to find out what he would like to name his miracle son.
63. He motioned for a writing tablet and, to everyone's utter astonishment, he wrote, "HIS NAME IS JOHN!"
64. And when Zechariah did this—when he and Elizabeth came into agreement with the word of God which the angel had delivered—his mouth was immediately opened and he began to speak, audibly, praising God!
65. Well, the neighbors were just awestruck and astounded by all this, and the news of it spread like wildfire throughout the entire region.
66. It was the main topic in every conversation in every home in the area, and everyone was asking, "What in the world is this child going to grow up to be?" No one could understand it, yet no one doubted that God's hand was on him.
67. Meanwhile, Zechariah was filled with the Holy Spirit and began to prophesy, saying:
68. "All praise rightfully belongs to the Lord, the God of Israel, because He has come to His people and redeemed them...

69. He has revealed the power of salvation for us right here in the very house of His servant David...
70. it is exactly as He said through His Holy prophets of long ago...
71. deliverance from our enemies and from the wrath of all who hate us...
72. to show mercy and benevolence to our ancestors and to remember His holy covenant...
73. the sacred oath He swore to our father Abraham...
74. to rescue us from the hand of our adversaries and to enable us to serve Him without any fear at all...
75. in wholeness and righteousness before Him throughout our whole lives!
76. "And you, my son, will be called a prophet of the Most High...for you will go on before the Lord to literally prepare the way for Him...
77. to bring to His people the full revelation of salvation through the forgiveness of their sins...
78. because of the tenderness and mercy and kindness of our God...the real God...by which the sun of redemption and reconciliation will rise to bring the dawn of a new day...
79. to shine in warmth and light on those living in the cold, dark shadow of death...to guide our feet into the path of peace!"
80. And, indeed, that baby boy grew and became strong in spirit. He was very different...an unusual child...because the message he was born to carry made him unique. Basically, he grew up in solitude, living out in the wilderness until he appeared publicly to Israel.

Chapter 2

1. Anyway (getting back to where I was in the story) right about this time, for some reason, Caesar Augustus decided to order a census to be taken throughout the entire Roman Empire.
2. This enrollment was unprecedented—the first ever of its kind, at least on such a grand scale—and it was made when Quirinius was governor of Syria.
3. It meant that everyone in the Empire—regardless of where they lived at the time or of what their current conditions were—had to make the journey to their own ancestral hometown to be accounted for.
4. This, in turn, meant that Joseph had to leave the Galilean town of Nazareth, where he lived, and travel all the way up to Bethlehem in

Judah, the City of David, to participate in the census. As a descendant of David, that's where he had to go.

5. And he took Mary, his pregnant fiancée, with him on the long journey, even though she was in the third trimester of her pregnancy.

6. Their plan was to move as quickly as possible to Bethlehem and then attempt to get back home in time for the baby's delivery. But it turned out that, while they were there, she went into labor and there was nothing they could do about it. She was going to have to give birth right there in this overcrowded city of strangers…with no connections, no acquaintances, no family, no doctor, no midwife, no place to stay…just lots and lots of inconvenienced people who were also there only because of the census.

7. And so Mary gave birth to a son, her firstborn, and she swaddled Him in a blanket and laid Him in a feeding trough for animals. It was her only alternative because she and Joseph ended up having to go into a stable for the delivery. There was absolutely no vacancy in any of the local inns or hostels, so they just did what they had to do with what was available to them.

8. As it turned out, there were some nomadic shepherds who had set up camp out in the nearby fields to keep watch over their flocks throughout the night.

9. And as they sat, sleepy, silent and still, an angel…a celestial being… just manifested right in front of their surprised eyes. At the angel's appearance, the very glory of God completely enveloped them, glowing and vibrating like an intense, electric force field, and they were utterly shocked and terrified.

10. But the angel spoke immediately and authoritatively, saying to them, "Do not be afraid! I am here to announce Good News to you…Good News of a great and joyful event, and of a new reality! And this Good News…this new reality…is for all people everywhere…it is for the entirety of humanity!

11. "This very night a Savior has been born in the City of David…a Savior Who will perfectly embody the Christ and will be known as the Lord!

12. "If you seek Him you will find Him, and this is what you're to look for: a baby swaddled in a blanket and lying in a feeding trough for animals!"

13. As soon as the angel made this declaration, the sky above the shepherds' heads lit up and was filled with a seemingly infinite

number of angels who formed a thunderous mass choir, singing God's praises, and shouting,

14. *"GLORY TO GOD IN THE HIGHEST PARTS OF THE HEAVENLY REALM...AND IN THE EARTHLY DIMENSION, PEACE...PEACE TO EVERY SINGLE PERSON ON THE EARTH...AND A REVELATION TO THEM THAT GOD'S WILL TOWARD ALL OF HUMANITY IS ONLY GOOD!"*

15. And then, just as suddenly as they had appeared, they were gone. When the stunned shepherds eventually regained their composure, they said to one another, "Well, let's go to Bethlehem right now and see for ourselves this thing that the Lord has revealed to us!"

16. And they did just that, leaving the sheep, the campsite and all of their belongings behind. They literally took off running all the way into the city and were able to locate the stable. And, sure enough, there they found Mary and Joseph and, lying in the trough as the angel had said, the infant Savior.

17. They gazed at Him, transfixed, for an indefinite period of time, until they eventually felt released to go. But as they returned to their campsite, they told everyone with whom they came into contact what they had just witnessed.

18. And their delivery of the news was so compelling that all who encountered them on their way were simply amazed at how these common shepherds—men who were normally quiet, isolated and reserved—carried on about what they had just seen.

19. But Mary was not as expressive...she just remained silent and contemplative, treasuring up all the mysteries of the night in her heart and thinking about what the future would hold for her newborn baby boy.

20. The shepherds returned to their campsite and their sheep, but they couldn't settle down for the rest of the night. They praised and glorified God on into the morning light for all the things they had heard and seen. Everything that the angel had told them was true.

21. When the eighth day of His earth-life arrived—the traditional day when Jewish boys were circumcised—the baby was officially named Jesus, the name given by the angel before His conception.

22. And when the number of days stipulated by Moses for the mother's purification and the baby's dedication were complete, His parents brought Him up to Jerusalem to ceremonially offer His life to God.

23. This was in accordance with the Law of the Lord, which states,

"Every firstborn male that opens the womb shall be set apart, dedicated, and called holy to the Lord."

24. And they also came to offer a sacrifice of "a pair of turtledoves or two young pigeons" as prescribed in the same Law.
25. Now there was a man in Jerusalem at this time whose name was Simeon—a good and devout man who lived in prayerful expectancy for the help and consolation of Israel—and the anointing of the Holy Spirit was on him.
26. And the Holy Spirit had personally assured him that he would not die before he had the opportunity to see with his own eyes the physical manifestation of God's Christ in the earth.
27. So, led by the Spirit, he entered the Temple just as the parents of the baby Jesus brought Him in to carry out the rituals of the Law.
28. And when Simeon saw them, he immediately recognized the Christ and approached them, took the baby into his arms, and began to bless God, saying,
29. "Now, God, You may release Your servant from this present earthly dimension, and I will be released in peace, just as You promised.
30. "With my own two eyes I have seen the manifestation of Your Salvation;
31. "I first saw it prophetically...by the Spirit...but now that Your Salvation has come in the physical form of this man-child, all of humanity will be able to see it for themselves;
32. they will see the Light…a Light for the revelation of God to the non-Jewish nations…a Light to disclose what was before unknown to the people of Israel, so that they may see Your glory."
33. Even though Mary and Joseph had heard and seen so many amazing things since the day Gabriel first appeared to her, they were still speechless with surprise at these prophetic words.
34. But Simeon went on to bless them and said to Mary, His mother, "This Child is destined to cause many in Israel to fall, but He will be a joy to many others. He has been sent as a sign from God, but many will oppose Him as He will be a figure often misunderstood and contradicted...
35. as a result, the deepest thoughts of many hearts will be exposed, but God will reveal who they really are, as they are forced into honesty by their very rejection of Him. And this rejection will affect you as His mother, causing the pain of a sword thrust through your very soul."

36. And there was also a prophetess there, Anna, the daughter of Phanuel, of the tribe of Asher. She was very old, having lived with her husband for only seven years before being widowed,
37. and she had been a widow for eighty-four years. Her entire life was in the Temple...she didn't go out from the Temple enclosure and worshipped night and day with fasting and prayer.
38. And she also came up at the same time, and gave thanks to God and talked of the promise and potential of Jesus to all who were looking for the redemption and deliverance of Jerusalem.
39. And when His parents had done everything according to the Law of the Lord given through Moses, they went back into Galilee to their own town, Nazareth.
40. And there Jesus experienced a relatively normal childhood, growing into boyhood and on into early adolescence. He became strong in spirit, and was filled with wisdom as He gradually walked into His destiny as the earthly embodiment of the Christ. Through it all, the grace and favor of God was upon Him.
41. Now His parents went to Jerusalem every year to celebrate the Passover Feast.
42. And, when Jesus was twelve years old, they went there as usual...as was their custom.
43. But when the Feast was over and they were returning to Nazareth, young Jesus remained behind in Jerusalem. His parents were completely unaware that He had initiated this significant act of independence, as He had given them no indication of it, whatsoever.
44. In fact, they just assumed that He was somewhere in the caravan in which they were traveling and went on a full day's journey before they actually realized that He was not with them. Then they looked everywhere for Him among their relatives and acquaintances, but none of them had any idea of Jesus' whereabouts.
45. So when He didn't turn up anywhere in the caravan, they went back to Jerusalem, frantically looking for Him all the way.
46. After three whole days of nonstop searching, they finally found Him in the court of the Temple, calmly sitting among the teachers, listening to them and asking them thought-provoking questions.
47. And all of these learned, seasoned, full-grown men were absolutely astonished and overwhelmed at His intelligence, understanding, and insightful, articulate replies to them.
48. When Joseph and Mary saw Him, they exploded emotionally with a

mixture of feelings...anger...relief...joy...bewilderment. And His mother blurted out to Him, "Jesus! Why have You treated us like this? Do You know what You've put us through? Your father and I have been in sheer torment, looking for You everywhere for three whole days!"

49. The twelve year old very matter-of-factly turned to look at her and said, "What do you mean you've been looking for Me? And why were you in torment? You should have known that I would be in My Father's house, doing My Father's business. How could you have assumed otherwise?"

50. But they did not grasp or comprehend at all what He was saying to them.

51. So He returned with them to Nazareth, and was obedient to them as His natural parents, but the dynamics of their relationship were never the same after this. He had clearly defined Himself by stating that God, not Joseph, was His Father...and had made it clear that He would ultimately be actualized in the business of His Father and not in that of His stepfather. His mother never brought it up again or really ever dealt with it at all...she just guarded all these things in her heart.

52. And Jesus increased in wisdom and self-awareness as He grew in physical stature and in years. At the same time, He also grew in favor with God and man.

Chapter 3

1. In the fifteenth year of Tiberius Caesar's reign (when Pontius Pilate was governor of Judea and Herod was tetrarch of Galilee, and his brother, Philip, was the tetrarch of the region of Ituraea and Trachonitis and Lysanias was tetrarch of Abilene,

2. and when Annas and Caiaphas were the high priests), the word—the revelation...the message concerning the manifestation of the Christ and of His Kingdom...and of His complete salvation—came to John, the son of Zachariah, out in the desert wilderness.

3. And when this revelation overtook him, he was compelled to go into the country on both sides of the Jordan, preaching the necessity of a paradigm shift and illustrating his message of change by baptizing people in the river.

4. And this portion of his life was a fulfillment of Isaiah's prophecy

which declares, *"The voice of one crying in the wilderness...shouting in the desert, 'Prepare the way of the Lord, make His beaten paths straight.*

5. *'Every valley, every ravine, shall be filled in and filled up, and every mountain, every hill, shall be completely leveled, and the crooked places shall be straightened out and the rough roads shall be made smooth;*

6. *and when this process is at last complete, all of mankind...the entirety of humanity...will see, behold, comprehend and understand the absolute salvation of God!'"*

7. But when he saw many of the religious leaders in the crowd coming to where he was baptizing, he said to them: "You brood of vipers! Who warned you to flee from the coming wrath?

8. "Produce fruit in keeping with the real changing of your minds and do not think that you have the right to say to yourselves, 'We have Abraham as our father.' I tell you that out of these stones God can raise up children for Abraham.

9. "Even now, the ax is already poised at the root of the trees, and every tree that does not produce good fruit will be cut down and thrown into God's purifying fire."

10. And the crowd was greatly affected by the message and responded by saying to him, "Tell us, then, what we should do!"

11. And he replied to them, "Whoever has two tunics (or undergarments), let him share with him who has none...and whoever has food to eat, let him share it the same way."

12. Even tax collectors came to be baptized, and they said to him, "Teacher, tell us also what we should do!"

13. And he said to them, "Just collect no more than the fixed and legal amount appointed you."

14. Those serving in the military also came to him and asked him, "What about us? What should we do?" And he replied to them, "Never act as terrorists, don't abuse your power and authority, and always be satisfied with your rations."

15. And the people were so moved by his directness and by the simple yet profound way that he spoke about fairness and equality and ethical behavior, that everybody reasoned and questioned in their hearts concerning him whether he perhaps might be the Christ, the Messiah.

16. But John answered them all by saying, "Look, I baptize you in a

river of water for transformation through the changing of your minds. But after me comes One Who is much more powerful, Whose sandals I am not worthy to even carry. He will purify you, not in a physical river of water, but by baptizing you with the Holy Spirit in a spiritual river of consuming fire!

17. "His winnowing fork and fan are in His hand, and He will clear His threshing floor, gathering His wheat into the barn and burning up the chaff in your lives with His unquenchable fire."
18. So, with many other innovative appeals and admonitions, he preached the Good News to the people.
19. But Herod the tetrarch—who had been openly rebuked by John for having Herodias, his brother's wife, and for all the other dishonorable things that he had done—
20. added this to the list of corrupt deeds...he had John arrested and shut up in prison.
21. Now as all the other people were being baptized, Jesus also submitted Himself to John's message and was baptized, as well. And while He was praying, the visible heaven was opened,
22. and the Holy Spirit descended upon Him in the incarnation of a dove, and a voice came from the heavenly dimension, saying, "You are My Son, My Beloved, in Whom I take pleasure and with Whom I am completely and absolutely delighted!"
23. So this experience, in a sense, officially began the public ministry of Jesus, Who was thirty years of age at this time and was generally known to the community as the son of Joseph, the son of Heli.
24. (And to give the earth-life of Jesus proper historical context...) Heli, Jesus' stepgrandfather, was the son of Matthat, who was the son of Levi, who was the son of Melchi, who was the son of Jannai...the son of Joseph...
25. the son of Mattathias...the son of Amos...the son of Nahum...the son of Esli...the son of Naggai...
26. the son of Maath...the son of Mattathias...the son of Semein...the son of Josech...the son of Joda...
27. the son of Joanan...the son of Rhesa...the son of Zerubbabel...the son of Shealtiel...the son of Neri...
28. the son of Melchi...the son of Addi...the son of Cosam...the son of Elmadam...the son of Er...
29. the son of Jesus...the son of Eliezer...the son of Jorim...the son of Matthat...the son of Levi...

30. the son of Simeon...the son of Judah...the son of Joseph...the son of Jonam...the son of Eliakim...
31. the son of Melea...the son of Menna...the son of Mattatha...the son of Nathan...the son of David...
32. the son of Jesse...the son of Obed...the son of Boaz...the son of Salmon...the son of Nahshon...
33. the son of Aminadab...the son of Admin...the son of Arni...the son of Hezron...the son of Perez...the son of Judah...
34. the son of Jacob...the son of Isaac...the son of Abraham...the son of Terah...the son of Nahor...
35. the son of Serug...the son of Reu...the son of Peleg...the son of Eber...the son of Shelah...
36. the son of Cainan...the son of Arphaxad...the son of Shem...the son of Noah...the son of Lamech...
37. the son of Methuselah...the son of Enoch...the son of Jared...the son of Mahalaleel...the son of Cainan...
38. the son of Enos...the son of Seth...the son of Adam...the son of God.

Chapter 4

1. Then Jesus, full of the Holy Spirit, returned from the Jordan and was purposely led by the Spirit
2. for forty days into the solitude of the desert wilderness for an intentionally staged and personal confrontation with the devil (or the adversary) into a place where He could be tempted, tested and tried by him, one-on-one, for Kingdom purposes. And He ate nothing during those days, but when they were completed, He was hungry.
3. And, at that time, the adversary came and said to Him, "If You really are Who You believe and say that You are—the manifestation of God in the physical realm…His own Son—then command these stones to be made into loaves of bread."
4. But He replied, "It has been written, *'Man shall not live and be sustained by bread alone, but by every word that comes forth, in the now, from the mouth of God!'*"
5. Again, the adversary took Him up on a very high mountain and showed Him in panoramic view all the kingdoms of the world and the splendor and magnificence of them all in a moment of time.
6. And he said to Him, "I will give You all this power and authority, as well as their glory, for it has been turned over to me and I give it to

whomever I will.
7. "If You will simply prostrate Yourself before me and sincerely worship me it will all be Yours."
8. But Jesus replied to him, "You get behind Me now! It is written, *'You shall do homage to and worship the Lord your God, and Him only shall you serve.'"*
9. Then the adversary took Him into the holy city and placed Him on a high gable (or turret) of the Temple sanctuary and said to Him, "If You really are the Son of God as You say You are, then throw Yourself down off this tower;
10. for it is written, *'He will give His angels charge over you, to watch over you closely and carefully;*
11. *and they will bear you up on their hands, lest you strike your foot against a stone.'"*
12. Jesus said to him, "Yes, but it is also written, *'You shall not tempt, test, or try the Lord your God!'"*
13. And when the adversary had ended the complete cycle of temptation (or, once these adversarial issues were settled in the mind of Jesus), he left Him (or, this thought process was ended) until the temptations of Jesus took on another form at another time.
14. After this, Jesus returned to Galilee, full of the power of the Holy Spirit, and His fame spread through the whole region and surrounding area.
15. And He conducted a series of well-received teachings in their synagogues because, at this point in His ministry, He was being accepted, recognized and highly honored by just about everyone.
16. So, one particular day, He came to Nazareth where He had been brought up and entered the synagogue as was His custom on the Sabbath. And, at the appropriate time in the service, He stood up to read in the congregation.
17. Without hesitation they handed Him the scroll of the book of the prophet Isaiah and He reverently, but authoritatively, unrolled it. Then He immediately found the place where it was written,
18. *"The very Spirit of the Lord is resting upon Me, because He has anointed and qualified Me to proclaim the Good News to the disenfranchised; He has sent Me to announce release to the captives and total recovery of sight to the blind...to bring relief to those who are oppressed, outcast and broken down by the hardships of life;*
19. *to reveal the true meaning of the Year of Jubilee and to become its*

physical fulfillment...to personify the year of God's favor in the now."

20. Then He calmly rolled up the book and gave it back to the attendant and sat down. But, on this day, the service didn't progress as usual. On this day, something was very different about the reading of Isaiah's prophecy. Something about the way Jesus read those familiar words made them seem simultaneously eternal and fresh... both ancient and newborn. You could hear a pin drop in the place as everyone fixed their attention on Him, waiting for Him to say something else. No one could take their eyes off Him.

21. So He responded to their expectancy and stood back up to speak. Looking around the room He boldly said something that had never been said before in the Synagogue: "Today this Scripture has actually been fulfilled in your presence...right here...right now...the Word has been made flesh in your hearing."

22. Everyone was taken aback at these words, but they were initially open and receptive to them, in general. But as His statement began to sink in with them, and as they considered the implication of it, they weren't exactly sure how to respond. It wasn't just the boldness of the declaration but, when they considered the source, they said among themselves, "Isn't this Joseph's son? Isn't this man the boy that we saw grow up right here in the neighborhood?"

23. He answered them, "I suppose now you're going to quote to Me the proverb, 'Doctor, go heal Yourself. Do here in Your hometown what we heard You did in Capernaum.'

24. "Well, let Me tell you something...it's a fact that no prophet is ever welcomed in his hometown.

25. "I mean, isn't it true that there were many widows in Israel at the time of Elijah during that three and a half years of drought when famine devastated the land?

26. "But isn't it also true that the only widow to whom Elijah was sent was in Zarephath in the country of Sidon?

27. "By the same token, there were many lepers in Israel in the time of Elisha the prophet, but the only one of them that was cleansed by being healed was Naaman, the Syrian."

28. With these statements, Jesus went from being provocative to being antagonistic...even blasphemous, as far as they were concerned...and all the people in the synagogue were instantly filled with rage for Him.

29. And they jumped up and grabbed Him, carrying Him to the projecting upper part of the hill on which their town was built, with the intention of hurling Him headlong over the cliff to His death.
30. But when they got there, He somehow miraculously passed right through their midst without injury and went on His way.
31. Without missing a beat, He went down to Capernaum, a town in Galilee, and on the Sabbath He taught the people, undaunted by what had just happened in Nazareth.
32. And the people there were absolutely amazed at His teaching, because His words had authority; He had a command and understanding of His own message that was undeniable.
33. In the synagogue, there was a man under the influence and control of a rebel spirit and, recognizing Who Jesus really was (as the spirits always did), he cried out at the top of his voice,
34. "Go away! What do You want with us, Jesus of Nazareth? Have You come to destroy our authority and domain? I know Who You are...You are the Holy One of God!"
35. *"All right, that's enough...be quiet!"* Jesus said, directly. *"Get out of this man's life!"* Then the spirit threw the man down before them all and released him without injury.
36. All the people were even more amazed at this and said to each other, "What's this all about? How does this man control the environment by simply using His words? He even tells rebel spirits what to do, and they obey Him!"
37. And the news about Him spread like wildfire throughout the surrounding area.
38. After this, Jesus left the synagogue and went to the home of Simon, where Simon's mother-in-law was suffering from a high fever. He went because they asked Him to help her.
39. So He bent over her and rebuked the fever, and it left her...just like that. She got right up and began to wait on Jesus and those who were with Him.
40. At sunset, the people brought to Jesus a steady stream of people who had all kinds of sicknesses and diseases and, laying His hands on every one of them, He healed everyone that He touched.
41. And many rebel spirits yielded to His authority, leaving the people that they had been controlling, and shouting, "You are the Son of God!" But He rebuked them and would not allow the revelation of His true identity to come through them.

42. This went on all through the night, but at daybreak, Jesus went out to a solitary place. And the people were looking for Him and, when they finally found Him, they tried to prevent Him from leaving them.
43. But He said, "Listen, I need to proclaim the Good News of the Kingdom of God to the rest of the population; it's My destiny to do so."
44. And He continued to preach in the synagogues of Judea.

Chapter 5

1. On one particular day, Jesus was preaching on the shore of the Lake Galilee and great crowds pressed in on Him there so that they could hear the message of God.
2. And as the crowd got bigger and closer, He noticed two empty boats at the water's edge...boats that the fishermen had left while they were washing their nets.
3. Without asking permission or explaining what He was doing, He stepped into one of the boats and asked Simon, its owner, to push it out into the water a few feet. Then He sat in the boat and taught the crowds from there.
4. When He had finished His message, He turned to Simon and said, "Now I want you to go out where it's deeper and let down your nets there to catch some fish."
5. "Teacher," Simon replied, "You should know that we fished here all night long...we worked really hard...and we didn't catch a thing." Jesus had no response to his words, so after a short, awkward pause, Simon said, "But if You say so, I'll let the nets down again."
6. As soon as Simon did what Jesus told him to do, he started catching fish immediately...and he continued to catch so many that the nets he used began to tear from the enormous amount of fish!
7. In fact, the haul was so big that he had to yell for his partners to come help him with it, and when they brought out the other boat, both boats became filled to capacity with fish...filled to the point that they were on the verge of sinking.
8. When Simon Peter perceived what had happened, he fell on his knees before Jesus and said, "Oh, Lord, please just leave me...I'm too much of a sinner to be around You...You're out of my league and I don't know how to handle this kind of thing."
9. He was overwhelmed and awestruck by the number of fish they had

caught, as were his fishing partners.

10. James and John, the sons of Zebedee, were there, too, and they were equally amazed and engulfed with awe at the miracle. Jesus calmly replied to Simon, "Hey...don't be afraid! From now on you'll be fishing like this all the time...but you'll be fishing for people!"

11. When they got back to shore, they just left everything they had and started following Jesus.

12. While Jesus was ministering in a certain town, a man came along who was covered up with leprosy. As soon as he saw Jesus, he literally fell on his face to the ground and, with great emotion, started begging Him, "Lord, if You are willing, You can heal me... You can make me clean!"

13. Immediately Jesus reached out His hand and touched the man that society considered untouchable, and said to him, "Hey...I'm totally willing...you don't have to beg...be clean!" And, just like that, the leprosy completely left him.

14. Then Jesus said to him, "Look, don't tell anyone about this...but go, show yourself to the priest and offer the sacrifices that Moses commanded for your cleansing as a testimony to them."

15. But, of course, there was no way to keep something like this quiet. The news about Him spread even more, and very fast. As a result, huge crowds of people came to hear Him and to be healed of their sicknesses and diseases.

16. But when the crowds got bigger and more demanding like this, Jesus withdrew to lonely places to pray and to meditate.

17. One day as He was teaching in the home of someone, some Pharisees and teachers of the Law came to listen to Him. People had come from every village of Galilee, from Judea, and Jerusalem on this occasion, and the tangible power to heal the sick was present and unusually strong that day.

18. And some men came carrying a paralyzed friend of theirs on a mat and tried to get him into the house to lay him before Jesus.

19. But the crowd was too thick and tightly packed into the house so, when they realized that they couldn't find a way to get through, they just went up on the roof and lowered him on his mat through the tiles, into the middle of the crowd, right in front of Jesus.

20. When Jesus saw their innovation and the proactive way that their faith manifested into action, He said to the man, "My friend, all your sins are forgiven!"

21. The Pharisees and the teachers of the Law were offended, even scandalized, at these words and began thinking to themselves, "Who does this upstart think He is? And why does He so glibly speak blasphemy? Who can forgive sins but God alone?"
22. Jesus instinctively knew what they were thinking and asked them, "Why are you thinking these things, internally?
23. "I mean, which is easier...to say, 'Your sins are forgiven,' or to say, 'Get up off of that stretcher and walk'?
24. "Allow Me to demonstrate this concept to you and show you that the Son of Man has authority on earth to forgive sins." Then He said to the man, "Get up! Pick up your mat and go home, whole!"
25. And immediately he stood up in front of all of them, picked up what he had been lying on, just as Jesus instructed him, and went home praising God.
26. Everyone there was amazed by the whole scenario and gave praise to God. They were all filled with awe and said to one another, "Remember what took place on this day; we have seen remarkable things here!"
27. Not long after this, Jesus encountered a tax collector named Levi, sitting at the tax office, as he did every day. When He saw him, He focused His entire attention on him and, without wasting any words, said to him, "I want you to join Me right now as a disciple and follow Me wherever I go."
28. These words were so direct, authoritative, and inexplicably compelling to Levi, that he completely left everything in his life as a tax man and got up right then and there to follow Jesus into a completely new and different reality.
29. One evening, Levi (also known as Matthew), hosted a great banquet in Jesus' honor at his own house and invited a large company of tax collectors and others of dubious reputation. And all of these people were comfortably reclining at the table with Jesus, laughing and talking with Him.
30. Now the Pharisees and their scribes were complaining about this, and protesting to Jesus' disciples, saying, "Why are you all eating and even drinking with these tax collectors and openly sinful people?"
31. Jesus overheard them and said, "It is not those who are healthy who need a doctor, but those who are sick.
32. "I haven't come to invite and call the ones that everyone assumes are

righteous, but the ones who are perceived as the unrighteous...the ones who are considered the worst of the worst...and the ones who, indeed, need to change their ways by changing their mindsets."

33. Then they said to Him, "Well, the disciples of John practice fasting often and offer up prayers and petitions...and so do the disciples of the Pharisees...but Yours spend all their time at parties, eating and drinking with riffraff!"
34. And Jesus said to them, "Do you think you can make the wedding guests fast as long as the bridegroom is with them?
35. "Look, the days will come when the bridegroom will be taken from them and then, believe Me, they will do their fasting."
36. He also told them a proverb, saying, "No one puts a patch from a new garment on an old garment, because, if he does, he will tear the new one and the patch from that garment will not match the old one.
37. "In the same way, no one pours new wine into old wineskins. If they do, the fresh wine will burst the skins and it will be spilled everywhere, and the skins will be ruined.
38. "The bottom line is this: new wine must be put into fresh wineskins!
39. "No one, after drinking fine, aged wine immediately desires new wine, for he says the old is good or better. So, in other words, I am having to show you a whole new way to think about how you perceive right and wrong...about how you discern what is 'acceptable' and what is 'unacceptable'...about who you think is fit or unfit. My intention is to turn your minds into new wineskins and to create within you a taste and a craving for the new wine!"

Chapter 6

1. On a particular day—a day which just happened to be the Sabbath—Jesus and His disciples were walking through some grain fields. As they moved along, casually talking with one another—not really thinking about anything, other than how hungry they all were—His men began to pick some heads of grain, rub them together in their hands and pop the kernels in their mouths.
2. Some of the ever-present and always vigilant Pharisees somehow saw them doing this and asked, "Why are you rebels doing what is unlawful on the Sabbath?"
3. Jesus quickly answered them, "Gentlemen, have you never read what David did when he and his men were hungry?

4. "If not, let Me remind you: he entered the house of God, took the consecrated bread, and ate what is lawful only for the priests to eat. And if that wasn't bad enough according to religious standards, he also served it to his companions!"
5. Then Jesus said to them, "The bottom line is this: the Son of Man is Lord of the Sabbath."
6. On yet another Sabbath, He went into the synagogue to teach, as He did so often during this period of His ministry. And there was a man there that day whose right hand was shriveled and deformed.
7. The Pharisees and the teachers of the Law by this time were constantly looking for a reason to accuse Him of something... anything...so they watched Him closely to see if He would be so bold as to heal on the Sabbath.
8. But, as always, Jesus knew what these predictable men were thinking, so He said to the man with the shriveled hand, "Sir, please get up and stand in front of the people where everyone can see you." So, without asking any questions, the man got up and stood there.
9. Then Jesus looked at the Pharisees and said to them, "All right, let Me ask you all a question: Which is lawful on the Sabbath...to do good or to do evil...to save life or to destroy it?"
10. No one said anything so, after He had stared at them blankly for a few moments, He turned to the man and said, "Stretch out your hand." And the man did just that and, as he did, his hand was completely restored and made normal.
11. But instead of being impressed or moved by the miracle or by Jesus' power and authority, the Pharisees and the teachers of the Law were infuriated by this. He had embarrassed them one too many times and had made their cherished rules and regulations seem silly and irrelevant. From this point, they began to seriously discuss with one another what they might do to Jesus and how they could effectively put a stop to Him, completely.
12. On another day, Jesus went out to a mountainside to pray and ended up spending the entire night in deep prayer.
13. At daybreak, He descended the mountain and called all of His disciples to Himself and, out of the whole number of them, He chose twelve, whom He also designated as apostles.
14. The final group consisted of Simon (whom He named Peter), his brother Andrew, James, John, Philip, Bartholomew,
15. Matthew, Thomas, James (son of Alphaeus), Simon (who was a

Zealot),
16. Judas (son of James) and Judas Iscariot (who was destined to be used as a traitor).
17. Then He took His newly-appointed group of twelve and stood out on a level place where a large crowd of His other disciples surrounded Him. Soon a great throng began gathering there...people from all over Judea, from Jerusalem, and from the coastal region around Tyre and Sidon.
18. When the news got out that He was appearing like this, people came from everywhere to hear Him and to be healed of their diseases...and they got what they came for. Even those who were harassed by rebel spirits were made well and whole.
19. And the people all tried to get up close enough to touch Him, because power was exuding from Him and He was healing them all.
20. Then He began to teach. Looking at His disciples, He said: "Blessed are you who have lost everything, for in having to change your perspective on owning things in the material world, you are able to own the realities of the Kingdom of God.
21. "Blessed are you who hunger now, for in identifying what it is that you really crave, you will ultimately be satisfied. Blessed are you who weep over what is missing in your life now, for the gift of laughter is coming with the revelation of all that is in the Kingdom.
22. "And even consider yourself blessed when it seems that people hate you and exclude you from their religious systems...when they insult you and reject your name as evil because of your affiliation with the Son of Man.
23. "Rejoice in the day that you experience this kind of thing; yes, rejoice to the point that you literally leap for joy! Because when you survive such attacks and come out on the other side of them even stronger...wiser...free from bitterness, all of heaven applauds! Remember, that is how their ancestors treated the prophets and that kind of treatment actually shaped those men into greatness.
24. "But there's a rude awakening ahead for those of you who have become rich through this present world system...those who have become selfish and smug to the point that you think your money can fix everything for you. What you have now is all you'll ever get.
25. "There's also trouble ahead for those of you who are self-absorbed and self-satisfied; in the days to come you'll realize that a selfish life will only leave you empty and hollow in the end. And woe to you

who don't take human relationships seriously...who laugh at the idea of making investments into the lives of others. It won't be so funny when you find yourself disconnected and all alone.

26. "And watch out if you're only living for the approval of others...if you're so emotionally needy that you refuse to speak your own truth for fear of repercussions. Remember, your ancestors appeased and flattered false prophets, but in the end they turned on them for not being authentic.

27. "But this is the main thing I want to say to those of you who are really hearing Me now, because it's the introduction to a whole new way of thinking...the door to a whole new world...and let Me tell you, it's a radical concept: Love your enemies...treat well those who detest you and pursue you with hatred...

28. invoke a flood of blessings upon those who openly curse you, and sincerely pray for their happiness; ask for God's blessing and favor upon those who abuse and misuse you…

29. if someone slaps you on the cheek, offer the other one to him or her, also...from whoever takes away your outer garment, don't withhold your undergarment...

30. if someone begs you for something that you have, give it to them...of him who takes away your goods, do not demand or require them back again.

31. "Here is the summation of all of it: as you would like and desire that people would do to you, do exactly that to them!"

32. "You must think this way if you want to create a new world, because if you only love those who love you, what's new and world-changing about that? Why should you even be commended for it? Even those who have no Kingdom mentality whatsoever, love those who love them.

33. "And if you're only kind to those who are kind to you, and only do favors for those who do favors for you, what's new and innovative about that? Any average sinner can do that.

34. "Furthermore, if you lend money at interest to those from whom you hope to receive, why should anyone even pay attention to that? Every day sinners lend money at interest to other sinners, so as to recover as much again. There's nothing about that that is going to turn things around.

35. "But love your enemies—I don't mean just tolerate and coexist with them—I mean love them! Be kind and do good so that someone is

blessed, whether you think they deserve it or not. And lend, expecting and hoping for nothing in return...and don't complain and whine about it, either...consider nothing as lost! If you can do these things, you will tap into a whole new dimension, and it's from that realm that you will be rewarded. And your abundant reward will be rich and intense and, most importantly, you will be bona fide sons of the Most High—thinking like He thinks, living like He lives, doing what He does—for He is kind and charitable and good, even to the ungrateful and the selfish and wicked.

36. "So be mercifully empathetic and responsive to the needs of people...become energized with the power of compassion...even as your Father exists in this realm.

37. "And while I'm on the subject of the operation of this new world order, I will also tell you not to pronounce judgment on anyone and you will live beyond the authority of anyone's judgment on your life...do not condemn or pronounce guilt on anyone and you will exist beyond the reach of condemnation and personal guilt...acquit, forgive and release others from your agendas and opinions and you will never be limited by the agendas and opinions of others.

38. "And give...give generously and freely...because if you do, gifts will be lavished upon you...and these gifts will be abundant (to demonstrate the infinite possibilities of the Kingdom), packed down (to make room for more), shaken together (to make sure that you never receive filler), and running all over the place (so that you never have a sense of lack)! People will come into your life just to give to you, and this is the way that they will pour into the pouch formed by the bosom of your robe and used as a bag. You define your own terms in this, for with the same measure you deal out—with the measure you use when you confer benefits on others—it will be measured back to you!"

39. He went on to tell them a proverb: "Can a blind person guide and direct another blind person? Won't they both stumble into a ditch or a hole in the ground?

40. "You see, a pupil is not superior to his or her teacher, but every individual, when he or she is completely trained and properly readjusted, will be like his or her teacher.

41. "With that in mind, let Me ask you: Why do you so easily notice the tiny speck that is in the eye of your brother or sister, when you are oblivious to the beam of timber that is in your own eye?

42. "And how can you have the nerve to say to that brother or sister, 'Hey, allow me to take out the splinter of wood that is in your eye,' when you do not even notice the enormous log that is in your own eye? What kind of phony game are you playing? First take the timber out of your own eye, and then you will see clearly how to perceive whatever is in your brother's or sister's eye.
43. "For there is no healthy tree that bears diseased fruit...on the other hand, a diseased tree can't produce healthy fruit...it's just that simple.
44. "Furthermore, each tree is identified by its own fruit. Figs are not gathered from thorn bushes, nor is a cluster of grapes ever picked from a bramble bush.
45. "The person who is known as honorable and virtuous, out of the good treasure stored in his or her heart, produces what is honorable and virtuous...and the evil person who manifests as evil, out of the evil storehouse brings forth that which is unacceptable. For out of the abundant overflow of the inner individual, the mouth speaks.
46. "Speaking of being honorable, let Me ask you: Why do you call Me 'Lord, Lord' and do not simply practice what I tell you?
47. "Everyone who comes to Me and listens to My words—I mean really listens and understands My Intentions—I will demonstrate to you what he or she is like:
48. That person is like a man who built a house...who dug and went down deep and laid a good foundation upon the rock. And when a flood arose and all manner of inclement weather beat upon the house, the basic structure could not be shaken or moved at all, because it had been securely built on bedrock.
49. "But, by the same token, he or she who merely hears, but does not practice doing My words, is like a man who built a house on the ground without a foundation...a man who built on sand. When the bad weather came against what he had built, immediately it collapsed and fell...and the fall of that house was dramatic and complete."

Chapter 7

1. When Jesus finished this important and revolutionary teaching, He entered Capernaum.
2. There in the city was a Roman centurion's servant, whom his master

valued very highly, and this servant was sick and at the point of death.
3. So when the centurion heard of Jesus, he sent some elders of the Jews to Him to ask Him to come and heal his servant.
4. So they did as he requested and, when they came to Jesus, they were insistent that He help the man. They said, "Look, this man deserves to have You do this...
5. You must help him because he loves our nation and has built us a synagogue!"
6. So Jesus was persuaded and went with them. But when He got near the centurion's house, the man sent friends to Him with this message: "Lord, I didn't mean for You to trouble Yourself...it wasn't even necessary for You to come in person...in fact, it's not even appropriate, since I don't worship Your God.
7. "That's why I didn't even consider myself worthy to come to You. I am just asking that You say the word, because I know that if You do, my servant will be healed.
8. "See, I myself am a man under authority, with a hundred soldiers under me. I tell this one, 'Go,' and he goes...I don't ever have to worry that one of my men won't carry out my orders...and to another one I say, 'Come,' and he comes...I never have to do any guesswork about it...I say to my servant, 'Do this,' and he does it...no questions asked."
9. When Jesus heard this message, He was amazed at the man's ability to perceive the concept of authority and the abstract idea of the power and function of words. So He turned to the crowd following Him and said, *"I tell you, I have not found faith this great even in Israel."* Then He sent the centurion's friends back to him with the same message.
10. When the men who had been sent returned to the house, they found the servant completely well.
11. Right after this, Jesus went to a town called Nain, and His disciples and a big crowd accompanied Him.
12. As He neared the gate of the city, He saw that a dead person was being carried out to be buried. Upon inquiry, He discovered that the body was that of a mother's only son and that she was a widow. A large group of people from the town made up the funeral entourage.
13. This crowd of mourners was too big to be missed, but when He finally saw the grieving mother, His heart immediately went out to

her and made a compassionate connection. Without hesitation He walked right up to her and said, "Dear lady, please don't cry."

14. Then He walked over and touched the bier on which they were carrying her son's lifeless body, and the pallbearers froze in their tracks. He said, "Young man, I say to you...get up right now!"

15. And the boy sat up and began to talk, virtually in mid-sentence, as if he had only been gone for a second or two. Then Jesus personally escorted him over to his amazed mother and presented him to her.

16. Of course, all the people who witnessed this were completely awestruck and began to praise God, saying, "A great and mighty prophet has appeared among us! God has come to personally help His people!"

17. And this news about Jesus spread throughout Judea and the surrounding country like wildfire.

18. Being aware of all that was happening with Jesus, John's disciples went to visit him in prison to tell him everything that they had heard about it. After listening to their reports, he called aside two of them

19. and sent them to Jesus to ask, "Are You really the One Who was to come...the One we've been expecting...or should we face the reality that we need to expect someone else?"

20. When the men came to Jesus, they said, "John the Baptist sent us to You to ask this...are You really the One Who was to come…the One the prophets talked about…the One we've been expecting…the Christ? Or should we part with our illusions concerning You and start to look for someone else who fits that description?"

21. Ironically, they were asking this while Jesus was in the middle of conducting a meeting...a meeting in which He was curing many who had diseases, releasing those who were under the control of rebel spirits, and giving sight to many who were blind.

22. So Jesus temporarily stopped ministering to the sick and replied to the messengers, "Go back and report to John what you have seen and heard: the blind are receiving their sight, the lame are walking, those who have leprosy are being cleansed, the deaf are hearing, even the dead are being raised, and the Good News is being proclaimed to the disenfranchised and the destitute.

23. "And blessed is anyone who accepts this as My validation, without offense because of their perception of Me, and does not even think of asking such a question."

24. After John's messengers left, Jesus began to speak to the crowd

about John, before anyone could form a negative opinion because of this exchange of words…before anyone could bring an accusation against John due to his obvious doubt and insolence. He said to them, "Just what did you think you were going to see out there in the wilderness? A little, non-confrontational weakling who doesn't speak his mind…a reed swayed by the wind?

25. "If not, then what did you go out to see? A man dressed in expensive clothes…a sellout for the religious establishment? No, those who wear fine and expensive clothes…who indulge in luxury…are found in palaces. A shaky reed would never have the nerve to challenge Me in this way.

26. "So then, what did you go out to see? A prophet? No doubt…that's what you wanted to see and that's indeed what you did see. But I tell you, this man—regardless of the mental battle he may be having right now in that lonely prison cell—is still a prophet…more than a prophet, in fact…he is a prophet and then some!

27. "This is the man about whom Malachi wrote: *'I will send my messenger ahead of You, who will prepare Your way before You.'*

28. "Here's the truth about John: Among those born of women, there has not risen anyone greater in history. Yet, in this Kingdom, which he, in fact, introduced to you…in this new paradigm where the first shall be last, and the last shall be first…the order of things will be so radically changed that whoever is perceived to be the least important…the least significant…the least worthy in the Kingdom of God, is actually greater than he!

29. "The ordinary people…the disreputable…even the tax collectors…all the people who heard John, by being baptized by him into Kingdom-consciousness, are the clearest evidence that he was the genuine article.

30. "But the Pharisees and religious leaders would have nothing to do with such a baptism and paradigm shift…they wouldn't think of giving up their place in line to those whom they considered to be their inferiors."

31. Jesus went on to say, "To what, then, can I compare the people of this generation? How can I describe and account for them?

32. "They are like spoiled children sitting in the marketplace and calling out to each other, saying, 'We played instruments for you, but you didn't dance; and then we sang a funeral dirge, but you didn't cry.'

33. "These people, and people like them, are never satisfied. Think

34. "The Son of Man, on the other hand, accepted the invitation to every party and socialized with every segment of society, and you called Him an unrestrained, gluttonous alcoholic...a friend of lowlifes.
35. "But wisdom is proved right by all her children...vindicated by the lives of those who follow her."
36. One day something totally unprecedented happened...one of the Pharisees actually invited Jesus to his home to dine with him. And Jesus, in spite of His strained and often volatile relationship with the religious leaders, graciously accepted the man's invitation and went to his house for dinner. The meal went smoothly...nothing controversial was brought up at the table...the atmosphere during the entire dinner party was harmonious and conciliatory...and afterward Jesus reclined at the table with his host and the others who were there, simply enjoying the evening and relishing its promise of the possibility of a new relationship between them all.
37. But then something happened that interrupted the flow of the night's events and completely changed the dynamics of everything that was happening in the Pharisee's house. Somehow, a woman, who was generally known as the town's leading and most infamous prostitute, had heard that Jesus was in the house and had found her way into the dining area where He was. Suddenly, she was standing right in front of Him, holding an alabaster flask of perfumed ointment.
38. None of the surprised people at the table said anything as she moved around behind Him and suddenly burst into a flood of tears. Then, moving back to where she was, she collapsed on the floor in front of Him, took His bare feet into her hands, and pressed her face onto them so that the flow of her tears could physically wet them. Then she began to wipe them with her own long hair, while she affectionately kissed them and anointed them with the ointment.
39. Now the Pharisee who had invited Him saw what was happening but, because he didn't want to embarrass his dinner guest (mainly because he knew who she was), he just let it happen. Initially, he didn't say anything, assuming that she would finish up this unusual and provocative demonstration quickly and then just leave his house. But after a few awkward moments of watching this display (which Jesus seemed perfectly fine with), he began to feel uncomfortable and, then, offended. He said to himself, "If this man were really a

(continued: about it...John came into the public eye fasting, and you called him a raving lunatic because of his hermetic lifestyle.)

prophet, He would surely know who and what sort of woman this seductress is who is touching Him in this way. If He had any sense of propriety or discernment at all, He would put a stop to it...not only is she doing this in my home without my consent...she is a woman who pleasures men for money...she shouldn't even be here and she certainly shouldn't be touching a holy man!"

40. And Jesus, knowing what the man was thinking, said to him, "Simon, I want to say something to you." And he answered, "All right, Teacher...say it."

41. "A certain man who lent money at interest had two debtors...one owed him five hundred denarii, and the other fifty.

42. "When it became clear that neither of them had any means of paying him back, he freely forgave them both. Now which of them do you think will love him more?"

43. Simon answered, "I suppose the one for whom he forgave and cancelled more." And Jesus said to him, "You're exactly right."

44. Then, turning back toward the woman who was still caressing His feet in her hands, He said to Simon, "Do you see this woman? When I entered your house this evening, you didn't even offer Me any water for My feet...but she has wet My feet with her own tears and has wiped them with her own hair.

45. "You didn't greet Me with a kiss, but she, from the moment she came in, has not ceased to tenderly kiss My feet.

46. "You didn't anoint My head with oil—not even with cheap, ordinary oil—but she has anointed My feet with costly and rare perfume.

47. "So this is My conclusion...I know who she is, and I know what she does for a living...but her sins, many as they obviously are, are forgiven her, simply because she loves so much and has proved it here. But he who is forgiven little, loves little."

48. Then He said to her, "Sweetheart, your sins are all forgiven!"

49. And this statement undid any and all relationship building that may have occurred that night between Him and the Pharisees. Those who were at the table were scandalized by the whole scenario...for them, it was wrong on so many levels...and they began to say among themselves, "Who does this man think He is that He can even forgive sins?"

50. But Jesus, undeterred as usual by the religious leaders and their lack of understanding, ignored them and said to the woman, "You washed My feet with your own tears and dried them with your own hair, so

I say to you that your own faith has saved you! Go from here and enter into peace in your life!"

Chapter 8

1. After this experience at the Pharisee's house, Jesus traveled from one town and village to another, proclaiming a singular message...the Good News of the Kingdom of God. As He focused entirely on doing this, the Twelve were with Him, as usual;
2. but there was also another group of disciples who accompanied Him...a large female following...women who had been released from the influence of rebel spirits and cured of diseases through Him. This group consisted of Mary (called Magdalene), from whom seven rebel spirits had been expelled;
3. Joanna, the wife of Chuza, the manager of Herod's household, Susanna, and many others who are not named here. These women ministered to Jesus, and helped to support His ministry, financially, out of their own means.
4. One day, while a large crowd was gathering and people were coming to Jesus from town after town, He began to teach, using this illustration:
5. "A certain farmer went out to sow his seed and, as he was scattering it, some of it fell along the path. Whatever seed was not trampled under foot there was quickly eaten up by the birds.
6. "Some of the other seed fell on rock, or gravelly ground, and when it came up, the vegetation quickly withered because it had no available moisture to sustain it.
7. "Other seed that he scattered fell among thorns, which grew up right along with it, and choked the life out of the plants.
8. "And still other seed fell on good soil that was conducive to growth. It came up as it should and produced a beautiful, healthy crop...a hundred times, in fact, more than was sown." After He had said this, He added, "Whoever has a perceptive and discerning ear to hear, let him or her really hear this with comprehension."
9. His disciples weren't sure they met that criteria, so they came to Him, privately, and asked Him to interpret His illustration.
10. So He said to them "Look...you've been given insight into the mysteries of God's Kingdom...a revelation of its inner workings and an understanding of its day-to-day operation. You know more about

it than you think you know. But those who can't see it yet (intrigued as they may be by My story-telling) only hear My stories as entertainment...that's all they are to them at this point...stories... 'illustrations without introspection'...'metaphors without meaning.'

11. "But I'll spell it out for you: the seed is the Word of God.
12. "Those along the path are the ones who hear, but the Adversary (or any adversarial individual or circumstance) comes and takes away the Word from their hearts so that they may not believe and get results from it.
13. "Those who are on the rock, or gravelly ground, are the ones who very happily receive the Word when they first hear it, but they have no root connection to it...no real root in themselves or sense of covenant relationship to the Word...and so they endure for a little while, but when trouble or persecution arises on account of the Word, they immediately become resentful and basically fall apart.
14. "Then the seed that fell among thorns stands for those who hear with comprehension...even with revelation...but as they go on their way, the daily cares and anxieties of the world wear them out and they easily get distracted by the illusions of the age...looking for pleasure and false glamour elsewhere...being deceived by the empty promises of riches. Without even noticing it, the craving and passionate desire for other things creep in and strangle the Word, so that they never fully mature.
15. "But the seed on good soil stands for those who hear the Word and openly receive it, accepting the personal responsibility for their own soil maintenance. They welcome it and have a mature relationship to it, and so they bear fruit and produce a bumper crop in their lives!
16. "Obviously, no one lights a lamp and then covers it up with a vessel or crams it under a bed to obscure its radiance. On the contrary, a lamp is made to be lit and then fixed somewhere up high on a lamp stand, so that it may burn brightly to illuminate everyone who enters the house.
17. "When the light is embraced, there is nothing hidden that will not be disclosed...nothing concealed that will not be revealed.
18. "So consider carefully how you listen...how you hear. See, it's not just *what* you hear that affects you, it's *how* you hear it. Your perception determines what you attract to yourself...in this way, those who have will be given more. By the same token, the way you hear can also repel certain things and move them away from you so

that those who do not have, even what they think they have will be taken from them."

19. One day Jesus' mother and brothers came to see Him, but they were not able to get near Him because He was surrounded by a big crowd.
20. So someone came to Him and said, "Your mother and brothers are standing outside, wanting to have a word with You."
21. Jesus replied to the man, "You know what? My real mother and brothers are those who hear God's word and put it into practice." And nothing more was said about it.
22. Another day He said to His disciples, "Hey, let's go over to the other side of the lake." So, without question, they all piled into a boat and launched out.
23. As they sailed, Jesus dozed off and, while He slept, a squall abruptly converged on the lake. In practically no time, the boat was being flooded and they were in great danger of sinking.
24. The frightened disciples went and woke Him up out of His peaceful, undisturbed sleep, saying, "Master! Master! Don't You know that we're about to drown?" Without saying a word, Jesus calmly opened His eyes, sat up and rubbed them for a moment, and then stood up and told the wind to settle down. Immediately, the storm subsided and the water became like glass.
25. Then He turned around and asked them, "Where in the world is your faith?"...and went back to His nap. In fear and amazement they asked one another, "Who is this? He even tells the winds and the water what to do, and they obey Him!"
26. After this they sailed to the region of the Gerasenes, which is across the lake from Galilee.
27. And as soon as He stepped out of the boat, a madman under the influence of a rebel spirit came right up to Him from out of the cemetery. This man actually lived naked, outside among the tombs.
28. But when he saw Jesus from a distance, the spirit controlling him recognized Him (as the spirits always did) and, crying out with a loud voice, the spirit spoke through the man, saying, "What business do You have here with me, Jesus, Son of the Most High? Why has the Son of God come here? I beg You not to torment me!"
29. For Jesus had commanded the rebel spirit to release the man, because many times it had harassed him. And though he was chained hand and foot and kept under guard, he had broken his chains and had been driven by the dark spirit into solitary places.

30. Jesus asked him, "What is your name?" And the spirit responded simultaneously in the singular and in the plural, because in the spirit realm they are most always the same. And, mixing his pronouns, he said, "'My' name is Legion, for 'we' are many in this man's life!"
31. And they begged him repeatedly not to order them back into the unseen realm.
32. Now an enormous herd of hogs was grazing there on the hillside while this exchange was happening. So "Legion" begged Him, saying, "Please, Sir, grant us permission to go to the hogs that we may go into them!" So He gave them the permission, being fully aware that they could do nothing without it.
33. And the spirits left the man and took control of the hogs. And the entire herd immediately rushed headlong down the steep slope, into the lake and were drowned in the water.
34. When those who were tending the hogs saw what had happened, they ran off and reported this bizarre event in the town and all over the countryside,
35. and the people went out to see for themselves what had happened. And they came to Jesus and looked with amazement at the man who had been previously controlled by the spirits, just sitting there, clothed, calm, and completely lucid—the very same man who had been controlled by the Legion of spirits called demons—and they were seized with alarm and struck with fear.
36. Those who saw it firsthand told the people how the insane man—the man who seemed to be controlled by the spirits—had been completely restored to mental health and wellness.
37. Then all the people of the region of the Gerasenes asked Jesus to leave them, because the whole thing was just too much for them; they were overcome with fear because of it. So He got into the boat and left.
38. The man who had been liberated kept begging Him that he might go with Him and be with Him...now worshipping Him on his own accord and not under the influence of any other entity. But Jesus went away, saying,
39. "No, friend...you'll be more effective if you go home to your own family and friends and tell them all that the Lord has done for you and how He has had mercy on you. They need to see for themselves what has happened to you!" And the man departed and immediately began to publicly proclaim all over town how much Jesus had done

for him.

40. When Jesus returned to the other side, a throng welcomed Him, because they were all expecting Him.

41. And from out of the crowd, a man named Jairus, a well-known synagogue leader, came and literally fell at Jesus' feet, pleading with Him to come to his house.

42. He made this request because his only daughter, a girl of about twelve, was sick and at the point of death. Jesus immediately agreed to accompany the man back to his house, but, as He was on His way, the desperate and excited crowds almost crushed Him.

43. But there was a certain woman in the crowd who, despite the mass hysteria that often manifested when Jesus was in healing mode, had the intention of making personal, physical contact with Him. This particular woman had been subject to a serious hemorrhaging situation for twelve years, and no one in that whole time had been able to help her get any relief.

44. So, believing that this was her last chance at wholeness, she made her way through the sea of people and came right up behind Him. When she got within arm's reach of Him, she grabbed the edge of His cloak and clutched it with all her might. Immediately her bleeding stopped.

45. "Who touched Me?" Jesus asked. Peter replied to Him, "What do You mean? People are crowding in and pressing against You... they're all touching You!"

46. But Jesus said, "No, no...this was different. Someone *touched* Me... I mean really touched Me...and something unusual just happened in that touch, because I could feel power and energy drain out of Me through the connection."

47. Then the woman, realizing that she could not remain anonymous, came trembling and fell at His feet. And in the presence of all the people, as a reverent hush fell on them, she told why she had touched Him and how she had been instantly healed through it.

48. Then, smiling, He said to her, "My daughter, your own faith has healed you. Go in absolute peace."

49. But while Jesus was in mid-sentence, someone came from the house of Jairus, the synagogue leader, and said to him, "Sir, your daughter is dead...don't bother the Teacher anymore."

50. Upon hearing this, Jesus grabbed Jairus by the shoulders and said, "Look at Me! Before you react to the news...before you say a

word...before you respond with any emotion whatsoever...*just believe*...don't say anything...don't feel anything...don't grieve...don't cry...don't be seized with alarm or struck with fear. Do one thing and one thing only...*only believe!*" So Jairus did as he was told.

51. When they arrived at the house of Jairus, Jesus refused to let anyone go in with Him except Peter, John and James, and the girl's father and mother.

52. Meanwhile, all the people there were wailing and mourning for her. Jesus instantly put a stop to all the drama and said, "Stop wailing! This girl is not dead...she's only sleeping!"

53. The mourners and wailers in the room switched, almost automatically, from crying to laughing...laughing at Him—that is...jeering at Him—and sarcastically telling Him that He was out of touch with reality.

54. But, unfazed by their negative reaction to His creative words, He gripped her firmly by the hand and said, "Little girl, I say to you, arise!"

55. And at these simple words, her spirit returned and she jumped right up and started walking around! Then Jesus said to her parents, "She's alive! Give her something to eat!"

56. They were totally astonished, but He instructed them not to tell anyone what had happened.

Chapter 9

1. When Jesus had called His official Twelve disciples together, He gave them power and authority, personally, to drive out and expel all rebel spirits and to cure diseases.

2. And He commissioned and authorized them to proclaim the Kingdom of God and to validate the message by healing the sick.

3. Then He told them, "Basically, I want you to take nothing with you on your journey...no external equipment...you must learn to rely, solely, on the internal gifts which I have imparted to you.

4. "Whatever house you enter, if it's friendly, stay there until you leave that town.

5. "But if any house or community will not receive, embrace and welcome you...if they refuse to listen to you...then get out of there. And when you depart, make a grand and symbolic gesture of shaking

6. off the dust from their streets that is on your feet, for a visible testimony against them."
6. So they all obediently set out on their Kingdom-adventure, going from village to village, proclaiming the Good News and healing people everywhere.
7. Now when Herod, the tetrarch, heard about all that was going on, he was very disturbed by it because some were saying that John had been raised from the dead.
8. Others believed that the reincarnation of Elijah had manifested, and still others were saying that one of the prophets of long ago had come back to life in the present dimension.
9. But Herod said, "I personally saw to it that John was beheaded! So Who, then, is this amazing person I keep hearing about?" And he made it his intention to see Him for himself.
10. When the disciples returned from their travels, they reported to Jesus everything they had done on their own. After hearing from them what had happened, He took them with Him in order to mentor them further, and they withdrew by themselves to a town called Bethsaida.
11. But, as usual, the crowds found out about it and followed Him wherever He went. But, even though they interrupted His plans with His disciples, He didn't rebuke them. In fact, He welcomed them and used the opportunity to unveil to them the mysteries of the Kingdom of God. He also healed everyone who needed healing.
12. But late in the afternoon, the disciples came to Him and said, "You need to send this crowd away so that they can go to the surrounding villages and find food and lodging before sundown. We're in a very remote place here and they need to go take care of themselves."
13. But Jesus said, "No...I don't want to send them away. Why don't you just give them something to eat?" They answered, "Well, that's impossible. We have only five loaves of bread and two fish among us. That's it, unless we go into town and buy food for all of them."
14. What makes the story even more interesting is that there were about five thousand men there, along with women and children! But, undaunted by the enormity of the situation, Jesus said to His disciples, "Just have them sit down in groups of about fifty each."
15. Without question or argument, the disciples did as He said, and everyone sat down.
16. Then, taking the five loaves and the two fish, and looking up into the heavenlies, He gave thanks for what He had in His hands and began

to break off pieces of both the bread and the fish. As He broke off piece after piece, He gave them to the disciples to serve to the people.

17. And they all ate...every one of them...and were completely satisfied. When the miraculous meal was over, the Twelve disciples went around and filled up twelve whole baskets of broken pieces that were left over!

18. Once, when Jesus was off praying by Himself, He became aware that His disciples had moved close to where He was. So He stopped and, before they could speak, He said to them, "Let Me ask you something...who do the crowds say I am?"

19. They replied, "Well, some say John, the Forerunner...others say Elijah in another form...still others presume that one of the prophets of long ago has come back to life."

20. "All right...fine...but what about you?" He replied. "Who do you say that I am?" Without missing a beat, Peter answered, "Easy...You are God's Christ!"

21. Jesus then warned them to be careful with that information. They were to be discreet to the point of telling no one what Peter had said.

22. He explained this warning to them by saying, "You see, the Son of Man must suffer many things and be repudiated and rejected on the part of the elders and priests and scribes. Eventually, He will even be put to death...but on the third day He will rise again."

23. And He went on to say, "So if any person wants to follow Me on this journey, he or she is going to have to give up his or her own personal agendas and selfish interests. You're actually going to have to fulfill your own destiny in taking up your own cross daily, so that you can follow Me as I take up Mine.

24. "For whoever is obsessed with self-preservation at the expense of others will end up losing his or her life, anyway. But whoever releases his or her life for My sake—whoever embraces sacrifice and service for the greater good as I do—will ultimately preserve and save his/her life.

25. "The bottom line is this: what does it profit a person if he/she gains the whole world through self-exaltation and ends up losing his/her very essence in the process?

26. "Your actions will define your terms with Me because of the universal laws of sowing and reaping. So if anyone is ashamed of Me and My words, the Son of Man will be ashamed of him when He

is revealed in the glory of His Kingdom, which is validated by the Father and the holy angels.

27. "But here's the truth about that revelation: some of you who are standing here will not experience death before they see the Kingdom of God manifested."

28. About eight days after this, Jesus took Peter, John and James with Him and went up onto a mountain to pray.

29. And as He was praying, His appearance began to undergo a complete metamorphosis right before their very eyes, causing the appearance of His face to change, dramatically. Even His clothing began to morph into a surrounding aura that was as bright as a flash of lightning!

30. Suddenly, two men, Moses and Elijah, were standing there conversing with Him!

31. They appeared in glorious and radiant splendor, similar to that of His appearance, and they spoke about His imminent departure from the physical realm, which He was about to bring to realization at Jerusalem.

32. Peter and his companions were very sleepy, but while they were in between being fully awake and being in a dream-like state, they were able to see clearly into the realities of the spirit world. Suddenly, they saw His glory, as well as the two men standing with Him, and somehow, inexplicably, they just knew who the two men were! They had obviously never seen them before (since both men had lived on the earth centuries before this) and, yet, as these two prophets continued to commune with Jesus, the disciples not only recognized them, but they were totally comfortable in their presence…not at all alarmed or surprised that they were seeing living people from another time and era right there on the mountain…in the now!

33. The whole thing was over in a flash, but as the men were de-materializing and leaving Jesus, Peter said to Him, "Master, this is an amazing and unforgettable moment in time and it is good for us to be here! If You approve, I'd like to put up three booths right here… to build three memorials…one for You and one for Moses and one for Elijah!" Of course, this notion of memorializing the moment with mere mementos was nonsense.

34. But while he was speaking, a shining cloud, completely composed of transcendent light, just emerged and sort of overshadowed all of

them, and it terrified them.

35. Then, a deep, thunderous voice from within the cloud began to speak, saying, "This is My Son…My Beloved, with Whom I am and have always been delighted! Listen to Him!"
36. When the voice had spoken, they saw that Jesus was no longer in an altered state, and they realized that He wasn't accompanied by the other two men any longer. The disciples kept this to themselves and told no one at that time what they had seen.
37. The next day, a crowd of needy people was waiting for them at the foot of the mountain.
38. As they approached the throng, a man from the crowd shouted out, "Lord, please have mercy on my only son!
39. "He has a terrible condition…a harassing spirit that causes severe, epileptic-type seizures which manifest frequently…and when they do, he foams at the mouth and convulses…and this thing won't leave him alone.
40. "I brought him to Your disciples to see if they could help him, but they weren't able to do a thing for him."
41. Frustrated, Jesus answered, "Oh, you unbelieving, clueless, and backward generation! How long am I supposed to demonstrate dominion before you? How many miracles is it going to take before you realize the power that you already have?! Bring him here to Me."
42. But while he was coming, the spirit threw him down and convulsed him. So Jesus calmly told it to stop showing off and then expelled it. He also healed the boy of any physical damage caused by the manifestations and restored him to his father.
43. Everyone there was astounded at this amazing demonstration of God's obvious power. But while they were all marveling at everything Jesus was doing, He turned to His disciples, seemingly unaffected by the amazement of the crowd, and said,
44. "Listen, you must comprehend this: the Son of Man is about to be betrayed and turned over into the hands of carnal men."
45. But they weren't able to grasp it…it was as if it was kept hidden from them so that they couldn't understand…and on some level they were afraid to ask Him anything about the statement. It was as if He never even said it.
46. Not long after this, a controversy arose among them as to which of them might be the greatest and the most superior.

47. But Jesus, perceiving their selfish ambition and hidden agendas by the Spirit, took an unpretentious little child and put him at His side.
48. Then He said to them, "You should know that I am so identified with these little ones, I can tell you that whoever receives and loves and welcomes and celebrates one little child like this for My sake and in My name, receives and loves and welcomes and celebrates Me. And whoever so receives Me so also receives Him Who sent Me, because, in this new Kingdom-reality, he who is perceived to be the least and lowliest among you all, is the one who is truly great."
49. Changing the subject entirely, John spoke up and said, "Lord, we saw a man driving out rebel spirits in Your name, and we commanded him to stop it because he is not one of us...we didn't approve or sanction him, so we told him that he was completely out of order to do such things."
50. But Jesus said to him, "You really shouldn't have done that...you need to change your paradigm of people like him and realize that whoever is not against you is for you!"
51. Now as the time approached for Jesus to leave the physical world and re-enter the heavenly realm, He made it His intention to make the journey to Jerusalem.
52. So He sent messengers before Him and they entered a Samaritan village to make preparations for His visit.
53. But when the local people in Samaria learned that His ultimate destination was Jerusalem, they refused Him hospitality.
54. When His disciples, James and John, observed this, they were incensed and said, "Lord, do You want us to command fire to come down from heaven and consume them, as Elijah did?"
55. But He instantly snapped at them, saying, "You don't even know of what sort of spirit you are;
56. "you should know by now that the Son of Man did not come to destroy people's lives, but to save them!" And without any confrontation, they journeyed on to another village.
57. And it occurred that as they were going along the road, a man came up to Him and said, "Lord, I want to follow You wherever You go!"
58. And Jesus replied, "Oh? Do you really? Listen...foxes have holes in which to lurk and the birds of the air have nests in which to roost... but the Son of Man lives the life of a vagabond...when He is in ministry mode, He has no physical place to lay His head."
59. Then He said to another, "I want you to become My disciple and

accompany Me!" But the man replied, "Lord, permit me first to go and await the death of my father so that I can give him a decent burial."

60. But Jesus said to him, "Let the dead bury their own dead...but as for you, in the meantime, go and publish abroad throughout the whole area the Kingdom of God."

61. Yet another approached Him and said, "I will follow You, Lord, and become Your disciple...become one of Your very own...but let me first say good-bye to those at my home."

62. Jesus said to him, "No, you won't...no one who puts his hand to the plow and looks back to the things behind is fit for the stewardship of the Kingdom of God."

Chapter 10

1. So after this—after sending out the original Twelve—Jesus appointed seventy others (or other type ministries) and sent them in partnerships of two ahead of Him into every town and place where He intended to go, to saturate the entire area with the message and to prepare the way for Him.

2. And He told them, "The harvest is huge, but the harvest hands, in the natural, are few. Ask the Lord of the harvest, therefore, to send out workers into His harvest field.

3. "And just go! As I have told you that you have a cross to embrace (even as I do), I also tell you that I am sending you out like sacrificial lambs (even as I am) among the wolves of religion.

4. "And I reiterate that you are not to take external equipment with you...depend, instead, entirely on your internal gifts. Be careful how you greet those you pass on the road, and don't waste a lot of time engaging in non-essential small talk.

5. "When you do enter a house, first declare a blessing of peace on it, saying, 'Peace to this house!'

6. "If, indeed, a man of peace is in authority there, he will receive your blessing, connect with it, and open up to you. But if it's not received, take it for yourself, knowing that no verbalized blessing is ever wasted. And get out...don't impose yourself, or waste your time on people who don't want peace.

7. "But if you do find a house of peace, stay in that house, eating and drinking whatever they serve you, for the worker deserves his wages.

Build relationships if you can...don't move around from house to house.

8. "When you enter a town and are welcomed, eat what is set before you, without getting into disputes with your hosts about customs and laws regarding food. In other words, when you are in any given town, become like the people in that town, and accept their way of doing things.

9. "Most importantly, heal the sick who are there and tell them, 'The revelation of the Kingdom of God is very near you right now!'

10. "But, by the same token, if you enter a town and are not welcomed, go out into its streets and say, publicly,

11. 'The dust of your town that sticks to our beautiful feet...feet that bring Good News to you...we openly and symbolically wipe off against you! And yet, you should still know that the Kingdom of God is very near you!

12. 'It is so near, in fact, that it will be more bearable on that day for Sodom than for that town.

13. 'Be warned of destruction, Korazin! You, too, Bethsaida! For if the miracles that were performed in you had been performed in Tyre and Sidon, they would have had a complete paradigm shift long ago, demonstrating it in the traditional way.

14. 'But it will be more bearable for Tyre and Sidon than for you when judgment comes on this nation.

15. 'And you, Capernaum...will you be lifted up to the heights? On the contrary...you will go down to the depths.'

16. "The simple truth is this...whoever listens to you, listens to Me; whoever rejects you rejects Me; whoever rejects Me rejects Him Who sent Me."

17. A little later, the seventy returned with great excitement, saying, "Lord, even the rebel spirits submit to us in Your name!"

18. But He replied, "I don't understand why you're so elated about that—I saw the Adversary fall like lightning from heaven—of course the spirits are subject to you...what else did you expect?

19. "You need to embrace this truth about yourselves: I have given you authority to trample on snakes and scorpions and to overcome all the power of the Adversary, or of anyone that you perceive to be an adversary! Absolutely nothing can harm you.

20. "But get it in perspective...don't rejoice that the spirits submit to you...that's really not anything to get all that excited about. Rejoice,

rather, that your names are written in the heavenlies!"

21. When He said that, Jesus became elated...exuberant in the Holy Spirit...and He cried out, joyfully, "I thank you, Father, Master of heaven and earth, that You hid these things from the presumptuous ones who think they know it all and revealed them to these innocent ones...these children, untainted by the cynicism of religion...these newcomers to the mysteries of the spirit realm. Yes, Father, it pleased You to do it this way."

22. He went on to say, "All things have been committed to Me by My Father...no one fully comprehends Who the Son is except the Father...no one fully comprehends Who the Father is except the Son and those to whom the Son chooses to reveal Him."

23. Then He turned to His disciples and said, privately, "Do you have any idea how blessed you are to be able to see what you are seeing?

24. "There are plenty of prophets and sages...even kings...who would have literally given anything to witness something like this but never got so much as a glimpse of anything like it...they longed to hear what you are hearing but were never able to tap into it."

25. On a particular occasion an expert in the Law approached Jesus with the intention of testing Him. "Teacher," he asked, "what must I do to realize the benefits of eternal life?"

26. "Well, what is written in your Law?" He replied. "How do you perceive and interpret it?"

27. He answered, "It's simple...'Love the Lord your God with all your heartfelt passion, your willed intention, and with all your energy, and with all your intellect or intelligence'; and, 'Love your neighbor as unconditionally as you love yourself.'"

28. "You have answered correctly...that's all it is," Jesus replied. "Do this and you will manifest the full potential of eternal life."

29. But that wasn't enough for this religious expert...he wanted to justify himself, so he asked Jesus, "All right...but who, exactly, is my neighbor?"

30. Jesus replied, "Let Me explain it this way: A certain man was going down from Jerusalem to Jericho when he became the victim of merciless robbers. They stripped him of all his clothes, beat him up, and went away, leaving him for dead.

31. "A priest just happened to be traveling down the same road, and when he saw the man lying there, bruised, bloody and naked, he was repulsed by the sight and passed by on the other side.

32. *"Then a Levite going the same way passed him and had the same reaction as the priest. Not wanting to get involved or touched by the man's condition, he also passed by on the other side.*
33. *"But a Samaritan, as he traveled, came to where the man was and, when he saw him, was moved to compassionate action.*
34. *"Without hesitation, he went to the man, bandaged his wounds and poured oil and wine on them. Then he picked the man up and put him on his own donkey, took him to a nearby inn and spent the night personally taking care of him.*
35. *"The following morning, he took out two silver coins and gave them to the innkeeper. 'I have to leave', he said, 'but I want you to look after him...and, when I return, I will reimburse you for any extra expenses.'*
36. *Now, which of these three do you think was a neighbor to the man who was victimized by inhumane robbers and indifferent holy men?"*
37. The expert in the Law replied, "Well, I suppose the one who had mercy on him." Jesus told him, *"Then go and do likewise."*
38. Then Jesus and His disciples went on their way, and they came to a village where a woman named Martha opened her home to Him in a show of hospitality.
39. And Martha had a sister named Mary, who sat at Jesus' feet, listening intently to everything He said.
40. But Martha, in an effort to be a good hostess and to make Jesus and His disciples feel comfortable in her home, became distracted by all the preparations that had to be made for dinner. So she came to Him and said, "Lord, does it not bother You to see that my inconsiderate sister has left me to do the work in the kitchen all by myself? It certainly bothers me! Tell her to get busy and help me!"
41. Unmoved, Jesus replied, *"Oh Martha, Martha...you are worried and upset about so many trivial and unimportant things.*
42. *"You should re-prioritize and embrace the fact that only one thing is really necessary...and your sister, Mary, has chosen that one, superior thing! And the thing that she has chosen will never be taken away from her."*

Chapter 11

1. One day Jesus was praying in a certain place and, when He finished, one of His disciples approached Him and said, "Lord, please teach us

to pray, just as John taught his disciples."

2. So He said to all of them, "All right, when you pray, say something like this: 'Our Father—not My Father…not your Father…but our Father Who is in the heavenly realm—may Your name be hallowed by us and always kept holy in our collective consciousness…may Your Kingdom continue to come to us, and in us, and through us. May Your will be done on earth…in the physical realm…as it is in heaven…in the spiritual realm.

3. 'Give us—not Me, not you, but us—give us this day, our daily bread…just the provision that we need in the now…no more…no less.

4. 'Forgive us, collectively, our sins, as we also forgive everyone who sins against us, collectively. And lead us…together…not into temptation.'"

5. Then He said to them, "Imagine that you have a friend and you go to him at midnight and say, 'Hey, buddy…lend me three loaves of bread.

6. "I'm asking because a friend of mine on a journey has come to visit me, and I have nothing to serve him to eat tonight.'

7. "And then suppose that your friend answers, 'Go away…don't bother me! The outer door to my front courtyard is already locked, and my entire household, including the children, is in bed. I can't get up right now and give you anything.'

8. "Here's the thing: even though he won't get up and give you the bread because of the obligation of your friendship, because of your shameless audacity…your absolute persistence…he will, no doubt, get up and give you as much bread as you need.

9. "So I say to you…keep on asking—never stop expressing your desires or challenging the boundaries of your faith—and it will ultimately be given you. Keep on seeking—never abandon your sense of wonder or your inquisitive interest in the mysterious—and you will ultimately find. Keep on knocking—never believe that your possibilities are exhausted or that your opportunities are finite—and the door will ultimately be opened to you.

10. "Do it because everyone in this life who keeps on asking keeps on receiving. And he or she who keeps on seeking keeps on finding. And to him or her who keeps on knocking, doors will continue to be opened.

11. "Look…what father is there of you, if his hungry son asks him for a

12. "Or if he asks for an egg, will give him a scorpion for dinner?
13. "If you then, with all of your potential for evil, know how to give good and beautiful gifts to your children, how much more will your Father Who is in the heavenly realm lavish the Holy Spirit on those who keep making a demand on Him!"
14. Once Jesus was expelling a spirit that was mute from a man. When the spirit left, the man spoke and the crowd was absolutely amazed.
15. But some of the cynics who were present said, "It is only by Beelzebub, the Lord of the Flies, that this charlatan exorcises spirits."
16. Others, unimpressed by this show of His authority, tested Him by asking for a sign from heaven.
17. Jesus saw right through them, knowing what they were thinking, and said to them, "Every kingdom divided against itself will be ruined, and every city or household divided against itself will not stand.
18. "If Beelzebub is divided against himself, how can he maintain his domain over the flies of the dunghill? I say this because you claim that I drive out spirits by his authority.
19. "Now, if I expel darkness by his authority, then how do your exorcists drive it out? So then, they will be your judges.
20. "But if it is by the Spirit of God that I drive out darkness, then the now-ness of the Kingdom of God has been revealed to you.
21. "When a fully armed strong man guards his own house, his possessions are safe.
22. "But when someone even stronger attacks and overpowers him, he takes away the armor in which the man trusted and divides the spoils.
23. "Whoever is not in the flow with Me rejects the authority of My Kingdom. So if you're not helping to bring about Kingdom purposes, you're making things worse for everybody.
24. "When an evil spirit comes out of a person, it goes through arid places—places that have not been watered by the water of the Word—seeking rest, and does not find it. Then it says, 'I think I will return to the house I left.'
25. "And when it arrives, it finds the house vacant and unoccupied, swept clean and put in order.
26. "Then it goes and takes with it seven other spirits even more wicked than itself, and they go in and live there. And so the final condition

of that person is actually worse than the first."

27. As Jesus was saying these provocative words, a woman in the crowd became overcome with emotion and called out, "Blessed is the womb of the mother who gave birth to You...and blessed are her breasts that nursed You!"
28. Without missing a beat, He replied, "No...blessed are those who hear the Word of God and fully embrace it!"
29. As the crowds increased, Jesus said, "This is an immature and manipulative generation. It asks for a miraculous sign, but none will be given it except the sign of the prophet Jonah.
30. "For as Jonah in his day was a sign to the Ninevites, so also will the Son of Man be to this generation in the now.
31. "The Queen of the South will rise in judgment with this generation and sentence it; for she came from a faraway land to listen to Solomon's wisdom, and now One greater than Solomon is here.
32. "The people of Nineveh will stand up when this generation is judged and accuse it; for they had a paradigm shift at the preaching of Jonah, and now One greater than Jonah is here.
33. "Look...no one lights a lamp and then puts it in a place where it will be hidden, or under some kind of covering. Instead, he puts it on its stand so that those who come in may be illuminated.
34. "In the same way, your perception is the lamp of your entire existence. When your perception is made right, your whole life will be enlightened. But when it is unhealthy, your life will be full of darkness.
35. "So see to it that you do not allow the light within you to be darkened.
36. "Therefore, if your whole life—your way of thinking and being—is full of light, and no part of it dark, it will be totally and absolutely enlightened. Your life will be illuminated in the same way that a room is made bright by the lighting of a lamp."
37. When Jesus had finished saying these things, a Pharisee came up to Him and invited Him to eat at his house. Being in the habit of accepting just about every social invitation, Jesus went with the man and reclined at his table.
38. But the Pharisee couldn't get past the fact that Jesus didn't first wash before the meal in the customary way.
39. Being aware of this, He said to him, "You know what? You Pharisees make such a production out of cleaning the outside of cups

and dishes, while you completely ignore the obvious truth that inside yourselves you are full of greed and wickedness.

40. "Your religion has made you people ridiculous! Didn't the One Who made the external world make the internal world, also?

41. "If you'd stop worrying for one minute about the superficial rules and start caring about what's happening with real people—if you'd give what's inside the dish to the poor, for example—then everything that actually matters would be clean for you.

42. "You Pharisees sicken Me! You are so faithful to tithe to God a tenth of all your produce, but you completely neglect things like speaking out about justice and tolerance, and ministering on the love of God! I'm not saying that you shouldn't tithe; I'm saying that you should have practiced tithing without it having become a mechanical ritual...a thing that causes you to leave these other important things undone.

43. "You Pharisees are going to face ruin because you love the attention...the applause...the notoriety of having the most important seats in the synagogues and being treated like celebrities out in the marketplaces.

44. "You Pharisees are going to become absolutely obsolete...you are like unmarked graves, which people walk over without knowing it."

45. One of the experts in the Law who was present at the table answered Him, "Teacher, when You insult the Pharisees like this, You insult us, also."

46. Jesus replied, "You experts in the Law...I say the same things to you! You load people down with burdens that they can hardly carry...rules and regulations that didn't even come from God...religious observations that are self-serving for you, which prop up your agendas...and you yourselves will not lift one finger to help them!

47. "Calamity is coming to you, too, because you build extravagant tombs for the prophets, and it was your own forefathers who killed them.

48. "In so doing, you testify that you approve of what your forefathers did...they killed the prophets, and you build their tombs.

49. "This is why God, in His foreknowledge, said, *'I will send them prophets and apostles, some of whom they will kill and others they will persecute and run off.'*

50. "Therefore, this generation will be held responsible for the blood of all the prophets that has been shed...not just the ones you know

about, but all the ones since the beginning of the world.
51. "I'm referring to everything and all of them, from the blood of Abel, to the blood of Zechariah who was killed between the altar and the sanctuary. I'm telling you the truth, this generation will reap the bitter harvest for it all.
52. "Destruction is coming to you experts in the Law because your legalism and closed-minded perspective and influence has taken away the very key to knowledge from your people. It's bad enough that you yourselves have not entered the door of revelation...worse yet, you have hindered those who were entering on their own."
53. When Jesus left there that day, the Pharisees and the teachers of the Law began to aggressively and openly oppose Him...and from that point on they bombarded Him with controversial questions at every opportunity.
54. They had made it their goal to get Him to entrap and condemn Himself with His own words.

Chapter 12

1. Meanwhile, an enormous crowd began to gather...thousands trying to get close to Him, literally trampling on one another. Before addressing or even acknowledging them, Jesus began to speak to His disciples, saying: "Beware of the yeast or leaven of the Pharisees... it's nothing but sheer hypocrisy.
2. "The truth is, there is nothing concealed that will not be ultimately revealed...nothing hidden in the now that will not eventually be made known.
3. "Everything that you have said in the secrecy of the night will be heard in the bright light of daybreak...what you have whispered in the ear in the secret rooms will be proclaimed from the rooftops."
4. Then He began to speak to the larger crowd, saying, "I'm speaking to you all as My dear friends...don't be intimidated into silence or forced into phoniness by the threats of religious bullies. It's true that, with the cooperation of this present government, they have the power to destroy your physical life, but then what can they really do? There's nothing that they or anyone else can do to your real self...your inner being.
5. "If you're really going to be in awe of someone to the point that it makes you tremble and shake, be in awe of God...the God Who

holds both your entire external and internal realities in His hands.
6. "Look, aren't five sparrows sold for just two pennies in the open market? Do you realize that not one of them is forgotten by God?
7. "You are so important...your existence so valuable...that every single hair that grows out of your scalp has its own, personal inventory number. So you have nothing to fear...you are worth much more than many sparrows!
8. "You define your terms with Me...public acknowledgment brings public acknowledgment...if you act like you really know Me, I will act like I really know you, even before the angels of God.
9. "But when persecution comes on this nation, if you act like you don't know Me to save yourself, I will treat you the same way...even before the angels of God who can protect you in the hour of persecution.
10. "And speaking of the power of words...everyone who speaks a word against the Son of Man will be forgiven, but anyone who blasphemes against the Holy Spirit will not be forgiven. Let Me explain...it's all about the power of your words to create by the ability and influence of the Holy Spirit. Every sin and blasphemy can be automatically forgiven people because of the mercy extended to the limited flesh, but, when you are filled with the Holy Spirit, your words become so effective that they literally create your reality. So when you speak things out of your mouth which are contrary to the purpose and nature of the Holy Spirit, you actually speak blasphemy against Him...and He can't forgive you in order to prevent those words from coming to pass, because He has empowered you to have what you say. You'll just have to deal with the consequences of whatever you've said, whether for good or for evil. You can speak against Me as the Son of Man and I'll automatically forgive you of your wrong words; but when you are empowered by the Holy Spirit, the words that you speak against His nature will have to stand just as you said them. They will not be erased through forgiveness.
11. "And when the persecution comes, and you are brought before synagogues, rulers and authorities, that same Holy Spirit will be there for you. Don't even worry about how you will defend yourselves at that time or what you will say.
12. "The Holy Spirit will inspire your words and teach you at that time what you should say."
13. Then someone in the crowd called out to Him, "Teacher...command

my brother to divide the inheritance with me."
14. Jesus replied, "Who appointed Me to be an arbiter between the two of you in these matters?"
15. In response to this, He said to them, "You all need to watch out! You must be on your guard against all kinds of greed, because real life doesn't consist of an abundance of material possessions."
16. To underscore His point, He told them this illustration: "There was a certain rich landowner whose crops yielded an abundant harvest.
17. "So when he realized how much he had, he thought to himself, 'What am I going to do with all of this? I don't have adequate facilities to store my crops.'
18. "After giving it some thought, he said, 'All right, this is what I'll do. I'll tear down my barns and build bigger ones, and I'll store all my surplus grain there.
19. 'And then I'll say to myself, "Self, you have plenty of grain laid up for many years...more than enough to take care of yourself. Take life easy...don't worry about anyone else...don't even think about someone else's needs...just spend your time eating and drinking and having one big party!"'
20. "But God said to him, 'You foolish, selfish clown! Tonight your physical life will be terminated...now who will get what you have prepared for yourself, seeing as how you cared more about things than about relationships?'
21. "This is how things will turn out for those who only store up things for themselves, but never acquire spiritual prosperity."
22. Then Jesus said to His disciples: "This is why I keep telling you not to worry about your physical life...about what you will eat...or about your body...what you will wear.
23. "Real life...authentic life...is more than natural food, and the body is more important than clothes.
24. "Pay attention to the birds of the air. They don't sow or reap, they don't have storerooms or barns, but they never go hungry, because God feeds them. And, as I've told you before, you are so much more valuable than birds!
25. "Anyway, who of you by worrying can add even a single hour to your life?
26. "So, since you can't even do that, what's the point of worrying about anything?
27. "Pay attention, also, to how the wild flowers grow. They don't labor

or obsess about what they're going to wear, and I tell you that not even Solomon in all his splendor was dressed as well as one of them.

28. "So think about it...if that's how God clothes the flowers and the grass of the field—plants which are here today and thrown into the fire tomorrow—how much more will He clothe you, you of small faith!

29. "And don't fixate on what you're going to eat or drink...don't even worry about it.

30. "People who don't know anything about God, or about His paternal love and affection for humanity, are preoccupied with such things...your Father knows full well that you need them.

31. "But seek out and search for a revelation of His Kingdom in and through every circumstance and in every situation. When you prioritize the Kingdom in this way, then you can be sure that everything in your personal world will come into order and that all you need for your daily provision will just automatically flow into your life and will be added to you as a result of your quest.

32. "Don't be afraid of anything, little flock, because it pleases your Father to no end to give you the abundance of the Kingdom.

33. "When you can, sell some of your possessions and give the money to the poor. Create a spiritual bank for yourselves that will not ever be emptied...treasures in the heavenly dimension that will never be devalued...a secure place that no bank robber can penetrate and no pest can destroy.

34. "The bottom line is this: where your treasure is, there your affections and thoughts will be, also.

35. "Stay prepared...ready for service...keep your lights on.

36. "Be like people waiting for the owner of their company to return from his honeymoon, so that when he arrives and knocks on the door of the business, they can immediately open up for him.

37. "Those employees whose boss finds them watching for him will be glad that they were prepared. The truth is that, not only will he be glad to see them, he will actually dress himself to serve them and personally wait on them at his own special table.

38. "It will be advantageous for those employees whose employer finds them ready to see him, even if he comes at an unexpected or inconvenient time.

39. "Furthermore, you know that if the office manager had been aware that a burglar or vandal was coming, he wouldn't have stayed out

late and left the place untended and unlocked.

40. "So don't be careless or clueless...just when you don't expect Him, the Son of Man will be revealed."

41. Peter asked Him, "Lord, are You trying to get a message to us with this illustration, or is this story for everyone?"

42. Jesus answered his question indirectly, saying, "So, who is a qualified and trustworthy manager whom the owner of the company puts in charge of his employees to make sure that they have everything that they need, when they need it?

43. "It will be good for that employed man or woman whom the owner finds faithfully doing his or her job anytime he decides to return to take inventory of his company.

44. "The truth is that he will promote such an employee and put him or her in charge of his entire corporation.

45. "But let's say, hypothetically, that such a manager (perhaps a man) says to himself, 'My boss is going to be gone a long time,' and he then begins to physically abuse the men in the company, and harass the women and be inappropriate with them...maybe he even begins to drink on the job and get drunk in the middle of the day.

46. "Inevitably, the owner of the company will show up on a day when he does not expect him and at an hour that is the most inopportune for him. The boss will no doubt cut him down to size and utterly demote him.

47. "That manager who is very familiar with his boss's way of doing things, his standard of excellence and the company policies, and still doesn't conduct himself in the way that he should, might even get mysteriously beaten up in an alley somewhere.

48. "But the one whose poor job performance is simply the result of ignorance or inexperience won't be dealt with so harshly. Let Me put it this way: from everyone who has been given much, much will be expected and demanded...and from the one who has been entrusted with a lot of responsibility, much more will be asked of him or her.

49. "I'm telling you this because I have come to baptize the earth with fire, and I am ready to get the fire started!

50. "I have My own personal fiery baptism ahead of Me, and I'm ready to go ahead and face it...ready to deal with it now!

51. "So do you suppose that I have come to only bring peace to the earth? Definitely not...sometimes before there can be peace, there

has to first come a division.

52. "In the days ahead, especially when the persecution on this nation begins, in one house there will be five divided among themselves... three against two and two against three.

53. "Families will even be divided...father against son and son against father...mother against daughter, and daughter against mother... mother-in-law against her daughter-in-law and daughter-in-law against her mother-in-law."

54. He went on to say to the crowd of people, "Look...when you see a cloud rising in the west, you automatically say, 'It's going to rain!' And, indeed, it does.

55. "In the same way, when you see that a south wind is blowing, you say, 'It's going to be so hot today!' And, sure enough, it occurs.

56. "You bunch of misguided phonies! You know how to intelligently discern and interpret the appearance of the earth and sky, but you have absolutely no idea how to discern and interpret the times! You're completely unaware that a whole new world is coming!

57. "Why can't you just personally decide what is right?

58. "But since you can't seem to do that, let Me give you some advice to help you through the transition that is on its way...as you go with your accuser before a magistrate, on the way to see the judge, make a real effort to settle out of court. If you don't do that, but instead inflexibly hold onto your irrelevant religion and your obsolete laws and your antiquated customs, the judge will turn you over to the officer and the officer will put you in prison.

59. "And don't be naive...you won't get out until you have paid the very last penny of your fine."

Chapter 13

1. Around this time, Jesus was informed that Pilate had had some people from Galilee executed as they were offering sacrifices in the Temple. There was a lot of rumor and innuendo swirling around the incident; it wasn't clear what had actually happened, but for some reason they had mixed their own blood with the blood of the sacrifices on the altar. Whatever the case, there seemed to be some sentiment among those who heard about it that those who were killed had it coming to them.

2. "Do you honestly think that those Galileans were worse sinners than

all the other people from Galilee?" Jesus asked. "In your self-righteous opinion, is that why they suffered like this?

3. "Absolutely not! First of all, you need to be much more concerned about your own need for a paradigm shift...about your own sins...about your own relationship with God.
4. "But what about the eighteen people who died when the tower in Siloam fell on them? That was just a random thing that happened; they weren't killed for any particular reason on their part, as far as anyone knows. Were they the worst sinners in Jerusalem?
5. "Certainly not...and I say again that, unless you change the way that you think about things like this, you are going to bring destruction upon yourselves."
6. Then He told them this illustration: "A certain man had a fig tree growing in his vineyard, and one day he went to look for fruit on it but didn't find any.
7. "So he said to the man who was responsible for taking care of the vineyard, 'Look, I've been coming to inspect fruit on this fig tree for three years now and haven't ever found any. I think it's time to cut it down! Why should it use up the good soil?'
8. "The man replied, 'Sir, please leave it alone for one more year; in the meantime, I'll dig around it and fertilize it.
9. 'If next year it finally bears fruit, fine! If not, then I'll personally cut it down.'"
10. On a particular Sabbath, Jesus was teaching and ministering in one of the local synagogues.
11. There was a woman there that day who was completely bent over with crippling arthritis and she had been that way for eighteen years.
12. When Jesus saw her, He called her up in front of the crowd and said to her, "Ma'am, I announce to you that today you are set free from your infirmity!"
13. Then He placed His hands on her, and immediately she straightened right up and began to praise God.
14. Furious that Jesus had once again healed on the Sabbath, the leader of the synagogue said to the people, "You know, there are six whole days for work in a week...come and be healed on one of those days...not on the sacred Sabbath!"
15. But Jesus openly rebuked him in front of his congregation, saying, "You hypocritical phonies! You all do your menial tasks on the 'sacred' Sabbath, don't you? You untie your ox or donkey from its

16. "So, should not this sweet lady—this daughter of Abraham who has been cursed with devilish arthritis for eighteen long years—be set free on the Sabbath day from the condition that bound her?"
17. When He said these confrontational words, His usual opponents were clearly and openly humiliated. But His audience saw Him as a hero that day...a champion of the people who cared about them more than about proper protocol on the Sabbath...and they were delighted with all the wonderful things He was doing.
18. Then Jesus asked, "How can I explain the Kingdom of God to you? What illustration will make it understandable?
19. "All right, think of it this way: It's like a seed, say a tiny mustard seed, which a man took one day and planted in his garden. And that insignificant seed eventually grew and became a huge tree...so big, in fact, that the birds of the air were able to perch in its branches."
20. Then He said, "Let Me see...how else can I describe it to you? How can I fully reveal the mysteries of the Kingdom and its progressively increasing influence in the earth?
21. "Here's another comparison: it's like yeast that a woman took and mixed into about sixty pounds of flour until it worked all through the dough. And then she waits for all the dough to rise."
22. He went on teaching that basic message of the Kingdom from town to village...village to town...but, little by little, He was really making His way toward Jerusalem.
23. On the way, someone asked Him, "Lord, in the end, will only a few be saved?" And He said to them,
24. "You need to be thinking about the now...about making the effort to enter into the Kingdom mentality by the narrow door that provides access to it. Many will try to grasp the concept of it, trying to enter it without repentance or revelation, but they will not be able to get in.
25. "It's just like when the master of a household gets up and officially closes the door for the evening. You may stand outside and knock on the outer door again and again, saying, 'Sir, open up to us!' But he will most likely answer you, 'I don't know what household you come from...certainly not mine.'
26. "And then you may reply, 'Hey...we ate and drank with you...you were a familiar voice in our community.'
27. "But he will say, 'Seriously, I don't know what household you come

from...you're definitely not a part of this one. Get out of here and go to your own homes, you strangers!'

28. "And you will have to stand outside all night in the cold, where your teeth will chatter from the cold and where you will grind them in anger as you see Abraham, Isaac, Jacob, and all the prophets enter the house because they understand what is happening in the Kingdom of God in the now. Your anger will be increased because you yourselves will be driven away by your own lack of understanding.

29. "And if that's not enough to set you off, you will also see people come from eastern lands and western lands, from the north and the south—all the people that you thought were not invited to the celebration at all—sit down and feast at the table in the Kingdom of God.

30. "You don't realize this and don't believe it when I say it, but there are some who are now 'last,' as it were, who will then be 'first'...and there are some who are now considered 'first' who will then be 'last.'"

31. Within an hour of hearing Him speak these words, some Pharisees came up to Him and said, "You need to get out of here...run for Your life! Don't You know that Herod is determined to kill You?"

32. And He replied in a very direct manner, "Please...feel free to go and tell that fox for Me that I expel rebel spirits and perform healings today and tomorrow...and on the third day I will triumphantly finish My course. I don't have time for him or his empty threats.

33. "I'm going to do what I'm going to do, today and tomorrow and the day after that. Besides, it's not proper for a prophet to come to a bad end outside Jerusalem...the whole thing will have its consummation there...and it won't happen until I get there!"

34. But then, in a moment of feeling the conflict between being simultaneously connected and disconnected from them, He said wistfully, "O Jerusalem...Jerusalem...you who continue to kill the prophets and to stone those who are sent to you! You have no idea how often I've desired...yearned, even...to gather your children together around Me as a hen gathers her young under her wings. I'll fulfill My own destiny (with or without your support), but, truth be told, I truly wanted to embrace you, but you just wouldn't have it!

35. "But it doesn't matter now; what's about to happen is about to happen and your house is forsaken. You won't see Me again until

the day of reconciliation when you all confess together, 'Blessed is He Who comes in the name of God.'"

Chapter 14

1. Regardless of previous experiences, Jesus once again went to eat in the house of a prominent Pharisee on a particular Sabbath. And, as was always the case in such an environment, He was being carefully watched and scrutinized.
2. Right there in front of Him was a man who was suffering from a condition like dropsy, which caused abnormal swelling in his body.
3. So Jesus said to the Pharisees and the experts in the Law who were present, "Let Me ask you gentlemen something...is it lawful to heal on the Sabbath or not?"
4. Even though this was a repeat of a previous scenario, the men still didn't have a reasonable answer to Jesus' provocative question, so they remained completely silent. Then Jesus authoritatively but compassionately took hold of the man, healed him, and sent him on his way.
5. Once the man was gone, He asked them, "If one of you has a child, or even an ox, that falls into a well on the Sabbath day, won't you immediately pull it out?"
6. But still they had nothing to say. They just sat there in silence, unable to be even the slightest bit objective about their tradition and belief system.
7. So, moving on from this dead-end of a subject, He noticed how the guests picked the places of honor at the table, and spoke to that, instead. He told them this illustration:
8. "Listen...when someone invites you to a formal wedding feast, don't be presumptuous enough to take the place of honor. You never know if a person more distinguished than you may have been invited and that place was intended for him or her.
9. "If, indeed, that is the case, the host who invited both of you will have to come and say to you, 'Please give this person your seat.' Then, humiliated, you will have to take the least important place, creating an awkward situation for everyone involved.
10. "So when you are invited, just automatically take the lowest place. That way, when your host comes to greet you, he will say to you, 'Friend, please...I insist that you move up to a better place.' Then

you will be honored and admired right there in the presence of all the other guests.

11. "You see, all those who exalt themselves will be humbled...and all those who humble themselves will be exalted."

12. Then Jesus turned to His host and said, "When you give a luncheon or a dinner, don't invite your friends...don't invite your brothers or your sisters...in fact, don't invite any of your relatives...and, by all means, don't invite your rich neighbors. If you invite any of them, they will most likely invite you back, and so you will be repaid.

13. "No...when you give a banquet, invite the poor and the disenfranchised...invite the crippled and the helpless...invite the lame...invite the blind;

14. "if you do that, you will be fully blessed. And although these people can't repay you, you will be repaid in the bigger picture with resurrection life and the benefits of righteousness."

15. When one of the guests at the table heard Him say this, he blurted out, "How blessed are those who will eat at the celebration feast in the Kingdom of God!"

16. This prompted Jesus to expound some more on the subject. He said, "There was a certain man who prepared an extravagant banquet and invited many guests.

17. "When it was time for the banquet to commence, he sent his personal servant to tell those who had been invited, 'Come now...the table is set...everything is ready.'

18. "But each of the invited guests that he approached began to make ridiculous excuses. The first one to whom he spoke said, 'You know what? I've just bought a field, and I have to go right now and see it. Please send my regrets.'

19. "The next one said, 'Listen, I've just bought five yoke of oxen and I'm on my way, even as we speak, to try them out. Thanks, anyway.'

20. "Still another said, 'Hey, I just got married, so I obviously can't come.'

21. "So the servant came back and reported all of this to his employer. Then the owner of the house felt insulted and became incensed. So he ordered his servant, 'Go out immediately into the streets and back alleys of the city and bring in the poor, the crippled, the blind and the lame.'

22. "In a short while the servant responded, 'Sir, what you've ordered

has been done, but there is still room at your table.'
23. "Undaunted, the host told his servant, 'All right then, go out to the dirt roads and country lanes and compel the rest of them to come in...drag them in if you have to...I want my house to be full!'"
24. Then Jesus said, "I tell you the truth...not one of those who were privileged to be originally invited to My feast will get so much as a taste of the food at My Kingdom-banquet."
25. Right after this, a huge crowd was walking along with Jesus on a particular day, and He stopped, turned to them, and said,
26. "Listen...if anyone comes to Me and does not make God his or her top priority, he or she can't be My disciple. Let Me put it this way: if you don't have a relative disregard for your parents, wife, husband, children, or siblings, in comparison with your attitude and affection toward God...even if you love your own life more than Him...you can't really follow Me.
27. "And whoever does not persevere and carry his or her own cross, even as I carry Mine, can't be My true disciple.
28. "I mean, which of you, planning to build a building on your farm or for your business, doesn't first sit down and calculate the cost to see whether or not you have sufficient means to finish it?
29. "You know full well that if you don't do that, when you've laid the foundation and are unable to complete the structure, everyone who sees it will begin to mock and jeer at you.
30. "They'll say, 'This man began to build something, but was not able to finish what he started.'
31. "Or, to put it another way, what king going out to engage in war with another king will not first sit down and consider the big picture? No, he'll take counsel with his advisers to see whether he is able, even with ten thousand men, to meet the one who opposes him with possibly twenty thousand.
32. "And, if after the war counsel has examined the situation from every angle, he realizes that it just can't be done, he devises another strategy. When the other king is still very far away, he sends an envoy to appease him, and begins peace talks with the enemy.
33. "The bottom line is this for any and all of you: if you do not forsake all—or if you're not at least willing to do whatever has to be done for the Kingdom—you just can't be My disciple.
34. "Look...salt is good; in fact, it's an excellent thing when it's used properly. But if salt loses its strength and becomes flat, how can its

saltiness ever be restored?
35. "It's not fit for anything....completely useless. I'm speaking in abstract terms, but I ask you to listen with real comprehension...hear this with your spiritual ear."

Chapter 15

1. Jesus' charisma and anointing regularly attracted a wide array of people-types, but, at this point in His ministry, an unusually large number of characters of dubious reputation seemed to be surrounding Him all the time. The hated tax collectors who were friendly with the oppressive Roman government—along with a variety of sinners of scandalous notoriety—were with Him constantly, hanging on to His every word and hearing Him with apparent comprehension.
2. The self-righteous Pharisees and teachers of the Law were shocked by His tolerance of them and by their obvious mutual familiarity. They whispered among themselves, "This man makes reprobates feel accepted and right at home...He openly socializes with them all the time."
3. So Jesus answered them with this illustration:
4. "Imagine that a shepherd has a hundred fine sheep and loses one of them. If he's a good shepherd, wouldn't he leave the ninety-nine in the open country and go after the lost one until he finds it?
5. "And when he finds it, wouldn't he joyfully put it on his shoulders?
6. "Wouldn't he then bring it home and call his friends and neighbors together and say to them, 'Come celebrate with me...I have found my lost sheep!'
7. "The truth is that, in the very same way, there will be more celebration in the heavenly realm over one transgressor who has a paradigm shift, than over ninety-nine people who think that there is no room for improvement in their own lives and stay exactly the same as they were.
8. "Or let's say a woman has ten silver coins and loses one of them. In that case, doesn't she light a lamp, sweep the whole house, and search it thoroughly until she finds the money?
9. "And, just like the shepherd, when she finds it she calls all her friends and neighbors together and says, 'Come celebrate with me... I have found my lost coin!'

10. "Just like with the lost sheep, I reiterate, there is rejoicing in the presence of the angels of God over one rebel who changes his or her mindset."
11. Then, to further make His point about recovery, He told this story: "There was a certain wealthy landowner who had two sons.
12. "One day, the younger of the two of them came to his father and said, 'Sir, I want you to give me my inheritance now...all of it...the money and the part of the property that will eventually be mine, anyway.' And without protest, the father did exactly as his son had requested, dividing the estate between them.
13. "In almost no time, the younger son gathered up everything that he had and started out on a grand adventure, journeying into a distant country. Once he arrived at a place that suited him—a place that could accommodate his desire for an extravagant and hedonistic lifestyle—he started throwing money at anything and everything that could bring him pleasure. Before he knew it, he had recklessly wasted his entire fortune in the prodigal pursuit of his passions.
14. "As it turned out, when he had spent everything that he had, a terrible famine came upon that country and he became destitute.
15. "Desperate, he went and forced himself on one of the citizens of that country, begging for work. So that man took pity on him and sent him into his fields to feed his hogs.
16. "His situation continued to deteriorate to the point that he would gladly have fed on the carob pods that the hogs were eating (because they were eating better than he was at the time), but they couldn't satisfy his extreme hunger. But there was no alternative...nobody could provide him with anything better.
17. "Then he came to himself...he looked objectively at the picture of what he had become and compared it to the picture in his mind of what he knew he was supposed to be. And with that he said, 'How many hired servants on my father's estate have enough food...more than enough to eat, in fact...but here I am, dying of hunger in a land of strangers!
18. 'I'm going to get myself up, and I'm going to go to my father. And when I see him, I'm going to say to him, "Father, I have sinned against God, and in your sight.
19. "I'm not even worthy to be called your son any longer, seeing as how I have selfishly squandered the inheritance you freely gave me, disgracing your family's good name. Please, sir...if you see fit, just

make me like one of your hired servants, and I will work hard for everything I earn.'"

20. "So he got up out of the hog pen, and returned to his father, practicing his repentance speech the whole way there. But while he was still a long way off, his father recognized his emaciated frame, staggering up the road, and was moved with pity and tenderness for him. So, instead of proudly waiting for the son to come all the way to him...and without judgment...and without even thinking about anything that had happened in the past...he just started running toward his boy. And when he reached him, he grabbed him and held him tight, ignoring the stench of the hogs that was still on him, and started kissing him all over his thin, mud-smeared face.

21. "And the surprised son went into his rehearsed repentance speech, saying, 'Father, I have sinned against God and in your sight...I'm no longer worthy to be treated as your son...I don't even deserve to be recognized as a son of yours!'

22. "But the father didn't need to hear a word of it. He immediately said to one of his bond servants, 'Bring me, this instant, the very best robe...the festive robe reserved for guests of honor...and put it on him...cover him with it. And give him a family signet ring for his hand and sandals for his feet.

23. 'And not only that...go bring out that fine, wheat-fattened calf that we've been saving for a special occasion, and butcher it. Tonight we'll pull out all the stops, have a feast fit for a king, and raise the roof with celebration!

24. 'Don't you see? This is my son who was dead and is alive again...he was lost and is found!' And with those words, the entire household went into a state of revelry.

25. "But while all of this was happening, his older son was out working hard in the field. At the end of a long day's work, he returned to the main house and, as he approached, he heard music and dancing.

26. "So he called one of the servant boys to him and asked him what was going on.

27. "The boy excitedly said to him, 'Oh! Haven't you heard? Your little brother has come home, and your father has killed that wheat-fattened calf that he's been saving and has thrown him a huge party! He's so happy that his son is back, safe and well.'

28. "But the elder brother was furious at this news and began to make a scene. He refused to go inside the house, so his father came out and

began to reason with him, trying to calm him down.

29. "But he pushed his father away and said, 'Are you kidding me with this?! You can't be serious! All these many years I have served you and I've never once disobeyed any of your directives. But you've never given me so much as a young goat, so that I might have just a little get-together with my friends.
30. 'But all of a sudden, when this ungrateful, undisciplined, irresponsible son of yours shows up here, after having devoured your estate by spending everything you gave him on whores and God knows what else, you have killed for him the special wheat-fattened calf!'
31. "And the father said to him, 'Oh, buddy...don't you realize that you're always with me and that everything I have is yours? You can have anything you want at any time...just ask for it.
32. 'But I'm not going to make any apology for having this feast for your brother. If the celebration goes on all night long, so be it...it's the right thing to do. This brother of yours was dead and is alive again! He was lost and is found!'"

Chapter 16

1. Then Jesus told His disciples a very different type of story. He said, "There once was a certain rich businessman who had reason to believe that the manager of his entire operation was exploiting his place of authority by running up huge, personal expenses, and was just basically wasting his possessions.
2. "So one day he called the manager in and said, 'All right...what's going on with you? Something's not adding up with your accounting. I want you to give me an updated report of all your transactions, and an audit of all your books, because I'm going to have to terminate your position here.'
3. "Going into immediate damage control, the manager said to himself, 'What in the world am I going to do now? My employer is taking away my wonderful job, and I don't have any alternative prospects. I'm not strong enough to do manual labor, and I'm definitely too proud to beg.
4. 'All right...I know what I'll do, so that, when I do lose my job and income and am possibly living on the street, people will welcome me into their houses.'

5. "So he called in each of his employer's debtors and asked the first one, 'How much do you owe my boss?'
6. 'Nine hundred gallons of olive oil,' he replied. So the manager told him, 'This is what I want you to do...take your bill, sit down right here, and re-write it for four hundred and fifty.'
7. "Then he asked the second one, 'And how much do you owe him?' The man replied, 'A thousand bushels of wheat.' He told him, 'Then take your bill and make it out for eight hundred.'
8. "When the dishonest manager's employer found out what he had done, he actually commended him because of the shrewd way in which he dealt with the situation. The point is that the people who operate in this present world system are generally more savvy in dealing with their own kind...and of understanding their own generation...than are the people who walk in the Light.
9. "This is what I'm telling you: Be streetwise when you need to be. Don't be reluctant to use worldly wealth to gain friends for yourselves, so that when your money runs out, you can call in some favors and be welcomed into permanent dwellings.
10. "Whoever is trustworthy with very little will most likely be trustworthy with very much...and whoever is dishonest with very little will also be dishonest with much.
11. "So think about it...if you haven't been trustworthy in dealing with worldly wealth, who will trust you with true riches?
12. "Furthermore, if you haven't been trustworthy with someone else's property, who is going to give you property of your own?
13. "The bottom line is this: No one can serve two masters. You basically will hate the one and love the other, or you will be committed to the one and reject the other. You can't be submitted and servile to both God and the god of the world system called Mammon."
14. The Pharisees, who were submitted to Mammon (the money god), heard all this and dismissed Jesus as being hopelessly naive.
15. Unaffected by their disdain, He said to them, "You are the ones who justify yourselves in the eyes of others, but God knows what's really behind the masks. Besides, what people generally value highly is just gross in God's sight.
16. "The Law and the prophets were proclaimed until the days when John the Forerunner was at the height of his influence. Since that time, the Good News of the Kingdom of God is being preached and

people are still trying, in one way or another, to literally force themselves into it through their own efforts. Men of passion, like John, have demonstrated this effort and, frankly, it has been allowed because there was basically no alternative until now.

17. "But, even though the Kingdom is now so easily accessible, the Law is still going to be completely fulfilled, in a sense. In fact, it's easier for both the heavenly realm and the earthly dimension to totally disappear, than for the least stroke of a pen to drop out of what's written in the Law.

18. "For example, the Law says that whoever divorces his wife must simply give her a certificate of divorce…no questions asked. But I tell you that whoever just casually dismisses and divorces his wife for no good or valid reason, such as unfaithfulness or infidelity, will inadvertently cause her to go out and commit adultery herself. And whoever marries a woman who has been divorced in this way will inadvertently commit adultery with her, seeing that she will more than likely still consider herself married to her previous husband."

19. While He was still in the mode of changing their paradigms and creating new realities through the use of fictitious stories about rich men, He told them this allegory: "There was a certain rich man who was in the habit of clothing himself in purple and fine linen—the wardrobe of the wealthy in his world—and he regularly reveled and feasted fabulously, basically throwing an extravagant party for his snobbish clique every single day.

20. "Meanwhile, at the gate of his mansion there was an indigent and impoverished man named Lazarus who had been left there to beg. Not only was he utterly destitute, but he was also diseased and covered with ulcerated sores.

21. "Day after day he begged for any leftovers that might come from the rich man's abundantly furnished table, being in such poor physical condition that he couldn't even care for himself. The only relief that he had from the pain, itching and burning of his abscesses was when the stray dogs came and licked his sores, providing a natural antiseptic that canines carry within their saliva.

22. "Anyway, it happened that the pitiful beggar finally died on the rich man's doorstep and was mercifully carried by the angels into the realm where Abraham watched over the captive, departed spirits of men and women until they could be reconciled. Ironically, the rich man also died right about that same time and was buried.

23. "And in the realm of the dead which the Jews call *Sheol* and the Greeks call *Hades,* he lifted up his eyes in torment and saw Abraham far away, and Lazarus in his company.
24. "And he cried out and said, 'Father Abraham, have pity and mercy on me, and send Lazarus to dip the tip of his finger in water and cool my tongue, for I am in anguish in this purifying flame.'
25. "But Abraham said, 'Child, remember that in your lifetime you fully received an endless flow of comforts and delights, and Lazarus had nothing in his life but discomfort and distress...but now he is comforted here with me, and you are there in anguish.
26. 'Besides, between us who have been purified through suffering, and you who are indifferent to those who suffer, a great chasm has been fixed in order that those who want to pass from this place to you may not be able...and no one may pass from there to us without going through the fire. You didn't even notice the suffering going on all around you in life so, in your callousness, you have violated the most basic principles of the Kingdom of God in which the first will be last and the last will be first! So, all those, like you, who are uncaring... indifferent...unfeeling...will go into the fire for a period of time...into a fiery trial that will ultimately burn out everything in them that causes them to be blind to the needs of others.'
27. "And the man said, 'Then, Father Abraham, I beg you to send him to my father's house.
28. 'I have five brothers there who are just like me—selfish and self-indulgent—and I want him to warn them so that they can avoid this place of torment.'
29. "But Abraham said, 'They have Moses and the prophets...let them hear and listen to them for themselves.'
30. "But he answered, 'No, Father...if someone from the dead goes to them, they will have a paradigm shift and will embrace the Kingdom in their lifetime: feeding the poor, caring for the dying, creating a new way to look at the condition of the world.'
31. "But he said to him, 'Listen, if they don't hear Moses and the prophets, they won't be persuaded and convinced, even if someone should rise from the dead.'" And in giving them this extended metaphor, He revealed to them the new way of thinking that would be required of them if they desired to live the Kingdom-life.

Chapter 17

1. Then Jesus said to His disciples, "Look, it's inevitable that people are going to do things that cause other people to stumble, but it's so regrettable for that one who causes it to happen.
2. "In fact, it would actually be better for an individual to have one of those huge grinding stones that they use in the mills fastened around his neck, and then be sunk in the depth of the sea, than to hurt one of these precious, little ones…or to abuse them in any way…or take advantage of their simple trust…or cause them to grow up and become less than what they should have been.
3. "So watch yourselves. Furthermore, if your brother or sister wrongs you in any way, you should have the integrity to go and tell him or her about it, directly, and keep the conversation and the whole matter between the two of you. And if he or she gets what you're saying and has a change of heart and apologizes, you have no choice but to forgive them.
4. "I mean, even if they offend you seven times in a day, and seven times come back to you saying 'I sincerely apologize,' you must forgive them."
5. When the disciples heard how high His standard was for them in this area, they said to Him, "Lord, increase our faith to be able to deal with people in this way!"
6. He replied, "If you have faith, even as small as a mustard seed, you can say to this mulberry tree, 'Be uprooted and be re-planted in the sea,' and the thing will actually obey you. In other words, you can do this.
7. "This is how I want you to look at it: Suppose one of you has a servant who comes in from plowing in the field or tending the sheep. Would you take his coat, set the table, and just say to him, 'Sit down here and eat'?
8. "Wouldn't you be more likely to say, 'Prepare my supper first, get yourself ready and wait on me while I eat and drink…and after that you may have your supper'?
9. "Now, does the servant get special thanks for simply doing what's expected of him?
10. "Well, it's the same with you. When you've done everything that's expected of you, you should simply say, 'We're just doing our job…carrying out what we were told to do.'"

11. Later, on His way to Jerusalem, Jesus was traveling along the border between Samaria and Galilee.
12. And as He was going into a certain village, ten men who were stricken with leprosy came to meet Him, but they stood at a distance.
13. And they all called out together in one loud voice, "Jesus...Master...have compassion on us!"
14. When He saw and heard them, He said, "All right, go...show yourselves to the priests." And they did as He said and, as they went, they were completely cleansed from their disease.
15. But one of them, when he realized that his body was healed and made like new, came right back to find Him, all the while praising God in a loud voice.
16. When he at last saw Jesus, he ran up to Him, threw himself at His feet, and thanked and praised Him profusely. And, for the record, the man was a Samaritan.
17. Jesus said to him, "Sir, your praise is excellent...but were not all ten men cleansed as you were? Where are the other nine?
18. "Seriously...was no one able or thoughtful enough to return and give praise to God except for this one foreigner?"
19. Then He said to the man, "All right, get up and go into your new life as a well man...re-enter society...and know that your own faith has made you well."
20. On another occasion, the Pharisees asked Jesus when the Kingdom of God would come. He replied, "The Kingdom of God does not come with your careful observation...with setting dates...or counting the days on the calendar...in fact, you can't even see it with the physical eye.
21. "And no one can ever say, 'Here it is' or 'There it is,' because the Kingdom of God is within human hearts and minds...why, it's even within you Pharisees!"
22. Then He turned and said to His disciples, "The time will come when you'll want to see one of the days of the Son of Man, but you won't see it.
23. "People will, no doubt, tell you, 'There He is!' or 'Here He is!' Don't bother to go running off after them.
24. "For the Son of Man in His day will be revealed, and His revelation will come like lightning flashing...the kind that lights up the sky from one end to the other.
25. "But first, it is inevitable that He must suffer many things, and even

26. "Then, destruction will come on this nation and it will be just as it was in the days of Noah. But the end result will be the days of the revelation of the Son of Man.
27. "Prior to the flood, people were eating, drinking, marrying and being given in marriage, right up to the day that Noah entered the ark. Then the flood came and brought destruction.
28. "The same was in the days of Lot. People were eating and drinking, buying and selling, planting and building. Life there was going on as usual.
29. "But the very day that Lot left Sodom, fire and sulfur rained down from the sky and destroyed them all.
30. "It will be like this on the day the power of the Son of Man is revealed to this nation.
31. "When that destruction comes, no one who is on the roof of his house with his goods inside should even take the time to go down to get them. In the same way, no one who is out working in the field should go back for anything.
32. "To sum it up...just remember Lot's wife!
33. "As I've said before, whoever tries to keep his life will end up losing it, and whoever loses his life will ultimately preserve it.
34. "I tell you that when that happens, 'two men,' as it were, will be in one bed...one will be taken, one left behind. The full revelation of the Son of Man will take away from you the man that needs to be purged, and will leave behind the real you...the righteous you...the man that He has chosen.
35. "In the same way, 'two women' will be grinding at the mill...one will be taken in the Son of Man's flood, so to speak—the part of that woman that is subject to His judgment—but one...the real one...will be mercifully left behind, safe in the ark of His redemption.
36. "And 'two men' will be working in the field...likewise, one will be taken, and the other will be left intact, safe and sound."
37. "Where is that place of redemption, Lord?" they asked. He replied, "Where the carcass is; in the same way that a gathering of vultures indicates that there is something dead nearby, so these signs will reveal that the end of an era is near."

Chapter 18

1. Then Jesus told His disciples another illustrative story to show them how prayer should become their lifestyle, and to reiterate to them that they should never give up on believing for the best.
2. He said, "In a certain town, there was a judge who had no regard whatsoever for God and was uncaring, unfeeling and unsympathetic toward people.
3. "In the same town was a widow who was involved in a legal dispute with someone, and this lady kept coming to him with the same plea: 'I demand that you grant me justice against my adversary!'
4. "For awhile he completely ignored her, but finally he said to himself, 'It's quite obvious that I don't care what God or people think.
5. 'But it's also obvious that, clearly, this woman is not going to give up...she refuses to let this thing go...and I believe that she will keep harassing me until I give her what she wants. I'm going to personally see to it that she receives justice, so that she won't eventually come and attack me!'
6. Then Jesus said, "Listen to what the corrupt judge said.
7. "I mean, if an unjust man like him will ultimately respond to the relentless pursuit of a tenacious, little widow, how much more will God, Who is loving and kind, bring about justice for those in this nation who cry out to Him day and night? Why would He, in His benevolence, put them off?
8. "My point is, they will certainly receive justice, and quickly. But the question with which I am most concerned is this: when the Son of Man is revealed, will He find faith on the earth?"
9. Then He told another story, but this one was directed to those in the audience who were smugly self-righteous and to those who felt superior to everyone else. He said:
10. "One day, two men went up to the Temple to pray...one was a Pharisee and the other was a tax collector.
11. "The Pharisee stood by himself and, in a pretentiously pious and grandiose fashion, prayed loudly, saying, 'Oh God, I thank You that I am not like other people: scofflaws, riffraff, robbers, evildoers, adulterers...and I especially thank You that I'm not remotely like this tax collector.
12. 'You know that I fast twice a week and that I am a tither, even giving a tenth of my gross income.'

13. "But the tax collector stood at a distance, out of the spotlight. He wouldn't even look up, but totally humbled himself and said, 'God, have mercy on me, a rebel.'
14. "The truth is that this man, rather than the other, went home justified before God. For all those who exalt themselves will eventually be humbled, and those who humble themselves will ultimately be exalted."
15. Right around this time, people were beginning to bring their little children to Jesus for Him to place His hands on them and bless them when He was ministering. But the disciples saw this and started insulting them by preventing them to do this.
16. When Jesus saw what the disciples were doing, He said, indignantly, "You let these little children come right to Me, and don't you dare tell them that they aren't allowed or welcome! Childlikeness is the standard for the Kingdom of God, so, in essence, the Kingdom belongs to such as these.
17. "The truth is that anyone who will not perceive and receive the Kingdom of God like a little child will never enter it in the first place."
18. One day a certain ruler came up to Jesus and asked, "Teacher, You're good…so I ask You…what good thing must I do to be in full possession of eternal life?"
19. Jesus answered, "Why do you question Me about what's good; in fact, why do you even call Me good? God is the only One Who is good.
20. "If you want to enter the life of God, just practice His precepts… keep His commandments…and you will manifest His goodness in your life. You know them: 'You shall not commit adultery'…'You shall not murder'…'You shall not steal'…'You shall not give false testimony'…'Honor your father and mother.'"
21. "That's it?" asked the man, "That's all there is? I've kept all those commandments practically my whole life, and I'm still not good."
22. When Jesus heard this, He said to him, "Look, if you're really that serious about manifesting the character of God in your life, you still lack one thing. Go sell everything that you have, give everything that you make from the sale to the poor, and the entirety of your possessions will then be in the Kingdom and all that you own will be deposited into the heavenly realm."
23. When he heard this, he became very sad. The idea of selling

everything…this suggestion of total abandon…just seemed too extreme for him, especially because he was wealthy and had a lot of possessions. Jesus' words not only caught him off guard, they also overwhelmed and depressed him.

24. Jesus looked at him and said, "I tell you, truthfully, it is really quite difficult…extremely hard…for a rich man to become a subject in the Kingdom of God.
25. "In fact, it's easier for a camel to go through that little gate that they leave open at night in the walls of Jerusalem called 'The Needle's Eye'—the gate that is so low and narrow that a large animal can only pass through it on its knees, unencumbered with baggage—than for the rich to enter the Kingdom of God."
26. For some reason, those who heard this were staggered by these words. They said to Him, "Well, then, if that's the case, who has any chance of being fit for the Kingdom, at all?"
27. Jesus replied, "Things like this are virtually impossible when only using human strength…but with God's help, anything and everything is really possible!"
28. Then Peter spoke up and said, "Well, now that You mention it…we may not have had the kind of wealth that man has, but we've left everything that we did have to follow You. What are we going to get for our sacrifice?"
29. "Truthfully, no one who sacrifices home, wife, brothers, sisters, parents or children because of their desire to follow Me and to manifest the Kingdom-life
30. will fail to get every bit of it back many times over! And this is in addition to the promise of the full blessings of eternal or 'now'-life."
31. Then Jesus took the Twelve aside and said to them, "All right…we're going to Jerusalem now, and everything that has been written by the prophets about the Son of Man will be fulfilled there.
32. "You should all know that He will be delivered over to the Gentiles, and they will mock Him, insult Him and spit on Him.
33. "They will also flog Him, and then they will kill Him…but on the third day, He will rise again."
34. The disciples weren't able to grasp any of this. Even though this wasn't the first time He had told them about it, they just had no comprehension…no idea of what He was talking about.
35. But they started out for Jerusalem anyway and, as Jesus approached Jericho (which was on the way), He saw a blind man sitting by the

36. roadside, begging. When the man heard the crowd that was following Jesus going by, he asked someone what was happening.
37. They said to him, "Don't you know? Jesus of Nazareth is passing by!"
38. Without missing a beat, he called out, "Jesus...Son of David...have mercy on me!"
39. The ones at the front of the entourage rebuked him and told him to shut up, but he shouted even louder, "Son of David...have mercy on me!"
40. Jesus heard him and stopped in His tracks. Then He ordered the man to be brought to Him. When he was brought near, Jesus asked him,
41. "What do you want Me to do for you?" And he replied "Lord...I just want to see."
42. Then Jesus said, "All right, then...receive your sight...your own faith has healed you."
43. And, sure enough, he immediately received his sight and started following Jesus, praising God with a loud voice. When all the people around saw what had happened, they praised God, too.

Chapter 19

1. Jesus entered Jericho, although He was just passing through to Jerusalem where His earthly destiny would soon be fulfilled.
2. There was a man who lived in the city by the name of Zacchaeus who was a chief tax collector. Zacchaeus was infamous for having built his fortune through the exploitation of the people in that area. He had illegally overtaxed them for years, had stolen from them, and had used the system to oppress and abuse them.
3. He had heard some of the buzz about Jesus and wanted to see Him for himself as He passed by, but, because he was short in stature, he couldn't see over the curious crowd.
4. So he, being the innovator that he was, ran ahead of the crowd and climbed a sycamore-fig tree to see Him up close, since the route that Jesus was taking would lead Him that way.
5. When Jesus reached the spot where the tree stood, He looked up at Zacchaeus and, without asking anyone who he was, called him by name, saying, "Zacchaeus, come down from there immediately! I must stay at your house today!"

6. So Zacchaeus jumped down from the tree at once and welcomed him, excitedly.
7. All the people in the crowd heard and saw them make this connection and, scandalized by it, began to gossip and complain about it. They said to one another, "Can you believe this? He has publicly embraced a known criminal and has publicly invited Himself to the man's house!"
8. But later, after Jesus had graced his home with His presence and unconditional friendship, Zacchaeus stood up and said, "Lord! Your goodness to me has caused me to have a change of heart! Here and now I pledge to give half of my possessions to the poor...and if I have cheated anybody out of anything, I will pay him or her back four times the amount!"
9. Jesus said to him, "That's beautiful, My friend. And I announce that today salvation has come to this house because this man, too, is a son of Abraham.
10. For the Son of Man came to seek and to save what was lost in man's self-perception in relationship to God and the world around him."
11. While those who were also at Zacchaeus' house that day were listening to this exchange between him and his self-invited Guest, Jesus proceeded to tell them an illustration. He used this opportunity to tell it, because He was near Jerusalem and the people thought that the Kingdom of God was going to visibly appear all at once.
12. He said, "There once was a man, a descendant from a royal house, who went to a distant country to have himself appointed king...to get authorization for his rule...and then return.
13. "But first he called his ten servants together and gave them each a sum of money. Then he said to them, 'Operate with this until I return.'
14. "However, the citizens there hated him, so they sent a commission with a signed petition to oppose his rule. They made no bones about their feelings and their petition simply stated, 'We don't want this man to rule over us.'
15. "When he returned, bringing the authorization of his rule with him, he called those ten servants to whom he had given the money to find out how they had done with what he left them.
16. "The first one said, 'Sir, while you were on your journey, I doubled your money.'

17. "He said to him, 'Excellent! Good for you! Now, because you've been trustworthy and productive in this small job, I'm going to make you governor of ten towns.'
18. "Then the second one stepped up and said, 'Sir, while you were gone, I made a fifty percent profit on your money.'
19. "He said to him, 'Great! Because of this I'm going to put you in charge of five towns.'
20. "Then a third one came and said, 'Here's your money, just as you left it. I've kept it tied up in a handkerchief and hidden away while you were gone.
21. 'I thought that it was the right thing to do. Besides, I was really afraid of you. I know you are a stern and severe man. I know that you pick up what you didn't lay down and that you reap what you didn't sow.'
22. "He said to this one, 'Oh, really? You think you know a lot about me, don't you? Well, your own lack of perception is going to be your downfall! I'll show you how stern and severe I really can be. You knew, did you, that I pick up what I didn't lay down and reap what I didn't sow?
23. 'Then why didn't you at least put my money in a bank so that, when I got back, I might have collected it with some interest?'
24. "Then he said to the bystanders, 'Take the money away from him and give it to the man who doubled what I gave him.'
25. "But they said to him, 'Sir, he already has double!'
26. "But he said, 'This is the way it works...to everyone who gets and has will more be given, but from the man or woman who does not get and does not have, even what he or she has will be taken away from him/her.
27. 'Oh, and one more thing,' said the indignant king, 'as for these enemies of mine who didn't want me to reign over them, bring them here and execute them in my presence!'"
28. When He finished this story, Jesus went on toward Jerusalem, walking ahead of His disciples.
29. On the way, He came to the towns of Bethphage and Bethany on the Mount of Olives, and He sent two disciples ahead.
30. And He said to them, "Go into that village over there, and as you enter it, you will see a young donkey tied there that no one has ever ridden. I want you to untie it and bring it here.

31. "If anyone should ask you, 'Why are you untying the colt?' just say to them, 'We're taking it because the Lord needs it.'"
32. So they did exactly as He said and went and found the colt.
33. And, indeed, the owners saw them taking it and asked them, "Why are you untying that colt?"
34. And, according to instructions, the disciples simply replied, "We're taking it because the Lord needs it."
35. Then they brought the colt to Jesus and threw their garments over it for Him to ride on into Jerusalem.
36. And as He rode along, the crowds spontaneously began to spread out their garments on the road ahead of Him.
37. And when He reached the place where the road started down the Mount of Olives, His followers began to shout and sing as they walked along, praising God for all the wonderful miracles that they had seen manifested through His ministry.
38. They sang, "Blessings on the King Who comes in the name of the Lord! Peace in the heavenlies and glory in the highest part of the heavenly dimension!"
39. But some of the Pharisees were in the crowd, as usual, and, as usual, they were displeased with Him. They said, "Teacher, You should rebuke Your followers for saying things like that!"
40. But He replied, "You know what? If they were to keep quiet, the stones along the road would burst into shouts of praise!"
41. But as He approached Jerusalem and saw the city, He burst into tears and wept over it.
42. And He said, "Jerusalem, if you had only known in this present day what would bring you peace...but right now your religious tradition has hidden it from your eyes.
43. "And so the days will come in the not-too-distant future when your enemies will build an embankment against you and encircle you. They will hem you in on every side.
44. "Destruction will be everywhere within your walls, even to you and your children. Your enemies will not leave one stone on another in this city, because you did not recognize the time of God's visitation to you as a nation."
45. Then He continued on into the city, and when He entered the Temple courts, He began to personally drive out those who were there selling.

46. He said to them *"It's written that 'My house is designed to be a house of prayer!'...but you have degraded it into a 'den of robbers.'"*
47. For the next several days after this, He was teaching there in the Temple. But the chief priests, the teachers of the Law and the leaders among the people were, at this point, completely focused on trying to kill Him.
48. But they couldn't find any opportunity or way to do it, because the people were surrounding Him constantly, hanging on to His every word.

Chapter 20

1. One day Jesus was teaching in the Temple courts, proclaiming the Good News and, as He finished up, the ever-vigilant chief priests and teachers of the Law, together with the elders, approached Him to talk to Him.
2. And they challenged Him, demanding, "By what power of authority are You doing these things, and who gave You this power of authority?"
3. He replied, *"I will answer your question with another question and, if you give Me the answer, then I also will tell you by what power of authority I do these things.*
4. *"The baptism of John...from where did it originate? Did it come from heaven, or did it come from men?"*
5. This question immediately set a private meeting among them into motion, in which they said to one another, "Watch out...this is a trick question...if we say that the baptism originated in the heavenlies, He will no doubt ask us, 'Then why did you not believe him?'
6. "On the other hand, if we say, 'It is of mere human origin,' we're going to receive so much flak from the people...they may even stone us...for they all regard John as a prophet."
7. So they answered, "We don't know where it was from."
8. And He said to them, *"Fair enough...so neither will I tell you by what power of authority I do these things."*
9. Then He went on to tell them this illustration: *"A prominent landowner planted a vineyard, rented it out to some tenants, and moved somewhere else for a long time.*
10. *"When it was time to harvest the grapes, he sent his servant back to*

collect his profits. But the tenants took the servant and beat him up, and sent him away empty-handed.

11. He then sent another servant, but they also beat that man and severely abused him, then they sent him away empty-handed, as well.

12. "He even sent a third, and they also met him with violence, wounded him, and threw him out.

13. "Finally, he sent his own son to them, saying, 'Surely, they will respect my own son whom I love and not treat him the way they have treated my servants.'

14. "But, as it turned out, when the tenants saw the son, they said to themselves, 'This is the heir to the fortune…let's kill him so that we can have his inheritance!'

15. "And, sure enough, they took him and threw him out of the vineyard and killed him right then and there. Now when the owner of the vineyard comes back, what do you think he'll do to those horrible, murderous tenants?

16. "He will come and put those tenants to death and give the vineyard to others." When the people heard this, they said, "God forbid that he would do something like that!"

17. Jesus looked intently at them and asked, "Have you never read in your Scriptures: *'The very Stone which the builders rejected and threw away has become the Cornerstone'?*

18. "Everyone who stumbles on this Stone will be shattered to pieces, but he on whom it falls will be crushed to powder, scattering him like dust."

19. When the religious leaders heard His dark, illustrative story that day, they perceived that He was talking about them and began to aggressively look for a way to arrest Him as soon as possible. But they didn't know how to do it, because they were cowards.

20. But from that point on they kept a close watch on Him. They even sent spies, pretending to be sincere, in hopes of catching Him in some verbal trap...waiting for Him to snare Himself with His own words so that they might hand Him over to the authorities.

21. These spies came to Him and questioned Him, saying "Teacher, we know that You certainly speak and teach what is right...and we also know that You have integrity, that You teach the way of God truthfully, regardless of possible consequences, that You are uncompromising in Your ethics, and that You don't pander to Your

audience.
22. "So tell us...is it right for us to pay taxes to Caesar or not?"
23. Of course He saw right through them, and said, "Do you phonies honestly think that I don't know what you're up to? Surely you can't be simple enough to assume that I would be rendered gullible by your empty compliments. That kind of flattery may work on you, but it doesn't work on Me; why do you keep trying to trap Me with these tired old tricks?
24. "All right...I'll play along with your silly game. Show Me a coin and tell Me whose image and inscription are on it." "Caesar's," they replied.
25. "Well, then, it should be obvious, shouldn't it? Pay to Caesar the things that are due to Caesar, and pay to God the things that are due to God. It's that simple."
26. The Pharisees didn't have a comeback. Once again the profound simplicity of His words had left them speechless, and they were again unable to entrap Him. Astonished by His answer, they were completely silenced.
27. Then some of the Sadducees, who say that there is no resurrection of the dead, came to Him with a question of their own.
28. "Teacher," they began, "Moses said that if a man dies leaving no children, his brother should marry his widowed sister-in-law and raise a family for his brother with her.
29. "Let's say, hypothetically, that there were seven brothers, and the first married and died and, having no children, left his wife to his brother.
30. "The same with the second brother;
31. and then the third brother married her, and so on until all seven died, leaving no children.
32. "Now...stay with us on this...let's say that, last of all, the woman died also.
33. "This is our question: in this scenario...in the resurrection...to which one of the seven brothers will she be wife, since she was married to all of them?"
34. Jesus replied, "Your premise is implausible, if not preposterous. Anyway, the people in this age and dimension marry and are given in marriage.
35. "But in the reality of the resurrection, neither men nor women get married, nor are they considered married when they enter the

resurrected state.

36. "In that sense, they are like the angels who live in the heavenly realm and they can no longer die. They are God's children...children of the resurrection.
37. "But as to your larger question...in the account of the burning bush, even Moses showed that the dead rise, in that he called the Lord *'The God of Abraham...and the God of Isaac...and the God of Jacob.'*
38. "Don't you see that He revealed something in the way that he phrased that? Because he spoke of God being the God of all of them in the present tense, he was declaring that He is not the God of the dead, but of the living, for to Him all are ultimately and eternally alive."
39. Some of the teachers of the Law who heard this responded, "Excellent...well said, Teacher!"
40. But whether they liked His answer or not, no one dared to ask Him any more questions.
41. But Jesus went on to say to them, "Why do you think it is said that the Messiah is the son of David?
42. "I mean, David himself declares in the Book of Psalms: *'The Lord said to my Lord, sit at My right hand,*
43. *until I make Your enemies a footstool for Your feet.'*
44. "Think about it...if David calls Him 'Lord,' how then can He be his son?"
45. While the people were trying to comprehend all this, Jesus turned to His disciples and said,
46. "Always remember to beware of the teachers of the Law. They love to walk around in flowing robes, looking pious and important...love to be greeted with respect in the marketplaces and treated like celebrities...love to have the most important seats in the synagogues and the places of honor at all the banquets.
47. "But while all this high profile show is going on, behind the scenes they devour the fortunes of gullible widows and, for a pretense, make lengthy prayers. These men will be justly and severely punished."

Chapter 21

1. After saying these things, Jesus looked up and saw the rich making a big show of putting their financial gifts into the Temple treasury.

2. At the same time, He saw a poor, little widow put in two very small copper coins.

3. "I want to tell you a truth about perception," He said, "This poor widow has actually put in more than all the rest.

4. "These others gave their gifts out of their vast wealth, but, in this sense, everything is relative...she, out of her poverty, put in all she had to live on, so, in reality, she gave the most."

5. And this exchange led to a conversation about the Temple, itself. Some of His disciples were remarking about how it was adorned with beautiful stones and with gifts dedicated to God, and they began to discuss the buildings of the Temple complex and how imposing and impressive they thought the architecture to be.

6. "You may be rightfully impressed with what you see before you," He said to them, "the Temple is, indeed, something to behold. But the truth is, there is not one stone in that magnificent building that is not going to end up in a massive pile of rubble."

7. "Teacher," they asked, "when are these things going to happen? Will that be the sign of Your fully coming into power and of the completion and consummation of this age and era?"

8. He said to them, "Be careful that no one deceives or misleads you on these points…understand these beginning events marking the period between My resurrection and the Temple's destruction. For during this time, many will come in falsehood claiming, 'I, alone, am the Christ,' and they will lead many away from the truth of Who and what the Christ truly is. Do not follow them.

9. "Also, during this time you will hear of wars and rumors of wars; see that you are not frightened or troubled, for this must take place…wars will come and go as they always have…but the end of the Temple age is not yet.

10. "Nation will rise against nation…ruler will fight ruler…kingdom will invade kingdom…the usual earthly conflicts will continue to occur as they always have. These things are nothing new.

11. "There will be great earthquakes, famines and pestilence in various places, and fearful events which are a part of the natural order of things…activity in the sky above you which can be seen as the birth pangs of the destruction that is coming on this nation.

12. "But before all this, they will lay hands on you and persecute you. They will deliver you to synagogues and prisons, and you will be brought before kings and governors, and all on account of your

association with My reputation and name.

13. "But this will provide an opportunity for you to be witnesses to them and to the whole world...a chance to give your testimony...to show that, as the Temple era comes to an end, the true Kingdom of God will be simultaneously revealed.

14. "But determine now within your own minds not to worry beforehand how you will defend yourselves when all this happens.

15. "For I, as the Spirit, will personally give you wise words that none of your adversaries will be able to resist or contradict.

16. "As this natural, physical nation is replaced by a supernatural, spiritual one, you may very well be betrayed even by parents, brothers, relatives and friends—the closest people to you who reject the change that the Kingdom will inevitably bring—and they will even put some of you to death.

17. "At one point, the conflict will become so intense that it will seem as if the entire world hates you because of your revelation of Me.

18. "But as you continue to embrace this revelation, not a hair of your head will perish.

19. "By standing firm in what you have received and perceived, you will gain a more excellent life.

20. "When you see armies coming to destroy both Jerusalem and the Temple, take notice and realize that this is the fulfillment of this nation's time of desolation.

21. "If you're living in Judea at the time, you'll need to run for the hills. If you're in the city, get out as soon as possible. If you're out in the country, stay where you are.

22. "Heed this advice, because this is the time of retribution, in fulfillment of all that has been written.

23. "Unfortunately, pregnant and nursing mothers will have it especially hard during this distressful time of persecution.

24. "The inhabitants of this city will fall by the sword and will eventually be taken as prisoners to many other nations. Jerusalem will be trampled on by the Gentiles until the time of the fall of the Roman Empire.

25. "It will be a time of utter chaos, with the sun, moon and stars becoming prophetic symbols of the downfall of rulers and authorities and of the total upheaval of this nation's current government. On the earth, it will seem as though all the surrounding nations are in anguish...as if the whole world is one big storm-tossed sea.

26. "The people of this city will faint from terror as they witness their world, as they now know it, coming to an end. Everything, including the sky above them and the celestial bodies, will seem to be off course and out of order.
27. "At that time, they will see a great manifestation of the authority of the Son of Man. To them He will no longer be shrouded in a cloud of mystery, but will be revealed to them with power and great glory.
28. "So when these things begin to take place, stand up and lift up your heads. Even though your present national reality and religious system are coming to an end, in the big picture, your redemption is actually drawing near."
29. Then He told them this illustration: "From the fig tree learn this lesson:
30. "As soon as its young shoots become soft and tender and it starts to put out leaves, you know for a fact that summer is near.
31. "In the same way, when you see these things happening, you will know that the manifestation of the Kingdom of God is about to appear in its fullness.
32. "I'm telling you the truth, so do not take this lightly or assume this is some far-off, futuristic prophecy that has no relevance to you. I'm not saying all this for some generation that will live hundreds of years from today. This is for all of you who are alive right now... these are things that will happen in your lifetime! And this era continues until all these things take place.
33. "The sky and the earth will fade away before any of My words do, because My words are eternally and absolutely true.
34. "Remain alert and aware, or your hearts will be weighed down with drunkenness and the anxieties of life, and that day will close in on you suddenly like a trap.
35. "For the downfall of this nation will ultimately have an effect on all those who live on the face of the earth.
36. "Be vigilant at all times and pray that you may personally be able to escape the inevitable destruction that is coming on this nation...and that you may be able to look, face to face, at the Son of Man."
37. Jesus continued, for a season, to teach every day at the Temple. And each evening during that time, He went out to spend the night on the hill called the Mount of Olives.
38. But every morning, all the people came early to hear Him again in the Temple.

Chapter 22

1. By this time, the Festival of Unleavened Bread (called the Passover) was fast approaching.
2. The chief priests and religious leaders were now looking for any and every opportunity to get rid of Jesus, but their fear of the people made it virtually impossible for them to initiate anything.
3. Then satan (to confirm God's purposes and to fulfill prophecy) entered the mind of Judas Iscariot (one of the original Twelve)...and Jesus did nothing to stop it, even though He had proven, time after time, that He had complete authority over the entire spirit-realm.
4. So Judas went to the chief priests and the officers of the Temple guard and discussed with them a strategy of how he might betray Jesus and hand Him over to them.
5. And this was the opportunity that they had been waiting for. They were delighted with him and the satanically-inspired idea that he pitched to them. They even agreed to give him money for it.
6. So Judas sealed the deal with them and began to watch for the perfect occasion and method of delivering Jesus over to them when no crowd was present.
7. Then the actual day of Unleavened Bread, on which the Passover lamb had to be sacrificed, finally came.
8. So Jesus sent Peter and John, saying to them, "I want the two of you to go and make preparations for us all to eat the Passover together."
9. They replied, "Absolutely. Where do You want us to prepare for it?"
10. He said to them, "As soon as you enter the city, you'll see a man carrying a jar of water. When he approaches you, follow him to the house that he enters.
11. "When you get there, say to the owner of the house, 'The Teacher wants to know where your guest room is, because that's where He wants to eat the Passover with His disciples.'
12. "He'll show you a large upper room, which will be all furnished. Make the preparations for this important celebration there."
13. So they left immediately, found the exact scenario which Jesus had described, and went right into making preparations for the Passover.
14. When the designated hour arrived, Jesus and His disciples came and ate and reclined at the table.
15. During the dinner, He said to them, "Boys, I've really been

anticipating this evening...it was important to Me to have this opportunity to eat the Passover with you before I suffer.

16. "You should know that I won't eat it again until it finds spiritual fulfillment and manifestation in the Kingdom of God."
17. After taking the cup, He gave thanks for it and said, "Take this and pass it among yourselves.
18. "For neither will I drink wine again with you until the Kingdom of God comes in revelation and in power."
19. Then He took bread, gave thanks for it and broke it...and He personally handed a portion of it to each of them at the table. As He distributed the broken pieces around the unbroken circle of His closest followers, He said to them, "THIS...this broken bread...this special night...this unique experience...this holy celebration...this final gathering in the physical realm of those I love...all of 'this' is My body, given for you. Do this...celebrate this...comprehend this...understand this...embrace this...in remembrance, or rather, in 're-member'-ance—in a re-assembling of the disconnected members of the Christ—do this in remembrance of Me."
20. Then, in the same way, after the supper He took the common cup, saying, "THIS cup is the ratification of the New Covenant in My blood...this life...this substance...this connection...this kinship and common bloodline...this is the blood which is poured out for you.
21. "But the very hand of him who is going to betray Me is with Mine on this table.
22. "The Son of Man will and must pass through the door of physical suffering to reveal the Son of God as it has been prophesied. But, even though it must happen according to what has been decreed by God, Himself, the man who betrays the Son will still be traumatized by the acting out of his role in this drama."
23. They immediately began to question among themselves which of them it might be who would do this thing.
24. And in their confusion, a ridiculous and immature dispute arose among them as to which of them was considered to be the greatest.
25. Jesus said to them, "Stop it! Wake up! Don't you realize that insecure kings need to throw their weight around to feel superior and worthy of their thrones and crowns...that people with authority in the current world system like to hide behind the fancy titles that they've conferred upon themselves?
26. "After all that I've revealed to you about the Kingdom-life, you

should realize by now that you can't ever be like that! The greatest among you should be the humblest...the one who actually rules should be the one who really serves.

27. "For who is greater...the one who is at the table, or the one who serves? Isn't it typically the one who is at the table? But look...I'm among you all as the One who serves you all.

28. "And as I serve you, I also honor and bless you for standing by Me in all My trials; you were more or less apprehended by this whole thing...plucked out of your normal, natural lives and thrust into the supernatural realm and all that it entails...and yet you have stuck with Me through thick and thin.

29. "That's why I confer on you all a Kingdom...just as My Father conferred one on Me.

30. "And all twelve of you will eat and drink at My table in My kingdom and sit on thrones with Me, leading and guiding even those outside of the Kingdom...those who are represented by the twelve Tribes of Israel."

31. Then Jesus spoke to Peter, calling him by his natural, pre-revelation name, saying, "Simon, Simon...satan has asked permission to sift you as wheat.

32. "And permission has been granted him...you will, indeed, be sifted in the next few hours. But I have prayed for you, Simon, that your faith may not fail and that, through this sifting process, the 'Simon' in you will be removed and 'Peter, the Rock' will finally emerge, fully intact. As I have said before...one man will be taken and one man will be left behind. And when the chaff of Simon is gone and the wheat of Peter is defined and refined, go back and strengthen your brothers."

33. But this concept basically went over his head, and he replied, "Lord, I don't know about satan's request, and I don't understand all this talk of sifting, but You should know that I'm ready right now to go with You to prison...I'm even prepared to follow You to death."

34. But Jesus, declaring the end from the beginning, called him Peter again, and said, "Buddy, I know you think you mean that, but I tell you, Peter, that before the rooster crows this morning, you will deny three times that you even know Me."

35. Then Jesus asked them all, "When I sent you out with nothing but the internal, spiritual gifts that had been imparted to you, did you lack any physical thing?" "No...not a thing," they answered.

36. "Well," He said to them, "now, if you have some things to help you get by, take them with you...and if you don't have a sword, pawn your coat and buy one.
37. "It is written: *'And He was numbered with the rebels'*...and I tell you that this Scripture must be confirmed in Me. Please try to understand that what is written about Me is about to be fulfilled."
38. The disciples said, "Look here, Lord, we already have two swords among us." "Well, on second thought," He said, "that's probably enough protection for you...and that's really enough talk about it."
39. Then Jesus went out to the Mount of Olives, as He had been doing every night for a while, and His disciples followed Him there.
40. Once they were at the desired spot, He said to them, "Pray that you will remain strong, especially in the next few hours."
41. Then He walked a short distance away from them and knelt down and prayed, saying,
42. "Father, if there is any alternative at this hour to what is already unfolding, then take this cup away from Me...but that is the Son of Man in His humanity speaking...the Son of God, in His divinity says, 'never mind what the voice of human, self-preservation says'...may Your will be done in this."
43. And immediately a ministering spirit from the heavenly realm manifested to Him and assisted Him in His transition from flesh to spirit.
44. But the process was difficult...painful...and His mind kept going in and out of the revelation of the Divine Purpose. So, being in anguish as the temporal engaged in fierce battle with the eternal, He prayed even more earnestly. And as He contended with the conflict between His two worlds...His two realities...the struggle caused His perspiration to morph into drops of blood. But as He gradually and ultimately yielded to the Will of Love, He began to bleed the atonement...before He was scourged...before He was beaten...before He was wounded. He bled because He said 'yes.'
45. And with this final resolution, He rose from prayer and went back to His disciples, but found them asleep...filled with wine and exhausted from sorrow.
46. "Why are you sleeping?" He asked them. "Get up and pray that you will remain strong!"
47. But that was all He could say to them because, while He was in mid-sentence, a mob led by Judas appeared, seemingly from out of

nowhere. And once they had converged upon them, Judas immediately went right up to Jesus and, without word or warning, kissed Him.

48. Jesus just looked at him and asked, "Judas...this is how you're going to do it? You're betraying the Son of Man with a kiss?"
49. When the disciples realized what was happening, they said, "Lord, should we fight with our swords?"
50. But before He could even answer, one of them (who will now remain nameless) just started clumsily wielding a sword, managing to strike the servant of the high priest, cutting off his right ear.
51. But Jesus called out, "No...stop it! It doesn't matter now...the fulfillment has begun...there's no reason to fight it now!" And He stooped and picked up the startled man's bloody, severed ear from off the ground, re-attached it, and healed him. This was His last miracle performed as the Son of Man.
52. Then He turned to the chief priests, officers of the Temple guard, and the elders who had come for Him, and said, "Is all this really necessary? Do you honestly perceive that I'm leading some kind of physical rebellion that demands you come for Me with swords and clubs?
53. "I mean, every single day I was with you in the Temple courts and you didn't lay a hand on Me then. But I suppose that this is appropriate...this is fitting for you and for how you think...acting out your methods of control when darkness reigns, depending on physical weapons to protect your interests."
54. But His words fell on deaf ears. They seized Him as a criminal, anyway, led Him away and took Him straight to the house of the high priest. Peter followed along after them, at a safe distance.
55. And when he arrived at the house, he saw that some people there had kindled a fire in the middle of the courtyard and had sat down together, so he sat down with them.
56. One of the high priest's serving maids walked outside to where they were sitting, and when she saw Peter warming himself, she just stopped in her tracks and stared at him. Unable to take her eyes off him, she said, "Hey...this man was with Him."
57. But he completely denied it, saying, "Lady, I don't even know what you're talking about."
58. A little later someone else saw him and said, "You are definitely one of them...one of Jesus' close followers!" Agitated, Peter replied,

"Man, I'm telling you...I am not!"

59. About an hour later another bystander spoke up and said, "Come on...admit it...you really are one of them...you are a Galilean...your dialect gives you away!"
60. Peter replied, "Look...I'm telling you for the last time...I don't know Him...never did...you people don't even know what you're talking about...shut up and leave me alone!" And as these words were still lingering in the air, a rooster crowed.
61. When this happened, Peter instinctively looked up to try to see Jesus, and when he spotted Him, he saw that Jesus was already standing there, staring at him. As they made eye contact, Peter remembered how Jesus had said to him, "Before the rooster crows twice, you will utterly deny Me...you will deny any connection to Me three times."
62. And when the realization of what had just happened came crashing in on him, Peter went out and broke down and cried loud and hard.
63. Then the men who were guarding Jesus began to mock Him and pummel Him with their fists.
64. As a kind of frenzy set in among them, they blindfolded Him and began to say while striking Him, "Prophesy, Prophet!...tell us who hit You!" They did this until they grew tired of it, then the guards took Him away and started another round of beatings.
65. And they also continued the verbal abuse, peppered with constant insults and obscenities.
66. This went on all through the night but, at daybreak, the Council of the Elders of the people, the chief priests and religious leaders all met together. Jesus was then led before them.
67. They said to Him, "If You really are the Messiah, tell us!" Jesus answered, "You men have proven that there's nothing I could tell you that you would believe;
68. and there's no question that I could ask you that you would actually answer.
69. "But whether you believe Me or not, from now on, the Son of Man will be seated at the right hand...the place of authority...with God."
70. They replied, "So now You're saying that You are the Son of God?" He answered, "To you I am Whoever you say that I am."
71. Then they said, "We obviously don't need any more testimony... we've heard the blasphemy from His own lips."

Chapter 23

1. With this phase of the impromptu trial over, and with the events now taking on an indefinable urgency and life of their own, the entire assembly rose and led Him off to stand before Pilate.
2. As soon as they arrived, the accusations began to fly. "We've found this rabble rouser...this demagogue...subverting our nation and all that it stands for!" they exclaimed. "He flagrantly opposes payment of taxes to Caesar and, most disturbing of all, claims to be a Messiah and a king!"
3. So Pilate said to Jesus, "Tell me, sir...is this true? Are You the King of the Jews?" *"To you I am whoever you say that I am,"* Jesus replied.
4. Then Pilate, initially dismissing the whole thing as something harmless...even amusing—certainly something with which he didn't want to be involved—announced to the chief priests and the crowd, "Look...I just don't find any basis for a charge against this Man."
5. But they were insistent, saying, "Governor...with all due respect, you don't seem to understand. He stirs up the people all over Judea by His anarchistic rhetoric and blasphemous teaching. He started spreading His poison in Galilee and has brought it all the way here!"
6. On hearing this, Pilate asked if Jesus was a Galilean.
7. When they answered in the affirmative, he ruled that Jesus was under Herod's jurisdiction, and then sent Him to stand before the king, who was also in Jerusalem at that time.
8. So they brought Him to Herod, who was actually quite pleased to see Him. For quite some time, Herod had been hoping for a chance to meet Him because of all that he had heard about the signs and wonders He performed. In fact, he hoped to see Him perform one right in front of him.
9. So he plied Him with a plethora of questions but, at this point, Jesus had said all He was going to say.
10. But the chief priests and religious leaders kept standing there, vehemently accusing Him, anyway.
11. Herod and his soldiers then began to ridicule and mock Him, dressing Him in an elegant robe. Then they sent Him back to Pilate.
12. Somehow, during all this circus-like atmosphere of mockery, false accusations and sending Jesus back and forth from trial to trial, Herod and Pilate became friends. Prior to this they had been hostile

enemies.
13. Then Pilate called together the chief priests, the rulers, and the people,
14. and said to them, "Listen...you brought me this Man, claiming that He was inciting the people to rebellion, but I've thoroughly examined Him in your presence and just haven't found any basis for these charges.
15. "And neither has Herod, obviously, because he sent Him right back here to us. In all honesty, you must realize that He hasn't really done anything to deserve death.
16. "So, to help you save face...to make you feel satisfied that you've made your point...I'm going to have Him publicly flogged. But then I'm going to release Him. That way, no one has to die, and He'll probably just disappear after all this beating and humiliation."
17. [Verse 17 doesn't exist in the original text.]
18. But they wouldn't hear of it. With one voice they cried out, "We want this Man done away with! Release the prisoner Barabbas to us if you need to pardon someone for the feast!"
19. Barabbas was serving a prison sentence for an insurrection in the city, and for murder.
20. But Pilate really wanted to release Jesus and made the same appeal to them again.
21. But they refused to acknowledge his words and just kept shouting, "Crucify Him! Crucify Him!"
22. Then Pilate spoke to them a third time, saying, "Why are you people so adamant about this? Seriously...what crime has this Man committed, really? There just aren't any legitimate or valid grounds for the death penalty that I can find here. He's already been beaten up, and I'm going to have Him severely punished for whatever you think He's done, but enough is enough...I intend to release Him!"
23. But they just got louder with the shouts and the insistent demands for His crucifixion. Eventually they wore Pilate down, and their shouts prevailed.
24. So he reluctantly decided to grant them what they wanted.
25. And he released the man who had been thrown into prison for insurrection and murder. He gave them the one they asked for and provided consent for them to do to Jesus whatever they wanted.
26. So the soldiers led Him away, forcing Him to carry the heavy beam that would later form the horizontal part of His cross. But He had

stood all night long and had been beaten repeatedly throughout the night, so He collapsed under the weight of the solid piece of wood, weakened from exhaustion and the loss of blood. So they seized Simon from Cyrene (who was passing by on his way in from the country) and made him carry the cross-beam and follow along behind Jesus as He staggered toward the place of His execution.

27. By this time, a large number of people followed Him on His death-march, including women who mourned and wailed loudly for Him.

28. Jesus turned to some of them who were crying hysterically, and said, "Daughters of Jerusalem, don't weep for Me...weep for yourselves and for your children.

29. "For the time will come in this nation when you will say, 'Blessed are the women without children...the barren wombs and the breasts that never nursed!'

30. "Then it will be fulfilled: *'They will say to the mountains, "Fall on us!" and to the hills, "Cover us!"'*

31. "For if people do this kind of thing to a living, green tree, can you imagine what they'll do with deadwood?"

32. And two other men, both convicted criminals, were also led out with Him to be publicly put to death.

33. When they arrived at the place called 'The Skull' (a rock formation in the side of a hill that eerily resembled the face of a human skull), they crucified Him there beside the road in front of it, along with the criminals. One was on His right, the other on His left.

34. Jesus said, "Father, forgive them...for even though this is ultimately the fulfillment of Your will, they don't understand why they are acting with such physical cruelty." Then the soldiers divided up the clothes that they had stripped off Him, by casting lots.

35. And then the people just stood there and watched...some wept, vehemently...others gawked, vacantly... the relentless religious rulers sneered at Him and mocked Him right up to the very end. They said, "He saved others...let Him save Himself if He is God's Messiah, the Chosen One!"

36. The soldiers also came up to Him and piled on with their unique brand of mockery. They offered Him wine vinegar

37. and said to Him, "Hey! You! If You're really the King of the Jews, save Yourself!"

38. They nailed a written notice above His head, which read: THIS IS THE KING OF THE JEWS.

39. One of the two criminals who hung there beside Him kept hurling insults at Him. He yelled, "Aren't You the Messiah? Why don't You save Yourself...and us!"
40. But the other one rebuked him, saying, "Don't you have any respect for God? How can you say that, seeing that you are under the same sentence?
41. "We're being punished justly...getting what our deeds deserve...but everyone knows this Man hasn't done anything wrong."
42. Then he looked over at Jesus and said, "Sir...please remember me when You come into your Kingdom."
43. Jesus raised His head and answered him, "Friend, I'm telling you the truth...this will soon be over, and today you'll be with Me in paradise."
44. Around noon, a strange darkness settled in over the entire area and remained until about three in the afternoon.
45. At one point, the darkness became so thick that it seemed as though the sun had stopped shining. Then the curtain of the Temple was torn in two, opening up the Holy of Holies to the entire world.
46. Right about then, Jesus cried out with a loud voice, "Father...into Your hands I commit My spirit." And with these words, He took His last breath in the physical body.
47. A Roman centurion, standing close by and seeing what had happened, praised God and said, "No doubt...this Man was just, righteous and innocent."
48. All the people who had gathered to witness the whole thing were, for the most part, overcome with sorrow when everything was said and done. They responded and reacted, each in his or her own way, and then left the scene of the execution.
49. But all those who actually knew Him, including the women who had followed Him all the way from Galilee, stood at a distance, keeping vigil.
50. Now there was a man named Joseph who was a member of the Council...a sincere man...a man of conscience...a man full of integrity.
51. He hadn't consented to the decisions and actions of the rest of the Council. He came from the Judean town of Arimathea and had been open to the ministry of Jesus, because he himself had pursued and waited for the manifestation of the Kingdom of God.
52. So he went to Pilate, personally, and asked for permission to be the

caretaker of Jesus' body.

53. Pilate allowed it, so he went and carefully took the lifeless corpse down off the cross, wrapped it in clean, linen cloth, and placed it in a tomb cut into the rock. The place was his own, personal property...a new tomb in which no one had yet been laid.
54. It was the day before Sabbath, known as Preparation Day, and the Sabbath was about to begin.
55. The women who had come with Jesus from Galilee followed Joseph, saw the tomb, and observed how His body was laid in it.
56. Then they went home immediately and began to prepare spices and perfumes which they could use to anoint the body. But, in obedience to the commandment, they rested on the Sabbath.

Chapter 24

1. But on the first day of the week, at the first light of dawn, the women took the spices which they had carefully prepared for His body, and made their way to the tomb.
2. But when they got there, they discovered that the huge, flat stone which fit down into the slot that ran along the front of the sepulcher, had been rolled away from the door of it.
3. Without hesitation they entered the enclosure, but the physical remains of Jesus which they had come to anoint were nowhere to be found.
4. The women were stunned by this...they didn't know what to think...didn't know what to say...they just stood there, dumbfounded and confused, staring in disbelief at the empty slab where His body had been just hours earlier. Then, suddenly, two men who were dressed in clothes that seemed to gleam like lightning, appeared and stood right beside them.
5. The sight of these beings from another dimension sent the women into a state of sheer panic. Completely overcome with fear, they collapsed, face forward, onto the stony ground and lay there in dead silence. But the men in the lightning-lit clothes said to them, "Ladies, why have you come looking for the living among the dead?
6. "He is not here! He has risen! Don't you remember how He told you while He was still with you there in Galilee:
7. 'The Son of Man must be delivered over to the temporary custody of rebels, be crucified, and on the third day be raised again'?"

8. And then, as the messengers repeated Jesus' own self-prophecy to them, the women settled down. The peace that was still attached to those words enveloped them, and soon they became ecstatic as they remembered and finally understood them.
9. When they came back from the tomb, they shared all of these amazing things with the remaining Eleven, and with all the others who were connected to them.
10. The women who went to the tomb were Mary Magdalene, Joanna, Mary, the mother of James, and some others who came with them. They all went together to find the disciples.
11. But the disciples didn't believe the women at all, because their words seemed to them to be the utter nonsense of hysterical women.
12. Peter, however, wanted to believe them, so he sprang up and ran, by himself, all the way to the tomb. When he got there, he went in, bent down, and saw the strips of linen lying by themselves. After awhile, he left the empty structure, realizing that something had definitely happened there, but he had no idea what.
13. Later that very same day, two of the disciples who were not a part of the remaining Eleven were going to a village called Emmaus, which was about seven miles from Jerusalem.
14. They were still somewhat in a state of shock from all that had transpired over the weekend and, as they walked along the road together, they could speak of nothing else.
15. In fact, they were so engrossed in deep conversation about their take on the events of the previous few days, that they didn't even notice when the freshly-resurrected Jesus, Himself, came up and walked along with them.
16. But they were unable to recognize Him in His post-resurrection incarnation.
17. So He said to them, "Pardon Me, but may I ask what in the world you gentlemen are discussing so intently as you walk along?" The sound of His voice penetrated their intense communication and jarred them into stopping in their tracks. But they just stood there for a few moments in silence with their faces downcast.
18. Then one of them, Cleopas by name, asked Him, "What are we discussing? Are you serious? You must be the only visitor to Jerusalem that doesn't know about or isn't talking about the things that have happened there in the last few days!"
19. "What things?" He asked. "Terrible things." they replied, "Terrible

events...the things surrounding the arrest, trial and execution of Jesus of Nazareth. He was a prophet with a powerful message...a miracle-worker Who was blessed by God and all the people.

20. "But the chief priests, and those in cahoots with them, found a reason and a way to hand Him over to be sentenced to death...and they crucified Him.
21. "We're devastated by the whole thing, mainly because we had hoped that He was the One Who was going to redeem Israel. And today is the third day since all of this took place.
22. "To make matters worse, this morning some of our women presented us with this far-fetched story that has us totally confused. They went to the tomb at daybreak to anoint the body of Jesus,
23. but didn't find it in its tomb. They came and told us that they had seen a manifestation of spirit-beings who claimed that He was alive.
24. "Then some of our colleagues went to the tomb to see for themselves and found it exactly as the women had said. But they didn't see Jesus anywhere, dead or alive."
25. Then He said to them, "How clueless you are...and how slow to believe all that the prophets have spoken!
26. "Isn't it written that the Messiah had to suffer these things and then enter into the fullness of His glory?"
27. But they had no response to His words, so, beginning with Moses and all the prophets, He patiently and methodically explained to them what was said in all the Scriptures concerning Himself.
28. And this continued throughout the entire seven-mile trek, until they approached the village to which they were going. Jesus, however, just kept walking as if He were going farther.
29. But they urged Him to remain with them saying, "No...don't go... stay with us and continue with what You were saying. Besides, it's nearly evening...the day's almost over." So He obliged and went in to stay with them.
30. They had dinner together and, when He was at the table with them, He took the initiative and began to act as the host. He took bread, gave thanks, broke it and began to give it to both of them.
31. And that's when it happened. They hadn't recognized Him in His current physicality (even though He had been walking and talking with them all afternoon), but somehow here...at the table...with the bread...in the communion...they had a revelation of Him. Their eyes were opened and they recognized Him in the now. But as soon as

this happened, He disappeared from their sight.
32. They sat there for a moment and then, when they were able to speak, they asked each other, "Wasn't it as if our hearts were on fire while He talked with us on the road and opened up the meaning of the Scriptures to us?"
33. They didn't even finish the meal...instead, they got right up and made the seven mile trip back to Jerusalem. When they finally got there, they found the Eleven and those with them, all together in one place.
34. They said to them, "Everybody...it's true! The Lord really has risen and has appeared to Simon Peter!"
35. Then the two of them began to unfold the story of how He had appeared to them, as well. They told all that had happened on the way to Emmaus and how that Jesus, in His current incarnation, was revealed to them in the breaking of the bread.
36. And while they were in the process of trying to explain all this, Jesus actually materialized in their presence, stood in the middle of the group, and said to them, "Peace...peace be with all of you."
37. Everyone in the room was startled and frightened, reacting as if they were seeing a ghost; in fact, most of them believed that they were, indeed, seeing an apparition.
38. But He said to them, "Why, after all this time—after everything that you've all seen, especially in the last few days—are you still so quick to be upset and easily spooked? But the bigger question is: Why are you still so prone to have doubts about Me in your minds?
39. "Look at Me! Look at My hands and My feet! It really is Me! Touch Me and see for yourselves. Don't be afraid...a ghost doesn't have flesh and bones, as you obviously can see that I have."
40. As He said this, He showed them His hands and feet.
41. But they still just couldn't grasp it...couldn't believe their eyes; they were excited to see Him, but it just seemed too good to be true. So He said to them, "All right...do you have anything here to eat?"
42. And one of them had the presence of mind to respond to His request and give Him a piece of broiled fish.
43. And He took the fish and ate it in front of them to further prove that He was real.
44. Then He said to them, "Remember...this is what I told you while I was still with you in the earthly dimension. Every single thing must be fulfilled that has been written about Me in the Law of

Moses, in the Prophets, and in the Psalms."

45. Then His presence, words, and anointing opened their minds to revelation so that they could understand the Scriptures.
46. He reminded them, "This is what is written...whether you like it or not...whether you understand it, fully, or not...the Messiah will suffer terribly and then rise triumphantly from the dead on the third day.
47. "And a global paradigm shift for the realization of His forgiveness of the world's sins will be preached in His name to all the nations of the earth. What happened in Jerusalem is just the beginning.
48. "And you in this room are privileged to be witnesses of the beginning of these things.
49. "So, I'm going to send you what My Father has promised...but stay here in the city until you have been inundated and infused with power from on high."
50. Then He led them out of that place to the vicinity of Bethany and, once they were there, He lifted up His hands and blessed them.
51. And while He was still speaking a blessing over them, He de-materialized and was translated into the heavenly dimension.
52. Then they instinctively worshiped Him, even though He was no longer physically in their presence. At last they understood that His being...His reality...was greater and more transcendent than anything that could be contained in a finite, physical body. And they returned to Jerusalem with great exuberance.
53. And for the days immediately following, they stayed continually in the Temple, praising, exalting and increasing in their comprehension of the one, true God.

John In The Now

John In The Now

Chapter 1

1. In the beginning, or in the eternal "now" before the creation of time, was the Word...the Logos...the Christ. And that timeless Christ/Word existed with God and, in fact, that Word actually was God, Himself.
2. He was originally omnipresent with God.
3. All things in the realm of space and time came into existence through the specific expression of that "now" Word, and without the expression of that Word was not even one thing made that has come into being in the material universe.
4. In His being was housed the source of life, and that life was the light that illuminates all of humanity.
5. And the light shines on in the darkness, for darkness has never been able to absorb the light, nor will it ever be able to overpower it or put it out.
6. There was a man who was God-sent, and his name was John.
7. John came to bear witness of the light that everyone, everywhere, might believe in it through him.
8. He was not the Light, but came that he might verify the truth that is in the Light.
9. And there it was, the true Light, coming in perfection to illuminate every individual on the planet.
10. He came into the world that He, Himself, had created, but that same world did not recognize Him, initially.
11. He appeared to that which already belonged to Him; He entered into His own domain and creation. But that creation did not welcome or receive Him.
12. Yet, to all who did receive and welcome Him by believing in the power of His name, He granted the authority to walk in the full reality that they were the children of God...
13. children born divinely of God...not merely of natural descent, nor of human decision or will.
14. And the eternal Word morphed into flesh—into a manifested incarnation with human attributes and authority in the natural

world—so that He could live with and among us human beings. And He did live with us here in our world, limiting Himself to the constraints of the human condition without reservation, but we could still plainly see His eternal, divine glory. It was obvious that He shined with the glorious light of a unique, firstborn son Who was miraculously like His Father Who had sent Him. The illumination from that glory revealed that He was literally filled with grace and that He overflowed with absolute truth.

15. John identified Him by boldly and publicly declaring, "This is the One! This is the One Who I said was coming after me! But, in reality, He was and is actually *before* me—He already existed in the now—and that is why He is superior to me!

16. "For out of the flow of His fullness we have all received gift after gift, grace upon grace, one spiritual blessing after another, favor heaped upon favor.

17. "For while the limited and limiting Law was laid down by Moses, amazing grace—undeserved, unmerited, unearned, *un*limited—along with the full revelation of the truth which has freely appeared to everyone, came through Jesus, the Christ.

18. "No one in this realm has ever really seen God in His fullness, but the unique Son, Who is Himself God and is in closest relationship with and to the Father, has revealed Him and has made Him known to us."

19. And this was John's testimony when the Jews sent priests and Levites to him from Jerusalem to ask him, "Who are you?"

20. He was quick to confess to them that he, by himself, was not the Christ.

21. They asked him, "Then who are you? Are you the reincarnation of Elijah?" He said, "No, I am not." Then they asked, "Are you the Prophet?" He answered, "No."

22. Finally they said, "Well, then, who are you? Answer us so that we can answer those who sent us to you. What do you say about yourself and your mission?"

23. He answered them by paraphrasing the words of the prophet Isaiah, saying, *"I am essentially nothing more than a voice...the voice of one crying in the wilderness or shouting out in the desert...to prepare the way of the Lord!"*

24. The messengers had been sent from the Pharisees,

25. and they asked him, "Why, then, are you baptizing people if you are

not the Christ, or Elijah reincarnated, or the prophet? What is the point that you are trying to make?"

26. John answered them, "I only baptize by using the familiar and recognizable symbolism of water, but One stands among you Whom you do not recognize and with Whom you are not familiar—and His baptism will change everything.

27. "He is the One Who comes after me in the realm of time, the thongs of Whose sandals I am not worthy to untie."

28. These conversations took place in Bethany, at the Jordan crossing where John was then baptizing.

29. The next day, John saw Jesus coming toward him and cried out, "See, recognize, discern and perceive the Lamb of God Who takes away the sin of the whole world!

30. "This is He of Whom I said would come after me in *time*, but is actually superior to me because He existed, as He is, in the *now*. He was before me because He *is* before me.

31. "I myself did not recognize Him at first, but now that I can see Who He is, I am baptizing with water as a means to reveal Him to the nation of Israel."

32. Then John went on to say, "I saw the Spirit come from the eternal realm, like a dove that appeared to fly down out of the limitless sky and light on Him. And it, or He, remained on Him and filled Him, making His home in Him.

33. "And that is how I recognized Him, because the One Who sent me to baptize with water said to me, 'The Man on Whom you see the Spirit come down and remain is He Who will baptize with the Holy Spirit.'

34. "And so I confidently make this testimony because there is no doubt in my mind that He is the Son of God."

35. Again the next day, John was in the same place with two of his followers,

36. and he looked at Jesus walking along and said to them, "Look at Him! He is the Lamb of God!"

37. When the two disciples of John heard this, they were so impacted by it that they immediately stopped following John and began to follow Jesus.

38. Jesus, aware that they were following Him, turned around and asked, "What do you want?" They said, "Teacher, we want to see where You live, or at least where You are staying; we want to go to Your house."

39. "Come," He replied, "and you will see." So they went to His house and spent the whole day with Him. It was about four in the afternoon.
40. Andrew (Simon Peter's brother) was one of the two who had followed Jesus after hearing John's words.
41. Immediately after visiting Jesus' house, Andrew found his brother Simon and told him, "We have found the Christ—the One anointed to be the Messiah!"
42. And he brought him to Jesus, Who took one look at him and said, prophetically, "You see yourself simply as Simon, the son of John, but I see that you are a foundation stone, so I am calling you *Cephas*, which is translated 'Peter, the Rock.'"
43. The next day Jesus decided to travel to Galilee. There He found Philip and He said to him, "I want you to follow Me."
44. Philip had a connection with Andrew and Peter, because they were all from the town of Bethsaida.
45. Philip then found Nathanael and told him, "We have found the One that Moses wrote about in the Law—the One about Whom the prophets also wrote—and He is Jesus of Nazareth, the legal son of Joseph, the carpenter!"
46. "Nazareth!" Nathanael exclaimed. "Has anything good ever come from there or *can* anything good ever come from there?" Philip said, "You need to come and see it for yourself."
47. When Jesus saw Nathanael approaching, He said of him, "Look at that! An authentic Israelite indeed, in whom there is no guile, falsehood or pretense."
48. Nathanael asked, "How do You know me, the *real* me?" Jesus answered, "Before Philip ever called you, I saw you. You were under a fig tree and I could see you right there where you were standing."
49. Then Nathanael, remembering that he was, indeed, standing under a fig tree right before Philip had approached him, declared, "Teacher, You are the Son of God! And I say that You are the King of Israel!"
50. Jesus said, "You believe because I told you that I saw you under the fig tree, but let Me tell you, you will see greater things than that!"
51. Then He said to him, "I'm telling you the truth—all of you—that the eternal or heavenly realm is about to be completely opened up, and the angels of God will interact with the Son of Man by ascending and descending upon Him, and you will see it all in the now!"

Chapter 2

1. On the third day, a wedding took place at Cana of Galilee, and Mary (Jesus' mother) was there.
2. And Jesus was also invited to the wedding, along with His newly chosen disciples.
3. At a certain point in the celebration, Mary came to Jesus and said to Him, pointedly, "You should know that the hosts of this reception have no more wine to serve their guests, and there is no place for the caterers to get more."
4. Jesus replied, *"That really is none of our business, Mother, so why are you telling Me? Don't try to draw Me into a natural situation in an attempt to push Me into doing the supernatural. I will not perform a miracle prematurely or before My time."*
5. Mary, completely ignoring Jesus' words of protest, turned to the caterers and said, "Just do whatever He tells you to do."
6. Now there were six stone water jars right there in front of Him (the kind used by the Jews for ceremonial washing), each holding twenty to thirty gallons.
7. So Jesus said to the servants, *"Very well, then…fill up these big vessels with water."* So they filled them all the way to the brim.
8. Then He said to them, *"Now take a sample to the host of the banquet."*
9. When the host tasted the water transformed into wine, he called the bridegroom aside and said, "I don't know where you've been keeping all of this very fine wine, but it is exquisite!
10. "And what impresses me is that, usually, at these events the people who hire me want me to serve the choice wine first and then the cheaper stuff after the guests have had too much to drink and don't notice or care. But you have the class and good taste to save the best until now!"
11. And this miraculous sign (that Jesus was more or less forced into performing) was the first among many of His wonders and, as a result, His disciples put their faith in Him, without reservation.
12. After this He went down to Capernaum with His mother and brothers and His disciples, and they spent several days together there.
13. When it was almost time for Passover, Jesus traveled to Jerusalem.
14. Upon entering the Temple courts there, He became enraged with what He saw going on inside. It looked more like an out-of-control

stock market than a Temple, with people all over the place selling cattle, sheep and doves. And in the middle of it all was an operation of loan sharks and money exchangers loudly doing business.

15. So, transferring His righteous anger into action, He took disciplinary matters into His own hands and fashioned a whip out of many leather cords. Then He took the whip and actually began chasing the business owners around, threatening them with it. He drove them all from the Temple courts and then scattered the coinage of the moneychangers by violently flipping over the tables they had set up for their transactions.

16. As He ran after them He shouted, *"Get all of this garbage out of here and stop turning My Father's beautiful house into an ugly place of shady commerce!"*

17. The scenario caused His disciples to remember that it is written in the Psalms, *"The zeal for your house will literally consume me!"*

18. Then the people there in Jerusalem challenged Him, saying, "Show us a sign to validate Your authority to do such a thing! Who do You think You are, and why do You presume to be in charge of the Temple operation?"

19. Jesus answered them, *"If you want a sign, then destroy this Temple and I will raise it up again in three days!"*

20. They replied, "Are You serious? It has taken forty-six years to build this Temple and You think that You can rebuild it in three days?"

21. What they didn't realize was that Jesus, speaking prophetically, was changing the whole concept and paradigm of the Temple. On one level He was answering them about the Temple as they saw it, but He was actually referring to the Temple of His own body that would be raised back to life after being dead for three days.

22. After the resurrection, His disciples recalled what He had said that day. And it really wasn't until then that they believed that His words had fulfilled the Scriptures.

23. Now while He was in Jerusalem at the Passover Feast, many people saw His miraculous signs and entrusted their lives to Him.

24. But Jesus would not entrust Himself to them, for He really knew people—all people—on a deep, personal level.

25. He did not need anyone's explanation or warning about humanity, for He Himself was more than just perceptive and intuitive. He could actually read the hearts of people and could discern—even empathize with—all of the complexities of human nature, including

its dark side.

Chapter 3

1. Now there was a man named Nicodemus who was a Pharisee, a member of the Jewish ruling council.
2. He secretly approached Jesus under the cover of night and said to Him, "Rabbi, it is obvious to all of us that You are a God-sent, God-ordained teacher, for no one could perform the amazing signs You are doing if God were not with him."
3. Jesus replied, "*This* is what is important—even more important than the signs—*this* truth is absolute: no one can perceive the concept of the kingdom of God without experiencing a rebirth of sorts…without having actually revisited the human birth process."
4. "What are You talking about?" Nicodemus asked. "How could any adult be born *again*? They obviously couldn't return to the womb, so how could *rebirth* possibly happen?"
5. Jesus answered, "I'm telling you, unreservedly, that no one can access the kingdom of God unless they are first physically born of water (the natural birth that begins when a pregnant woman's water breaks) and then have their thought processes *reborn* by having them washed with the *water* of the Word, which is the result of the birth of the Spirit.
6. "Every living thing in the physical realm gives birth to, or recreates, a physical manifestation, and everything spiritual gives birth to a spiritual reality. Whatever is birthed from the Spirit is the essence of spirit.
7. "Look, you shouldn't be so surprised to hear Me say 'You must be born again.'
8. "Think of it this way: the wind blows wherever it wants to blow…it has a mind of its own. You can hear it, but you can't locate its place of origin and you can't predict its destination. This is how it is with everyone who is birthed out of the Spirit-wind."
9. Nicodemus said, "I don't understand. What exactly are You talking about?"
10. Jesus said to him, "How can you be such a great teacher of truth—one who deals with abstract thought…one of the greatest in Israel, in fact—and not be able to grasp this concept?
11. "Here's the truth: I only speak of what I know by experience and

verify what I have seen with My own eyes. My revelation is organic. But you who are overly-educated and pretentiously religious do not accept My testimony.

12. "If I have told you of things that happen right here in the finite, earthly realm and none of you believes Me, how can you possibly comprehend My description of the infinite…the eternal things that are in the now?

13. "No one has ever gone into the eternal realm called heaven except the One Who came from there, namely, the Son of Man.

14. "And just as Moses lifted up the snake in the wilderness for all to see, so the Son of Man must be lifted up in the same way,

15. so that everyone who believes in Him may walk in the fullness of their eternal life.

16. "You see, God's love for the whole world—His paternal affection for the entire cosmos—was so all-encompassing and complete that He freely gave His unique Son to it, so that anyone from that world who believes in Him would not perish, but would awaken to the fact that eternal life is theirs.

17. "It certainly was never God's intention to send His Son into the world to pronounce a sentence of condemnation upon it. Rather, He was perfectly focused on saving it…on redeeming the whole of humanity…everyone and everything on the planet…through the gift of that unique, manifested Son.

18. "Those who believe in the Son never come up for judgment because their faith causes them to be acquitted. Those who do not believe live their lives as though they were under a death sentence, because they do not embrace a faith in the name of the unique Son of God.

19. "The bottom line is this: Light has come into the world, but people loved darkness instead of light because their deeds were evil.

20. "Those who ignorantly practice evil hate the Light and will not come into it because they fear that the Light will expose them and their deeds.

21. "But those who desire to live truthfully come into the light with no fear. They welcome the Light and are not afraid for the Light to reveal who they really are."

22. After this, Jesus and His disciples went out into the countryside of Judea to spend some bonding time together, and Jesus also baptized some people there.

23. But John was also baptizing at Aenon near Salim, because there was

a lot of water there and people kept coming to him to be baptized.
24. This was before John was thrown into prison and everything was still good between him and Jesus.
25. And an argument developed between some of John's disciples and a local Jewish man over the matter of ceremonial washing.
26. And they approached John and said to him, "Teacher, the man who was with you on the other side of the Jordan—the One that you've been talking about so much—is also baptizing, and everyone seems to be going to Him instead of you."
27. And John replied, "A spiritual man can receive nothing except it has been granted to him from the spirit-realm. By that, I mean he must be content to receive the gift that has been given him from heaven because there really is no other source for gifts.
28. "And you yourselves know that I have freely admitted that I, alone, am not the Christ and that I have not been anointed to be the Messiah. My mission is simply to be His forerunner and to prepare the world for His reign.
29. "The bride belongs to the bridegroom. The bridegroom's 'best man' at the wedding listens for him and waits on him; in fact, he is full of joy for his friend's happiness. And so, if you follow my analogy, you should know my joy is now full. I am happy to have been a part of the wedding ceremony, but I know that I am only the 'best man,' as it were.
30. "What I am saying is that, even though I have fulfilled my destiny in this respect, His influence must become greater now. The attention needs to be more on Him and less on me, from this point on.
31. "The One Who comes from the now, or the eternal, heavenly realm (or from what you perceive as *above*), is, in fact, above all. Whoever is from the earth belongs to the earth, speaks the language of the earth, is limited to earthly constraints of space and time, and speaks entirely from an earthly paradigm. The One from heaven is transcendent.
32. "It is the One from heaven Who relays what He has seen and heard *in the now*, but no one limited by the material world accepts His testimony.
33. "The individual who has accepted it, however, has certified and declared, once and for all, that God is absolutely real and His words are completely true.
34. "For the One Whom God has sent speaks the words of God, for God

gives Him His Spirit without measure or the limits of time or space. He holds within Himself the infinite universe of the Spirit.

35. "The Father loves the Son and has placed everything in His hands, committing all things to His dominion.
36. "And he or she who believes in the Son by perceiving Who He is, understands the reality of his or her eternal life. But whoever does not believe in the Son does not enjoy the benefits of eternal life, but lives as though the wrath of God were hanging over him or her, continually."

Chapter 4

1. When Jesus became aware that the Pharisees had heard that He was gaining and baptizing more disciples than John, He realized that they were trying to turn John and Him into rivals in the eyes of the people.
2. (For what it's worth, Jesus didn't actually baptize the people...His disciples did.)
3. So He left Judea and went back again to Galilee.
4. Now He had to go through Samaria to get there.
5. And He came to a town in that country called Sychar, near the plot of ground that Jacob had bequeathed to his son Joseph.
6. The famous and historical "Jacob's Well" was there and, because everyone who lived in the village had to get their water from that location, it also served as the hub and focal point of all the town's communication and social life.
7. When He saw a certain anonymous Samaritan woman come to draw water from the well, Jesus said to her, "Excuse Me, but will you please give Me a drink?"
8. He was sitting there alone because His disciples had gone into the town to buy food.
9. The Samaritan woman replied, "Mister, do You realize how many things are wrong with the statement You just made? You are a Jew. I am a Samaritan. You are a man. I am a woman. And You are a *stranger*, no less, so how is it that You think You can ask me for a drink, especially since Jews have nothing to do with Samaritans?"
10. Jesus answered her, "Listen, if you could discern the gift of God...if you could comprehend Who it is that asks you for a drink...you would have seized the opportunity to ask *Him* and He would have

given you water that is literally alive and life-giving."
11. The woman said to Him, "Is that so? Well, You have no bucket to draw with and the well is very deep, so how can You get to Your so-called 'living water?'
12. "Do You presume to be greater than our father Jacob...the one who really made this well live? His well has been sustaining life for generations, just like it did for his own sons and flocks and herds."
13. Jesus answered, "Everyone who drinks the water from this well will be thirsty again,
14. but those who drink the water that I have to give will never experience thirst...ever! See, I am actually able to tap into a spring of life-giving water from within a person. In the same way that Jacob put this well here in Sychar, I can locate and dig an artesian well within your spirit and mind that will become a constant source of eternal life for you!"
15. Intrigued with this mysterious stranger and His unusual proposition, she said, "Sir, give me this water so that I won't get thirsty and have to come here every morning to get my water for the day."
16. He said to her, "All right, but I want you to go and get your husband and bring him back with you, and then I'll tell you more about it."
17. "Well," she said, "The thing is...I don't have a husband." Jesus said to her, "I'm glad that you admitted that you have no husband,
18. because the truth is that you have actually had five husbands in all, and the man that you're currently living with as your husband is not even married to you. You have very readily and succinctly spoken the truth about yourself."
19. "How could You possibly know that?" she asked in astonishment. "You must truly be a prophet!"
20. "Let me ask You something: our ancestors worshipped on this mountain, but you Jews claim that the place where we must worship is in Jerusalem."
21. "Lady," Jesus replied, "believe Me when I tell you that a time is coming when you will worship the Father neither on this mountain nor in Jerusalem.
22. "The truth is, you Samaritans are basically clueless about worship. We Jews do understand the dynamics of it, for salvation, before becoming universal, is going to originate in Israel through the Jews. But there is another and greater dimension of worship that is opening up...one that transcends nationality or ethnicity or religion or

ancestry.

23. "In fact, you may find this hard to believe because of your past and present lifestyle, but the Father is actually looking for worshippers just like you…people who are candid and honest about their lives and histories, without making any bogus attempt to justify themselves. Transparent people like you—no matter where you have come from or how many failed marriages you've had—who are able to worship in the Spirit, regardless of the truth about themselves.

24. "And the reason is that *God is spirit* and His worshippers must worship Him *in the Spirit*, which means that they must worship Him truthfully, honestly, with the same candor that you demonstrated in being honest about your life. Worship in the Spirit requires that you free yourself of the façade of flesh…that the real you worships the real God."

25. The woman said, "I don't know about all that, but I do know that the Messiah, or the Christ, is coming, and when He comes He will explain God and the realities of the spirit world to us."

26. Then Jesus said to her, "Isn't it obvious to you, yet? I, the One sitting here at this well talking to you about all this, am He! I am the One you've really been looking for all these years, and I can supply you with something superior to anything any of these other men in your life could ever give you."

27. While He was speaking these words, His disciples returned and were, frankly, surprised to find Him just blatantly ignoring propriety and the cultural mores of the day by talking so freely with a strange, native woman of Samaria…one who could, most likely, be another man's wife…right out in the open like that. But no one made it their business to ask Him anything about it.

28. Then suddenly, leaving her water jar there, the woman jumped up from where she had been sitting and talking with Jesus, headed back to town, and started telling everyone that she could find about what had just taken place.

29. She said to anyone who would listen, "You've got to come meet this man that I just met at the well! He is definitely a prophet because He told me everything that I ever did. But He is more than a prophet. In fact, He says He is the Messiah and I think that He just might be!"

30. She was so convincing…her testimony so compelling…that the people from town just started following her back to where she had left Jesus, and some even made their own way to meet Him for

themselves.

31. As they began to flock to Him, His disciples said, "Teacher, a crowd is forming to hear from You, but before You minister to them, You should eat something."
32. But He said to them, "I appreciate your concern for Me, but you should know that what sustains Me…what satisfies My hunger…is something you know nothing about, yet."
33. So His disciples, missing the point, asked Him if someone had already brought Him something to eat.
34. Jesus said to them, "My nourishment comes from doing the will of Him Who sent Me and to finish His work. Whether it's one-on-one, as with this woman at the well, or ministering to this gathering crowd, this is what feeds and sustains Me!
35. "Stop limiting your concept of food to the natural. Do you not say, 'It is still four months until harvest time comes?' Well, I'm talking about the harvest of spiritual produce…a crop in the now. Lift up your eyes and look at these fields right now! These people here are the field…our field of harvest…and the harvest is ripe right now!
36. "Already the reaper is getting his wages. The one who does the harvesting has his reward *now*, for he is gathering a crop of eternal lives. And the one who does the planting rejoices with one who picks the crop, because it all happens—sowing *and* reaping—together *in the now*!
37. "For in this the saying holds true about the synergy of harvesting: one sows and another reaps, and together they produce what neither could produce individually.
38. "I have sent you to reap a crop for which you have not labored. Others, like the prophets and those who have preached about the coming Messiah, have toiled in the field, and you are able to step in to reap the results of their work."
39. By this time many Samaritans from the town began to believe in Him, mainly because of the power of the testimony of this woman who said, "This man told me everything I ever did." She obviously seemed to be amazed by His prophetic ability, but what really impressed them is that she didn't appear to be put off at all by a Jewish stranger so matter-of-factly reading her mail, so to speak. On the contrary, she came across as being positively changed for the better by it…like she was relieved that someone, at last, had so clearly seen right through her. It was as if her parched soul,

dehydrated by the effects of a life besieged by bad relationships, had somehow been refreshed and revived with living water!
40. The Samaritans who believed then came to Him and asked Him to remain there with them, so He ended up staying there two days.
41. Then even more people in town began to believe that He was the Messiah because of the things that He said.
42. And they told the woman that they no longer believed just because of what she had initially told them, but because of the things that they heard Him say first hand during those two days. They declared to her that they were convinced that He was, indeed, the Savior of the world, the Christ, Himself, as she had suggested.
43. But after those days He went on from there into Galilee, which was His original plan and destination,
44. although He Himself acknowledged and declared that a prophet generally is dishonored in His own natural habitat.
45. But as it turned out when He got into Galilee, He actually found that the people sincerely welcomed Him there. It was apparent that their hearts had been completely opened up to Him, and they took His claims seriously because they had attended the feast in Jerusalem and had seen everything that He did there. The Jerusalem experience changed them, and they were ready to receive Jesus as the Christ.
46. So Jesus came again to Cana of Galilee where He had turned the water into wine. And there He encountered a certain royal official whose son was lying ill in Capernaum.
47. The man had heard that Jesus had returned from Judea and was again in Galilee, so He came to meet Him there and began to literally beg Jesus to come and heal his son because the boy was about to die.
48. Jesus said to him, "Unless you see signs and miracles, you people will never believe or have faith, at all."
49. The king's officer pleaded with Him, "Sir, I do have faith. That's why I have come to You to ask for Your help. You're my only hope at this point because if You don't come and heal him, my boy is going to die."
50. Jesus answered him, "All right. Go in peace. Your son will live!" And the man just took Jesus at His word, without seeing anything... no sign...no miracle. He simply put his trust in what Jesus had said and started home.
51. While he was still en route to his house, his servants met him on the

52. way and said to him, "Your son is alive and well!"
52. When he inquired as to the exact time that his son had taken a turn for the better, they said to him, "The fever left him at one o'clock yesterday afternoon."
53. And the man immediately realized that that was exactly when Jesus had spoken the words, "Your son will live!" Needless to say, he and his whole household believed from that point on.
54. This was the second wonder that Jesus performed after He had come out of Judea into Galilee.

Chapter 5

1. A while later, Jesus traveled to Jerusalem for one of the Jewish festivals.
2. And there was in the city, near the Sheep Gate, a pool that is called Bethesda (in the Aramaic language).
3. This area was a well-known apparition site where a great number of sick people—the blind, the crippled, the paralyzed—did nothing every day but wait near the edge of the pool.
4. [Verse #4 does not appear in the original manuscript.] They waited there because of a widely believed myth about an angel that would periodically and unexpectedly make the water in the pool bubble up, thereby giving it healing properties.
5. One who was there was a man who had been an invalid for thirty-eight years.
6. When Jesus saw him lying there at the pool and learned that he had been in that condition for so long, He asked him, "Would you like to be well and whole?"
7. The man said, "Sir, I have no one to help me into the pool when the water is stirred by the angel. As soon as I try to get in by myself, someone else always goes down ahead of me."
8. Jesus said to him, "Stop wasting your time by putting all your hope in this urban legend. You don't need to wait for some angel to make the water bubble up. Just stand up on your own two feet, take up your cot, and walk!"
9. As soon as Jesus spoke these words, the man was instantly healed. Now the day on which this took place was the Sabbath,
10. and, true to form, that technicality was all that the religious leaders noticed or cared about. They said to the man who had been healed,

"It is the Sabbath and the Law forbids that you carry your own cot."
11. But he replied, "The man Who made me well said to me, 'Pick up your bed and walk,' and so I did!"
12. So they asked him, "Who told you to pick it up and walk?"
13. The man who was healed had absolutely no idea Who it was, for Jesus had vanished into the crowd.
14. Later, Jesus found him at the Temple and said to him, "Look at yourself! You are completely well! Now stop committing the sin of believing in myths and legends…of limiting your options by just focusing on one thing, like some magical, bubbling water, to help you. Repent, also, of the sin of believing that you are totally dependent on others to get you to where you need to be in your life. This mindset of yours is more of a disability than anything that you've dealt with physically, and if you don't stop this sinful thinking, a worse thing will eventually come on you."
15. The man went away and told the Jewish leaders that it was Jesus Who had caused him to be healed.
16. So, because Jesus was doing these things on the Sabbath, the religious leaders began to persecute Him.
17. Defending Himself to them, Jesus said, "My Father is always at work—every day, around the clock—and I am simply imitating His work patterns."
18. This is why they began to try to kill Him. He was not only trampling all over their limited concept of the Sabbath, He was just glibly calling God His own Father and, ultimately, making Himself equal with God.
19. Jesus answered them, "Look, here's the absolute truth about how I operate. The Son can do nothing by Himself; He can only do what He sees His Father doing. The Son just imitates the Father, that's all,
20. because the Father loves the Son and shows Him everything He does and how to do it. And He will even show Him greater works to perform in what you perceive to be the future – things that will totally amaze you.
21. "And just as the Father raises the dead, giving them life, so the Son creates life in whomever He pleases.
22. "Furthermore, the Father judges no one, but has entrusted all judgment to the Son, entirely.
23. "He has done this so that all people, everywhere, may honor the Son

just as they honor the Father. Whoever does not honor the Son, does not honor the Father Who sent Him.

24. "In all honesty I say to you, whoever hears My word, and believes in Him Who sent Me, is walking in the fullness of eternal life and will never live out his or her life under a sentence of judgment.

25. "And, believe Me when I tell you this, the time is coming—in fact, the time is now—when those who have been dragging themselves through their days on earth like dead people because of the oppression of religion, will hear the Son's voice and will begin to really live for the first time in their lives.

26. "For as the Father has life in Himself, so He has granted the Son also to have life in Himself.

27. "And He has given Him authority to judge because He is the Son of Man—the One Who empathizes with the human condition.

28. "Do not be amazed at this idea, for the time will come when all people—both the dead and the living—shall hear His voice

29. and shall ultimately be held accountable to Him for the way in which they live (or lived) out their lives.

30. "By Myself I am powerless; I judge only as I hear, and My judgment is fair and just because I have no selfish, hidden agenda. My entire motivation is to please Him Who sent Me.

31. "If I testify only about Myself, My testimony is invalid and irrelevant.

32. "But there is another who testifies on My behalf and I know that his testimony about Me is all true.

33. "You have personally sent an inquiry to John, and he freely and publicly testified on My behalf.

34. "Not that I am dependent upon human testimony. I only mention it that you may have a point of reference for your own salvation.

35. "John was the lamp that burned…shining for all to see…illuminating the path to show you the way. And for a short time you were more than happy to bask in the warmth of that bright and unique light.

36. "But I have a mandate and a testimony that is weightier than that of John. For the very work that the Father has given Me to finish, which I am doing, confirms the fact that the Father has sent Me.

37. "And the One Who sent Me—the Father Himself—has testified concerning Me. You have never heard or seen Him, no matter in what form He has appeared to you. You have never recognized any of His manifestations or revelations, so it stands to reason that you

do not recognize His incarnation in Me.
38. "And you do not have His word living in your hearts because you do not acknowledge the Word that has become flesh, living and moving all around you.
39. "You religiously search the Scriptures because you believe that they produce life in you, but you do not recognize that the Scriptures are all about Me, the very source of life!
40. "You see Me and the works that I do, but you refuse to approach Me to find out how to really live your life.
41. "Look, I don't crave human validation. I don't have an overwhelming need to be famous or adored, or even accepted for that matter, because I already know Who I am, whether you ever do or not. I do not need your approval.
42. "So I can tell you this without any fear of your rejection: I know you more than you can even understand. In fact, I know you better than you know yourselves, and I clearly see that there is no evidence of the love of God in you, whatsoever.
43. "I have come to you in My Father's name and you do not accept Me. But, interestingly, if someone else comes in his own name, speaking in no one's authority but his own, you don't seem to have any problem accepting him.
44. "But, really, it's not surprising. You all are so accustomed to living to please one another—to heaping glory and honor only on those who are in the loop, as it were, who are connected to the arc of your religious circle—that it never occurs to you that you should only be seeking the praise and glory of the Father, God, alone.
45. "But I have no need or intention to accuse you to the Father. You already have an accuser, and his name is Moses, the one on whom you have built your entire religious system.
46. "The bottom line is this: If you believed Moses, you would believe Me, for he wrote about Me, personally.
47. "But if you do not really believe his writings, how can you ever believe My teachings?"

Chapter 6

1. After this, Jesus crossed to the other side of the Sea of Galilee, or Tiberias as it is also known,
2. and a great number of people began to follow Him because they

were so amazed by the signs that they saw Him continually perform on the sick.
3. Then Jesus ascended to a mountainside and sat down with His disciples there.
4. It was near the time of the Passover Festival.
5. When Jesus noticed that a great crowd was coming toward Him, He said to Philip, "Listen, we have a situation; these people are hungry and we need to feed them right here, right now. Do you have any thoughts or suggestions about where we can buy bread for all of them to eat?"
6. He asked this only to test his faith and capacity for a big vision, for He already had a plan in His mind about what He was going to do.
7. Philip answered Him, "Do You realize that there are several thousand people here? I mean, we could feasibly do it, but it would take a great deal of planning and almost a year's wages to buy enough for each one to just have a bite!"
8. Another of His disciples, Andrew (Simon Peter's brother), spoke up and said,
9. "I don't know if this means anything or not, but You may want to know that there is a boy here with a lunch of five small barley loaves and two small fish. I know that this little bit of food certainly won't go very far among so many, but it's *something*. Just a thought…."
10. Jesus said, "All right then, have all the people sit down." It was a large, grassy area, and they all sat down there as they were instructed (if you counted just the men, there were about five thousand of them).
11. Then Jesus took the loaves, gave thanks, and began distributing bread to those who were seated. Thousands of them took as much as they wanted because there was no enforced rationing; literally, they had all they could eat! Then He took the fish and did exactly the same thing with it.
12. When everyone there had eaten all they could hold, He said to His disciples, "Now, gather up all the leftovers. Don't let anything go to waste."
13. So they gathered the scraps and excess food and filled up twelve whole baskets with thousands of pieces of bread and fish that were uneaten.
14. After the people saw this amazing sign, they began to say to one another, "You know, this man must surely be the Prophet whose

coming the whole world has been expecting!"
15. Jesus, becoming aware of how profoundly affected the people were by this miracle, realized that they were going to try to apprehend Him and forcibly make Him their king. So He resisted the temptation to settle for any earthly kingship and withdrew again to a mountain by Himself. He needed to be alone to regain a little perspective on maintaining the balance between His humanity and His divinity.
16. When evening came, His disciples went down to the lake together,
17. where they boarded a boat and set off across the water for Capernaum. It was now dark and Jesus had not yet joined them.
18. And a very strong wind started to blow hard across the water and began to produce extremely high, choppy whitecaps.
19. When they had rowed the boat out between three and three and a half miles, the disciples were astonished to see Jesus approaching the boat on foot! He was walking on top of the rough waves as if they were little hills on dry land! When they realized what He was doing, they just became totally paralyzed by overwhelming fear.
20. But He said to them, "Don't be afraid, boys! It's just Me!"
21. Then, as their initial panic began to subside, they were able to gather their wits enough to take Him into the boat. And in virtually no time, the vessel reached the shore where they were heading, landing in exactly the right spot.
22. The following day, the crowd that had stayed on the other side of the lake began to realize that only one boat had been there and that Jesus had not boarded it with His disciples. They remembered that the disciples had left without Him.
23. Then several boats from Tiberias arrived near the place where the people had eaten the miraculously-multiplied bread after the Lord had given thanks and blessed it.
24. As soon as the crowd realized that neither Jesus nor His disciples were there, they got into the boats and went to Capernaum, aggressively searching for Jesus.
25. When they finally found Him on the opposite side of the lake, they asked Him, "Teacher, when did You get here?"
26. Jesus answered, "Let Me tell you the truth: You are looking for Me, not because you saw the signs that I performed, but because you liked the fact that you ate the bread and fish until you were full.
27. "You shouldn't strive so hard to find food that is only going to spoil

in a couple of days; you should be using your energies to constantly search for the source of eternal food…the bread in the now…which the Son of Man will freely give you! And He gives you this bread because it is on Him that the Father has placed His unique seal of approval."

28. Then they asked Him, "How can we best use our energies to do the works that God requires of us?"
29. Jesus answered them, "The work of God, basically, is only this: to simply believe in the One Whom He has sent."
30. So they said, "We assume that You are referring to Yourself, and if believing in You really is all that we should do to meet God's requirements, then what sign will You give to convince us of that? What supernatural wonder will You perform before our eyes that will leave us no choice but to believe in You?
31. "You see, our ancestors saw all manner of amazing signs in the wilderness, not the least of which was the manna that they ate daily, just as it is written: *'He gave them bread from heaven to eat.'*"
32. Jesus said to them, "Surely, you must realize that it is not Moses who has given you the bread from heaven. Only My Father can give you the true, eternal bread in the now...the nourishment that comes from the heavenly realm...and He is serving you that real bread today.
33. "For the bread of God is He Who has come from the eternal now, the One Who has descended from the heavenly realm to give life to the whole world."
34. Jesus' words came across with such conviction and authority that the people who heard them enthusiastically responded by saying, "Then give us this heavenly bread now and forever!"
35. Jesus said to them, "You still don't get it! Don't you understand that this bread is not something that I can give you – it is what I am! I literally *am* the Bread of Life, and he or she who believes in Me will never go hungry or thirsty again…ever!
36. "But, as I have told you again and again, you have seen Me and My miracles, but somehow you can't seem to really believe that I am Who I say that I am! You can't see beyond the limited boundaries of your preconceived, religious ideology!
37. "But everyone that the Father enlightens will come to Me, unrestricted by religion. And when they do come, no matter what and no matter from where, I will never, ever reject them in any way.
38. "For I have come down from the heavenly realm into this dimension

not to do My will, but to do the will of Him Who sent Me.

39. "And this is the will of Him Who sent Me: that I should not lose anyone that He has given Me, but that I should give new life to them all, that I should raise them all up, even if bringing them all to salvation requires that I seek for them until there are no more days.

40. "For this is My Father's will—it is His ultimate purpose—that everyone who looks to the Son and believes in Him shall experience all the potential of eternal life, even if they don't see the fullness of it until the very last day."

41. Then suddenly He began to somehow lose favor with His audience. For the most part they had been somewhat open-minded to His message up until He said, "I, Myself, am the Bread that came down out of heaven!" For some reason, that particular statement seemed to rub everyone the wrong way, and the whole crowd began to turn on Him from that point.

42. They kept saying, "Isn't this Jesus, the Son of Joseph the carpenter? Doesn't He realize that we know both of His parents and that we know where He came from? How can He have such delusions of grandeur; how can He be so out of touch with reality that He could say, 'I have come down from heaven'?"

43. So Jesus said to them, "Look, I know what you're thinking and I can hear the things that you are saying against Me to one another, and I want you to stop it right now!

44. "I'll say it again, whether you like it or not: No one is able to come to Me unless the Father Who sent Me attracts them to Me, and I will eventually raise them all up, even if it requires a continual effort on My part, all the way up to the very last day!

45. "And this reconciliation is what the prophets of old referred to when they said, *'And they shall all be personally taught by God, Himself.'*

46. "No one has seen the Father in His fullness except the One Who is from God; only He has really seen the Father in all His glory.

47. "I am telling you the truth: He or she who believes in Me walks in the full blessings and benefits of everlasting life.

48. "And I reiterate, I *am* the Bread of Life!

49. "Look, I know that the manna in the wilderness is one of your most cherished and sacred iconic images, but you must face the fact that your forefathers ate it for years and died anyway!

50. "But I am talking about the bread that comes down out of heaven, which a person may eat and, as a result, will never die.

51. "Whether you are ready to receive it or not, it is a fact: I am the Living Bread that came out of the heavenly realm, or down from heaven, as you perceive it. If anyone eats this bread, he or she will live abundantly forever, and this bread literally is My *flesh*—the flesh that contains the life that I will lay down for the whole world."
52. Now the people became angry at Him because they were scandalized and appalled at this talk of "eating flesh." They considered the idea at once bizarre and grotesque and said to one another, "How is He able to give us His flesh to eat?"
53. And Jesus said to them, "This is the truth, regardless of how strange it may sound to your ears: You cannot have any life in you unless you devour the flesh of the Son of Man. And not only that, but you must also drink His blood if you want to live!
54. "The person who is hungry enough to feed on My flesh and thirsty enough to drink My blood, will walk in the full potential of eternal life and I will ultimately and personally raise him or her up.
55. "For My flesh is real, genuine food, and My blood is real, genuine drink.
56. "He or she who feeds on My flesh and drinks My blood dwells continually in Me and I will dwell continually in him or her.
57. "Just as My living Father sent Me and I live because of Him, so the one who feeds on Me will live because of Me. I am the sustainer of life!
58. "You're literally looking at the bread that came down out of heaven. And this bread is not like the manna which your and My ancestors ate and still died. The individual who relies on this bread for his or her primary food source will live now and forever."
59. He said all this while He was teaching in the synagogue in Capernaum.
60. When His disciples heard this, many of them said, "He's just gone too far this time with this strange doctrine. His self-exaltation alone is blasphemous enough to be deemed inappropriate and unacceptable for most people, but this allusion to cannibalism and vampirism is, frankly, just too hard for anyone to stomach!"
61. Aware that His disciples were having this conversation, He confronted them, asking, "Do we have a problem? Is My teaching offensive to you?
62. "I mean, if My revelation is too radical for you to receive, then how are you going to deal with it when you see the Son of Man literally

ascend to where He was before?
63. "My teaching is transcendent and spiritual, and it is the Spirit that gives life. Speaking about the trivialities of dead religion and the superficiality of the flesh does not profit you in any way. It is a waste of time. The words that I speak, however, are literally filled with the Spirit and they are full of the essence of life!
64. "And yet, in spite of the accessibility to the spirit-world that My words provide, there are still some of you, amazingly, who do not believe."
65. He went on to say, "This is why I have told you that no one can come to Me unless they can embrace the broader scope—the bigger picture if you will—where the Father can attract them to Me."
66. At this time many of His disciples disassociated themselves from Him and had nothing more to do with Him.
67. But Jesus made no effort to explain Himself or to qualify His offensive statements to the remaining disciples. And, without any apology, retraction or attempt at clarification, He asked the Twelve, flatly, "Well? Are you leaving with the rest of them?"
68. Peter spoke up and said, "Are You joking? Where would we go? There's nothing else to look for after finding You because You alone have the words of life for us; for us, You are the journey's end.
69. "We don't have to understand everything that You say with our minds because we believe in You with our hearts. Regardless of anything You throw at us, and no matter how new or strange it may sound to our ears, we have come to know, without a doubt, that You are the Christ...the Anointed One...the Son of the living God."
70. Then Jesus said, "Well, you Twelve are the original ones that I personally chose in the beginning. You are special to Me because you are the ones I started out with, even though I know that one of you is My adversary."
71. He was referring to Judas (the son of Simon Iscariot), who eventually betrayed Him, even though he was one of the originals.

Chapter 7

1. After this, Jesus went around in Galilee, intentionally avoiding Judea because the locals there were wanting to kill Him.
2. But when the Jewish Feast of Tabernacles was near,
3. Jesus' brothers took Him aside and said to Him, "You know, this

really is no place for You. The masses are never going to see You here. You really ought to leave this small town and go to Judea, so that more of Your followers there can see the miracles that You perform.

4. "No one who wants the publicity that it takes to become a public figure does anything low profile or in secret. If You feel You must do these things…if You're determined to keep acting like this…then go all the way with it! Make it work for You and reveal Yourself to the world!"

5. They had this little talk with Him, basically, because they did not believe in Him or take Him seriously. His very own brothers couldn't recognize His divinity or His uniqueness.

6. So, He replied to them, "My time has not come, yet. But because you, My brothers, do not understand the delicacy of timing or the importance of seasons…and really because you do not understand Who I really am…any time is suitable for you. You think that the window of opportunity is always open.

7. "You don't have any idea what it is like to be hated by the world. You blend in so well with the status quo that society has no reason to form any opinion, positive or negative, about you. But the larger society, especially the part that has been shaped by the conformity of religion, definitely hates Me. It hates Me, not just because of My individuality, but because I expose it for what it is, with all of its hypocrisy and phoniness.

8. "Please feel free to go to the feast yourselves. There will be a lot of people there who think just like you do, so you should be able to enjoy yourselves. But I have no intention of going because it is premature for Me to go public, and there is no way that I can go there privately or without being noticed. You couldn't possibly understand this because you don't lead public lives, but I have to strategically plan My every move so that I can stay in My proper time."

9. Having said this to them, He stayed behind in Galilee.

10. But afterward, when His brothers had gone up to the feast without Him, He actually did go there, also. Without traveling in their caravan, and without being a part of any entourage, it was more possible for Him to maintain anonymity and not draw attention to Himself.

11. But, of course, He was the One that everyone was already talking

about…the One that everyone had come there to see. They kept asking, "Where is that man, that radical, that miracle-worker? Is He here? Is He coming?"

12. And there was an amazing amount of buzz about Him everywhere at the celebration. Little groups were huddled all over the place, arguing about Him in hushed tones so that the Jewish religious leaders could not hear, but in hot dispute over Him, nonetheless. Some said, "He is good!" Others said, "No, He is a deceiver Who spreads false ideas!"

13. But no one had the courage to make any public statement about Him one way or the other.

14. But when the feast was about half over, to everyone's surprise, Jesus went up into the Temple court and just began to teach.

15. The Jews there were astonished at His presentation. They said, "How is it that this unlearned man can sound so intelligent and inspired? How can He be so eloquent when speaking of the sacred and the spiritual, especially when He expounds on theology and the Holy Scriptures?"

16. Jesus overheard them and said, "I can't take any credit for My teaching, because it is not My own but is the teaching of Him Who sent Me.

17. "If anyone desires to please God by doing His will, he or she will be illuminated to recognize whether or not My teaching is from God. Those who desire to hear from God will have the insight and discernment to properly judge My doctrine and to be able to identify its supernatural source.

18. "He who speaks on his own authority does so with a hidden agenda, to gain honor for himself. But He Who speaks for the honor of the One Who sent Him is a man of truth and integrity. There is nothing false—nothing to be mistrusted—about Him.

19. "And while I'm on the subject of integrity, let Me ask those of you who want to kill Me a question. We all agree that Moses gave you the Law, but you all know good and well that not one of you keeps it, so why do you think that you should kill Me because you presume that I don't keep the Law? What is the source of this hypocritical and irrational anger towards Me?"

20. Immediately the attitude of the crowd went negative, and they answered Him, "You are a paranoid lunatic! Who wants to kill You? You must be demon-possessed!"

21. Jesus answered them, "Look, I did one miracle and you were all astounded by it.
22. "Now Moses established the rite of circumcision, although he did not originate it (the Patriarchs did), and you are totally fine with performing it on baby boys on the Sabbath.
23. "So explain to Me how you can circumcise one part of a child's body on the Sabbath so that Moses' Law will not be broken, and yet be so angry at Me because I healed a man's whole body on the Sabbath?
24. "I mean, think about it! If you can stop judging everything by the superficial appearance of religion for one minute, you can see how absurd and pointless religion can be. Only then can you judge Me fairly."
25. Just then, ironically, some other people from Jerusalem joined the crowd and inadvertently confirmed His initial accusation by saying, "Hey, isn't that the man that they're trying to kill?
26. "And here He is speaking right out here in the open…in the Temple…right in front of the religious leaders! Did we miss something? Have the authorities now concluded that He is the Messiah?
27. "But the fact *is* that we know where this man is originally from, and we know that when the Messiah comes, no one should be able to know where He comes from!"
28. Then Jesus, still in the middle of His teaching in the Temple courts, cried out to them, "You think you know Me because you think you know where I am from. What you don't know is that I am not here on My own authority, but He Who sent Me is true—the consummation of all the truth—and because you don't know His truth, you don't know Me or understand where I am really from!
29. "But that does not affect My self-awareness because I do know Him, and I know without a doubt that He sent Me here."
30. These words were like a cue to the crowd to become aggressively violent with Him. They actually tried to personally seize Him with their own hands, but no one could get a grip on Him because His time had not come yet.
31. But somehow, in spite of all this, there actually were many in the crowd who began to believe in Him that day. They made this point, saying, "When the Messiah does come, does anyone really think that He could perform more extravagant and impressive signs and wonders than this man does and has?"

32. By this time the Pharisees had become aware of what the people in the Temple courts were saying about Him, both pro and con, so they decided to put a stop to all of it. The chief priests, along with the Pharisees, sent the Temple guards to arrest Him on the spot so that He would no longer be the controversial center of attention at this traditional celebration.
33. But Jesus made this final statement for that day: "I am only with you here in this dimension for a short time, and then I am going back to be reunited with the One Who sent Me.
34. "You will look for Me then, but you will not be able to find Me because where I am going, you cannot come."
35. Upon hearing this dramatic statement, the people there said, "Where does this man think He can go that we can't find Him? Will He go to where the Jews live scattered among the Greeks so that He can teach the Greeks?
36. "And what does He mean by saying, 'You will look for Me, but you will not find Me'? And why did He say, 'Where I am, you cannot come'?" And they argued and speculated and tried to interpret His words for the rest of that day. But He was nowhere to be found.
37. But on the final and most important day of the feast, Jesus just stood up right where He was and, without any timidity or self-consciousness at all, began to yell out at the top of His lungs these words: "Let anyone who is thirsty come to Me and drink!
38. "Whoever believes in Me, as the Scriptures have stated, living rivers of life will continuously and freely flow from within their inner beings!"
39. This was His way of introducing them to the ministry of the Holy Spirit, Whom those who believed in Him would later receive. The era of the Holy Spirit had not yet begun at this time, since Jesus had not yet been glorified.
40. On hearing these startling words spoken so loudly, some of the people said, "Surely this man is the Prophet!"
41. Others said, "No, He is the Messiah!" Still others argued, "But, how can the Messiah come from Galilee?
42. "Doesn't the Scripture say that the Messiah will come from the descendants of David…from Bethlehem, the town where David lived?"
43. So the people, forced into forming an opinion about Jesus with their limited understanding of how His life had already confirmed the

Scriptures, were ultimately divided because of Him.
44. Some wanted to seize or arrest Him, but no one had the courage to lay a hand on Him.
45. Finally, the Temple guards went back to the Pharisees and chief priests, who asked them, "Well, where is He? Why didn't you bring Him in?"
46. "It's hard to explain," the guards replied. "If you could only hear Him for yourselves—if you could see the way that the people relate and respond to Him…even the way that He invokes all kinds of reactions from them—you would understand that there has just never been a person, anywhere or anytime, who speaks like this man!"
47. "Don't tell me that He has deceived you, also!" retorted one of the Pharisees.
48. "You certainly don't see any of us believing in Him, do you?
49. "It's only this stupid crowd—gullible people who are ignorant of our precious Law—that even considers His ridiculous claims. And may they be damned for it!"
50. Nicodemus, who had gone to Jesus earlier and was one of the Pharisees, said,
51. "Surely our Law does not condemn a man without giving him a fair trial first! Shouldn't we at least hear Him ourselves to find out what He is actually doing?"
52. They replied, "Nicodemus, we don't care how open-minded you may be about the prospect of a Prophet or Messiah coming out of Galilee; the fact remains that, if you look into it from a theological or historical viewpoint, you will clearly see that it is impossible for such a man to come from there!"
53. That being said, the meeting broke up and they all went home.

[The earliest manuscripts, and many other ancient witnesses,
do not contain John 7:53 - 8:11.]

Chapter 8

1. Instead of returning to His home after the feast as everyone else did, Jesus went to the Mount of Olives.
2. But first thing the next morning, He was right back again in the Temple courts drawing a crowd to Himself. And when the people who were there at that hour began to gather around Him, He sat

down to teach them.

3. While He was in the middle of His talk, a group of some of the scribes and Pharisees dramatically interrupted His message by bringing a woman up to Him that they had somehow managed to catch in the act of adultery. They made her stand before Him in the middle of the court as if she were on trial in front of a judge.

4. And, with obvious sarcasm, they called Him, "Teacher," and said, "this woman has been caught in the very act of adultery" (of course, no one made any mention of the *man* with whom she was caught "in the act").

5. But they continued, "In our Law, Moses commanded us to stone such adulterous women to death. But we have brought this woman to You because we want to know what *You* have to say about her fate."

6. They were using this question to trap Him, intellectually and theologically, in front of an audience. But Jesus, instead of getting into a heated debate with them, just stooped down and began to write rather mysteriously on the ground with His finger, as if the religious men weren't even there.

7. But His ignoring them in this manner only caused them to become more persistent in their questioning. So He stood back up, looked around at all of them, and said, "Yes. I would say that it is both appropriate and necessary to stone her with stones until she is dead, as Moses commanded. And I also think that since you are the ones who discovered her in her indiscretion, then you are the ones most qualified to perform the execution…so step right up and start the killing! And whichever one of you is absolutely sinless should have the honor of hurling the first stone at her."

8. Then He bent down again and went on writing on the ground with His finger.

9. His words just seemed to hang, suspended in the air, and the power of them deflated the pompous arrogance of the men who had apprehended the woman. Conviction gripped their hearts and, while Jesus paid no attention to them as He continued His writing, they just began to silently file out of the Temple court, one by one, from the oldest down to the last one.

10. When Jesus stood back up, He looked straight at the woman and said to her, "Ma'am where are your accusers? Has no man in this crowd pronounced a sentence of condemnation on you?"

11. She looked around and then answered Him, "Apparently no one, Sir." "Then I don't condemn you, either," He replied. "You see, condemnation for the sin of adultery, or any other sin for that matter, doesn't come from above—from My Father or from Me—it comes from the people around you. People remit sins and people retain sins, depending on how they feel about you and on how they interpret their religion. My advice to you is that you change your adulterous lifestyle, because it's only going to bring you pain, and people can be very unforgiving of your mistakes. Now go, and don't get yourself into this kind of trouble again."
12. Then He turned His attention back to the crowd who was still there listening and said, "I am the Light of the world. Whoever follows Me will never stumble around in darkness, blinded by the hypocrisy and self-righteousness of religious thinking, but will have the Light of life."
13. But there were other Pharisees there in the crowd who defied Him by saying, "You are testifying on Your own behalf, so Your testimony is invalid. We can't just be expected to take Your word for it that You are Who You claim to be."
14. Jesus answered, "My testimony is true, even if I do testify on My own behalf. And I can speak up for Myself with authority because I know where I came from and I know where I am going. You just can't receive it because you don't know where I came from and so you don't know where I am going. You have no real comprehension of Me because of your lack of perception.
15. "You evaluate everything by human standards, setting yourselves up to judge according to the flesh. You have no point of reference other than what you can see with the natural eye. But I do not set Myself up to judge anyone or to pass a sentence of condemnation on them.
16. "But even if I take the liberty to sit in judgment, My judgment will be true and undisputed and I will always make the right decision. I say that with all confidence because I am not alone in the decision-making process…there are two of us. The Father Who sent Me is in complete harmony with Me. We confer on everything and We agree on everything.
17. "And in your own Law it is written that the corroborating testimony of two witnesses is reliable enough to stand up in court.
18. "I am one of the two necessary parties bearing testimony concerning Myself. The other validating witness is My Father Who sent Me,

and He is consistent with His testimony in My behalf."

19. Then they said to Him, "You keep talking about this Father of yours…well, where is He?" Jesus answered them, "You have no perception of My Father because you have a misguided perception of Me. If you could see and know Me, you could see and know My Father. It's that simple."

20. This session took place in the Treasury, the place where the offerings were put in the Temple court. But even though His teaching was not received there, no one ventured to arrest Him because His hour had not yet come.

21. Then once again He said to them, "I am leaving this dimension and returning to the heavenly realm, and you will look for Me, but you will die in the sin of your rebellion. With your state of mind, you cannot go where I am going."

22. At these words, the religious leaders began to ask among themselves, "Is He trying to tell us that He plans to commit suicide? Is that why He says that we cannot go where He is going?"

23. But He said to them, "You are from below…from the natural realm...bound by space and time…bound in your thinking by religion and the limitations of the Law. I am from above…from the superior spirit-realm…the eternal now…the ultimate dimension. You are the prisoner of this world order. I am not of this world.

24. "That is why I have told you that you will die, having lived your entire life under the curse of your sins. If you do not believe that I am Who I claim to be, that will be your fate."

25. So they said to Him, "Who are You, anyway? What are You really all about?" Jesus replied, "You know, speaking to you is just a waste of My time. I am exactly Who and what I have been telling you over and over again. Why do you need for Me to keep repeating Myself?

26. "I could say a lot about you—words of harsh judgment that would all be true—but He Who sent Me is faithful and trustworthy and so I choose to use My energies in telling the world the beautiful things that I have heard from Him, instead of spinning My wheels trying to convince you of something that you refuse to believe."

27. But even after all of this exchange, they still did not perceive that He was speaking to them of the Father.

28. So Jesus added, "When you have finally lifted up the Son of Man (He was speaking of being lifted up on the cross), then you will

know that I am Who I have said all along that I am. I have no reason to lie to you, nothing to gain by misleading you. Eventually, you will understand that I do nothing that is self-motivated or on My own authority. I only say what My Father has taught Me. I have no other agenda.

29. "And He Who has sent Me is always with Me. I'm not out here on My own, because I always only do what pleases Him."

30. While all of this conflict was going on between Jesus and the religious leaders, there were many in the crowd who, amazingly, began to believe in Him that day. Somehow, in spite of the negative atmosphere and extreme tension in the air, the truth of His message got through to them.

31. So He said to those who opened their hearts to Him then and there, "If you simply believe My words and wholeheartedly embrace My ideas, you will truly be My disciples.

32. "Then you will be freed from the bondage of religious thinking. Your knowledge of Me will become your key of truth...the key that opens the door to your mental and spiritual prison. In other words, you shall know the truth and the truth that you know will set you free!"

33. But others in the crowd answered Him, "We are the descendants of Abraham and have never been in bondage to anyone or to any ideology. What do You mean by saying that we will be 'set free'?"

34. Jesus replied, "Everyone who sees the world through the paradigm of the Law and its consequences, eats from the tree of the knowledge of good and evil. So, when he or she sins, that person automatically becomes the slave of sin.

35. "And a slave has no permanent place in the family, but a son is a son indefinitely, no matter what he does. I have come to deliver you from the bondage of slavery and to bring you into the Father's own family.

36. "You have a certain concept of freedom in your collective consciousness, but the Son is offering you a whole other and greater dimension of freedom. And if the Son liberates you, you will be liberated indeed…completely! You will no longer eat from the tree of the knowledge of good and evil, but you will eat from the tree of life! No longer slaves, you will know freedom in a way that you know nothing about at this point.

37. "I appreciate the fact that you are Abraham's descendants, but some

of you would rather kill Me than to open your hearts to the freshness of My word! Don't you see how warped religious thinking can be?

38. "I tell you things that I have seen and heard, first hand, from being in the presence of My Father. Your actions reflect that you are just repeating what you have heard from *your* father."

39. Indignant, they retorted, "Abraham is our father!" But Jesus replied, "If you really were the children of Abraham, then you would live like Abraham lived…you would do what he did. Abraham was open to change and had a real relationship with God. He actually conversed with the Father and could receive revelation from Him. He didn't just mindlessly follow a form of rules and regulations.

40. "But now there are some of you who are looking for an efficient way to kill Me…One Who has told you things that I heard fresh from God, Himself! Abraham would have had an open mind and would have listened to Me.

41. "You are actually acting like your real father." They said to Him, "Are You calling us bastards? You should know that we have no Father but God!"

42. Jesus said to them, "No, if God were your Father, you would love Me and receive Me as your own brother. I came from God, straight from His very presence. I am not self-appointed. The One that you say is your Father is the One Who sent Me!

43. "Why are My words so confusing to you? Why do they make you so angry? It's because your rigid, religious mindset will not allow you to hear Me with your heart!

44. "You are the offspring of your father, that devil called religion! You carry out the devil's desires, which have always culminated in murder—from Cain's murdering Abel over the proper way to offer the sacrifice, to your current plans to assassinate Me! That murdering devil is the father of lies; lying is his natural inclination, and when he lies, he speaks in his native tongue!

45. "So when I tell you the *truth,* you don't believe Me. You are so saturated with lies that the truth sounds false to your religious ears.

46. "Not one of you can prove Me guilty of sin, so why don't you believe Me when I tell you the truth?

47. "Whoever belongs to God hears the voice of God. You can't recognize My voice because you do not really belong to God."

48. They answered Him, "Do You know what we think? We think that You are a Samaritan and that You are demon-possessed!"

49. Jesus said, "Well, I'm definitely not a Samaritan and, no, I am not possessed by a demon. All I am is One Who honors My Father and, for that, you dishonor Me.
50. "I have no desire to seek glory for Myself. There is only One Who does that and He, alone, is the Judge.
51. "And the truth is that whoever receives and obeys My word will never see death."
52. At this they exclaimed, "Well, You may not be a Samaritan, but You definitely are demon-possessed! Now we know that You are because of what You just said. Abraham died and so did all the prophets, yet You say that whoever obeys Your word will never die!
53. "Are You claiming to be greater than our father Abraham? Hello…he died! The prophets died! Who do You think You are to say such an outrageous thing?"
54. Jesus replied, "Look, here's the bottom line: If I glorify Myself, My glory is empty and meaningless. But My Father, Whom you claim is your God, is the One Who glorifies Me, and that's all the validation that I need.
55. "You do not know Him, but I do. I can't say that I don't because then I would be lying like you. It's the truth, whether you believe it or not. I know that I know Him and that I obey His word.
56. "Furthermore, your father Abraham rejoiced at the thought of seeing My day and hour, and he did actually see it and it was everything that he hoped it would be."
57. The Jewish leaders then shouted out, "You are not even fifty years old! How could You have personally seen Abraham who lived centuries ago...and how could he possibly have seen You or Your 'day?' You're unbelievable!"
58. "I'm just telling you the truth," Jesus calmly replied. "And the truth is that, before Abraham was even born, I AM!"
59. Well, that statement just pushed them over the edge. They not only considered it an insanely arrogant thing to say, but it struck them as being blatantly blasphemous to use the holy words "I AM" when referring to Himself. They became so infuriated that they started picking up stones to stone Him with, but Jesus, once again, was miraculously able to slip away from the midst of the people on the Temple grounds.

Chapter 9

1. As He was walking along one day, Jesus saw a man who had been blind since birth.
2. His disciples, picking up on the object of His attention, asked Him, "Teacher, whose sin caused this man's blindness? Was his own sinfulness the source of the problem, or did he inherit some generational curse from his sinful parents?"
3. Jesus answered them, "Why do you assume that his blindness is the direct result of sin? And even if it *were* the result of sin, why is it so important to you to know *whose* sin it was? You need to change your perspective and your priorities. When you see someone in need like this, your immediate response should be to look for a way for the works of God to be displayed in his or her life, and nothing more.
4. "As long as it is daylight, we must do the work of Him Who sent Me, and His work is to heal the whole of humanity, not to punish people who are already suffering. God's business is the order of the day and it must be done before nightfall.
5. "And as long as I am in this dimension, I am the world's Light."
6. When He had said this, He did something quite unusual; He spat on the ground and made mud with His saliva, then He spread it all over the man's eyes.
7. After that, He sent the man to wash in the pool of Siloam (which, ironically, means "Sent"). So he went and did as Jesus had instructed him and he came back with fully restored vision.
8. When the neighbors and people who only knew him by sight as a blind beggar saw him, they said, "Hey, isn't that the man who used to sit and beg so pathetically?"
9. Some said, "Yes! I think it *is* him!" Others said, "No way! It has to be someone who just looks very much like that guy." But he, himself, settled the question by telling everyone, "Yes, I am the man who used to be blind!"
10. So they said to him, "What happened? How did you get your sight restored to you?"
11. He replied, "You know that man called Jesus? Well, He just made some mud and put it on my eyes and told me to go to Siloam and wash, which I did. And when I opened my eyes after flushing them out with water, I could see everything!"
12. Obviously excited, they asked, "Where is Jesus right now?" And he

said to them, "How should I know?"

13. So they just sort of overtook the man who had been blind and brought him immediately to the Pharisees.
14. Now it just so happened that it was on the Sabbath day that Jesus mixed the mud and healed the man's eyes with it.
15. So the Pharisees asked the man what everyone else had asked him. They wanted to hear from him how he had received his sight, so he recounted to them the whole story of the mud and the miracle.
16. Then some of the Pharisees said, "Well, this Jesus that everyone keeps talking about is obviously not from God because He has no apparent regard for the Sabbath." But others said, "Yes, but how could a sinner or an evil man do such wonderful signs and miracles? How could a bad man do such good things?" So, there was, again, the typical difference of opinion and division over Jesus among them.
17. So they asked the man who had been healed, "What do you have to say about Him, seeing that it was your eyes that He opened?" And he said to them, "Well, there's clearly something special about Him…He must be a prophet!"
18. But the Jewish religious leaders did not believe that he had really been blind and was now healed. So they called in his parents to verify the story.
19. When the parents arrived, the Pharisees said to them, "We have three questions for you: One, is this your son? Two, if he is your son, is it true that he was blind from birth? And three, if he was blind, how do you explain the fact that he can now see?"
20. The man's parents replied, "We can only answer the first two questions. He is definitely our son, and he has been completely blind from the day he was born.
21. "But, as for your third question, we have absolutely no idea what to tell you. We don't know how he is suddenly able to see after all these years, and we do not know who is responsible for this miracle. He is of age; you'll have to ask him about what has happened to him."
22. They said this in an effort to avoid acknowledging Jesus to the Pharisees. They were afraid of a confrontation, because the religious leaders had already agreed that if anyone should even hint that Jesus was the Christ, they would be banned from the synagogue.
23. So they dodged answering the question by saying, "He is of age; ask

him."

24. So the Pharisees summoned the man a second time and said to him, "In the future, when people ask you about your restored eyesight, you must simply say that it was the result of a mysterious act of God. Do not give any credit to this Jesus, because He is sinful and wicked and should not receive any credit or publicity."

25. The man replied, "Look, I don't know if He is a sinner or not. And I'm not personally qualified to determine whether He is good or bad. All I can tell you is that this time last week I couldn't see a thing, and this week I have perfect eyesight! I have no opinion about His morality, character or ethics, and I don't know what He thinks about the Sabbath. But one thing I can definitely vouch for is His ability to demonstrate the miraculous, even if His methods are unconventional! I mean, the man can heal people; in fact, He probably can do anything!"

26. So they said to him, "All right, off the record, tell us exactly what happened to you. Walk us through the entire encounter with Jesus from the beginning."

27. He answered, "Gentlemen, I've already told you this whole story! Why do you want me to repeat it? It sounds to me like you are interested only in Jesus, because you seem to be nearly obsessed with Him! If I didn't know better, I'd say that you are all considering becoming His disciples yourselves!"

28. Well, that did it! The Pharisees completely lost control at these words and cursed the man, railing at him with unbridled rage. "How dare you?" they snarled. "You're the one who is obsessed with Him! We are the disciples of Moses,

29. because we know that Moses was directly sent by God. We don't have any idea where this imposter, this Jesus, is from or what His wicked agenda is!"

30. The man replied, "You people are just too much! I mean, isn't this an amazing thing? Here this man has opened my eyes—you can't deny that—but you deny that you know where He came from! Amazing!

31. "Get serious! You have to know, deep down, that this Man is the Christ! You don't believe that God listens to sinners, so how can you explain God listening to Him?

32. "Since the beginning of time, no one has ever opened the eyes of a man born blind. You know that it's true.

33. "If this Man were not from God, there is no way that He could perform such miracles…pure and simple! There is nothing else that needs to be said about it."
34. They retorted, "You weren't just born blind…you were born in sin and you're still a sinner. How dare you presume to teach us! Who do you think you are? This conversation is over!" And with that, they literally threw him out of the Temple.
35. When Jesus heard that the man had been put out so dramatically, He went to meet him. When He found him, He asked, "Do you believe that the Son of Man is the Son of God?"
36. The man replied, "If He is Who I think that He is, then point Him out to me and I will believe in Him."
37. Jesus said to him, "I believe you know Who He is… He is talking to you right now!"
38. The man then cried out, "Lord, I do believe! And I worship You! You have not only given me my sight, You have given me back my life! You are the Christ, the Son of the Living God!"
39. Jesus responded, "I came to heal the blindness of the whole world and, in so doing, I have become a divider. I divide the light from the darkness so that those who have never seen can have their spiritual eyes opened and those who are supposedly the 'seers' will be exposed as the blind guides that they are."
40. Some nosy Pharisees were standing close by, eavesdropping on this conversation. They spoke up and said, "Are we to assume, then, that You are calling all of us blind?"
41. Jesus said, "No, actually, because if you all really were blind, you would be held blameless in your rejection of Me. But since you claim to have insight from God—because you are supposed to be the ones who can see the truth—you are held accountable. You are not blind...you just refuse to see.

Chapter 10

1. "Listen, all of you Pharisees, because I want to talk to you about so-called spiritual leaders who are really nothing more than thieves and robbers, and what I tell you about them is the absolute truth. Simply put, anyone who does not enter in by the door into the sheepfold, but climbs up some other way, exposes himself as being nothing but a thief and a robber.

2. "But he or she who enters by the door is a true shepherd of sheep.
3. "The gatekeeper will open the gate for that shepherd, and his sheep will listen for the sound of his voice. And that true shepherd will call his own sheep by name, and he will lead them from the safety and security of the sheepfold, out into the wide, open spaces where green pastures can be found.
4. "And once he has brought his sheep outside, he will walk on ahead of them on the journey and they will automatically follow him because they recognize his voice and have learned to depend on his leadership to guide them.
5. "There is no chance of them ever following a stranger, because they would not recognize his voice and would be unfamiliar with his call. In fact, they would run away from him."
6. Jesus used this parable to illustrate the relationship between leaders with insight and integrity and their faithful followers, but it went right over the Pharisees' heads.
7. So Jesus broke it down for them and said, "The truth is that I, Myself, am the door for the sheep.
8. "Anyone who ever came before or after Me claiming to be the door, was and is nothing but a dishonest thief and an opportunistic robber. But those sheep who are really hungry for spiritual food will not even listen to them.
9. "I am the Door. Anyone who enters in directly through Me, instead of trying to come in through his or her dogma, doctrine or denomination, will be saved. And that person will have the liberty to go in and out of different, progressive stages of truth to find pasture.
10. "But these 'thieves and robbers,' as I call them, who impose the agendas of their own particular religious ideas and their irrelevant, manmade laws on the sheep, only do so in order to steal, kill and destroy them. They come to steal any and all prophetic revelation available to the sheep, to kill any chance of them ever having a real, first-hand relationship with God, and to ultimately destroy their personal destinies. But I have come that the sheep, the true seekers, may have and enjoy life and have it in abundance! Overflowing life…rich and full and free of religious oppression…that's the kind of life I have to offer the sheep who follow Me.
11. "I am the Good Shepherd. The good shepherd doesn't just lead the sheep, he actually risks and even lays down his own life for them.
12. "But when a servant who is only a hired hand sees a wolf coming, he

deserts the flock and runs away, because he has no real relationship with the sheep. Then that wolf is able to catch the sheep and scatter them, and when they get separated from one another, they become particularly vulnerable.
13. "The hired hand flees because it's just a job to him. He doesn't have the connection with the sheep, nor the concern for them that a true shepherd does, because he does not own them and has no history with them.
14. "But I am the Good Shepherd, and I know and recognize My own sheep, and My own sheep know and recognize Me,
15. in the very same way that the Father knows Me and I know the Father. That is why I am able to give up My very life for the sheep.
16. "And not only that, but I also have other sheep besides these of whom I speak…sheep that you don't even know or believe exist because they are not of this fold. But I must bring them in, also, and they will listen to My voice and will respond to the call that is uniquely meant for them. And they will be brought in to unite with these so that, ultimately, there will just be one great flock under one good shepherd.
17. "The Father loves Me because I lay down My life for My own, only to take it back up again for them.
18. "But make no mistake about this: No one takes My life from Me! I am the only one authorized to lay it down, and I do so voluntarily. I, alone, have the power to give up My life, and I willingly offer it as a sacrifice. I will never be a martyr. And because I have the power to lay it down, I have the power to take it back up again. I have received this command to take authority over My own death and resurrection from My Father."
19. Once again his audience was divided over His bold declarations.
20. Many of them held to the rumors that He was demon-possessed. Others said, "Why are you still listening to Him? Don't you realize that He is just a raving lunatic?"
21. But still others said, "It's ridiculous and entirely too easy to dismiss this man as being nothing more than a madman. And if you really think about it, the 'demon-possessed' theory can't fly either, because a demon could never open the eyes of the blind!"
22. Then came the Festival of Dedication of the reconstruction of the Temple in Jerusalem.
23. It was winter, and Jesus was walking in the Temple area called

Solomon's Porch.

24. So the people who were there surrounded Him and began asking, "How long are You going to keep us in suspense? If You really are the Christ…the Messiah …then open up to us and tell us plainly."
25. Jesus answered them, "You're not in suspense! I've repeatedly told you Who I am; you just don't believe Me. And I don't even need to tell you with words in the first place because My actions speak much louder to this issue. The works that I do in the name of the Father testify of Me.
26. "But you do not believe because you are not My sheep.
27. "My sheep intimately know My voice; I know them completely, and they willingly follow Me.
28. "I cause them to walk in the full potential of eternal life, and they will never be stolen from Me, or killed, or destroyed…because no one, not even you thieves and robbers, can snatch them out of My hand!
29. "My Father, Who has given them to Me, is greater than anyone or any religious system; and no one can snatch them out of My Father's hand.
30. "The Father and I are one."
31. Once again, the people started picking up stones with which to stone Him when He said that.
32. But Jesus said to them, "I have shown you many amazing things and have done many good deeds in your presence because the Father has enabled Me to do so. For which miracle or act of mercy do you intend to stone Me?"
33. They answered, "We are not stoning You for any good work, but for Your blasphemy! You are a mere man, but You claim to be God!"
34. Jesus said to them, "Why do My claims shock and anger you so much? This isn't a new concept. Don't you know that in your own Law—in the Psalms of Asaph—God is recorded as saying, 'I said you were gods'?
35. "Now, if He called those who just received His message 'gods' in the Scriptures—in your own Law—and you say that you honor the Scriptures and that the Law cannot be set aside,
36. then how is it when I say that I am the Son of God Whom the Father has set apart and sent into this dimension, that you accuse Me of blasphemy?
37. "Look, don't believe Me unless I do the works of My Father.

38. "But if I do them, they alone should convince you that the Father is in Me and I am in the Father."
39. Once again, their anger was ignited and they tried to seize Him and, once again, He was able to escape their grasp.
40. After that, Jesus went back to the other side of the Jordan to the place where John had been baptizing earlier, and stayed in that location.
41. And many people came to Him there and said, "Although John never performed a sign, everything that he said about this man is true."
42. And in that place many people became believers in Him.

Chapter 11

1. Now Jesus had a personal friend named Lazarus, who was very sick. Lazarus lived in Bethany, the village of Mary and her sister, Martha.
2. This Mary was the one who, in this account of Jesus' life, anointed Him with perfume and wiped His feet with her hair. It was Mary's brother, Lazarus, who was sick, and Jesus was close to the whole family.
3. So when Lazarus became ill, his sisters sent word to Jesus, saying, "Lord, the friend whom You love so deeply is sick and needs Your help."
4. When Jesus received the message, He responded, prophetically, "This sickness will not end in death! In fact, it is for God's glory so that God's Son may be glorified through it."
5. Now it should be reiterated that Jesus loved these three people very much. He was close to them in a way that was rather unusual and unprecedented for Him, because He basically didn't build personal relationships with people outside of His circle of disciples.
6. But, in spite of the bond that He shared with Lazarus and his sisters, Jesus did not immediately rush to Bethany to see about His sick friend, as requested. On the contrary, He stayed where He was for two more whole days before even acknowledging the situation.
7. Then, finally, He said to His disciples, "We need to go back to Judea. I'm ready now."
8. "But Teacher," they said, "just the other day when You were there, the local people were attempting to stone You to death! Do You think it's a good idea to go back there right now?"
9. Jesus answered them, "Are there not twelve hours in the day?

10. Whoever walks around in the daytime does not stumble, because they see everything by this world's light.
10. "It is when people try to walk at night that they stumble, for they have no light for their path."
11. After saying this, He continued, "Our friend Lazarus has fallen asleep and I need to go there and wake him up."
12. His disciples replied, "Lord, if he is sick, it is good for him to get as much rest as possible. Sleep is therapeutic...the more he gets, the sooner he will get better."
13. But Jesus was speaking of something else entirely. Even though He didn't want to say it, and even though He had said that it wouldn't happen, Jesus knew within Himself that Lazarus had died. But His disciples didn't discern this and thought that He was referring to natural sleep.
14. So He spelled it out for them: "Lazarus is dead;
15. and, for your sake, I am actually glad that I was not there to prevent it from happening so that you may begin to believe on a whole new level. Now let us go to him."
16. Then Thomas (whose Greek name was Didymus), demonstrated how clueless they all were by chiming in with a bizarrely random and irrelevant suggestion. "Let us also go, that we may die with him!" he said. No one even responded to this strange response to Jesus' announcement that He was going to raise Lazarus up; they just started on their journey.
17. Upon His arrival, Jesus discovered that Lazarus had already been in the tomb for four days.
18. Now Bethany was less than two miles from Jerusalem,
19. and many people from there had come to visit Mary and Martha to comfort them in the loss of their beloved brother.
20. When Martha heard that Jesus was approaching the house, she went out to meet Him on the way. Mary, on the other hand, just stayed indoors.
21. "Lord," Martha said to Jesus, "where have You been? If You had just come when we called for You, my brother would be alive right now!
22. "But even though I am brokenhearted that You ignored our message, I know that God will give You whatever You ask."
23. Without apology Jesus said to her, "Martha, your brother will rise again."

24. She answered Him, "Yes, I know that eventually he will rise again in the resurrection, but that's little consolation to us in the here and now."
25. Jesus said to her, "You need to stop thinking of the resurrection as an event and begin to see it as a person, and that person is Me! I am the Resurrection and the Life! Whoever believes in Me will live, in spite of the fact that they experience the rite of passage called death.
26. "Whoever lives by believing in Me will not even be affected by death. Do you believe what I'm telling you?"
27. "Yes, Lord," she replied, "I do believe that You are the Messiah, the Son of God Who has come into our world!"
28. After she had said this, she went back to the house to speak privately with her sister. "Our Friend, the Teacher is here," she said, "and He is asking for you."
29. When Mary heard this, she gathered up her courage and went out to meet Him.
30. At this point, Jesus had not yet entered the village but was still at the place where Martha had met Him.
31. When the local people who had been with Mary in the house, comforting her, saw how quickly she got up from her place of mourning and went out, they followed her. They assumed that she was going back to the tomb and they wanted to be there for her.
32. But when Mary reached the place where Jesus was and saw Him face to face, she became overwhelmed with emotion and fell, prostrate, at His feet. Seeing Him brought it all home for her…the sorrow…the anger…the disappointment…the pain. "Lord," she sobbed, "if You had been here, my brother would not have died."
33. Mary's obvious grief affected the people who were with her, because they all started crying, as well. When Jesus saw Mary and all of her friends weeping so pitifully, it really hit Him hard. The whole scenario touched Him on so many levels that all He could do was deeply groan in His spirit. When it came to ministry, Jesus was usually able to keep some emotional distance between Him and those who needed Him, but this was different. This really troubled Him.
34. "Where have you laid him?" He asked. "Come and see, Lord," they replied, and they led Him to Lazarus' burial site.
35. When Jesus finally saw the tomb, He just broke down and wept. A few days before, He had boldly prophesied that Lazarus' sickness

was not going to end in death, and now He had every intention of supernaturally reversing time and making that prophecy come true. Only a short while earlier, He had even announced to Martha, very authoritatively, that He was the Resurrection and the Life. But when He experienced with His own two eyes the harsh reality of seeing a close friend's grave, He so identified with the human condition that all He could do was cry. His immediate reaction to the sight was not that of "the Resurrection and the Life," but that of a completely human being who was dealing with a sense of loss on a very personal level.

36. When the people saw Him crying, they were very moved and said, "Look at that…see how much He loved him!"

37. But some of them said, "Then why didn't He prevent this from happening? He can open the eyes of the blind; why couldn't He save the life of His own friend?"

38. Hearing all this talk only forced Jesus to groan even more deeply in His spirit. His human nature was competing here with His divine nature in a very profound way. The Son of God was ready to perform a miracle, but the Son of Man just wanted and needed to grieve for His friend. But, in spite of this inner conflict, He approached the tomb, which was really just a cave with a stone laid across the entrance, and said,

39. "Take away the stone." "But Lord," Martha protested, "his body has been in there for four days and by now is decaying and putting off a bad odor. Please, just let him be."

40. But at this point Jesus was neither groaning nor weeping. And with great conviction He declared to her, "Have I not told you that if you believe, you will see the very glory of God?"

41. Martha said nothing, but His words so dominated the atmosphere that they motivated some of the people to remove the stone. Then He looked up and said, "Father, I thank You that You have heard Me.

42. "And that goes without saying, because I know that You always hear Me; but I am speaking this out loud for the benefit of these standing here so that they may believe that You sent Me."

43. After saying these words, Jesus called in a loud voice, "Lazarus, come out of there!"

44. And in virtually no time, that dead man came out alive! His hands and feet were wrapped in linen strips and a cloth was tied around his

face, so Jesus said to the stunned people standing there, "Now, take off his grave clothes and let him go!"
45. Naturally, many of the people who had come to visit Mary, and had seen what Jesus did there, easily put their faith in Him at that point.
46. But some of them made it their business to go to the Pharisees to tell them what Jesus had done *this* time.
47. Then the chief priests and the Pharisees called a meeting of the entire Sanhedrin court to discuss the matter of this Miracle Worker. They said, "We've got to do something about Jesus of Nazareth, but what? He not only continues to perform these signs and wonders, but they seem to be getting increasingly more elaborate and dramatic!
48. "If we don't put a stop to His influence and magic, the whole nation will eventually believe in Him. And if that happens, the Romans will get involved and will come and suppress us and take away our holy place…our Temple…our city…our nation. He could potentially ruin everything for us!"
49. But one of them, Caiaphas, who was the high priest that year, spoke up and said, "You know nothing at all!
50. "You need to realize that it is better for all of us that one man die for the people, than that the whole nation perish."
51. He did not say this on his own; he was not self-motivated. But, as the high priest that year, he was authorized to prophesy, and so he prophesied that Jesus would die for the nation.
52. And not only for the Jewish nation, but also for the purpose of uniting into one body the children of God who have been scattered to all the nations of the earth.
53. So, from that day, they began to plot together how they could take His life from Him.
54. From then on, Jesus no longer publicly moved among those who could be influenced by the Jewish religious leaders. Instead, He withdrew to an area near the wilderness, to a village called Ephraim, where He stayed with His disciples.
55. When it was almost time for Passover, many went up from the country to Jerusalem for the traditional cleansing ceremony that was required for it.
56. They kept looking for Jesus there. People gathered in the Temple courts and asked one another, "Have you heard anything about Jesus? Do you know if He is coming to the festival at all?"
57. Everyone was interested in Him for one reason or another. But they

all knew that the chief priests and Pharisees had given strict orders that if anyone knew of Jesus' whereabouts, they were to report to them immediately because there was a warrant for His arrest.

Chapter 12

1. Six days before the Feast of Passover, Jesus went back to Bethany where He had raised Lazarus from death.
2. His main reason for returning to the village was that Martha had prepared a big meal to honor Him and to show her appreciation for Lazarus' miracle. So she served up a great feast and Lazarus sat right next to Him at the table.
3. It was a beautiful time of celebration and, after the meal, Mary brought in a jar of very expensive aromatic oils with which she anointed and massaged Jesus' feet. Then she wiped them with her hair and the sweet smell of the perfumed oils filled the whole house.
4. But one of his disciples, Judas Iscariot, who was already having thoughts of betraying Him, objected:
5. "Why wasn't this perfume sold and the money given to the poor? It was worth a year's wages...a small fortune."
6. He didn't say this because he cared about the poor, but because he was a thief. Even though he had been entrusted with the office of treasurer and accountant for Jesus' ministry, he was in the habit of helping himself to the money whenever he needed it for his own personal use.
7. "Leave her alone," Jesus replied. "She has done this in preparation for My burial. And, furthermore, you need to realize the truth about the poor. Even if you gave them all the money from the sale of this expensive oil and more, it would not eradicate their poverty. Only a change in their mindset can do that.
8. "In other words, you'll always have the poor with you, but you won't always have Me."
9. Now word got out that He was back in town, so a great number of people came to see Him. And, of course, everyone was extremely curious to see Lazarus, the man who had been raised from the dead.
10. So the chief priests plotted to put Lazarus to death, also.
11. He was added to their hit list because, on account of him and his amazing miracle, many of the local people were leaving their traditional faith and believing in Jesus.

12. The next day, a huge crowd assembled in Jerusalem for the Passover Feast. When they heard that Jesus was coming there for the festival,
13. they took palm branches and went out to meet Him, loudly shouting to Him, "Hosanna! Blessed is He Who comes in God's name. Blessed is the King of Israel!"
14. But Jesus found a young donkey and sat on it, to fulfill what was written:
15. *"Don't be afraid, people of Israel. Look, your King is coming, sitting on a donkey's colt."*
16. At first, His disciples didn't get it at all. But after Jesus was glorified, they remembered all this and realized that everything had happened exactly as the Scriptures had said it would.
17. Those in the crowd who had seen Jesus raise Lazarus from the dead, were talking about it incessantly. And as they kept recounting the story over and over, the excitement from the whole thing just spread like wildfire among the people.
18. And that's why the crowd was so huge and noisy that day. The whole town was so electrified with the news of Jesus' power and ability, that a kind of mania had set in among them.
19. So when the Pharisees saw what was happening, they said to one another, "This thing is out of control! Look! The entire world has gone after Jesus!"
20. Now there were some Greeks among those who went up to celebrate and worship at the Feast.
21. And they approached Philip (who was from Bethsaida in Galilee), with a request. "Sir," they said, "we've got to see this Jesus that everyone is talking about!"
22. Philip went to tell Andrew and, in turn, Andrew and Philip told Jesus.
23. But Jesus answered them, saying, "The hour has come for the Son of Man to be glorified.
24. "And this is the truth that you need to grasp: Unless a kernel of wheat falls to the ground and dies, it remains only a single seed. But if it dies, the course of nature sees to it that it is then able to produce innumerable seeds!
25. "Those who love their natural life more than their spiritual life will lose their natural life. But those who let go of this natural life will walk in the fullness of eternal life…a life in the now…and they will have it here and in the next dimension.

26. "All those who want to be My disciples must come and follow Me because My servants need to be where I am. And if they follow Me into full comprehension of eternal life, the Father will honor them.
27. "Now My soul is troubled...My inner conflict is intense...but what can I do about it? I can't say, 'Father, save Me from this hour of trial and agony,' because this is what I came for!
28. "At this point, all I can say is 'Father, glorify Your name through this!'" Just then a voice from the eternal realm manifested into the natural dimension and said, "I have glorified it by sending You there, and I will glorify it again by receiving You back here."
29. Everyone in the crowd heard it, but some of them dismissed it as nothing but a clap of thunder. Others surmised that an angel had spoken to Him.
30. But Jesus said, "This voice did not speak for My benefit, but for yours.
31. "Now the crisis point of this world has arrived, and now the administration of the so-called 'prince of this world' has come to an end. The one who has presented himself as the evil genius of this dimension is finished...finally cast down and cast out.
32. "And now begins the new era of My reign, the time for Me to be lifted up. And if I am lifted up from the earth, first in humiliation on the cross and then in triumph on the throne of My kingdom, I will personally draw all of humanity...every ethnicity, culture, and people group...to Myself!"
33. He said this to show the kind of death He was going to die, because a large part of the horror of crucifixion was the public humiliation and exposure of it. Jesus would be crucified naked, and elevated to a level where all could see him, so that He could bear the shame of every individual's sin consciousness. The Romans "lifted up" their victims on crosses to make public spectacles of them – the idea being that the visibility of those executed would serve as a deterrent to crime and rebellion. But Jesus would be lifted up so that everyone, everywhere, could identify Him, and identify *with* Him, so that they could see Him high above the crowd and be able to know where and how to find Him from any place on the earth.
34. But the crowd spoke up and said, "We have heard from the Law that the Christ will remain forever, so how can you say, 'The Son of Man must be lifted up'? And Who is this 'Son of Man' that you keep talking about, anyway?"

35. So Jesus said to them, "You will only have the Light in this way a little while longer. You must walk while you have the Light; walk before darkness overtakes you. Those who walk in the dark have no idea where they are going.
36. "Believe in the Light while you have the Light; your faith in the Light will cause you to become sons and daughters of the Light, beings of light who are filled with light." When He had finished speaking, Jesus left and hid Himself from them.
37. Even after Jesus had performed so many amazing signs and wonders in their presence—right before their very eyes—they still would not believe in Him.
38. And this phenomenon (the fact that they couldn't see Him because of the blindness of their religion, even though He revealed Himself to them) fulfilled Isaiah's words: "Lord, who has believed our message, and to whom has the mighty, muscled arm of the Lord been revealed?"
39. This explains why they could not believe, because Isaiah also said,
40. *"He has blinded their eyes and hardened their hearts, so they can neither see with their eyes nor understand with their hearts, nor turn around and face Me so that I could heal them."*
41. Isaiah said this because he saw Jesus' glory in the eternal now and spoke about Him in the dimension of time. And he prophesied these things because it was necessary for Israel, as a nation, to reject Jesus as being their Messiah, so that the gospel would be forced to become global, finding its universal manifestation in the diverse dimension of the Holy Spirit.
42. Yet at the same time, many, even among the religious leaders, believed in Him. But, because of the Pharisees, they would not openly confess it for fear they would be put out of the synagogue.
43. For they loved religious approval and human glory more than the glory of the true God.
44. Then Jesus cried out with a loud voice, "Those who believe in Me do not believe in Me only, but in the One Who sent Me!
45. "When they look at Me, they are really looking at the One Who sent Me here!
46. "I have come into this physical world to light it up—to illuminate it with the brightness of My shining truth—so that no one who believes in Me should continue to live in darkness.
47. "As for those who hear My words but do not observe to do them,

> I do not judge them because I did not come into this dimension to judge the world. My only reason for coming here was to save the world, the *whole* world.

48. "But anyone who consistently rejects My teachings already has his judge. My very message itself will ultimately convict him.
49. "And the reason I say this is that I have never spoken on My own authority, but the Father Who sent Me has commanded Me to say everything that I have said.
50. "And I know that His commandment activates the full potential of eternal life. So, whatever I speak, you can be sure that I am saying exactly what My Father has told Me to say—no more, no less—My words are in perfect accordance with His instructions."

Chapter 13

1. It was right before the Feast of Passover, and Jesus knew that the time had come for Him to physically leave the earthly dimension and return, full-time, to the spirit realm to be with His Father in the now. And having loved His own who were in the world, He continued to love them right up to the very end of His existence as the Word made flesh. He loved those twelve men with an intense and unfailing love, as much as any human being could possibly love another. He didn't simply have divine affection for them as an almighty Creator would have for His creation; His connection with them was more complex...more than that of God benevolently loving mankind. He actually cared for them with the very vulnerable, heart-felt emotion of a man who enjoyed their company and depended on them as His partners in the ministry. They were His friends, they were His confidants, they were His brothers, they were His sons. They had worked together, prayed together, fished together, changed people's lives together. They had all become a part of each other.
2. But as the evening meal progressed, Judas became increasingly adversarial toward Jesus in his attitude, giving in to his dark side in a way that made it seem as though the devil had entered him and had prompted him to betray Jesus. On another occasion, Jesus had referred to Judas as a devil (which simply means "adversary"), and now His prophetic words were coming to pass.
3. But Jesus, being completely confident in the fact that God had put Him in charge of everything that was happening and everything that

was about to happen, was not intimidated by what was going on inside Judas' mind. He was focused on the knowledge that, in the same way that He had come from God, He was about to return to God.

4. So He got up from the table, stripped down completely, and wrapped a towel around His waist. In so doing, He girded Himself in the manner that servant boys did at that time when they waited on houseguests.

5. Then He poured water into a basin and began to humbly and deliberately wash His disciples' feet, drying them with the towel that He had wrapped around His waist.

6. But when He got to Simon Peter, Peter objected, saying, "Lord, surely You do not intend on washing *my* feet!"

7. Jesus replied, "You aren't able to comprehend what I'm doing right now, but later it will make perfect sense to you."

8. "No!" Peter said emphatically. "It's not right. I will never permit You to be subservient to me in this way. I absolutely will not allow You to ever wash my feet!" Jesus answered, "Let Me put it to you this way, Peter. Unless I wash you, you have no part with Me."

9. "All right, then," Peter finally said. "If that's the way it is, if it is that important, then go ahead and do it, but don't just wash my feet...wash my hands and my head, as well!"

10. But Jesus answered him, saying, "Those who have had a bath only need to wash their feet after walking on a dirty floor, because the rest of their body is clean. This act is symbolic in that you, as a group, are clean, but not every one of you."

11. He said this because He knew who was going to betray Him, and that was why He said that not every one of them was clean.

12. When He had completed washing the feet of each disciple, He put His clothes back on and returned to where He had been sitting at the table. Then He asked them, "Do you have any idea why I have done what I just did?

13. "Let Me explain: You call Me 'Teacher' and 'Lord,' and it is appropriate that you do so because that is what I am.

14. "But the point is this: Now that I, your Lord and Teacher, have washed your feet, you should also serve one another in this same way. You should take every opportunity to wash one another's feet just as I have washed yours.

15. "I have set the example for you—the example of unconditional love,

16. because the truth is that servants are not greater than their master, and those who deliver a message are not greater than the one who sent them to deliver it.
17. "And now that I have demonstrated these principles to you, you are responsible for them, and you will be blessed if you do them.
18. "And you need to know that what I am saying applies to every one of you. I know those that I have chosen, and I never second-guess My choices. But what is happening, even as I speak, is the fulfillment of the Scripture that says 'He who shared My bread with Me has lifted up his heel against Me.'
19. "I am prepared for this, but I am telling you about it now, before it happens, so that when it comes to pass you will have another reason to believe that I am Who I am.
20. "Always remember how this truth works in this dimension: Whoever accepts anyone that I send, ultimately accepts Me, and, likewise, whoever accepts Me accepts the One Who sent Me."
21. But as soon as He said this, the reality of what was happening dawned on His human nature, and He became troubled and depressed in His spirit. The God part of Him was fully in control of the situation, even emotionally detached from it, in a way. But the part of Him that was a man—the part that loved Judas as a friend and a brother—suddenly cried out in sorrow, "The painful truth is that one of you sitting right here is going to betray Me!"
22. His disciples were so dumbfounded at this that they just stared at one another in disbelief. No one knew what to say.
23. But one of them, the one known as the disciple that Jesus loved, was reclining so close to Jesus that he was actually leaning on Him.
24. And Simon Peter motioned to this disciple and said to him, "Lean in a little closer so that He can whisper to you who He's talking about."
25. So, leaning back even closer into Jesus' personal space, he asked, "Lord, who is it? Who is going to betray You?"
26. Jesus responded to him, saying, "The one to whom I give this piece of bread after I have dipped it into the dish." Then He dipped the bread and handed it to Judas, the son of Simon Iscariot.
27. As soon as Judas took the bread, a sense of darkness overtook him and he completely surrendered to the devilish plan to betray Jesus.

And, being fully aware of what had just taken place in Judas' heart, Jesus said to him, "Don't put off what you are going to do any longer; go ahead and get it over with quickly."

28. But the disciples were so in denial of what was actually transpiring in that moment, that not one of them was able to understand what Jesus was talking about. It was too unthinkable for them to grasp that anyone in that room, including Judas, was capable of actually turning against Jesus.
29. So, since Judas was in charge of the finances, they just assumed that Jesus was telling him to buy what was needed to celebrate the festival or to give something to the poor. That was the end of it as far as they were concerned.
30. But nothing was ever the same after Judas took that bread from Jesus, and they both knew it. There were no other words that needed to be said, so he just got up and quietly went out into the shadows of the night.
31. As soon as the door closed behind him, Jesus turned to the remaining disciples and said, "Now the Son of Man is glorified, and God is glorified in Him.
32. "And if God is glorified in Him, He will glorify the Son in Himself, and He will glorify Him in the now.
33. "Listen, My sons; I am only going to be with you a little while longer. You will look for Me, and as I told the people in the Temple so I tell you now, 'Where I am going you cannot come.'
34. "So this is what I need to leave with you—these are My last words to you—what I want, more than anything, for you to remember. I have given you many instructions and insights during our time together, but here is the new commandment, the new order, the thing that is superior to every other thing, in a word: LOVE ONE ANOTHER. In the way that I have loved you, so you must love one another. Do you understand?
35. "You see, this is the only way that people will know that you are My disciples. Your love for one another is the solitary thing that will validate My message in the long run—not the miracles, not the signs and wonders, not the teaching—but your unconditional love for each other. It is not optional."
36. Simon Peter asked Him, "Lord, where exactly are You going?" Jesus answered him, "Peter, where I am going, you cannot go. It is not possible for you to follow Me there now, but you will be able to

follow Me there later."

37. But Peter said, "I don't want to wait! Why can't I follow You now? Don't You realize how important You are to me? I mean, I would lay down my very life for You!"
38. Then Jesus answered, "I know that you think you really mean that, but the truth is that you will disown Me—you will actually deny that you ever even knew Me—three times before the rooster crows tomorrow morning.

Chapter 14

1. "But don't let your heart be troubled about this, Peter, and that goes for the rest of you, as well. Just believe in God and believe also in Me, and you will survive what is about to happen to all of us.
2. "Even though you will definitely deny Me three times, there will still always be a room for you in the Father's house—a room with your name on the door. And that room represents your secure and unique place of effectiveness in ministry, your guarantee of personally staying in good standing with Me, regardless of what you do in the next few hours, or for the rest of your life, for that matter. If this were not the case, you can be sure that I would tell you. In fact, I am going to the cross to personally prepare this place for you in My purpose.
3. "And if I go to prepare this room for you, I will come back from the grave and personally receive you to Myself...move you into the Father's house to live with Me indefinitely...so that where I am, you may be, also. In this way, you will never doubt your eternal place with Me again and will never again succumb to any pressure put upon you to deny Me.
4. "And really, you already know in your heart where I am going and how to get there for yourself."
5. Thomas spoke up and said, "Lord, don't take for granted that we know where You are going. We don't! How can we know the way to the Father's house if we don't fully understand what and where it is?"
6. Jesus said, to him, "I am the Way, and the Truth, and the Life. Ultimately, no one can find his or her way to the Father's house without Me personally taking them there. There are many paths one may take to find Me, but I am the way.

7. "By knowing Me, you are able to know the Father, so from now on, realize that you know Him…you actually know God and have seen Him in Me."
8. Philip, said to Him, "Lord, just show us the Father, that's all we ask. Only seeing Him will really satisfy us."
9. Jesus replied, "Did you not hear what I just said, Philip? How could I have been with you all this time and you still not be able to recognize Me? I'm telling you again: anyone who has seen Me has already seen the Father. How can you so ignorantly say then, 'Show us the Father'?
10. "Do you not believe that I am in the Father and that the Father is in Me?
11. "By now you should easily believe that the Father and I are completely integrated, if for no other reason than because of the wonderworks that I perform.
12. "And I'll tell you something else, something really important, and it's the absolute truth, even though you may find it hard to believe. Those who believe in Me will do the very same works that I have been doing, and they will actually do even greater things than I have done because I am going to be reunited with the Father in the eternal realm.
13. "And I will do whatever you ask in My name, or on the authority of My reputation, so that the Father may be glorified in the Son.
14. "We will walk in such harmony that you may ask Me for anything in My name, and I will do it.
15. "If you really love Me, keep these commands of Mine.
16. "And I will ask the Father to send you another Helper, just as He sent Me to you. And this Helper will be your Comforter, Advocate, Intercessor, Standby...and He will never have to leave you as I have to leave you now. He will be with you indefinitely…forever.
17. "He is the Spirit of Truth, and the world at large cannot comprehend or accept Him at this point because it has no perception of His reality. But you already know Him because He has been living *with* you, and as soon as I am released from this physical manifestation, He will begin to live *in* you.
18. "Just because I will no longer be seen by you in this incarnation, does not mean that you will be orphaned by Me. I will come right back to you as My Spirit-self.
19. "In a few hours the world will no longer see this flesh-man, but you

will still see Me with your spiritual eyes. You will not be limited any longer to only seeing this Jesus, but you will be freed and released to see this Christ! And because I will transcend and outlive the physical, you will also transcend and outlive the physical.

20. "When all this comes together for you, you will realize that I am in My Father, and you are in Me, and I am in you…all together…all connected…all one!

21. "And whoever holds on to My commands and does them, proves that they love Me. And those who love Me will experience the reality of the Father's love for them, and it will ultimately reveal to them Who I really am and Who I have been all along."

22. Then Judas (not Judas Iscariot) said, "But, Lord, what is the point of revealing Yourself to us if You're not going to reveal Yourself to the whole world?"

23. Jesus said to him, "Anyone who loves Me will obey My teaching and precepts, and they will experience the fullness of the Father's love. In this way, they will become the dwelling place of the Father in Me, or Me in the Father; in other words, those who are obedient will become the house of God.

24. "But anyone who does not love Me will not obey My teaching, so they will not enjoy this privilege. So, in answer to your question, Judas, the revelation is in the obedience, and anyone in the world who obeys can have the same revelation of Me that you have. These words are not My own...they are the words of the Father Who sent Me.

25. "I have told you as much as I can while I am still with you in the physical realm.

26. "But this Advocate/Helper that I'm telling you about—the Holy Spirit, Whom the Father will send in My behalf—will teach you all of this. He will remind you of everything that I have said to you and will make it all make sense to you. So don't be unsettled about these mysteries. I don't want to leave you in a state of turmoil.

27. "Peace I leave with you; I'm talking about My own, personal sense of peace, wholeness and well-being; I'm actually transferring it to you. You see, My peace is unlike the peace that comes from this realm...the peace that is reactionary and temporal, dependent on outward circumstances to determine its strength and presence. My peace is other-worldly, settled, absolute, causing you to be in harmony with your whole life—past, present, and future—and

ultimately with the whole of creation. It will empower you to refuse to let your heart (your inner world) become troubled, agitated, or upset, no matter what is happening around you, and you can be fearless because you will be at peace with the Father, with yourself, and with the universe.

28. "At this point, you should be comfortable with the idea that I am going away, because I have told you that I would be back. If you love Me properly and unselfishly, you will celebrate the fact that I am going to the Father, because the Father is greater and mightier than even I am.
29. "This is another thing that I have told you before it happens so that, when it comes to pass, you will believe.
30. "But I will not say much more to you from this point on because it is time for the final conflict between light and darkness to be consummated, and words are unnecessary now. In this way, the one who claims to be the prince of this world is coming to Me, but I have nothing more to say to him. He has no place in My consciousness.
31. "But he has a purpose to serve, and I will allow it. His coming to Me will cause the world to understand that I love the Father and do exactly what My Father has commanded Me, because everything that I have done and am about to do is because of My relationship to My Father. Now, I have a few more things to say to you, but let's leave this place. I will say the rest while we walk."

Chapter 15

1. Then He said to them, "I am the true vine – the real, authentic vine that produces life in this world – and My Father is the gardener and vinedresser.
2. "Any branch in Me that is not fruitful or productive, He purifies and cleans.
3. "But you have already been cleansed, thoroughly made clean through the word that I have spoken to you.
4. "Stay connected to Me in your mind and attitude, and I will continue to produce life in you. In the same way that a branch can't bear fruit by itself, but only by being joined to the vine, you can't bear fruit in your life without staying connected to Me in your consciousness.
5. "I really want you to understand this: I am the Vine, you are the branches. Whoever stays connected to Me, mentally and spiritually,

will bear much fruit and will continue to be productive. But disconnected from Me, you can do nothing.

6. "Whoever intentionally separates himself or herself from Me just dries up and withers like a dead branch that is only useful as firewood.

7. "But if you continue to stay mentally and spiritually connected to Me, and if My words, My teachings, My concepts, become a vital part of your everyday life, then you will have the confidence to ask for whatever you want and your desires will be granted.

8. "In this way, My Father is honored. He is exalted through your fruitfulness, and only those who are fruitful and productive are My true disciples.

9. "You need to realize that I have loved you with the same intensity with which the Father has loved Me, so remain faithful to My unfailing love for you.

10. "If you keep My commandments, you will maintain intimacy with Me. You will be confident in My love for you, as I am confident in the Father's love for Me. Your obedience will reinforce our covenant of love.

11. "And I am telling you all of this for one reason: that My joy may remain in you and that your joy may be full. In other words, I want you to be as completely happy as I am!

12. "And this is My essential and ultimate commandment that will bring you joy and happiness: that you love one another in the same way that I have loved and do love you…unconditionally, completely, wholly, eternally.

13. "And the utmost test of love is this: that a person lays down his or her life for his or her friends.

14. "You show that you are My friends by keeping My commandments, especially this main one.

15. "I think of you as My friends, not as My servants, because a servant does not necessarily know what his master is doing. But I call you friends, because I have made known to you everything that I have heard from My Father through the intimate, everyday conversation that friends have.

16. "You did not choose Me. I chose you, just like you were, and I sent you out to produce fruit in your life and ministry – the kind of fruit that will never spoil, but will last eternally.

17. "And again, I can't stress enough how important this commandment

is: LOVE ONE ANOTHER!
18. "If you find that the promoters of this world-system hate you, don't take it personally. Remember that they hated Me first, and their intense dislike is more about Me than it is about you.
19. "If you blindly followed the rules of the religious world-system, its proponents would love you. But you are non-conformists and iconoclasts like Me, so the people who feel threatened by you will hate you. People who do not walk in the light always hate and fight what they don't understand.
20. "So don't forget this: A servant is not greater than his master. If people mistreat Me, they will mistreat you. It comes with the territory. But if they have done what *I* told them, then they will do what *you* tell them to do.
21. "Basically, people will do to you exactly what they did to Me, because you belong to Me and they don't know the One Who sent Me.
22. "If I hadn't been so open and candid with them, they would not be guilty of the sin of closed-minded unbelief. But now they have no excuse; from now on there is no excuse for anyone refusing to walk in the light.
23. "But the bottom line is that whoever hates Me, hates My Father, also.
24. "You surely must realize that I have done things that no one else has ever done, and I have done them right before the eyes of the general public. If I had not been so visible – if I had not made the truth so accessible – they would not be guilty. But many of them have seen and heard it all and still hate both Me and My Father.
25. "That is why the Scriptures are true when they say, 'The people hated Me for no good reason.'
26. "But when The Helper comes, Whom I will send from the Father, He will be revealed as the Spirit of Truth, and He will tell you all about Me. He will fill in all the blanks for you and will make all of this make sense to your spirit and to your mind.
27. "Then you will be empowered to also easily tell others about Me, because you have been with Me from the beginning and you will know exactly what to say.

Chapter 16

1. "I am telling you all of these things before I leave you so that you will not be afraid and will not fall apart when things get rough.
2. "You need to be prepared for this: the religious people are going to evict you from their synagogues and meeting places. In fact, the time will come when some of them will become so self-righteous that they will be capable of killing you, thinking that they are doing God a service in doing so. Religion will make them so blindly intolerant that they will actually think that murdering you will be their way of doing God a favor!
3. "They will do these things only because they don't know Me and, therefore, do not know the Father.
4. "I am saying this to you now so that, when it happens, you will remember My words and will not be unprepared for it. I haven't told you these things before now because I've been with you every day, and I knew that I could take care of everything in person.
5. "But now I am going back to the Father—back into the eternal now—and yet not one of you seems to be curious about where I am going.
6. "You are too preoccupied with your own personal sadness about what you perceive to be something wonderful that is coming to an end.
7. "But you need to realize that this is really a new beginning for us all! It is to your advantage that I go away, because if I do not leave this fleshly incarnation, the Holy Spirit cannot come to you. But if I leave this realm, I will personally be able to send Him to you.
8. "And when He comes, He will show everyone around the world the truth about sin and God's justice and about how judgment works.
9. "The Spirit will show them that they were wrong about Me...that it was a sin to reject Me and not believe in Me.
10. "He will show them the truth about righteousness, and they will be able to understand it then because I will be with the Father, and you won't see Me in this present incarnation again.
11. "And He will show them the truth about judgment, because God has already judged the so-called ruler of this world.
12. "I really have so many more things to say to you, but I think that you are already saturated and a little overwhelmed with all this.
13. "But don't worry about it. When the Spirit of Truth is finally

revealed, He will guide you into all the truth that there is. He will not speak on His own and tell you something different than what I have told you. He will only tell you what He has heard from Me, and He will give you the insight to know what is ahead so that you can actually see into the future.

14. "The Spirit will glorify Me, because He will take My message and make it global and universal. And He will declare it to you, directly.

15. "Everything that the Father has is mine. That is why it is so important that the Spirit takes My message and integrates it into your consciousness.

16. "In just a short while you will not be able to see Me with the natural eye, but then you will be able to perceive Me by the Spirit because I am returning to the Father in the now."

17. Then some of His disciples really began to react to His words. "What does He mean by saying, 'In a little while you won't be able to see Me with the natural eye, but then you will see Me by the Spirit?' Why does He say, 'I am going to the Father'?"

18. They also asked, "What in the world does He mean by 'a little while'? We do not understand His mysterious words, at all!"

19. Jesus was fully aware of their confused curiosity, so He said to them, "Are you asking one another what I meant by saying, 'In a little while you will see Me no more, and then after a while you will see Me again'?

20. "Here's the truth about that: You will initially weep and mourn while the slaves to this world-system rejoice. You will grieve, but then your grief will be turned into joy!

21. "When a woman gives birth to a child, she has pain in her labor and delivery. But that pain is put into perspective when the baby is born, to the point that she seems to forget the physical altogether. The joy that the baby brings is so much greater than any suffering that it may have caused, that the hardship of labor becomes completely irrelevant and insignificant.

22. "So it is with you. You are about to feel your own pains of labor in grieving over My departure from this fleshly manifestation. But I will see you again when I am 'born' in the person of the Holy Spirit, and then you will have so much joy that you will forget this present sorrow, completely. And when that happens, no one will ever be able to take your joy away from you!

23. "There is a new era coming, and in that era you will no longer ask

Me anything. You will ask God the Father, directly, and He will give you whatever you ask for in My name or on behalf of My reputation.

24. "Until now you have not prayed with this mindset, but now you will be able to ask, and you will receive. And I want you to do this simply because it will make your joy complete; the miracle of answered prayer will grant you unsurpassed happiness.

25. "I have been speaking to you in parables and allegories, but the time is about to arrive when I will speak to you plainly about the Father. You are ready for real communication.

26. "When that time comes, you will be able to pray in My name, or on the strength of My reputation, and your words will go directly to the Father's ears. It will not even be necessary for Me to speak to the Father on your behalf, because you will already be in Me and I will be in Him.

27. "For the Father has a loving relationship with you—person to person…face to face—because you have loved Me and have believed that I came out of the Father.

28. "I came from the Father in the now and entered the dimension of space and time—or the natural world as you know it—and now I am leaving this dimension and going back to the Father…back to the now."

29. Then Jesus' disciples said, "Ah! Now we are beginning to understand! It seems as if You are suddenly speaking plainly to us… not in parables or mysteries or figures of speech. It's as if a veil has been lifted.

30. "We are at peace with the fact that You clearly know everything, including where You are going, and You don't need to be questioned any further. We get it: You really did come from God."

31. Jesus answered them, "Now do you believe?

32. "The time will come, in fact it is already here, when all of you will be temporarily scattered. You will all panic and leave Me alone, but I will not really be alone because the Father is always with Me.

33. "I have told you these things so that, in Me, you may have real peace and confident serenity. Now don't be naïve to the fact that, in the world, you will have trouble; it is a given. But, take heart! You can celebrate and live a joyful life, regardless of any circumstances in your life, because I have completely overcome the trouble of the world and have set the example to show how you can overcome it, as

well!"

Chapter 17

1. After Jesus had finished speaking to His disciples, He looked up toward the infinite sky and said, "Father, the time has come for You to bring glory to Your Son so that Your Son may glorify You.
2. "You have granted Him full authority over all the people of the earth, and You have given them to Him so that He might give them all eternal life.
3. "And this fulfills the purpose of eternal life, that they may know You, the only true God, and Jesus Christ, the manifestation of Your physical presence on the earth.
4. "I brought glory to You in this dimension by doing everything that You told Me to do.
5. "And now, Father, bring Me back into the eternal now so that I may exist in the glory that We shared before the world began.
6. "I have told these men who have followed Me all about You. Their perception was limited, having been shaped by the current world's system, but You gave them to Me and now they have been freed from the smallness of their previous mindset by obeying Your word.
7. "They know that everything that I have came from You.
8. "I just told them exactly what You told Me, and it convinced them that I came from You and that You sent Me here.
9. "Right now I am not praying for the whole world, but for those whom You have given to be My followers, because they know that they belong to You.
10. "All that I have is Yours, and all that You have is Mine, and the glory of that connection has now included them in its manifestation.
11. "I will no longer remain in this dimension or in this physical incarnation, but *they* are still in the physical realm of space and time. I am returning to the eternal now to be reintegrated with and in You, but I pray, Holy Father, that You keep, through Your name, those whom You have given Me. I pray that, even though they continue to live and move in the physical world, they will be able to transcend its finite limitations and be one with each other, even as We are.
12. "While I was with them in the physical world, I kept them safe and intact in Your name. I carefully guarded them, and not one of them was lost to My circle of influence, except for that one who just

seemed bent on destruction. But his rebellion only served to fulfill the Scriptures.

13. "I am on My way back into the eternal now, but I want to say these things while I am still in this physical incarnation. If I say these things as the Son of Man, it will make it possible for them to also say these kinds of things so that they can know the joy of being manifested as Sons of God.

14. "I have told them Your message, but they are hated by those mental prisoners of the world-system, because they don't belong to that system in any way, just as I don't.

15. "Father, I don't ask that you take My followers out of the world, because it would defeat the entire purpose of My coming here if You should allow them to become escapists. I only pray that they be kept safe from the phantom menace.

16. "They are misfits in this world—strangers to its present mindset—just like Me.

17. "So let them find shelter in the truth of Your word; it is the only place where they can live now that they have been with Me.

18. "As You sent Me into this dimension, I am sending them into it…into the fullness of it.

19. "I have given Myself completely for their sake…becoming absolutely absorbed into them, so that they may become absolutely absorbed into the truth.

20. "But I do not pray for these alone…these who know Me as I am, here and now. But I pray for those everywhere and in every dimension of time, including those in the future, who will ultimately believe in Me through their witness and their word.

21. "And I pray that they all may be one in the now…all around this world of Yours, not just the ones here in this time and place. Make them all one as You, Father, are in Me, and I in You. Integrate them as You and I are integrated: unified, in harmony, inseparable.

22. "I have actually given them the glory that You gave Me, so that it would be possible for them to be one, even as We are.

23. "I have become one with them in the same way that You are one with Me, so that they may become completely one. This unification—this melding and merging of separate entities into a perfect oneness—is the thing that will ultimately show the whole world that You sent Me. They will all see that You love My followers as much as You love Me.

24. *"Father, I truly want everyone You have given Me to be with Me…wherever I am…so that they will see, first-hand, the glory that You have given Me because You loved Me in the now…before the world of space and time was created.*
25. *"Righteous Father, the people of the world at large don't know the real You, but I know You, and now the ones who have followed Me know that You sent Me.*
26. *"And I have revealed You to them and will continue to reveal You through the coming manifestation of the Holy Spirit. I am committed to continuing this revelation so that your love for Me may be in them and that I, Myself, may be in them, as well."*

Chapter 18

1. When Jesus had finished speaking these words, He went out with His disciples over the Brook Kidron, across the Kidron Valley, to a place where there was a garden.
2. Jesus had often met there with His disciples, so they all knew where it was, including Judas.
3. So Judas came to the place with a whole battalion of soldiers and Temple guards that had been sent by the Pharisees. They were all carrying torches or lanterns, and they were all armed.
4. But Jesus knew everything that was about to happen to Him, and He had no fear of it at this point. He had already made complete peace with His destiny. So when He saw the men, He calmly approached them and said, *"Who are you looking for?"*
5. "Jesus of Nazareth," they answered Him. But instead of responding to them by saying "I am He" or "That's Me," He just looked straight at the crowd and simply said the very same words God had spoken to Moses at the burning bush…He said, *"I AM!"*
6. And when He said those profoundly holy words, the sheer impact of them just knocked the entire battalion right off their feet, and they all went limp and fell backwards on the ground like dead men.
7. So then, having made it quite obvious by this act that no one was going to take Him by force, He calmly asked them again, *"Now, who exactly did you say that you are looking for?"* As soon as they were able, they jumped back up on their feet, shook off their shock, regained their composure and said, "Jesus of Nazareth."
8. This time Jesus just said, *"You are looking for Me; let these other*

ones go."

9. In saying that, He fulfilled what He had just prayed when He said, "I have not lost a single one of those you gave Me."
10. Then Peter, in his typical reactionary way, drew a sword and tried to kill one of the high priest's servants. But as he swung his sword, he was only able to slash off the right ear of one of them named Malchus.
11. But Jesus shouted at Peter, "What do you think you're doing? Don't you know that I am fully prepared to drink this cup that the Father is serving Me? Put your sword away!"
12. Then the entire detachment of troops, along with the captain and the officers of the religious leaders, arrested Jesus and tied Him up.
13. And immediately they led Him away to Annas, the father-in-law of Caiaphas who was serving as that year's high priest.
14. Caiaphas was the one who had advised the Jewish leaders that it was to their advantage that one man die for the people.
15. And Simon Peter followed Jesus on the way, along with another disciple who was acquainted with the high priest. So when they got there, the disciple with the connections went right into the high priest's court.
16. But Peter had to wait outside by the door until the other disciple could speak about him to the girl who was on duty. Then that disciple gained permission from her to bring Peter inside.
17. And when the girl came to let Peter in, she asked him as he entered, "Aren't you a follower of that man?" But Peter answered, emphatically, "No, I am not!"
18. Now, it was a cold night, so several of the servants and Temple police had built a charcoal fire and were warming themselves by it.
19. Meanwhile, the high priest began interrogating Jesus about His followers and about His teaching.
20. But Jesus said to Him, "I have never conducted any underground meetings. Anything that I have said, I have said publicly...in the Temple, out in the open, in all the usual meeting places.
21. "So why are you questioning Me? Just ask anyone who has heard Me, because they all know exactly what I have said."
22. As soon as Jesus said this, one of the Temple guards stepped up and slapped Him hard across the face, shouting, "That's no way to talk to the high priest!"
23. Jesus looked at him and said, "If I have done or said something

wrong, just say so. But if not, why did you slap Me?"
24. Jesus was still tied up, and Annas sent Him to the high priest, Caiaphas.
25. And while Peter still stood warming himself by the fire, someone else asked him, "Aren't you one of Jesus' followers?" And again, Peter strongly denied it, saying, "No, I certainly am not!"
26. Then, one of the high priest's servants there, who was also a relative of the man whose ear Peter had cut off said, "Wait a minute; didn't I see you in the garden with that man? Yes, I'm sure that it was you and that you are connected to Him!"
27. Once again Peter denied it, but on this third time, while he was still speaking, a rooster outside the courtyard began to crow loudly.
28. Then they led Jesus from Caiaphas into the Praetorium (Pilate's official place of residence in the palace), just as the dawn was beginning to break. But they themselves did not enter the Praetorium so that they would not be defiled and could still eat the Passover later.
29. So Pilate went out to meet them and inquired, "What accusation do you bring against this Man?"
30. They answered him, "If He were not a criminal, a truly evil man, we would not have considered it so urgent that we bring Him to you."
31. Then Pilate said to them, "Whatever He has done that you think is so bad is really no concern of mine. Just take Him and judge Him according to your Law, and whatever you decide to do with Him is fine with me." "But we no longer have the legal right to put a man to death," the people objected. "Only you Romans have the authority to perform executions now."
32. And so, what Jesus had predicted about His own death was about to come to pass.
33. Then Pilate went back inside the palace, called Jesus over to him and asked, "Yes or no…are You the king of the Jews?"
34. Jesus replied, "Is this your own, original question, or are you asking on behalf of someone else who told you about Me?"
35. Pilate answered, "I'm not a Jew! I have no knowledge or opinion of You. Your own people, including the chief priests, have brought You here, and I am simply curious as to the reason why. What have You done that has caused all this drama?"
36. Jesus answered, "My kingdom is not bound to this dimension. If it belonged to this world-system, My followers would not have handed

37. Me over to the Jewish leaders. But it is not of this world, at least not yet."
37. "So You do say that You are a king," Pilate replied. Jesus answered, "Those are your words, not Mine, but, yes, I am a king—maybe not by your definition, but a king, nonetheless. I was born into this world to become the king over all truth, and everyone who is of the truth becomes a subject in My kingdom."
38. Pilate asked Jesus, "What is truth?" But Jesus at this point had nothing more to say to him. So Pilate went back out and said, "Look, I just don't believe this Man is legitimately guilty of anything!
39. "And since you have a custom that I should release someone to you at Passover, why don't you just allow me to release to you the 'King of the Jews' and we'll be done with this business?"
40. But this idea only served to enrage them, so they shouted back, "No! Not this man! If you're going to release someone to us, then give us Barabbas!" Now Barabbas was a known terrorist.

Chapter 19

1. Then Pilate gave orders for Jesus to be beaten thirty-nine times with a whip made up of many lead-tipped leather thongs.
2. And the soldiers made a big, spiky crown of long, sharp thorns and pushed it down hard on His head. It painfully scraped through His scalp, causing scores of little bloody rivers to begin flowing into His eyes. Then, to humiliate Him further, they threw a royal purple robe across His shoulders.
3. "Hail! King of the Jews!" they sarcastically mocked, and when they did, a sort of maniacal fury broke out among the hundreds of men there and they all began to take turns punching Him in the face, as hard as they could, with their fists.
4. Eventually, Pilate, assuming that this violent episode with the soldiers would satisfy the people, went outside again and said to them, "I am going to bring Him out to you now, but you should know that I absolutely find Him guilty of nothing. But just the same, He has been severely beaten to satisfy you."
5. Then Jesus stumbled out before them, wearing the thorny crown that was now lodged into the top of His bleeding head. He was also wearing the once purple robe that was now nearly completely

crimson, having been saturated by the blood from several hundred deep lacerations around His body. And Pilate, dramatically gesturing with his hand to suggest closure to this whole, horrible scenario, said, "Behold! Here is the Man!"

6. But when the chief priests and Temple police saw Him in this condition—bleeding profusely, eyes swollen shut from the severe pummeling that He had received to His face—it only incited them to call for more blood. They yelled, "Crucify Him! Nail Him to a cross! Crucify Him until He is dead!" Taken aback and somewhat sickened by their savagery, Pilate said to them, "You crucify Him! I find Him not guilty."

7. But the religious leaders replied, "By our laws He ought to die because He called Himself the Son of God."

8. This merciless insistence for the execution of a seemingly harmless man terrified Pilate.

9. So he re-entered the Praetorium, taking Jesus in with him. Inside, trying to understand the real situation at hand, he said to Jesus, "Where did You come from?" But Jesus did not answer him. He just stood there in silence, as the blood began to congeal all over His abused body.

10. Pilate asked, "Why won't You answer me? Don't You realize that I am trying to save Your life? I alone have the power to let You go free or to nail You to a cross until You are dead. Right now, I'm the only friend You have in this world, so You need to start talking to me."

11. Jesus then said to him, "You have no authority over Me or My life. Whatever power you may have in this situation is just what God has given to you, so don't be afraid to do what you have to do. Besides, the one who handed Me over to you did something worse than anything you can do."

12. At this point, Pilate determined in his mind to just override the people and let Jesus go free. He had no desire to let this thing go any further. But the religious leaders told him, "If you let this man go, you will show yourself to be disloyal and unfriendly to Caesar, because anyone who claims to be king is an enemy to the Emperor and a rebel against Rome."

13. When they said this, Pilate brought Jesus out to them once again and sat down on the judgment seat—a bench on the platform known as the Stone Pavement, or "Gabbatha" in the Aramaic language.

14. It was about noon on the day before Passover. And Pilate said to the people there, "Here is your King!"
15. Once again they yelled, "Kill Him! Crucify Him! Nail Him to a cross until He is dead!" Pilate said, "Do you actually want me to crucify and kill your King?" But they yelled even more loudly, "The Emperor is our king! We have no king but Caesar!"
16. So, realizing that he was completely incapable of persuading the people to have mercy, he gave in and handed Jesus over to the executioners, who led Him away to commence with the crucifixion.
17. And, despite the fact that Jesus had been beaten beyond recognition, with open wounds and eyes full of blood, He carried His own heavy cross of rough wood across the shredded flesh of His back and shoulders. Without protest, He carried it all the way to a place known as "The Skull," so named because of a weird rock formation in the side of the hill that looked very much like an actual human skull.
18. And, there, Jesus had large spikes driven through where His hands connected with His wrists and through His feet and ankles. When He was securely nailed to the cross, it was set upright between two men who were also being crucified.
19. And Pilate ordered that the charge against Jesus be written on a board and nailed to the top of the cross. It read in bold letters, "JESUS OF NAZARETH, THE KING OF THE JEWS," and was written in Hebrew, Latin and Greek.
20. Then many of the local Jewish people read this sign, for the place where Jesus was crucified was near the city, and the words were written in three languages.
21. So the chief priests went back to Pilate and said, "Why did you write that He is the King of the Jews? You should have written that He merely *claimed* to be the King of the Jews. We demand that you have that sign changed immediately."
22. But Pilate, being fed up with their obsessive hatred of Jesus said, "That's enough from you people about Him. Let it go. What has been written will not be changed."
23. Then the soldiers, after nailing Jesus to the cross, took His clothes and divided them into four parts, one for each of them. But the tunic that He wore as an outer garment was elegantly crafted from a single, seamless piece of cloth.
24. So they said to one another, "This is a fine garment; let's not tear it,

but rather gamble to see who gets it." And this fulfilled the Scripture that recorded David's prophecy when he said, *"They divided My garments among them, and for My robe they threw dice."*

25. So that is what the soldiers did. But standing by Jesus' cross were His mother and her sister, Mary (the wife of Clopas), and Mary Magdalene.
26. When Jesus saw His mother standing there, and the disciple that He loved standing nearby, He said to His mother, "Great lady, this man is now your son!"
27. Then He said to the disciple, "My brother, this woman is now your mother!" And from that moment on, that disciple took her into his own home and loved and cared for her as if she were his own mother.
28. After taking care of this last detail, Jesus knew that His work in the earthly dimension was now finished. And, as was prophesied in the Scriptures, He said, "I am thirsty." This thirst was the last human sensation that He felt before leaving the physical body.
29. And a jar of cheap, sour wine was there, so someone in the crowd soaked a sponge with it and held it up to Jesus' mouth on the stem of a hyssop plant.
30. So when Jesus received whatever He could of the sour wine, He said, "Everything is done now; it is completely finished!" And, bowing His head, He simply released His spirit.
31. Now, because the next day would be the Sabbath and especially because it was Passover, the local people did not want dying bodies up on crosses during their special day. So they asked Pilate to have the men's legs broken to expedite their deaths, and to have their bodies taken down.
32. So the soldiers came and broke the legs of the other two men on either side of Jesus who were already nearly dead.
33. But when they approached Jesus, it was obvious to them that He had died, so they did not break His legs.
34. But one of the soldiers pierced His side with a spear and, when he did, a fountain of blood and water gushed out of the opening.
35. And the disciple who recorded all of this saw it first hand and testifies that it is all true; not one bit of it is hearsay.
36. These last two things were the further fulfillment of prophetic Scripture, for it is written, *"Not a bone of Him shall be broken."*
37. And in another place it says, *"They will see the One in whose side*

they plunged a spear."

38. Joseph of Arimathea was a disciple of Jesus, but he had kept that fact a secret because he was afraid of the religious leaders. But now that Jesus was gone, he asked Pilate to grant him custody of His corpse, and Pilate gave him permission to take it down from the cross, which he did.
39. Nicodemus (the same Nicodemus who had come to Jesus by night) then came with about seventy-five pounds of spices made from myrrh and various aloes.
40. And the two men wrapped the body in linen cloths with the spices, following the traditional Jewish burial custom.
41. And right in the same place where Jesus had been nailed to a cross, there was a garden with an unused tomb.
42. And so, because it was the customary day of preparation before the Passover and since the tomb was conveniently close at hand, they laid Jesus' body there.

Chapter 20

1. Early on Sunday morning, while it was still dark, Mary Magdalene came to the tomb and was surprised to find that the stone that had been lodged into the entrance had somehow been rolled away.
2. As soon as she assessed the situation, she immediately ran to find Simon Peter and the other disciple whom Jesus loved, and when she got to them she blurted out, "They have taken the Lord out of the tomb and we don't know where they have put Him!"
3. When Peter and the other disciple heard this, they just took off running to the tomb to see for themselves.
4. The two disciples initially were running together, but then the other disciple picked up speed and outran Peter, arriving at the tomb first.
5. And when he got there, he stooped down to look inside and saw the linen grave clothes lying there, but he didn't enter the tomb.
6. But when Peter got there, he just went right in and also saw the little pile of linen material lying there.
7. Next to it was the piece of cloth that had been used to cover Jesus' face, neatly rolled up and in a place by itself.
8. The disciple who got there first then entered the tomb and, when he saw the whole scenario, he believed fully in the resurrection.
9. For, as yet, the disciples had not made the connection that the

Scriptures had said that He would rise from the dead.
10. But even though he believed, the disciple didn't know what to do about it, so he and Peter both just went back to their homes.
11. Mary Magdalene, on the other hand, remained there and just stood outside the tomb weeping. And at a certain point, while she was still in tears, she stooped down and looked into the interior.
12. Inside, she saw two men who appeared to be angels, all dressed in white, sitting where Jesus' body had been. One was sitting at the head, the other at the foot.
13. They turned and looked right at her and asked, "Why are you crying?" She answered, "Because they have taken away my Lord's body, and I don't know where they have put Him."
14. As soon as Mary said this, she became aware that someone was standing right behind her. So she quickly turned around and saw Jesus standing there, but she didn't realize that it was Him.
15. Jesus asked her "Why are you crying, Ma'am? Who are you looking for?" She just assumed He was the gardener and said, "Sir, if you have removed His body, please tell me so that I can go and get it."
16. Then Jesus said to her, "Mary!" Suddenly, the sound of His voice penetrated her stupor and, realizing Who He was, she cried out, "Teacher!"
17. When she reached out to embrace Him, He told her, "Don't try to hold on to Me, Mary. I am making the transition into the Father's dimension, and you can't keep Me here. I no longer belong in the physical body that you are used to seeing and holding, so don't touch Me. But tell My disciples that I am going to our Father and to our God."
18. So Mary Magdalene went immediately to the disciples and declared to them that she had seen the Lord. She also told them what He had said to her.
19. But the disciples were afraid of the religious leaders, so, on the evening of that same day, they assembled themselves and barricaded the doors of their meeting room. But as soon as they built the barricade, Jesus just appeared in the middle of the room and said to them, "Peace be with all of you!"
20. When He had said this, He showed them all His hands and His side and, when they got over the shock of seeing Him, they became exuberant and began rejoicing.
21. Once again He said to them, "Peace be to all of you; just as the

Father sent Me into this dimension, now I am sending you to all the people of world."

22. Then He took a deep breath and began to breathe and blow on them, and into them, in the same way that God had breathed into Adam in the creation. As He continued to blow on them, He began to say, "Receive…receive…receive the Holy Spirit.

23. "Receive the power to forgive sins; if you forgive the sins of any, they are forgiven; if you refuse to forgive them, they are unforgiven. You now have the same power and authority on the earth that I have had, not just to heal diseases, but to forgive sins, as well."

24. Now Thomas (called the Twin) was one of the Twelve, but he was not with them in the room that night.

25. So when the disciples recounted to him the story of Jesus' amazing appearance and the transfer of anointing that took place there with them all, he was more than a little skeptical. When they told him that they had seen the Lord, Thomas said, "Unless I see the holes in His hands made from the spikes and put my finger through them and put my hand into the opening in His side made by the spear, I will not believe."

26. So, a full week later the disciples were all together again, this time with Thomas, with the doors barricaded just like before. And in the same way, Jesus appeared in the middle of the room and said, "Peace be to all of you!"

27. Then He looked at Thomas, held up His hands in front of Him and said, "Go ahead, Thomas, put your finger through the holes in My hands and reach into the open place in My side. I don't want you to be an unbeliever, so if this is what it takes to get you to believe, then please explore all of My wounds; see for yourself and believe!"

28. But Thomas didn't have to touch Him. He knew immediately that it was Him and simply said, "My Lord and my God."

29. Jesus said to him, "Thomas, because you have seen Me with your natural eyes, you have believed. But there is a special blessing for those who have the faith, the vision, the imagination, to believe in what they can't see."

30. Jesus actually did many other miraculous signs in the presence of His disciples, miracles that are not even recorded in this book.

31. But the ones that are recorded here are written that you, the reader, may believe that Jesus was and is the Christ, the Son of God, and that by believing in Him you may live your life to the fullest in His

name.

Chapter 21

1. After this, Jesus appeared again to His disciples, this time at Lake Tiberias (also known as the Sea of Galilee).
2. And this is how it happened: Simon Peter, Thomas (called "The Twin"), Nathaniel (from Cana in Galilee), and the brother of James and John were all there, together with two other disciples.
3. They were all still in a sort of subdued state of shock over everything that had happened in the last several days, and nobody knew what to do...how to act...how to live. Now that Jesus was gone, should they just go back to doing whatever they were doing before He interrupted their lives? He really hadn't been that specific in His instructions about what they should do post-resurrection. So Peter looked at all of them just standing around and said, "Well, I've got to do something! Life has to go on; I'm going fishing." And the rest of them, relieved that someone had finally broken the awkward silence and had come up with a plan, said, "We'll come, too!" So they all piled into the boat and started fishing, finding comfort in the normalcy of a familiar activity. And they fished all night long, but nobody caught a thing.
4. Early the next morning, Jesus stood on the shore, but the disciples did not recognize Him or realize Who He was.
5. So Jesus called out to them, "Hey guys, have you caught anything?" And they answered Him with a simple, indifferent, "No."
6. Then He said, "Throw out your net on the right side of the boat and you will catch plenty of fish!" After staring blankly at Him for a minute, they all looked at each other and said, "Why not? What have we got to lose?" So they did what He said and almost immediately began catching so many fish that they couldn't even draw the net back into the boat.
7. Then the disciple whom Jesus loved said to Peter, "You know Who that is, don't you? It is the Lord!" When Peter heard this, he scrambled to put all his clothes back on and spontaneously plunged into the water, swimming as fast as he could to the shore. His immediate response to the thought of seeing Jesus was sheer elation; all he could think about was getting to Him, so much so that he forgot the fact they had not faced each other alone since the three denials.

8. The others stayed with the boat and tried to drag the overloaded net to the shore, for they were only out about three hundred feet.
9. When they got up on the beach, they saw that a charcoal fire was burning and fish was frying over it. There was also bread there to go with it.
10. "Bring up some of the fish that you've just caught," Jesus said.
11. So Simon Peter ran back to the boat and dragged the net to shore. There were one hundred fifty three large fish in it, but somehow the net didn't rip.
12. So Jesus Himself cooked breakfast for His friends and, when it was ready, He said, "Come on and eat!" But none of His disciples dared ask why He was there cooking for them, and they didn't have to ask Who He was, because they all knew that it was Him.
13. Then Jesus took the bread in His hands and gave some of it to His disciples and then He did the same with the fish.
14. This was now the third time that Jesus had appeared to the disciples...the third time that He had shown Himself alive to them since being raised from the dead.
15. When they all had finished eating, Jesus turned and looked directly into Peter's eyes and said, deliberately, "Simon, son of John, I want to know if you love Me more than the others do." Immediately, Peter's heart began beating faster because of the direct and serious tone in Jesus' voice. But he swallowed hard and, trying to sound as brave and as positive as he could, said, "Yes, Lord, You know that I love You!" Jesus replied, "Then feed My lambs."
16. Jesus then asked a second time, "Simon, son of John, do you love Me?" At these words Peter's heart was pounding so hard that he could feel his heartbeat in his temples. He began to tremble inside and with a softer, shakier voice said, "Yes, Lord, You know I love You." Jesus said, "Then take care of My sheep."
17. Then Jesus asked a third time, "Simon, son of John, do you really love Me?" At this third question, Peter just dropped his head and stared down at the ground. He could feel the sting of tears in his nostrils and his eyes began to well up. He knew what this confrontation was about—these three questions had to do with his three denials, but it was about more than that. This was about him being restored to the ministry—about being entrusted with the responsibility of feeding Jesus' beloved sheep—after doing something that should have disqualified him from ever having that

privilege again. And, on its most basic level, this was about a friend being reconciled to a friend…about the Man-Jesus somehow needing closure from a personal hurt before He could move into the next dimension of His divine reign. Peter was deeply pained that Jesus asked him this question three times and, with tears streaming down his face, he said even more softly, "Lord, You know everything. You know that I love You." Jesus said, "Then I want you to feed My sheep."

18. He went on to say, "The truth is, when you were young, you were able to do as you liked. You were able to dress yourself and go wherever you wanted to go. But when you are old, you will stretch out your hands because you will need others to dress and direct you, and they will take you where you don't want to go."

19. Jesus said this to tell Peter how he would be in his old age and how his eventual death would glorify God. Then He said to Peter, "Follow Me!"

20. Immediately Peter dried his tears and looked right over at the disciple who was perceived by everyone to be Jesus' favorite—the one who leaned on Jesus at supper and asked who was going to betray Him—and the competitive spirit rose up in him, triggering his old rivalry with this disciple. Instantly, his emotional mood changed. It didn't occur to him to question Jesus about this bleak prophecy that He had just spoken over him or to protest it in any way. All he could think about was what Jesus would say to the other disciple.

21. So Peter said to Jesus, "Wait a minute…what about him? What's going to happen to him in the future?"

22. Jesus answered him, "What is it to you? If I want him to remain alive on the earth until I come again, that is none of your concern. You just follow Me."

23. And so it seemed that Jesus pronounced the prophecy over Peter just to force a reaction out of him…just to cause his feelings of resentment toward the other disciple to rise to the surface so that they could be dealt with. In this way, Peter could be freed from this petty contention and move on to the important business of feeding Jesus' sheep. But then a rumor spread among the disciples that Jesus had said that *that* disciple would not die, which is not what He said, at all. The disciples desperately needed the Holy Spirit to come, because they were still misinterpreting Jesus' words, even after the

resurrection.

24. And this is that disciple who saw all of these events, first hand, and has personally recorded them here. All of us who actually lived this story know for a fact that this account of it is accurate, and now those who read it down through the ages will know that it is the truth, as well.

25. And Jesus actually did many other things that are not even recorded in this work, or in any other book for that matter. In fact, He was so prolific and innovative in His earthly incarnation that, if every ground-breaking thing that He did and said were recorded in detail, I imagine that the entire world could not contain all the volumes that would have to be written to cover the entirety of His amazing story! That's why His biography continues to be written through the vibrant lives of those who continue to follow Him...His story is still being written in the now!

Other books by Bishop Swilley . . .

A Year In The Now

a dynamic devotional dedicated to the daily discovery of destiny

Would you like to . . .

> . . . discover your destiny?
> . . . perceive your purpose?
> . . . validate your vision?
> . . . reinforce your relationships?
> . . . strengthen your self-esteem?
> . . . overcome your obstacles?
> . . . feed your faith?
>
> You can . . . this year!
> You can . . . by living in the now!
> You can . . . one day at a time!

God is on your side! He is available to assist you in the pursuit of your potential as you develop the diligence to seriously search out your personal path for growth into greatness! Through seeking first His Kingdom and righteousness, you can become the person that He created you to be!

You can ONLY find God's Kingdom in the eternal NOW as you endeavor to experience Him in your everyday existence. Kingdom-seeking consists of a constant effort to embrace the "now" and a commitment to the continual conforming of your consciousness to it. This empowers and enables you to escape the mental distractions produced by living in the past or in the future, so that you can comprehend a real Christ for your current real circumstances!

A YEAR IN THE NOW! is a devotional designed to deliver a doable format for the daily development of your eternal life—to help you think creatively, beyond your familiar, time-bound comfort zones. These positive and powerful affirmations will provide the help you need to progressively put your life on the right track in realistic increments. You don't have to become overwhelmed by the tremendous task of trying to lead a *now life* in a *yesterday/ tomorrow world*. You can do it day by day!

This is your year to change your world! You can change your world by changing your mind! You can change your mind one day at a time! It's time for a fresh start, and you can start right NOW!

What others have to say about *A Year In The Now*...

When my dear friend, Bishop Jim Swilley sent me a copy...I stopped everything I was doing and couldn't put it down...Jim is one of the most effective, prolific, and unique communicators I have ever met. He breaks down deep and profound truth and makes it palatable for all of us in such a practical way that just reading the principles and reciting the affirmations increases our life skills. The days are broken down into seven key principles a day, seven being the number of alignment between heaven and earth (four being the number of earth, and three of heaven), whereby applying the seven daily truths your heart and mind are aligned with heaven's best and you are automatically brought into the kind of agreement that gets results in your life. If you want to get the "more" out of your daily life that has been promised to you in Christ I want to encourage you to get your hands on *A Year In The Now!* and make it a part of your daily spiritual discipline and focus.

Dr. Mark J. Chironna
The Master's Touch International Church

A Year in the Now! reads as a personal message to me. Each day I am encouraged—God is doing a new thing in the NOW...This devotional reinforces that God is working His plan in all things....

Germaine Copeland
Author of Prayers That Avail Much Family Books

Deeply profound, yet 'DO-ably' practical...Bishop Jim's 'easy to read' style of communication, combined with his witty grouping together of words that start with the same letter, define this devotional as a delightful way to delve deeper into your divine destiny as a daily discipline. Profound and practical, it's the perfect proponent to promote your personal progress.

Doug Fortune
Trumpet Call Ministry

A Year In The Now!.is extraordinary and powerful, giving day by day guidance on how to be strong in the Lord through seven pearls of wisdom each day. Seven! This is God's number for completeness and fulfillment. Through *A Year In The Now!*, God is truly using Bishop Swilley in a mighty way to unlock the wonderful mystery of the gospel so that each of us can live abundantly and serve God abundantly, in the now!

David Scott
United States Congressman, Georgia

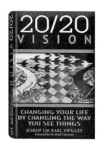

20/20 VISION

Changing Your Life
By Changing The Way You See Things

You really can live a larger life, starting now, by increasing your vision and improving your personal perception and your perception of the world around you. *20/20 VISION* is based on 20 daily affirmations that you can make concerning how you see yourself, and another 20 daily affirmations that you can make concerning how you see everything else. Each affirmation has commentary that expounds on its meaning for your life, with a plan to help you observe things in a better light and encourage you to say something good about what you see every day.

You can, in fact, change your life by changing the way that you see things. It has been theorized that there is no such thing as *reality,* there is only *perception*—a premise that can be argued, ad infinitum, by philosophers and physicists, alike. Whether or not it is actually and completely true, the fact remains that your perception of things really does determine how you think, feel and function every single day of your life. It is a fact that God *is,* but it is also a fact that God is to you how you *see* that He is.

You can determine your own happiness by learning how to properly view and discern the circumstances of your past and present. By learning how to see yourself correctly, you can become the person you've always really wanted to be or, better yet, you can reveal the best "you" that you already are. You have the ability to choose an attitude and vision for each day with the same confidence and ease that you have when choosing what to have for breakfast in the morning or what clothes to wear for the day. The more you are able to see how inner sight creates daily realities, the better skilled you will become in using it to your advantage.

Free your mind, open the eyes of your heart and prepare to change your life for the better. You **can** be happy. You **can** succeed. You **can** stop second-guessing your life choices, living in regret or blaming others. You **can** break all the limitations of your own mind and tap into an inner power that will enable you to do things that you never thought you could do before. And you can do it all by simply choosing to change your viewpoint and perception of the things pertaining to your life. As you begin to realize personal transformation, let these words take on new meaning for you: *I once was lost, but now am found; was blind, but now I see!*

[A separate 20/20 VISION Workbook is also available.]

What others have to say about *20/20 VISION*...

My friend, Bishop Jim Swilley, has written this masterpiece...and it is a sure invitation to a larger life by making that fundamental shift in your perception of reality. If you ever doubted whether God had more in store for you, this book will change your paradigm forever. Let the words of this book give you the permission you need to open the windows of your perception, change the way you view yourself and the world you live and, and watch both you and that world undergo incredible and remarkable transformation!

—**Dr. Mark J. Chironna**
Mark Chironna Ministries
www.markchironna.com

My friend, Jim Swilley, has successfully entered the marketplace of visualization and given correct spiritual understanding of a principle that literally creates success or failure, life or death, poverty or prosperity...Jim's book will change the lives of millions of people because he is adding vision to their sight.

—**Prophet Kim Clement**
Prophetic Image Expressions

In a way that only he can, Bishop Jim Swilley has taken the principles of Scripture and made them practical and doable. *20/20 VISION* challenges its readers to elevate their perception from being down-trodden, victimized and hopeless, to being empowered, capable and victorious....

—**Bishop Eddie L. Long**
Senior Pastor, New Birth Missionary Baptist Church

Bishop Swilley has done it again! His ability to provide daily insights for life is simply amazing...**20/20** is a must read for every believer!

—**Pastor Dony McGuire**
The River at Music City

Bishop Swilley shows us how we often view ourselves through lenses clouded by hurt, unforgiveness, bitterness and self-doubt. He reveals how we see ourselves through the lenses of others and believe that mirage, instead of the divine reality and purpose God has ordained for us.

—**Minister Steen "Newslady" Miles**
Senator, State of Georgia

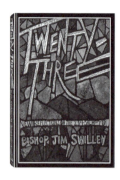

Twenty-Three

New Reflections on the 23rd Psalm and You

The beautifully simple lyrics to David's timeless masterpiece remain as life-affirming and culturally relevant today as they were thousands of years ago when he originally wrote them. In this accessible, topical devotional based on his song that we know as the 23rd Psalm, you will find a positive "now" word for your every situation. You will want to keep a copy handy at all times to remind you that you can live fearlessly, even when walking through your own valley of the shadow of death. And when you are stressed out or feeling intimidated by those who try to oppose you, you will find in these pages the grace to help you lie down in green pastures and the encouragement to eat at the very table that the Shepherd has prepared for you in the presence of your enemies. His rod and His staff will comfort you at all times, and *Twenty-Three* will help you to use that rod and staff more effectively and to enjoy a more fulfilling life as you learn to dwell in the house of the Lord forever.

From the Foreword: *"I wholeheartedly endorse both this book and the author. You will be encouraged, edified and uplifted with nothing but the good news. Bishop Swilley is a breath of fresh air in the religious climate of pretentiousness and egotism."*

— Bishop David Huskins

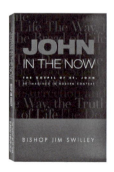

JOHN IN THE NOW

THE GOSPEL OF ST. JOHN
RE-IMAGINED IN MODERN CONTEXT

John's account of the greatest story ever told is in a class all by itself. It is the gospel written for nonconformists and individualists—for those who can comprehend Jesus outside the box

JITN will help you open your mind to a side of the real Jesus that you may not have noticed was there before. ***An audio version of John In The Now (read by Bishop Swilley) is also available.***

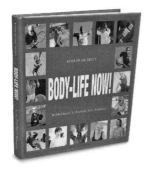

Body-Life Now!

Mini-Meditations for Maximum Fitness Motivation

Whether you're a serious body builder, competitive athlete, or just somebody who wants to drop a few pounds and be a little healthier than you are now, this power-devotional is for you! Inside you'll find 75 crisp little meditations on fitness, nutrition, attitude and lifestyle that will supercharge your workout and improve your outlook on your day.

You'll be doing yourself a big favor by incorporating these inspiring pages into your regular routine, *however* you choose to do so. Your spirit will be refreshed, your mind will be sharpened, and your body will thank you for the extra empowerment.

And if you're just getting *started* on the road to physical fitness, you'll find this book to be *especially* beneficial. It will serve as an easy-to-read road map for the journey designed to help you discover the new, improved *you*.

That journey can start right *here* . . . and it can start right *NOW!*

Activating the Power of Life and Death

It's your life . . .
It's your choice . . .
YOU CHOOSE!

God has given you the power to choose life or death, blessing or cursing. By the words of your mouth, you determine the quality of your life. This powerful book will help put you in charge of your life and your future.

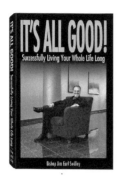

It's All Good!

Successfully Living Your *Whole* Life Long

Pursuing peace with your *past* . . .
Perceiving purpose in your *present* . . .
Fearlessly facing your *future* . . .

All these themes *and more* are explored in this provocative study of the powerful implications of Romans 8:28:

> *And we know that all things work together for good to those who love God, to those who are the called according to His purpose.*

Balancing the *secular* with the *sacred*, this candidly autobiographical and brutally honest book will make you *laugh* and make you *think*.

More importantly, it will help you begin to see how the plan for your life is unfolding every day and how God's "big picture" is revealing your destiny.

Every page contains good news and vital information about how to successfully live your **whole life long**. It's all here, and *it's all good!*

Keepin' It Real

Becoming a Real Person,
Experiencing the Real God,
in the Real World

You've never read a book quite like *Keepin' It Real!* In its pages, Bishop Swilley candidly examines an unusually wide array of subjects...the reality TV phenomenon...pop culture...history...politics ...self-esteem...prosperity... success...parenting...multiculturalism...New Age philosophy...world religions... political correctness...racism...sexism...tolerance... activism...technology... addiction...eschatology...dispensationalism...the antichrist...orthodoxy... prayer...the Holy Spirit... destiny...purpose...vision...and much more...and addresses how they all relate to the Kingdom of God in the now!

But *Keepin' it Real* is also about *you* and how you can develop the courage and confidence to be yourself at all times and to live your *real* life without compromise. Socially relevant, thought-provoking, and theologically edgy, *Keepin' it Real* is a modern manifesto for REAL PEOPLE EXPERIENCING THE REAL GOD IN THE REAL WORLD.®

If you're ready to get *real*, get this book!

School of the Bible Seminar Materials:

The School of the Bible seminars were one day meetings consisting of four sessions. In these sessions, Bishop Jim presents ideas about ancient truths for your consideration and answers some questions that have been asked of him. Above all, everything discussed in this material must be potentially summed up in these three words: **God Is Love!** This and all Gospel preaching/teaching must meet that criterion. If it doesn't demonstrate and exalt the love of God, it's not the Gospel. (All sessions available on DVD, CD and MP3; a corresponding Workbook is also available.)

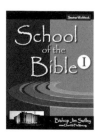

School of the Bible I Topics

- How We Got Our Bible
- What is Hell and Who is the Devil?
- Are We Living in the End-Times?
- God's Mercy to All

School of the Bible II Topics

- How to Study the Bible
- Overview of the Book of Revelation
- The Lake of Fire and the Second Death
- Christ Is All and Is In All: The Greatness of God

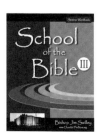

School of the Bible III Topics

- The Gospel of the Kingdom: Developing a Real Theology for Real People Living in the Real World
- A Global Vision: Understanding Christ and World Religions
- The Restoration of All Things: Understanding the Doctrine of Universal Reconciliation
- On Earth as it is in Heaven: The Manifestation of the Unconditional Love of God

School of the Bible IV Topics

- Behold the Lamb of God Who Takes Away the Sin of the World
- The Mark of the Lamb: Overcoming the Worship of the Beast
- Singing the "Uni-Verse": Global Reconciliation Revealed in the Psalms
- The Songs of Revelation: John's Vision of Universal Worship

Washed by the Word Music Products:
(the spoken Word over a background of live, instrumental music)

A distinctive quality of Bishop Swilley is his frequent practice of quoting Scripture and washing his congregation with the mind-renewing, life-changing Word of God. Finally, after many requests, the "Washed by the Word" series were recorded live at Church In The Now. You will be greatly blessed as you hear the anointed Word spoken into your life and will want to play them over and over again.

Washed by the Word track listing:

In His Presence • The Authority of the Word • The Psalms • The Word Concerning Your Righteousness • Your Blessing for Favor • Your Blessing for Prosperity and Success • The Healing Scriptures • Your Blessing for Peace • The Word Concerning Your Children • Your Blessing for Strength • Your Blessing for Joy • The Word Concerning Your Dreams and Visions • Faith Builders • The Word Concerning Your Destiny and Future • O Magnify the Lord With Me

Washed by the Word AM & PM track listing:

AM: *Morning Has Broken • Good Day Sunshine! • Give Us This Day Our Daily Bread • Carpe Diem! • The Mind of Christ • Attitude Adjustment • Great Expectations • The Whole Armor of God • I Can Do All Things Through Christ • Get In The Groove!*

PM: *Evening Praise • Count Your Blessings • Let It Go • Angels Watching Over Me • No Plague Comes Near My Dwelling • Take No Thought for Tomorrow • Cast All Your Care upon Him • Now I Lay Me Down to Sleep • Sweet Dreams • Sleep in Heavenly Peace*

Washed by the Word for Kids track listing:

Opening Prayer • This is the Day the Lord has Made! • You Are Special! • The Word Concerning Success in School • A Blessing for Girls • A Blessing for Boys • The Word Concerning Your Family • The Word Concerning Your Friends • The Blessing of Obedience • Overcoming Bad Memories • The Word Concerning Your Character • The Word Concerning Your Destiny and Future • Don't be Afraid of the Dark • Peaceful Sleep

For more information on these products, please visit the website at
www.churchinthenow.org

For large quantity purchases, please email:
info@churchinthenow.org